The

HISTORY

of the

AMERICAN

REVOLUTION

Volume II

David Ramsay

The
HISTORY
of the
AMERICAN
REVOLUTION

IN TWO VOLUMES

by David Ramsay, M.D.

EDITED BY LESTER H. COHEN

Volume II

LibertyClassics

INDIANAPOLIS

v

LibertyClassics is a publishing imprint of Liberty Fund, Inc., a foundation established to encourage study of the ideal of a society of free and responsible individuals.

The cuneiform inscription that serves as the design motif for our end-papers is the earliest-known written appearance of the word "freedom" (ama-gi), or "liberty." It is taken from a clay document written about 2300 B.C. in the Sumerian city-state of Lagash.

Frontispiece portrait of Dr. David Ramsay (1749–1815), oil on canvas, by Rembrandt Peale. Courtesy of The Gibbs Museum of Art/Carolina Art Association, Charleston, South Carolina.

Facsimile title pages for both volumes are courtesy of the Rare Books and Manuscripts Division, The New York Public Library, Astor, Lenox and Tilden Foundations.

Cover art for Volume I is of Paul Revere's ride, by an anonymous artist. Cover art for Volume II is a woodcut illustrating the battle at Lexington, by John W. Barber.

Library of Congress Cataloging-in-Publication Data

Ramsay, David, 1749–1815.
The history of the American Revolution / by David Ramsay ; edited by Lester H. Cohen.
    p.   cm.
    Originally published: Philadelphia : Printed and sold by
R. Aitken, 1789.
    Includes bibliographical references.
    ISBN 0-86597-078-5 (set).—ISBN 0-86597-081-5 (pbk. : set).—
ISBN 0-86597-079-3 (v. 1).—ISBN 0-86597-082-3 (pbk. : v. 1).—
ISBN 0-86597-080-7 (v. 2).—ISBN 0-86597-083-1 (pbk. : v. 2)
    1. United States—History—Revolution, 1775–1783.   2. United
States—Politics and government—1783–1789.   3. United States—
Constitution.   I. Cohen, Lester H., 1944–   . II. Title.
E208.R187   1989
973.3—dc20   89-14583
                                                      CIP

10 9 8 7 6 5 4 3 2 1

Contents

CONTENTS

HISTORY OF THE AMERICAN REVOLUTION

CONTENTS

CHAPTER XXIII

The

HISTORY

of the

AMERICAN

REVOLUTION

Volume II

HISTORY

OF THE

AMERICAN REVOLUTION.

By *DAVID RAMSAY*, M. D.

IN TWO VOLUMES.

VOLUME II.

PHILADELPHIA:

PRINTED AND SOLD BY *R. AITKEN & SON.*

M.DCO.LXXXIX.

The Campaign of 1777, in the Middle States.

[1] SOON AFTER THE DECLARATION of Independence, the au-   1777
thority of Congress was obtained for raising an army, that would be
more permanent than the temporary levies, which they had previously
brought into the field. It was at first proposed to recruit, for the
indefinite term of the war, but it being found on experiment that the
habits of the people were averse to engagements, for such an uncertain
period of service, the recruiting officers were instructed to offer the
alternative of, either enlisting for the war, or for three years. Those
who engaged on the first conditions were promised a hundred acres
of land, in addition to their pay and bounty. The troops raised by
Congress for the service of the United States, were called, continentals. Though in September 1776, it had been resolved, to raise 88
battalions, and in December following, authority was given to general

Washington to raise 16 more, yet very little progress had been made in the recruiting business, till after the battles of Trenton and Princeton. Even after that period, so much time was necessarily consumed before these new recruits joined the commander in chief, that his whole force at Morris-town, and the several out-posts, for some time, did not exceed 1500 men. Yet, what is almost incredible, these 1500 kept as many thousands of the British closely pent up in [2] Brunswick. Almost every party that was sent out by the latter, was successfully opposed by the former, and the adjacent country preserved in a great degree of tranquility.

1777

It was matter of astonishment, that the British suffered the dangerous interval between the disbanding of one army, and the raising of another, to pass away without attempting something of consequence against the remaining shadow of an armed force. Hitherto there had been a deficiency of arms and ammunition, as well as of men, but in the spring of 1777, a vessel of 24 guns arrived from France at Portsmouth in New-Hampshire, with upwards of 11,000 stand of arms, and 1000 barrels of powder. Ten thousand stand of arms arrived about the same time, in another part of the United States.

Before the royal army took the field, in prosecution of the main business of the campaign, two enterprizes for the destruction of American stores were undertaken, in an opposite direction to what proved eventually to be the theatre of the operations of Sir William Howe. The first was conducted by colonel Bird, the second by major general Tryon. The former landed with about 500 men at Peek's-kill, near 50 miles from New-York. General Washington had repeatedly cautioned the commissaries not to suffer large quantities of provisions to be near the water, in such places as were accessible to shipping, but his prudent advice had not been regarded. The few Americans, who were stationed as a guard at Peek's-kill, on the approach of colonel Bird, fired the principal storehouses, and retired to a good position, about two or three miles distant. The loss of provisions, forage, and other valuable articles, was considerable.

MARCH
23

Major general Tryon, with a detachment of 2000 men, embarked at New-York, and passing through the Sound, landed between Fairfield and Norwalk. They advanced through the country without interrup-

APRIL 26

338

tion, and arrived in about 20 hours at Danbury. On their approach the few continentals who were in the town withdrew from it. The British began to burn and destroy, but abstained from injuring the property of such as were reputed tories—18 houses, 800 barrels of pork and beef, 800 barrels of [3] flour, 2000 bushels of grain, 1700 tents, and some other articles were lost to the Americans. Generals Wooster, Arnold and Silliman, having hastily collected a few hundred of the inhabitants, made arrangements for interrupting the march of the royal detachment, but the arms of those who came forward on this emergency, were injured by excessive rains, and the men were worn down with a march of 30 miles in the course of a day. Such dispositions were nevertheless made, and such advantageous posts were taken, as enabled them greatly to annoy the invaders when returning to their ships. General Arnold, with about 500 men, by a rapid movement, reached Ridgefield in their front—barricadoed the road, kept up a brisk fire upon them, and sustained their attack, till they had made a lodgement on a ledge of rocks on his left. After the British had gained this eminence, a whole platoon levelled at general Arnold, not more than 30 yards distant. His horse was killed, but he escaped. While he was extricating himself from his horse, a soldier advanced to run him through with a bayonet, but he shot him dead with his pistol, and afterwards got off safe. The Americans, in several detached parties, harrassed the rear of the British, and from various stands kept up a scattering fire upon them, till they reached their shipping.

The British accomplished the object of the expedition, but it cost them dear. They had by computation 2 or 300 men killed, wounded, or taken. The loss of the Americans was about 20 killed, and 40 wounded. Among the former was Dr. Atwater, a gentleman of respectable character, and considerable influence. Colonel Lamb was among the latter: General Wooster, though seventy years old, behaved with the vigour and spirit of youth. While gloriously defending the liberties of his country, he received a mortal wound. Congress resolved, that a monument should be erected to his memory, as an acknowledgment of his merit and services. They also resolved, that a horse, properly caparisoned, should be presented to general Arnold, in their name, as a token of their approbation of his gallant conduct.

Not long after the excursion to Danbury, colonel [4] Meigs, an enterprising American officer, transported a detachment of about 170 Americans, in whale boats, over the Sound, which separates

Long-Island from Connecticut, and burned twelve brigs and sloops, belonging to the British, and destroyed a large quantity of forage and other articles, collected for their use in Sagg-Harbour on that island— killed six of their soldiers, and brought off 90 prisoners, without having a single man either killed or wounded. The colonel and his party returned to Guilford in 25 hours from the time of their departure, having in that short space not only completed the object of their expedition, but traversed by land and water, a space not less than 90 miles. Congress ordered an elegant sword to be presented to colonel Meigs, for his good conduct in this expedition.

As the season advanced, the American army in New-Jersey, was reinforced by the successive arrival of recruits, but nevertheless at the opening of the campaign, it amounted only to 7272 men.

Great pains had been taken to recruit the British army with American levies. A commission of brigadier general had been conferred on Mr. Oliver Delancey, a loyalist of great influence in New-York, and he was authorised to raise three battalions. Every effort had been made, to raise the men, both within and without the British lines, and also from among the American prisoners, but with all these exertions, only 597 were procured. Mr. Courtland Skinner, a loyalist well known in Jersey, was also appointed a brigadier, and authorised to raise five battalions. Great efforts were also made to procure recruits for his command, but their whole number amounted only to 517.

Towards the latter end of May, general Washington quitted his winter encampment at Morristown, and took a strong position at Middlebrook. Soon after this movement was effected, the British marched from Brunswick, and extended their van as far as Somerset court-house, but in a few days returned to their former station. This sudden change was probably owing to the unexpected opposition which seemed to be collecting from all quarters, [5] for the Jersey militia, turned out in a very spirited manner, to oppose them. Six months before that same army marched through New-Jersey, without being fired upon, and even small parties of them had safely patrolled the country, at a distance from their camp; but experience having proved that British protections were no security for property, the inhabitants generally resolved to try the effects of resistance, in preference to a second submission. A fortunate mistake gave them an opportunity of assembling in great force on this emergency. Signals had been agreed on, and beacons erected on high places, with the view of communicating over the country, instantaneous intelligence of the approach of the British. A few hours before the royal army began their march, the signal of alarm, on the foundation of a false report, had been hoisted. The farmers, with arms in their hands, ran to the place of rendezvous from considerable distances. They had set out at least twelve hours before the British, and on their appearance were collected in formidable numbers. Whether Sir William Howe intended to force his way through the country to the Delaware, and afterwards to Philadelphia, or to attack the American army, is uncertain, but whatever was his design, he thought proper, suddenly to relinquish it, and fell back to Brunswick. The British army, on their retreat, burned and destroyed the farm houses on the road, nor did they spare those buildings which were dedicated to the service of the Deity.

Sir William Howe, after his retreat to Brunswick, endeavoured to provoke general Washington to an engagement, and left no manoeuvre untried, that was calculated to induce him to quit his position. At one time he appeared as if he intended to push on without regarding the army opposed to him. At another he accurately examined the situation of the American encampment, hoping that some unguarded part might be found, on which an attack might be made that would open the way to a general engagement. All these hopes were frustrated. General Washington knew the full value of his situation. He had too much penetration to lose it from the circumvention of military manoeuvres, and too much temper [6] to be provoked to a dereliction of it. He was well apprized it was not the interest of his country, to commit its fortune to a single action. 1777

Sir William Howe suddenly relinquished his position in front of the Americans, and retired with his whole force to Amboy. The apparently retreating British, were pursued by a considerable detachment of the American army, and general Washington advanced from Middlebrook to Quibbletown, to be near at hand for the support of his advanced parties. The British general immediately marched his army back from Amboy, with great expedition, hoping to bring on a general action on equal ground, but he was disappointed. General Washington fell back, and posted his army in such an advantageous position, as compensated for the inferiority of his numbers. Sir William Howe was now fully convinced of the impossibility of compelling a general engagement on equal terms, and also satisfied that it would be too hazardous to attempt passing the Delaware, while the country was in arms, and the main American army in full force in his rear. He therefore returned to Amboy, and thence passed over to Staten-Island, resolving to prosecute the objects of the campaign by another route. During the period of these movements, the real designs of general Howe were involved in great obscurity. Though the season for military operations was advanced as far as the month of July, yet his determinate object could not be ascertained. Nothing on his part had hitherto taken place, but alternately advancing and retreating. General Washington's embarrassment on this account, was increased by intelligence which arrived, that Burgoyne was coming in great force towards New-York, from Canada. Apprehending that Sir William Howe would ultimately move up the North-River, and that his movements, which looked southwardly were calculated to deceive, the American general, detached a brigade to reinforce the northern division of his army. Successive advices of the advance of Burgoyne, favoured the idea, that a junction of the two royal armies near Albany, was intended. Some movements were therefore made by general Washington, [7] towards Peek's-kill, and on the other side towards Trenton, while the main army was encamped near the Clove, in readiness to march either to the north or south, as the movements of Sir William Howe might require. At length, the main body of the royal army, consisting of thirty-six British and Hessian battalions, with a regiment of light horse, and a loyal provincial corps, called the Queen's rangers, and a powerful artillery, amounting in the whole to about 16,000 men, departed from Sandy-hook and were reported to steer southwardly. About the time of this embarkation, a letter from Sir William Howe to general Burgoyne was intercepted. This contained intelligence, that the

British troops were destined to New-Hampshire. The intended deception was so superficially veiled, that in conjunction with the intelligence of the British embarkation, it produced a contrary effect. Within one hour after the reception of this intercepted letter, general Washington gave orders to his army to move to the southward, but he was nevertheless so much impressed with a conviction, that it was the true interest of Howe to move towards Burgoyne, that he ordered the American army to halt for some time, at the river Delaware, suspecting that the apparent movement of the royal army to the southward, was a feint calculated to draw him farther from the North-river. The British fleet having sailed from Sandy-hook, were a week at sea, before they reached cape Henlopen. At this time and place, for reasons that do not obviously occur, general Howe gave up the idea of approaching Philadelphia, by ascending the Delaware, and resolved on a circuitous route by the way of the Chesapeak. Perhaps he counted, on being joined by large reinforcements from the numerous tories in Maryland or Delaware, or perhaps he feared the obstructions which the Pennsylvanians had planted in the Delaware. If these were his reasons, he was mistaken in both. From the tories he received no advantage, and from the obstructions in the river, his ships could have received no detriment, if he had landed his troops at New-Castle, which was 14 miles nearer Philadelphia than the head of Chesapeak bay.

[8] The British fleet, after they had left the capes of the Delaware, had a tedious and uncomfortable passage, being twenty days before they entered the capes of Virginia. They ascended the bay, with a favourable wind, and landed at Turkey-point. The circumstance of the British fleet putting out to sea, after they had looked into the Delaware, added to the apprehension before entertained, that the whole was a feint calculated to draw the American army farther from the North-river, so as to prevent their being at hand to oppose a junction between Howe and Burgoyne. Washington therefore fell back to such a middle station, as would enable him, either speedily to return to the North-river, or advance to the relief of Philadelphia. The British fleet, after leaving the capes of Delaware, were not heard of for near three weeks, except that they had once or twice been seen near the coast steering southwardly. A council of officers

1777

AUG. 25

AUG. 21 convened at Neshaminy, near Philadelphia, unanimously gave it as their opinion, that Charlestown, in South-Carolina, was most probably their object, and that it would be impossible for the army to march in season for its relief. It was therefore concluded to try, to repair the loss of Charleston, which was considered as unavoidable, either by attempting something on New-York island, or by uniting with the northern army, to give more effectual opposition to Burgoyne. A small change of position, conformably to this new system, took place. The day before the above resolution was adopted, the British fleet entered the Chesapeake. Intelligence thereof, in a few days, reached the American army, and dispelled that mist of uncertainty, in which general Howe's movements had been heretofore enveloped. The American troops were put in motion to meet the British army. Their numbers on paper amounted to 14,000, but their real effective force on which dependence might be placed in the day of battle, did not much exceed 8000 men. Every appearance of confidence was assumed by them as they passed through Philadelphia, that the citizens might be intimidated from joining the British. About the 1777 same time a number of the principal inhabitants of that city, [9] being suspected of disaffection to the American cause, were taken into custody, and sent to Virginia.

Soon after Sir William Howe had landed his troops in Maryland, he put forth a declaration, in which he informed the inhabitants, that he had issued the strictest orders to the troops "for the preservation of regularity and good discipline, and that the most exemplary punishment should be inflicted upon those who should dare to plunder the property, or molest the persons of any of his majesty's well-disposed subjects." It seemed as though fully apprized of the consequences, which had resulted from the indiscriminate plunderings of his army in New-Jersey, he was determined to adopt a more politic line of conduct. Whatever his lordship's intentions might be, they were by no means seconded by his troops.

SEPT. 3 The royal army set out from the eastern heads of the Chesapeak, with a spirit which promised to compensate for the various delays, which had hitherto wasted the campaign. Their tents and baggage were left behind, and they trusted their future accommodation to such quarters as their arms might procure. They advanced with boldness, till they were within two miles of the American army, which was then posted near New-port. General Washington soon changed his position, and took post on the high ground near Chadd's Ford, on the Brandywine creek, with an intention of disputing the passage. It was the wish, but by no means the interest of the Americans, to try their strength in an engagement. Their regular troops were not only greatly inferior in discipline, but in numbers, to the royal army. The opinion of the inhabitants, though founded on no circumstances more substantial than their wishes, imposed a species of necessity on the American general to keep his army in front of the enemy, and to risque an action for the security of Philadelphia. Instead of this, had he taken the ridge of high mountains on his right, the British must have respected his numbers, and probably would have followed him up the country. In this manner the campaign might have been wasted away in a manner fatal to the invaders, but the bulk of the American people were so impatient [10]   1777 of delays, and had such an overweening conceit of the numbers and prowess of their army, that they could not comprehend the wisdom and policy of manoeuvres to shun a general engagement.

On this occasion necessity dictated, that a sacrifice should be made on the altar of public opinion. A general action was therefore hazarded. This took place at Chadd's Ford, on the Brandywine, a   SEP. 11 small stream which empties itself into Christiana creek, near its conflux with the river Delaware.

The royal army advanced at day break in two columns, commanded by lieutenant general Kniphausen, and by lord Cornwallis. The first took the direct road to Chadd's Ford, and made a shew of passing it, in front of the main body of the Americans. At the same time the other column moved up on the west side of the Brandywine to its fork, and crossed both its branches about 2 o'clock in the afternoon, and then marched down on the east side thereof, with the view of turning the right wing of their adversaries.

This they effected and compelled them to retreat with great loss. General Kniphausen amused the Americans with the appearance of crossing the ford, but did not attempt it until lord Cornwallis having crossed above, and moved down on the opposite side, had commenced his attack. Kniphausen then crossed the ford, and attacked the troops posted for its defence. These, after a severe conflict, were compelled to give way. The retreat of the Americans soon became general, and was continued to Chester, under cover of general Weeden's brigade, which came off in good order. The final issue of battles often depends on small circumstances, which human prudence cannot control— one of these occurred here, and prevented general Washington from executing a bold design, to effect which, his troops were actually in motion. This was to have crossed the Brandywine, and attacked Kniphausen, while general Sullivan and lord Stirling, should keep earl Cornwallis in check. In the most critical moment, general Washington received intelligence which he was obliged to credit, that the column of lord Cornwallis [11] had been only making a feint, and was returning to join Kniphausen. This prevented the execution of a plan, which, if carried into effect, would probably have given a different turn to the events of the day. The killed and wounded in the royal army, were near six hundred. The loss of the Americans was twice that number. In the list of their wounded, were two of their general officers—the marquis de la Fayette, and general Woodford. The former was a French nobleman of high rank, who, animated with the love of liberty, had left his native country, and offered his service to Congress. While in France, and only nineteen years of age, he espoused the cause of the Americans, with the most disinterested and generous ardour. Having determined to join them, he communicated his intentions to the American commissioners, at Paris. They justly conceived, that a patron of so much importance would be of service to their cause, and encouraged his design. Before he had embarked from France, intelligence arrived in Europe, that the American insurgents, reduced to 2000 men, were fleeing through Jersey before a British force of 30,000. Under these circumstances, the American commissioners at Paris thought it but honest to dissuade him from the present prosecution of his perilous enterprise. It was in vain that they acted so candid a part. His zeal to serve a distressed country, was not abated by her misfortunes. Having embarked in a vessel, which he purchased for the purpose, he arrived in Charleston, early in 1777, and soon after joined the American army. Congress resolved, that "in consideration of his zeal, illustrious family and connexions, he should have the rank of major general in their army."

1777

Independent of the risque he ran as an American officer, he hazarded his large fortune in consequence of the laws of France, and also the confinement of his person, in case of capture, when on his way to the United States, without the chance of being acknowledged by any nation, for his court had forbidden his proceeding to America, and had dispatched orders to have him confined in the West-Indies, if found in that quarter. This gallant nobleman, who under all these disadvantages [12] had demonstrated his good will to the United States, received a wound in his leg, at the battle of Brandywine, but he nevertheless continued in the field, and exerted himself both by word and example in rallying the Americans. Other foreigners of distinction also shared in the engagement. Count Pulaski, a Polish nobleman, the same who a few years before had carried off king Stanislaus from his capital, though surrounded with a numerous body of guards, and a Russian army, fought with the Americans at Brandywine. He was a thunderbolt of war, and always sought for the post of danger as the post of honour. Soon after this engagement Congress appointed him commander of horse, with the rank of brigadier. Monsieur du Coudray, a French officer of high rank, and great abilities, while on his way from Philadelphia to join the American army, about this time was drowned in the river Schuylkill. He rode into the flat-bottomed boat on a spirited mare, whose career he was not able to stop, and she went out at the farther end into the river, with her rider on her back.

1777

The evening after the battle of Brandywine, a party of the British went to Wilmington, and took president M'Kinley prisoner. They also took possession of a shallop, loaded with the most valuable effects of the inhabitants.

Howe persevered in his scheme of gaining the right flank of the Americans. This was no less steadily pursued on the one side, than avoided on the other. Washington came forward in a few days with a resolution of risquing another action. He accordingly advanced as far as the Warren tavern on the Lancaster road. Near that place both armies were on the point of engaging with their whole force, but were prevented by a most violent storm of rain, which continued for a whole day and night. When the rain ceased, the Americans found that their ammunition was entirely ruined. They therefore withdrew

SEP. 18

to a place of safety. Before a proper supply was procured, the British marched from their position near the White Horse tavern, down towards the Swedes Ford. The Americans again took post in their front; but the British, instead of urging an action, began to [13] march up towards Reading. To save the stores which had been deposited in that place, Washington took a new position, and left the British in undisturbed possession of the roads which lead to Philadelphia. His troops were worn down with a succession of severe duties. There were in his army above a thousand men who were barefooted, and who had performed all their late movements in that condition. About this time the Americans sustained a considerable loss by a night attack, conducted by general Grey on a detachment of their troops, which was encamped near the Paoli tavern. The outposts and pickets were forced without noise, about one o'clock in the morning. The men had scarcely time to turn out, and when they turned out they unfortunately paraded in the light of their fires. This directed the British how, and where to proceed. They rushed in upon them and put about 300 to death in a silent manner by a free and exclusive use of the bayonet. The enterprise was conducted with so much address, that the loss of the assailants did not exceed eight.

Congress, which after a short residence at Baltimore had returned to Philadelphia, were obliged a second time to consult their safety by flight. They retired at first to Lancaster, and afterwards to Yorktown.

The bulk of the British army being left in Germantown, Sir William Howe, with a small part, made his triumphal entry into Philadelphia, and was received with the hearty welcome of numerous citizens, who either from conscience, cowardice, interest, or principle, had hitherto separated themselves from the class of active whigs.

The possession of the largest city in the United States, together with the dispersion of that grand council which had heretofore conducted their public affairs, were reckoned by the short sighted as decisive of their fate. The submission of countries, after the conquest of their capital, had often been a thing of course, but in the great contest for the sovereignty of the United States, the question did not rest with a ruler, or a body of rulers, nor was it to be

1777

SEP. 20

SEP. 26

determined by the possession or loss of any particular place. It was the public mind, the sentiments and opinions [14] of the yeomanry of the country which were to decide. Though Philadelphia had become the residence of the British army, yet as long as the bulk of the people of the United States were opposed to their government, the country was unsubdued. Indeed it was presumed by the more discerning politicians, that the luxuries of a great city would so far enervate the British troops as to indispose them for those active exertions to which they were prompted, while inconveniently encamped in the open country.

1777

To take off the impression the British successes, might make in France to the prejudice of America, Doctor Franklin gave them an ingenious turn, by observing, "that instead of saying Sir William Howe had taken Philadelphia, it would be more proper to say, Philadelphia had taken Sir William Howe."

One of the first objects of the British, after they had got possession, was to erect batteries to command the river, and to protect the city from any insult by water. The British shipping were prevented from ascending the Delaware, by obstructions hereafter to be described, which were fixed near Mud-Island. Philadelphia, though possessed by the British army, was exposed to danger from the American vessels in the river. The American frigate Delaware, of 32 guns, anchored within 500 yards of the unfinished batteries, and being seconded by some smaller vessels, commenced a heavy cannonade upon the batteries and town, but upon the falling of the tide she ran aground. Being briskly fired upon from the town, while in this condition she was soon compelled to surrender. The other American vessels, not able to resist the fire from the batteries after losing one of their number, retired.

General Washington, having been reinforced by 2500 men from Peeks-kill and Virginia; and having been informed, that general Howe had detached a confiderable part of his force, for reducing the forts on the Delaware, conceived a design of attacking the British post at Germantown. Their line of encampment, crossed the town at right angles near its centre. The left wing [15] extended to the Schuylkill, and was covered in front by the mounted and dismounted chasseurs. The queen's American rangers and a battalion of light infantry were in front of the right. The 40th regiment with another battalion of light infantry were posted on the Chesnut-hill road, three quarters of a mile in advance. Lord Cornwallis lay at Philadelphia, with four battalions of grenadiers. A few of the general officers of the American army, whose advice was requested on the occasion unanimously recommended an attack; and it was agreed that it should be made in different places to produce the greater confusion, and to prevent the several parts of the British forces, from affording support to each other. From an apprehension, that the Americans from the want of discipline would not persevere in a long attack, it was resolved that it should be sudden and vigorous, and if unsuccessful to make an expeditious retreat. The divisions of Sullivan and Wayne flanked by Conway's brigade, were to enter the town by the way of Chesnut-hill, while general Armstrong with the Pennsylvania militia should fall down the Manatawny road, and gain the left and rear of the British. The divisions of Greene and Stephen's flanked by M'Dougal's brigade were to enter by the lime kiln road. The militia of Maryland and Jersey under generals Smallwood and Furman, were to march by the old York road, and to fall upon the rear of their right.

OCT. 4

Lord Stirling with Nathe's and Maxwell's brigade were to form a corps de reserve. The Americans began their attack about sunrise on the 40th regiment, and a battalion of light infantry. These two corps being obliged to retreat, were pursued into the village. On their retreat lieutenant colonel Musgrove with six companies took post in Mr. Chew's strong stone house, which lay in front of the Americans. From an adherence to the military maxim of never leaving a fort possessed by an enemy in the rear, it was resolved to attack the party in the house.

1777

In the mean time general Greene got up with his column and attacked the right wing. Colonel Mathews routed a party of the British opposed to him, killed several, [16] and took 110 prisoners, but from the darkness of the day lost sight of the brigade to which he belonged, and having separated from it, was taken prisoner with his whole regiment, and the prisoners which he had previously taken, were released. A number of the troops in Greene's division, were stopped by the halt of the party before Chew's house. Near one half of the American army remained for some time at that place inactive. In the mean time general Grey led on three battalions of the third brigade, and attacked with vigour. A sharp contest followed. Two British regiments attacked at the same time on the opposite side of the town. General Grant moved up the 49th regiment to the aid of those who were engaged with Greene's column.

The morning was extremely foggy. This, by concealing the true situation of the parties occasioned mistakes, and made so much caution necessary as to give the British time to recover from the effects of their first surprize. From these causes the early promising appearances on the part of the assailants were speedily reversed. The Americans left the field hastily, and all efforts to rally them were ineffectual. Lord Cornwallis arrived with a party of light horse, and joined in the pursuit. This was continued for some miles. The loss of the royal army, including the wounded and prisoners, was about 500. Among their slain were brigadier general Agnew, and lieutenant colonel Bird. The loss of the Americans, including 400 prisoners, was about 1000. Among their slain were general Nash and his aid de camp major Witherspoon.

Soon after this battle the British left Germantown, and turned their principal attention towards opening a free communication between their army and their shipping.

Much industry and ingenuity had been exerted for the security of Philadelphia on the water side. Thirteen gallies, two floating batteries, two zebeques, one brig, one ship, besides a number of armed boats, fire ships and rafts, were constructed or employed for this purpose. The Americans had also built a fort on Mud-Island, to which [17]   1777 they gave the name of fort Mifflin, and erected thereon a considerable battery. This island is admirably situated for the erection of works to annoy shipping on their way up the Delaware. It lies near the middle of the river, about 7 miles below Philadelphia. No vessels of burden can come up but by the main ship channel, which passes close to Mud-Island, and is very narrow for more than a mile below. Opposite to fort Mifflin there is a height, called Red-Bank. This overlooks not only the river, but the neighbouring country. On this eminence, a respectable battery was erected. Between these two fortresses, which are half a mile distant from each other, the American naval armament for the defence of the river Delaware, made their harbour of retreat. Two ranges of chevaux de frise were also sunk into the channel. These consisted of large pieces of timber, strongly framed together, in the manner usual for making the foundation of wharfs in deep water. Several large points of bearded iron projecting down the river were annexed to the upper parts of these chevaux de frise, and the whole was sunk with stones, so as to be about four feet under the water at low tide. Their prodigious weight and strength could not fail to effect the destruction of any vessel which came upon them. Thirty of these machines were sunk about 300 yards below fort Mifflin, so as to stretch in a diagonal line across the channel. The only open passage left was between two piers lying close to the fort, and that was secured by a strong boom, and could not be approached but in a direct line to the battery. Another fortification was erected on a high bank on the Jersey shore, called Billingsport. And opposite to this, another range of chevaux de frise was deposited, leaving only a narrow and shoal channel on the one side. There was also a temporary battery of two heavy cannon, at the mouth of Mantua creek, about half way from Red-Bank to Billingsport. The British were well apprized, that without the command of the Delaware, their possession of Philadelphia would be of no advantage. They therefore strained every nerve, to open the navigation of that river—to this end lord Howe had early taken the most effectual measures [18] for conducting the fleet and transports round from the Chesapeak to the Delaware, and drew them up on the Pennsylvania shore, from Reedy-Island to New-Castle. Early in October, a detachment from the British army crossed the Delaware, with a view of dislodging the Americans from Billingsport. On their approach, the place was evacuated. As the season advanced, more vigorous measures for removing the obstructions were concerted between the general and the admiral. Batteries were erected on the Pennsylvania shore to assist in dislodging the Americans from Mud-Island. At the same time Count Donop with 2000 men, having crossed into New-Jersey, opposite to Philadelphia, marched down on the eastern side of the Delaware, to attack the redoubt at Red-Bank. This was defended by about 400 men under the command of colonel Greene. The attack immediately commenced by a smart cannonade, under cover of which the Count advanced to the redoubt. This place

1777

was intended for a much larger garrison than was then in it. It had therefore become necessary to run a line in the middle thereof, and one part of it was evacuated. That part was easily carried by the assailants, on which they indulged in loud huzzas for their supposed victory. The garrison kept up a severe well directed fire on the assailants by which they were compelled to retire. They suffered not only in the assault, but in the approach to, and retreat from the fort. Their whole loss in killed and wounded was about 400. Count Donop was mortally wounded and taken prisoner. Congress resolved, to present colonel Greene with a sword for his good conduct on this occasion. An attack made about the same time on fort Mifflin by men of war and frigates, was not more successful than the assault on Red-Bank. The Augusta man of war of 64 guns, and the Merlin, two of the vessels which were engaged in it, got aground. The former was fired and blew up. The latter was evacuated.

Though the first attempts of the British, for opening the navigation of the Delaware, were unsuccessful, they carried their point in another way that was unexpected. The chevaux de frise, having been sunk some considerable [19] time, the current of the water was diverted by this great bulk into new channels. In consequence thereof the passage between the islands and the Pennsylvania shore was so deepened as to admit vessels of some considerable draught of water. Through this passage, the Vigilant, a large ship, cut down so as to draw but little water, mounted with 24 pounders, made her way to a position from which she might enfilade the works on Mud-Island. This gave the British such an advantage, that the post was no longer tenable. Colonel Smith, who had with great gallantry defended the fort from the latter end of September, to the 11th of November, being wounded, was removed to the main. Within five days after his removal, major Thayer, who as a volunteer had nobly offered to take charge of this dangerous post, was obliged to evacuate it.

This event did not take place till the works were entirely beat down—every piece of cannon dismounted, and one of the British ships so near that she threw granadoes into the fort, and killed the men uncovered in the platform. The troops who had so bravely defended fort Mifflin, made a safe retreat to Red-Bank. Congress voted swords to be given to lieutenant colonel Smith and commodore

1777

Hazelwood, for their gallant defence of the Delaware. Within three days after Mud-Island was evacuated, the garrison was also withdrawn from Red-Bank, on the approach of lord Cornwallis, at the head of a large force prepared to assault it. Some of the American gallies and armed vessels escaped by keeping close in with the Jersey shore, to places of security above Philadelphia, but 17 of them were abandoned by their crews, and fired. Thus the British gained a free communication between their army and shipping. This event was to them very desirable. They had been previously obliged to draw their provisions from Chester, a distance of sixteen miles, at some risque, and a certain great expence. The long protracted defence of the Delaware, deranged the plans of the British, for the remainder of the campaign, and consequently saved the adjacent country.

1777

About this time the chair of Congress became vacant, [20] by the departure of Mr. Hancock, after he had discharged the duties of that office to great acceptance, two years and five months. Henry Laurens, of South-Carolina, was unanimously elected his successor. He had

NOV. 1

been in England for some years, antecedent to the hostile determinations of parliament against the colonies, but finding the dispute growing serious, he conceived that honour and duty called him to take part with his native country. He had been warmly solicited to stay in England, and offers were made him not only to secure, but to double his American estate, in case of his continuing to reside there—but these were refused. To a particular friend in London, dissuading him from coming out to America, he replied on the 9th of Nov. 1774, when at Falmouth, on the point of embarking,

I shall never forget your friendly attention to my interest, but I dare not return. Your ministers are deaf to information, and seem bent on provoking unnecessary contest. I think I have acted the part of a faithful subject, I now go resolved still to labour for peace; at the same time determined in the last event to stand or fall with my country.

Immediately on his arrival in Charleston, he was elected a member, and soon after the president of the provincial congress—the president of the council of safety—the vice-president of the state—and a member of congress.

CHAPTER XIV

While Sir William Howe was succeeding in every enterprize in Pennsylvania intelligence arrived, as shall be related in the next chapter, that general Burgoyne and his whole army had surrendered prisoners of war to the Americans.

General Washington soon after received a considerable reinforcement from the northern army, which had accomplished this great event. With this increased force he took a position at and near Whitemarsh. The royal army having succeeded in removing the obstructions in the river Delaware, were ready for new enterprizes. DEC. 4 Sir William Howe, marched out of Philadelphia with almost his whole force, expecting to bring on a general engagement. The next morning he appeared on Chesnut-hill in front of, and about three miles distant from [21] the right wing of the Americans. On the day following the British changed their ground, and moved to the right. Two days after they moved still farther to the right, and made every appearance of an intention to attack the American encampment. Some skirmishes took place, and a general action was hourly expected: but instead thereof on the morning of the next day, after various marches and countermarches, the British filed off from their right, by two or three DEC. 9 different routes, in full march for Philadelphia.

The position of general Washington in a military point of view was admirable. He was so sensible of the advantages of it, that the manoeuvres of Sir William Howe for some days, could not allure him from it. In consequence of the reinforcement lately received, he had not in any preceding period of the campaign been in an equal condition for a general engagement. Though he ardently wished to be attacked, yet he would not relinquish a position, from which he hoped for reparation for the adversities of the campaign. He could not believe that general Howe with a victorious army, and that lately reinforced with four thousand men from New-York, should come out of Philadelphia only to return thither again. He therefore presumed that to avoid the disgrace of such a movement, the British commander would, from a sense of military honour, be compelled to attack him, though under great disadvantages. When he found him cautious of engaging and inclining to his left, a daring design was formed which would have been executed, had the British either continued in their position, or moved a little farther to the left of the American army.

This was to have attempted in the night to surprise Philadelphia. The necessary preparations for this purpose were made, but the retreat of the British prevented its execution. Soon after these events general Smallwood with a considerable force, was posted at Wilmington on the banks of the Delaware, and general Washington, with the main army retired to winter quarters at Valley Forge, 16 miles distant from Philadelphia. This position was preferred to distant and more comfortable villages, as being [22] calculated to give the most extensive security to the country adjacent to Philadelphia. The American army might have been tracked, by the blood of their feet, in marching without shoes or stockings over the hard frozen ground, between Whitemarsh and Valley Forge. Some hundreds of them were without blankets. Under these circumstances they had to sit down in a wood, in the latter end of December, and to build huts for their accommodation. This mode of procuring winter quarters, if not entirely novel, has been rarely if ever practiced in modern war. The cheerfulness with which the general and his army submitted to spend a severe winter, in such circumstances, rather than leave the country exposed, by retiring farther, demonstrated as well their patriotism as their fixed resolution to suffer every inconvenience, in preference to submission. Thus ended the campaign of 1777. Though Sir William Howe's army had been crowned with the most brilliant success, having gained two considerable victories, and been equally triumphant in many smaller actions, yet the whole amount of this tide of good fortune was no more than a good winter lodging for his troops in Philadelphia, whilst the men under his command possessed no more of the adjacent country than what they immediately commanded with their arms. The Congress, it is true, was compelled to leave the first seat of their deliberations, and the greatest city in the United States changed a number of its whig inhabitants for a numerous royal army; but it is as true that the minds of the Americans were, if possible, more hostile to the claims of Great-Britain than ever, and their army had gained as much by discipline and experience, as compensated for its diminution by defeats.

The events of this campaign were adverse to the sangine hopes which had been entertained of a speedy conquest of the revolted colonies. Repeated proofs had been given, that, though general

Washington was very forward to engage when he thought it to his advantage, yet it was impossible for the royal commander to bring him to action against his consent. By this mode of conducting the defence of the new formed states, two campaigns [23] had been wafted away, and the work which was originally allotted for one, was still unfinished.

1777

An account of some miscellaneous transactions will close this chapter. Lieutenant colonel Barton, of a militia regiment of the state of Rhode-Island, accompanied by about forty volunteers, passed by night from Warwick neck to Rhode-Island, and surprised general Prescot in his quarters, and brought him and one of his aids safe off to the continent. Though they had a passage of ten miles by water, they eluded the ships of war and guard boats, which lay all round the island. The enterprize was conducted with so much silence and address, that there was no alarm among the British till the colonel and his party had nearly reached the continent with their prize. Congress soon after resolved, that an elegant sword should be presented to lieutenant colonel Barton, as a testimonial of their sense of his gallant behaviour.

JULY 9

It has already been mentioned, that Congress in the latter end of November 1775, authorised the capture of vessels, laden with stores or reinforcements for their enemies. On the 23rd of March 1776, they extended this permission so far as to authorise their inhabitants to fit out armed vessels to cruise on the enemies of the united colonies. The Americans henceforth devoted themselves to privateering, and were very successful. In the course of the year they made many valuable captures, particularly of homeward bound West-India men. The particulars cannot be enumerated, but good judges have calculated, that within nine months after Congress authorised privateering, the British loss in captures, exclusive of transports and government store ships, exceeded a million sterling. They found no difficulty in selling their prizes. The ports of France were open to them, both in Europe and in the West-Indies. In the latter they were sold without any disguise, but in the former a greater regard was paid to appearances. Open sales were not permitted in the harbours of France at particular times, but even then they were made at the entrance or offing.

In the French West-India islands the inhabitants not only purchased prizes, brought in by American cruisers, [24] but fitted out privateers under American colours and commissions, and made captures of British vessels. William Bingham, of Philadelphia, was stationed as the agent of Congress, at Martinico, and he took an early and active part in arming privateers in St. Pierre, to annoy and cruise against British property. The favourable disposition of the inhabitants furnished him with an opportunity, which he successfully improved, not only to distress the British commerce, but to sow the seeds of discord between the French and English. The American privateers also found countenance in some of the ports of Spain, but not so readily nor so universally as in those of France. The British took many of the American vessels, but they were often of inferior value. Such of them as were laden with provisions, proved a seasonable relief to their West-India islands, which otherwise would have suffered from the want of those supplies, which before the war had been usually procured from the neighbouring continent.

The American privateers in the year 1777, increased in numbers and boldness. They insulted the coasts of Great-Britain and Ireland, in a manner that had never before been attempted. Such was their spirit of adventure, that it became necessary to appoint a convoy for the protection of the linen ships from Dublin and Newry. The general Mifflin privateer, after making repeated captures, arrived at Brest, and saluted the French admiral. This was returned in form as to the vessel of an independent power. Lord Stormont, the British ambassador, at the court of Versailles, irritated at the countenance given to the Americans, threatened to return immediately to London, unless satisfaction was given, and different measures were adopted by France. An order was issued in consequences of his application, requiring all American vessels to leave the ports of His Most Christian Majesty, but though the order was positive, so many evasions were practiced, and the execution of it was so relaxed, that it produced no permanent discouragement of the beneficial intercourse.

The Northern Campaign of 1777.

[25] TO EFFECT A FREE COMMUNICATION between New-York and Canada, and to maintain the navigation of the intermediate lakes, was a principal object with the British, for the campaign of 1777. The Americans presuming on this, had been early attentive to their security, in that quarter. They had resolved to construct a fort on Mount Independence, which is an eminence adjoining the strait on which Ticonderoga stands, and nearly opposite to that fortress. They had also resolved to obstruct the navigation of the strait by cassoons, to be sunk in the water, and joined so as to serve at the same time for a bridge between the fortifications on the east and west side of it; and that to prevent the British from drawing their small craft over land into lake George, the passage of that lake should be obstructed— that Fort Schuyler, the same which had formerly been called Fort

Stanwix, should be strengthened, and other fortifications erected near the Mohawk river. Requisitions were made by the commanding officer in the department for 13,600 men, as necessary for the security of this district. The adjacent states were urged to fill up their recruits, and in all respects to be in readiness for an active campaign.

The British ministry were very sanguine in their hopes, from the consequences of forming a line of communication between New-York and Canada. They considered the New England people to be the soul of the confederacy, and promised themselves much by severing them from all free communication with the neighbouring states. They hoped, when this was accomplished, to be able to surround them so effectually with fleets and armies, and Indian allies, as to compel their submission. Animated with these expectations they left nothing undone, which bid fair for ensuring the success of the plans they had formed for this purpose.

The regular troops, British and German, allotted to this service, were upwards of 7000. As artillery is considered to be particularly useful in an American war, [26] where numerous inhabitants are to be driven out of woods and fastnesses, this part of the service was particularly attended to. The brass train that was sent out, was perhaps the finest, and the most excellently supplied, both as to officers and men, that had ever been allotted to second the operations of an equal force. In addition to the regulars, it was supposed that the Canadians and the loyalists, in the neighbouring states, would add large reinforcements, well calculated for the peculiar nature of the service. Arms and accoutrements were accordingly provided to supply them. Several nations of savages had also been induced to take up the hatchet, as allies to his Britannic majesty. Not only the humanity, but the policy of employing them, was questioned in Great-Britain. The opposers of it contended that Indians were capricious, inconstant and intractable, their rapacity insatiate, and their actions cruel and barbarous. At the same time their services were represented to be uncertain, and that no dependence could be placed on their most solemn engagements. On the other hand, the zeal of British ministers for reducing the revolted colonies, was so violent as to make them, in their excessive wrath, forget that their adversaries were men. They contended, that in their circumstances

1777

every appearance of lenity, by inciting to disobedience, and thereby increasing the objects of punishment, was eventual cruelty. In their opinion partial severity was general mercy, and the only method of speedily crushing the rebellion, was to invelope its abettors in such complicated distress, as by rendering their situation intolerable, would make them willing to accept the proffered blessings of peace and security. The sentiments of those who were for employing Indians against the Americans, prevailed. Presents were liberally distributed among them. Induced by these, and also by their innate thirst for war and plunder, they poured forth their warriors in such abundance, that their numbers threatened to be an incumberance.

The vast force destined for this service was put under the command of lieutenant general Burgoyne, an officer whose abilities were well known, and whose spirit of enterprize [27] and thirst for military fame could not be exceeded. He was supported by major general Philips of the artillery, who had established a solid reputation by his good conduct during the late war in Germany, and by major general Reidesel, and brigadier general Speecht of the German troops, together with the British generals Frazer, Powell and Hamilton, all officers of distinguished merit.   1777

The British had also undisputed possession of the navigation of Lake Champlain. Their marine force thereon, with which in the preceding campaign they had destroyed the American shipping on the lakes, was not only entire, but unopposed.

A considerable force was left in Canada for its internal security, and Sir Guy Carleton's military command was restricted to the limits of that province. Though the British ministry attributed the preservation of Canada to his abilities in 1775 and 1776, yet by their arrangements for the year 1777, he was only called upon to act a secondary part, in subserviency to the grand expedition committed to general Burgoyne. His behaviour on this occasion, was conformable to the greatness of his mind. Instead of thwarting or retarding a service which was virtually taken out of his hands, he applied himself to support and forward it in all its parts, with the same diligence as if the arrangement had been entirely his own, and committed to himself for execution.

The plan of the British for their projected irruption into the northwestern frontier of New-York, consisted of two parts. General Burgoyne with the main body, was to advance by the way of Lake Champlain, with positive orders, as has been said, to force his way to Albany, or at least so far as to effect a junction with the royal army from New-York. A detachment was to ascend the river St. Lawrence, as far as Lake Ontario, and from that quarter to penetrate towards Albany, by the way of the Mohawk river. This was put under the command of lieutenant colonel St. Leger, and consisted of about 200 British troops, a regiment of New-York loyalists raised and commanded by Sir John Johnson, and a large body of savages.

1777

Lieutenant general Burgoyne arrived in Quebec [28] on the 6th of May, and exerted all diligence to prosecute in due time the objects of the expedition. He proceeded up Lake Champlain and landed near

JUNE 20, 21

Crown-Point. At this place he met the Indians—gave them a war feast, and made a speech to them. This was well calculated to excite them to take part with the royal army, but at the same time to repress their barbarity. He pointedly forbad them to shed blood when not opposed in arms, and commanded that aged men, women, children, and prisoners, should be held sacred from the knife and the hatchet, even in the heat of actual conflict. A reward was promised for prisoners, and a severe enquiry threatened for scalps, though permission was granted to take them from those who were previously killed in fair opposition. These restrictions were not sufficient, as will appear in the sequel, to restrain their barbarities. The Indians having decidedly taken part with the British army, general Burgoyne issued a proclamation, calculated to spread terror among the inhabitants. The numbers of his Indian associates were magnified, and their eagerness to be let loose to their prey described in high sounding words. The force of the British armies and fleets prepared to crush every part of the revolted colonies, was also displayed in pompous language. Encouragement and employment were promised to those who should assist in the re-establishment of legal government, and security held out to the peaceable and industrious, who continued in their habitations. All the calamities of war arrayed in their most terrific forms, were denounced against those who should persevere in a military opposition to the royal forces.

General Burgoyne advanced with his army in a few days to Crown-
Point. At this place he issued orders of which the following words
are a part: "The army embarks to-morrow to approach the enemy.
The services required on this expedition are critical and conspicuous.
During our progress occasions may occur, in which, nor difficulty,
nor labour, nor life, are to be regarded. This army must not retreat."
From Crown-Point the royal army proceeded to invest Ticonderoga.
On their approach to it, they advanced with equal caution and order
[29] on both sides of the lake, while their naval force kept in its
center. Within a few days they had surrounded three-fourths of the
American works at Ticonderoga and Mount Independence, and had
also advanced a work on Sugar Hill which commands both, so far
towards completion, that in 24 hours it would have been ready to
open. In these circumstances general St. Clair the commanding
officer, resolved to evacuate the post at all events; but conceiving it
prudent to take the sentiments of the general officers, he called a
council of war on the occasion. It was represented to this council,
that their whole numbers were not sufficient to man one half of the
works, and that as the whole must be on constant duty, it would be
impossible for them to sustain the necessary fatigue for any length
of time, and that as the place would be completely invested on all
sides within a day, nothing but an immediate evacuation of the posts
could save their troops. The situation of general St. Clair was
eminently embarrassing. Such was the confidence of the states in
the fancied strength of this post, and of the supposed superiority of
force for its defence, that to retreat without risquing an action could
not fail of drawing on him the execration of the multitude. To stand
still, and by suffering himself to be surrounded to risque his whole
army for a single post, was contrary to the true interest of the states.
In this trying situation, with the unanimous approbation of a council
of his general officers, he adopted the heroic resolution of sacrificing
personal reputation to save his army.

The assumption of confident appearances by the garrison, had
induced their adversaries to proceed with great caution. While from
this cause they were awed into respect, the evacuation was completed
with so much secrecy and expedition, that a considerable part of the
public stores was saved, and the whole would have been embarked,

had not a violent gale of wind which sprung up in the night, prevented the boats from reaching their station.

The works abandoned by the Americans, were as follow: The old French lines constructed in the late war [30] between France and England, which looked towards general Burgoyne's encampment had been repaired the year before, and were in good order. About the center was a battery of six guns. These occupied about two-thirds of the high ground from the strait to the old fort. The remaining third was open, but some fleches were thrown up for its security. The old fort was in ruins, but some guns were mounted on a ravelin thereof, that looked towards the lake. There was also a battery of four guns in the French lines, which had the same aspect. On the point above the bridge was a battery of four guns, and on Mount Independence another of six or eight. The fort on that side was nearly a mile from the battery, and was formed of piquets. The defence of it might have employed four hundred men, but it could not have resisted a six pounder. There were no barracks within it, nor a drop of water, but at a considerable distance. From the battery at the point, a line of entrenchment ran round the mount, upwards of a mile and a half in length. There had been a strong abbatis in front of this line the year before, but it had been consumed by fire, as was also that in front of the French lines. Towards the east of the mount was a block-house. Another was on the Ticonderoga side. New works were begun on the mount, but there was neither time nor strength of hands to complete them. A great deal of timber had been felled between the east creek and the foot of the mount, to retard the approaches of the British. All the redoubts on the low ground were abandoned, for want of men to occupy them. These works, together with 93 pieces of ordnance, and a large collection of provisions, fell into the hands of the British.

This evacuation of Ticonderoga was the subject of a severe scrutiny. Congress recalled their general officers in the northern department, and ordered an enquiry into their conduct. They also nominated two gentlemen of eminence in the law to assist the judge advocate in prosecuting that enquiry, and appointed a committee of their own body to collect evidence in support of the charges, which were on this occasion brought against them. General [31] St. Clair, from the necessity of the case, submitted to this innovation in the mode of conducting courts martial, but in behalf of the army protested against its being drawn into precedent. Charges of no less magnitude than cowardice, incapacity and treachery, were brought forward in court against him, and believed by many. The public mind, sore with the loss of Ticonderoga, and apprehensive of general distress, sought to ease itself by throwing blame on the general. When the situation of the army permitted an enquiry into his conduct, he was honourably acquitted. In the course of his trial it was made to appear, that though 13,600 men had been early called for as necessary to defend the northern posts, yet on the approach of general Burgoyne, the whole force collected to oppose him was only 2546 continentals, and 900 militia badly equipped, and worse armed. From the insufficiency of their numbers, they could not possess themselves of Sugar-hill, nor of Mount-Hope, though the former commanded the works both of Ticonderoga and Mount Independence, and the latter was of great importance for securing the communication with Lake George, and had been fortified the year before with that view. To the question which had been repeatedly asked, "why was the evacuation, if really necessary, delayed, till the Americans were so nearly surrounded, as to occasion the loss of such valuable stores?" It was answered, that

from various circumstances it was impossible for general St. Clair to get early information of the numbers opposed to him. They made no debarkation till they came to Gilliland's creek, which is about 40 miles to the northward of Ticonderoga, and from this they speedily reimbarked. The savages which they kept in front, deterred small reconnoitring parties from approaching so near as to make any discoveries of their numbers. Large parties from the nature of the ground, could not have been supported without risquing a general action, and that from the combined operation of these circumstances, the numbers of the approaching royal army were effectually concealed from the garrison, till the van of their force appeared in full view before it.

The retreating army embarked as [32] much of their baggage and stores as they had any prospect of saving on board batteaux, and dispatched them under convoy of five armed gallies to Skenesborough.

1777

Their main body took its route towards the same place by way of Castleton. The British were no sooner apprized of the retreat of the Americans than they pursued them. General Frazer, at the head of the light troops, advanced on their main body. Major general Reidesel was also ordered with the greater part of the Brunswic troops, to march in the same direction. General Burgoyne in person conducted the pursuit by water. The obstructions to the navigation, not having been completed, were soon cut through. The two frigates—the Royal George and the Inflexible, together with the gun boats, having effected their passage, pursued with so much rapidity, that in the course of a day the gun boats came up with and attacked the American gallies near Skenesborough falls. On the approach of the frigates all opposition ceased. Two of the gallies were taken and three blown up. The Americans set fire to their works, mills and batteaux. They were now left in the woods, destitute of provisions. In this forlorn situation they made their escape up Woodcreek to fort Anne. Brigadier Frazer pursued the retreating Americans—came up with, and attacked their

rear guard, at Hubbordton. In the course of the engagement he was joined by the German troops, commanded by general Reidesel. The Americans commanded by colonel Warner, made a gallant resistance, but after sustaining considerable loss, were obliged to give way. Lieut. colonel Hall, with the ninth British regiment, was detached from Skenesborough by general Burgoyne, to take post near fort Anne. An engagement ensued between this regiment and a few Americans, but the latter, after a conflict of two hours, fired the fort, and retreated to fort Edward. The destruction of the gallies and batteaux of the Americans at Skenesborough, and the defeat of their rear, obliged general St. Clair, in order to avoid being between two fires, to change the route of his main body, and to turn off from Castleton to the left. After a fatiguing and distressing march of seven days, he joined

[33] general Schuyler at fort Edward. Their combined forces, inclusive of the militia, not exceeding in the whole 4400 men, were not long after on the approach of general Burgoyne, compelled to retire farther into the country, bordering on Albany. Such was the rapid torrent of success, which in this period of the campaign swept away all opposition from before the royal army. The officers and men were highly elated with their good fortune. They considered their toils to

be nearly at an end; Albany to be within their grasp, and the conquest of the adjacent provinces reduced to a certainty. In Great-Britain intelligence of the progress of Burgoyne diffused a general joy. As to the Americans, the loss of reputation which they sustained in the opinion of their European admirers, was greater than their loss of posts, artillery and troops. They were stigmatised as wanting the resolution and abilities of men in the defence of their dearest rights. Their unqualified subjugation, or unconditional submission was considered as being near at hand. An opinion was diffused, that the war in effect was over, or that the farther resistance of the colonists would serve only to make the terms of their submission more humiliating. The terror which the loss of Ticonderoga spread throughout the New-England states was great, but nevertheless no disposition to purchase safety by submission appeared in any quarter. They did not sink under the apprehensions of danger, but acted with vigour and firmness. The royal army, after these successes, continued for some days in Skenesborough, waiting for their tents, baggage and provision. In the mean time general Burgoyne put forth a proclamation, in which he called on the inhabitants of the adjacent towns to send a deputation of ten or more persons from their respective townships, to meet colonel Skene at Castleton, on the 15th of July. The troops were at the same time busily employed in opening a road, and clearing a creek, to favour their advance, and to open a passage for the conveyance of their stores. A party of the royal army which had been left behind at Ticonderoga, was equally industrious in carrying gun boats, provision, vessels, and batteaux over land, into lake George. [34] An immensity of labour in every quarter was necessary, but animated as they were with past successes and future hopes, they disregarded toil and danger. 1777

From Skenesborough general Burgoyne directed his course across the country to Fort Edward, on Hudson's-River. Though the distance in a right line from one to the other is but a few miles, yet such is the impracticable nature of the country, and such were the artificial difficulties thrown in his way, that nearly as many days were consumed as the distance passed over in a direct line would have measured in miles. The Americans under the direction of general Schuyler, had cut large trees on both sides of the road, so as to fall across with their branches interwoven. The face of the country was likewise so broken with creeks and marshes, that they had no less than forty bridges to construct, one of which was a log-work over a morass, two miles in extent. This difficult march might have been avoided, had general Burgoyne fallen back from Skenesborough to Ticonderoga, and thence proceeded by lake George, but he declined this route, from an apprehension that a retrograde motion on his part would abate the panic of the enemy. He had also a suspicion that some delay might be occasioned by the American garrison at Fort George, as in case of his taking that route, they might safely continue to resist to the last extremity, having open in their rear a place of retreat. On the other hand it was presumed, that as soon as they knew that the royal army was marching in a direction which was likely to cut off their retreat, they would consult their safety by a seasonable evacuation. In addition to these reasons he had the advice and persuasion of colonel Skene. That gentleman had been recommended to him as a person proper to be consulted. His land was so situated, that the opening of a road between Fort Edward and Skenesborough would greatly enhance its value. This circumstance might have made him more urgent in his recommendations of that route, especially as its being the shortest, it bid fair for uniting the royal interest with private convenience. The opinion formed by general Burgoyne of the effect of his direct movement from Skenes-

1777 borough [35] to Fort Edward on the American garrison, was verified by the event; for being apprehensive of having their retreat cut off, they abandoned their fort and burnt their vessels. The navigation of Lake George being thereby left free, provisions and ammunition were brought forward from Fort George to the first navigable parts of Hudson's-River. This is a distance of 15 miles, and the roads of difficult passage. The intricate combination of land and water carriage, together with the insufficient means of transportation, and excessive rains, caused such delays, that at the end of fifteen days there were not more than four days provision brought forward, nor above ten batteaux in the river. The difficulties of this conveyance, as well as of the march through the wilderness from Skenesborough to Fort Edward, were encountered and overcome by the royal army, with a spirit and alacrity which could not be exceeded. At length, after incredible fatigue and labour, general Burgoyne, and the army under his command reached Fort Edward, on Hudson's-River. Their exultation on accomplishing, what for a long time had been the object of their hopes, was unusually great.

While the British were retarded in their advance by the combined difficulties of nature and art, events took place, which proved the wisdom and propriety of the retreat from Ticonderoga. The army saved by that means, was between the inhabitants and general Burgoyne. This abated the panic of the people, and became a center of rendezvous for them to repair to. On the other hand, had they stood their ground at Ticonderoga, they must in the ordinary course of events, in a short time, either have been cut to pieces, or surrendered themselves prisoners of war. In either case, as general St. Clair represented in his elegant defence:

> Fear and dismay would have seized on the inhabitants from the false opinion that had been formed of the strength of these posts, wringing grief and moping melancholy, would have filled the habitations of those whose dearest connexions were in that army, and a lawless host of ruffians, set loose from every social principle, would have roamed at large through the defenceless [36] country, while bands of savages would have carried havock, devastation and terror before them. Great part of the state of New-York must have submitted to the conqueror, and in it he would have found the means to prosecute his success. He would have been able effectually to have co-operated with general Howe, and would probably soon have been in the same country with him—that country where the illustrious Washington, with an inferior force made so glorious a stand, but who must have been obliged to retire, if both armies had come upon him at once—or he might have been forced to a general and decisive action in unfavourable circumstances, whereby the hopes, the now well founded hopes of America—of liberty, peace and safety might have been cut off forever.

Such, it was apprehended, would have been the consequences, if the American northern army had not retreated from their posts at Ticonderoga. From the adoption of that measure very different events took place. In a few days after the evacuation, general Schuyler issued a proclamation, calling to the minds of the inhabitants the late barbarities and desolations of the royal army in Jersey—warning them that they would be dealt with as traitors, if they joined the British, and requiring them with their arms to repair to the American standard. Numerous parties were also employed in bringing off public stores, and in felling trees, and throwing obstructions in the way of the advancing royal army. At first an universal panic intimidated the inhabitants, but they soon recovered. The laws of self-preservation operated in their full force, and diffused a general activity through the adjacent states. The formalities of convening, draughting and officering the militia, were in many instances dispenced with. Hundreds seized their firelocks, and marched on the general call, without waiting for the orders of their immediate commanders. The inhabitants had no means of security, but to abandon their habitations, and take up arms. Every individual saw the necessity of becoming a temporary soldier. The terror excited by the Indians, instead of disposing the inhabitants to court British protection, had a contrary effect. The friends of the royal cause, as well as its enemies, [37] suffered from their indiscriminate barbarities. Among other instances, the murder of Miss M'Crea excited an universal horror. This young lady, in the innocence of youth, and the bloom of beauty— the daughter of a steady loyalist, and engaged to be married to a British officer, was on the very day of her intended nuptials, massacred by the savage auxiliaries, attached to the British army.* Occasion was thereby given to inflame the populace, and to blacken the royal cause. The cruelties of the Indians, and the cause in which they

1777

* This, though true, was no premedidated barbarity. The circumstances were as follows: Mr. Jones, her lover, from an anxiety for her safety, engaged some Indians to remove her from among the Americans, and promised to reward the person who should bring her safe to him, with a barrel of rum. Two of the Indians, who had conveyed her some distance, on the way to her intended husband, disputed, which of them should present her to Mr. Jones. Both were anxious for the reward. One of them killed her with his tomahawk, to prevent the other from receiving it. Burgoyne obliged the Indians to deliver up the murderer, and threatened to put him to death. His life was only spared, upon the Indians agreeing to terms, which the general thought would be more efficacious than an execution, in preventing similar mischiefs.

were engaged, were associated together, and presented in one view to the alarmed inhabitants. Those whose interest it was to draw forth the militia in support of American independence, strongly expressed their execrations of the army, which submitted to accept of Indian aid, and they loudly condemned that government which could call such auxiliaries into a civil contest, as were calculated not to subdue, but to exterminate a people whom they affected to reclaim as subjects. Their cruel mode of warfare, by putting to death as well the smiling infant and the defenceless female, as the resisting armed man, excited an universal spirit of resistance. In conjunction with other circum- stances, it impressed on the minds of the inhabitants a general conviction that a vigorous determined opposition was the only alternative for the preservation of their property, their children and their wives. Could they have indulged the hope of security and protection while they remained peaceably at their homes, they would have found many excuses for declining to assume the profession of soldiers, but when they contrasted the dangers of a manly resistance, with those of a passive inaction, they chose the former, as the least of two unavoidable evils. All the feeble aid, [38] which the royal army 1777 received from their Indian auxiliaries, was infinitely overbalanced by the odium it brought on their cause, and by that determined spirit of opposition which the dread of their savage cruelties excited. While danger was remote, the pressing calls of Congress, and of the general officers, for the inhabitants to be in readiness to oppose a distant foe were unavailing, or tardily executed, but no sooner had they recovered from the first impression of the general panic, than they turned out with unexampled alacrity. The owners of the soil came forward with that ardor, which the love of dear connections and of property inspires. An army was speedily poured forth from the woods and mountains. When they who had begun the retreat were nearly wasted away, the spirit of the country immediately supplied their place with a much greater and more formidable force. In addition to these incitements, it was early conjectured, that the royal army, by pushing forward would be so entangled as not to be able to advance or retreat on equal terms. Men of abilities and of eloquence, influenced with this expectation, harangued the inhabitants in their several towns—set forth in high-colouring, the cruelties of the savage auxiliaries of Great-Britain, and the fair prospects of capturing the whole force of their enemies. From the combined influence of these causes, the American army soon amounted to upwards of 13,000 men.

While general Burgoyne was forcing his way down towards Albany, lieutenant colonel St. Leger was co-operating with him in the Mohawk country. He had ascended the river St. Lawrence, crossed Lake Ontario, and commenced the siege of Fort Schuyler. On the approach of this detachment of the royal army, general Harkimer collected about 800 of the whig militia of the parts adjacent, for the relief of the garrison.

St. Leger aware of the consequences of being attacked in his trenches, detached Sir John Johnson, with some tories and Indians to lie in ambush, and intercept the advancing militia. The stratagem took effect. The general and his militia were surprised, but several of the Indians were nevertheless killed by their fire. A scene of confusion [39] followed. Some of Harkimer's men run off, but others posted themselves behind logs, and continued to fight with bravery and success. The loss on the side of the Americans was 160 killed, besides the wounded. Among the former was their gallant leader general Harkimer. Several of their killed and wounded were principal inhabitants of that part of the country. Colonel St. Leger availed himself of the terror excited on this occasion, and endeavoured by strong representations of Indian barbarity to intimidate the garrison into an immediate surrender. He sent verbal, and written messages,

demanding the surrender of the fort, and stating the impossibility of their obtaining relief, as their friends under general Harkimer were entirely cut off, and as general Burgoyne had forced his way through the country, and was daily receiving the submission of the inhabitants," he represented "the pains he had taken to soften the Indians, and to obtain engagements from them, that in case of an immediate surrender every man in the garrison should be spared," and particularly enlarged on the circumstance, "that the Indians were determined, in case of their meeting with farther opposition, to massacre not only the garrison, but every man, woman or child in the Mohawk country." Colonel Gansevort, who commanded in the fort, replied, "that being by the United States entrusted with the charge of the garrison, he was determined to defend it to the last extremity, against all enemies whatever, without any concern for the consequences of doing his duty.

It being resolved maugre, the threats of Indian barbarities to defend the fort—lieutenant colonel Willet undertook, in conjunction with lieutenant Stockwell, to give information to their fellow citizens, of the state of the garrison. These two adventurous officers passed by night through the besiegers works, and at the hazard of falling into the hands of savages, and suffering from them the severity of torture, made their way for fifty miles through dangers and difficulties, in order to procure relief for their besieged associates. In the mean time the British carried on their operations with such industry, that in less than three weeks they had advanced within 150 yards of the fort.

[40] The brave garrison, in its hour of danger, was not forgotten. 1777 General Arnold, with a brigade of continental troops, had been previously detached by general Schuyler for their relief, and was then near at hand. Mr. Tost Schuyler who had been taken up by the Americans, on suspicion of his being a spy, was promised his life and his estate, on consideration that he should go on and alarm the Indians with such representations of the numbers marching against them, as would occasion their retreat. He immediately proceeded to the camp of the Indians, and being able to converse in their own language, informed them that vast numbers of hostile Americans were near at hand. They were thoroughly frightened and determined to go off. St. Leger used every art to retain them, but nothing could change their determination. It is the characteristic of these people on a reverse of fortune to betray irresolution, and a total want of that constancy, which is necessary to struggle for a length of time with difficulties. They had found the fort stronger and better defended than was expected. They had lost several headmen in their engagement with general Harkimer, and had gotten no plunder. These circumstances, added to the certainty of the approach of a reinforcement to their adversaries, which they believed to be much greater than it really was, made them quite untractable. Part of them instantly decamped, and the remainder threatened to follow, if the British did not immediately retreat. This measure was adopted, and the siege

raised. From the disorder, occasioned by the precipitancy of the Indians, the tents, and much of the artillery and stores of the besiegers, fell into the hands of the garrison. The discontented savages, exasperated by their ill fortune, are said, on their retreat, to have robbed their British associates, of their baggage and provisions.

While the fate of Fort Schuyler was in suspense, it occurred to general Burgoyne, on hearing of its being besieged, that a sudden and rapid movement forward would be of the utmost consequence. As the principal force of his adversaries was in front between him and Albany, he hoped by advancing on them, to reduce [41] them to the necessity of fighting, or of retreating out of his way to New-England. Had they to avoid an attack, retreated up the Mohawk river, they would, in case of St. Leger's success, have put themselves between two fires. Had they retreated to Albany, it was supposed their situation would have been worse, as a co-operation from New-York was expected. Besides, in case of that movement, an opportunity would have been given for a junction of Burgoyne and St. Leger. To have retired from the scene of action by filing off for New-England, seemed to be the only opening left for their escape. With such views general Burgoyne promised himself great advantages, from advancing rapidly towards Albany. The principal objection against this plausible project, was the difficulty of furnishing provisions to his troops. To keep up a communication with Fort George, so as to obtain from that garrison, regular supplies at a distance daily encreasing, was wholly impracticable. The advantages which were expected from the proposed measure, were too dazzling to be easily relinquished. Though the impossibility of drawing provisions from the stores in their rear, was known and acknowledged, yet a hope was indulged that they might be elsewhere obtained. A plan was therefore formed to open resources, from the plentiful farms of Vermont. Every day's account, and particularly the information of colonel Skene, induced Burgoyne to believe, that one description of the inhabitants in that country were panic struck, and that another, and by far the most numerous, were friends to the British interest, and only wanted the appearance of a protecting power to shew themselves. Relying on this intelligence, he detached only 500 men, 100 Indians, and two field pieces, which he supposed would be fully sufficient for the expedition. The command of this force was given to lieutenant colonel Baum, and it was supposed that with it he would be enabled to seize upon a magazine of supplies which the Americans had collected at Bennington, and which was only guarded by militia. It was also intended to try the temper of the inhabitants and to mount the dragoons. Lieutenant colonel Baum was instructed to keep the regular [42] force posted, while the light troops felt their way; and to avoid 1777 all danger of being surrounded, or of having his retreat cut off. But he proceeded with less caution than his perilous situation required. Confiding in the numbers and promised aid of those who were depended upon as friends, he presumed too much. On his approaching the place of his destination, he found the American militia stronger than had been supposed. He therefore took post in the vicinity, entrenched his party, and dispatched an express to general Burgoyne, with an account of his situation. Colonel Breyman was detached to reinforce him. Though every exertion was made to push forward this reinforcement, yet from the impracticable face of the country and defective means of transportation, 32 hours elapsed before they had marched 24 miles. General Starke who commanded the American militia at Bennington, engaged with them before the junction of the two royal detachments could be effected. On this occasion about 800 undisciplined militia, without bayonets, or a single piece of artillery, attacked and routed 500 regular troops advantageously posted behind entrenchments—furnished with the best arms, and defended with two pieces of artillery. The field pieces were taken from the party commanded by col. Baum, and the greatest part of his detachment was either killed or captured. Colonel Breyman arrived on the same ground and on the same day, but not till the action was over. Instead of meeting his friends, as he expected, he found himself briskly attacked. This was begun by colonel Warner, (who with his continental regiment, which having been sent for from Manchester, came opportunely at this time) and was well supported by Stark's militia, which had just defeated the party commanded by colonel Baum. Breyman's troops, though fatigued with their preceding march, behaved with great resolution, but were at length compelled to abandon their artillery, and retreat. In these two actions the icans took four brass field pieces, twelve brass drums, 250 dragoon swords, 4 ammunition wagons, and about 700 prisoners. The loss of the Americans, inclusive of their wounded, was about 100 men. [43] Congress resolved, "that their thanks be presented to gen. Stark, of the New-Hampshire militia, and the officers and troops under his command, for their brave and successful attack upon, and signal victory over the enemy in their lines at Bennington, and also, that brigadier Stark, be appointed a brigadier general in the army of the United States." Never were thanks more deservedly bestowed. The overthrow of these detachments was the first link in a grand chain of causes, which finally drew down ruin on the whole royal army. The confidence with which the Americans were inspired, on finding themselves able to defeat regular troops, produced surprising effects. It animated their exertions, and filled them with expectation of farther successes.

That military pride, which is the soul of an army, was nurtured by the captured artillery, and other trophies of victory. In proportion to the elevation of the Americans, was the depression of their adversaries. Accustomed to success, as they had been in the preceding part of the campaign, they felt unusual mortification from this unexpected check. Though it did not diminish their courage, it abated their confidence. It is not easy to enumerate all the disastrous consequences which resulted to the royal army, from the failure of their expedition to Bennington. These were so extensive, that their loss of men was the least considerable. It deranged every plan for pushing the advantages which had been previously obtained. Among other embarrassments it reduced general Burgoyne to the alternative of halting, till he brought forward supplies from Fort George, or of advancing without them at the risque of being starved. The former being adopted, the royal army was detained from August 16th, to September 13th. This unavoidable delay, gave time and opportunity for the Americans to collect in great numbers.

The defeat of lieutenant colonel Baum, was the first event which for a long time had taken place in favour of the American northern army. From December 1775, it had experienced one misfortune, treading on the heels of another, and defeat succeeding defeat. Every movement [44] had been either retreating or evacuating. The subsequent transactions present a remarkable contrast. Fortune, which previous to the battle of Bennington, had not for a moment quitted the British standard, seemed after that event, as if she had totally deserted it, and gone over to the opposite party.

After the evacuation of Ticonderoga, the Americans had fallen back from one place to another, till they at last fixed at Vansnaick's island. Soon after this retreating system was adopted, Congress recalled their general officers, and put general Gates at the head of their northern army. His arrival gave fresh vigour to the exertions of AUG. 19 the inhabitants. The militia flushed with their recent victory at Bennington, collected in great numbers to his standard. They soon began to be animated with a hope of capturing the whole British army. A spirit of adventure burst forth in many different points of direction. While general Burgoyne was urging his preparations for advancing towards Albany, an enterprize was undertaken by general Lincoln to recover Ticonderoga, and the other posts in the rear of SEPT. 13 the royal army. He detached colonel Brown with 500 men to the landing at Lake George. The colonel conducted his operations with so much address, that he surprised all the outposts between the landing at the north end of Lake George, and the body of the fortress at Ticonderoga. He also took Mount Defiance and Mount Hope, the French lines, and a block-house, 200 batteaux, several gun boats, and an armed sloop, together with 290 prisoners, and at the same time released 100 Americans. His own loss was trifling. Colonel Brown and colonel Johnson, the latter of whom had been detached with 500 men, to attempt Mount Independence, on examination found that the reduction of either that post or of Ticonderoga, was beyond their ability. When the necessary stores for thirty days subsistence, were brought forward from Lake George, general Burgoyne gave up all communication with the magazines in his rear, and crossed Hudson's river. This movement was the subject of much discussion. 13 & 14 Some charged it on the impetuosity of the general, and alledged, that it was premature before [45] he was sure of aid from the royal forces 1777 posted in New-York, but he pleaded the peremptory orders of his superiors. The rapid advance of Burgoyne, and especially his passage of the North-River, added much to the impracticability of his future retreat, and in conjunction with subsequent events made the total ruin of his army in a great degree unavoidable.

General Burgoyne, after crossing the Hudson, advanced along its side, and in four days encamped on the heights, about two miles from general Gates' camp, which was three miles above Stillwater. The Americans, elated with their successes at Bennington and Fort Schuyler, thought no more of retreating, but came out to meet the advancing British, and engaged them with firmness and resolution.

SEPT. 19 The attack began a little before midday, between the scouting parties of the two armies. The commanders on both sides, supported and reinforced their respective parties. The conflict, though severe, was only partial for an hour and a half, but after a short pause it became general, and continued for three hours, without any intermission. A constant blaze of fire was kept up, and both armies seemed to be determined on death or victory. The Americans and British alternately drove, and were driven by each other. Men, and particularly officers, dropped every moment, and on every side. Several of the Americans placed themselves in high trees, and as often as they could distinguish an officer's uniform, took him off by deliberately aiming at his person. Few actions have been characterised by more obstinacy in attack or defence. The British repeatedly tried their bayonets, but without their usual success in the use of that weapon. At length, night put an end to the effusion of blood. The British lost upwards of 500 men, including their killed, wounded, and prisoners. The Americans, inclusive of the missing, lost 319. Thirty-six, out of forty-eight British matrosses were killed, or wounded. The 62nd British regiment, which was 500 strong, when it left Canada, was reduced to 60 men, and 4 or 5 officers. This hard fought battle decided nothing, and little else

1777 than honour was gained by either army, but nevertheless [46] it was followed by important consequences. Of these one was the diminution of the zeal and alacrity of the Indians in the British army. The dangerous service, in which they were engaged, was by no means suited to their habits of war. They were disappointed of the plunder they expected, and saw nothing before them but hardships and danger. Fidelity and honour were too feeble motives in the minds of savages, to retain them in such an unproductive service. By deserting in the season when their aid would have been most useful, they furnished a second instance of the impolicy of depending upon them. Very little more perseverance was exhibited by the Canadians, and other British provincials. They also abandoned the British standard, when they found, that instead of a flying and dispirited enemy, they had a numerous and resolute force opposed to them. These desertions were not the only disappointments which general Burgoyne experienced. From the commencement of the expedition, he had promised himself a strong reinforcement from that part of the British army, which was stationed at New-York. He depended on its being able to force its way to Albany, and to join him there, or in the vicinity. This co-operation, though attempted, failed in the execution, while the expectation of it contributed to involve him in some difficulties, to which he would not have otherwise been exposed.

General Burgoyne received intelligence in a cypher, that Sir Henry Clinton, who then commanded in New-York, intended to make a diversion in his favour, by attacking the fortresses which the Americans had erected on Hudson's river, to obstruct the intercourse between New-York and Albany. In answer to this communication he dispatched to Sir Henry Clinton some trusty persons, with a full account of his situation, and with instructions to press the immediate execution of the proposed co-operation, and to assure him, that he was enabled in point of provisions, and fixed in his resolution, to hold his present position till the 12th of October, in the hopes of favourable events. The reasonable expectation of a diversion from New-York, founded on this intelligence, [47] made it disgraceful to retreat, and at the same time improper to urge offensive operations. In this posture of affairs, a delay of two or three weeks, in expectation of the promised co-operation from New-York became necessary. In the mean time the provisions of the royal army were lessening, and the animation and numbers of the American army increasing. The New-England people were fully sensible, that their All was at stake, and at the same time sanguine, that by vigorous exertions Burgoyne would be so entangled, that his surrender would be unavoidable. Every moment made the situation of the British army more critical. From the uncertainty of receiving farther supplies, general Burgoyne lessened the soldiers provisions. The 12th of October, the term till which the royal army had agreed to wait for aid from New-York, was fast approaching, and no intelligence of the expected co-operation had arrived. In this alarming situation it was thought proper to make a movement to the left of the Americans. The body of troops employed

SEPT. 21

OCT. 1

for this purpose consisted of 1500 chosen men, and was commanded by generals Burgoyne, Philips, Reidesel, and Frazer. As they advanced, they were checked by a sudden and impetuous attack; but major OCT. 7 Ackland, at the head of the British grenadiers, sustained it with great firmness. The Americans extended their attack along the whole front of the German troops, who were posted on the right of the grenadiers, and they also marched a large body round their flank, in order to cut off their retreat. To oppose this bold enterprise, the British light infantry, with a part of the 24th regiment, were directed to form a second line, and to cover the retreat of the troops into the camp. In the mean time the Americans pushed forward a fresh and a strong re-inforcement, to renew the action on Burgoyne's left. That part of his army was obliged to give way, but the light infantry, and 24th regiment, by a quick movement, came to its succour, and saved it from total ruin. The British lines being exposed to great danger, the troops which were nearest to them returned for their defence. General Arnold, with a brigade of continental troops, pushed for the works 1777 [48] possessed by lord Balcarras, at the head of the British light infantry; but the brigade having an abbatis to cross, and many other obstructions to surmount, was compelled to retire. Arnold left this brigade, and came to Jackson's regiment, which he ordered instantly to advance, and attack the lines and redoubt in their front, which were defended by lieutenant colonel Breyman at the head of the German grenadiers. The assailants pushed on with rapidity, and carried the works. Arnold was one of the first who entered them. Lieutenant colonel Breyman was killed. The troops commanded by him retired firing. They gained their tents about 30 or 40 yards from their works, but on finding that the assault was general, they gave one fire, after which some retreated to the British camp, but others threw down their arms. The night put an end to the action.

This day was fatal to many brave men. The British officers suffered more than their common proportion. Among their slain general Frazer, on account of his distinguished merit, was the subject of particular regret. Sir James Clark, Burgoyne's aid de camp, was mortally wounded. The general himself had a narrow escape, a shot passed through his hat, and another through his waistcoat. Majors Williams and Ackland were taken, and the latter was wounded. The loss of the Americans was inconsiderable, but general Arnold, to whose impetuosity they were much indebted for the success of the day, was among their wounded. They took more than 200 prisoners, besides 9 pieces of brass artillery, and the encampment of a German brigade, with all their equipage.

The royal troops were under arms the whole of the next day, in expectation of another action, but nothing more than skirmishes took place. At this time, general Lincoln, when reconnoitring, received a dangerous wound: An event which was greatly regretted, as he possessed much of the esteem and confidence of the American army.

The position of the British army, after the action of the 7th, was so dangerous, that an immediate and total change became necessary. This hazardous measure was executed without loss or disorder. The British [49] camp, with all its appurtenances, was removed in the course of a single night. The American general now saw a fair prospect of overcoming the army opposed to him, without exposing his own to the danger of another battle. His measures were therefore principally calculated to cut off their retreat, and prevent their receiving any farther supplies.

1777

While general Burgoyne was pushing on towards Albany, an unsuccessful attempt to relieve him was made by the British commander in New-York. For this purpose, Sir Henry Clinton conducted an expedition up Hudson's river. This consisted of about 3000 men, and was accompanied by a suitable naval force. After making many feints he landed at Stoney Point, and marched over the mountains to Fort Montgomery, and attacked the different redoubts. The garrison commanded by governor Clinton, a brave and intelligent officer, made a gallant resistance. But as the post had been designed principally to prevent the passing of ships, the works on the land side were incomplete and untenable. When it began to grow dark, the British entered the fort with fixed bayonets. The loss on neither side was great. Governor Clinton, general James Clinton, and most of the officers and men effected their escape under cover of the thick smoke and darkness that suddenly prevailed.

OCT. 5

6

The reduction of this post furnished the British with an opportunity for opening a passage up the North-River, but instead of pushing forward to Burgoyne's encampment, or even to Albany, they spent several days in laying waste the adjacent country. The Americans destroyed Fort Constitution, and also set fire to two new frigates, and some other vessels. General Tryon at the same time destroyed a settlement, called Continental Village, which contained barracks for 1500 men, besides many stores. Sir James Wallace with a flying squadron of light frigates, and general Vaughan with a detachment of land forces, continued on and near the river for several days, desolating the country near its margin. General Vaughan so completely burned Esopus, a fine flourishing village, that a single house was not left standing, [50] though on his approach the Americans had left the town without making any resistance. Charity would lead us to suppose that these devastations were designed to answer military purposes. Their authors might have hoped to divert the attention of general Gates, and thus indirectly relieve general Burgoyne, but if this was intended the artifice did not take effect. The preservation of property was with the Americans only a secondary object. The capturing of Burgoyne promised such important consequences that they would not suffer any other consideration to interfere with it. General Gates did not make a single movement that lessened the probability of effecting his grand purpose. He wrote an expostulatory letter to Vaughan, part of which was in the following terms: "Is it thus your king's generals think to make converts to the royal cause? It is no less surprizing than true, that the measures they adopt to serve their master, have a quite contrary effect. Their cruelty establishes the glorious act of independence upon the broad basis of the resentment of the people." Whether policy or revenge led to this devastation of property is uncertain, but it cannot admit of a doubt that it was far from being the most effectual method of relieving Burgoyne.

The passage of the North-River was made so practicable by the advantages gained on the 6th of October, that Sir Henry Clinton, with his whole force, amounting to 3000 men, might not only have reached Albany, but general Gates' encampment, before the 12th, the day till which Burgoyne had agreed to wait for aid from New-York. While the British were doing mischief to individuals without serving the cause of their royal master, it seems as though they might by pushing forward about 136 miles in six days, have brought

Gates' army between two fires, at least twenty-four hours before Burgoyne's necessity compelled his submission to articles of capitulation. Why they neglected this opportunity of relieving their suffering brethren, about thirty-six miles to the northward of Albany, when they were only about one hundred miles below it, has never yet been satisfactorily explained.

Gates posted 1400 men on the heights opposite the [51] fords of Saratoga, and 2000 more in the rear, to prevent a retreat to Fort Edward, and 1500 at a ford higher up. Burgoyne receiving intelligence of these movements, concluded from them, especially from the last, that Gates meant to turn his right. This, if effected, would have entirely enclosed him. To avoid being hemmed in, he resolved on an immediate retreat to Saratoga. His hospital, with the sick and wounded, were necessarily left behind, but they were recommended to the humanity of general Gates, and received from him every indulgence their situation required. When general Burgoyne arrived at Saratoga, he found that the Americans had posted a considerable force on the opposite heights, to impede his passage at that ford. In order to prepare the way for a retreat to Lake George, general Burgoyne ordered a detachment of artificers, with a strong escort of British and provincials, to repair the bridges and open the road leading thither. Part of the escort was withdrawn on other duty, and the remainder on a slight attack of an inconsiderable party of Americans, ran away. The workmen thus left without support, were unable to effect the business on which they had been sent. The only practicable route of retreat, which now remained, was by a night march to Fort Edward. Before this attempt could be made, scouts returned with intelligence, that the Americans were entrenched opposite to those fords on the Hudson's river, over which it was proposed to pass, and that they were also in force on the high ground between Fort Edward and Fort George. They had at the same time parties down the whole shore and posts, so near as to observe every motion of the royal army. Their position extended nearly round the British, and was by the nature of the ground in a great measure secured from attacks. The royal army could not stand its ground where it was, from the want of the means necessary for their subsistence; nor could it advance towards Albany, without attacking

1777

a force greatly superior in number; nor could it retreat without making good its way over a river in face of a strong party, advantageously posted on the opposite side. In case of either attempt, the Americans [52] were so near as to discover every movement, and by means of their bridge could bring their whole force to operate.

Truly distressing was the condition of the royal army. Abandoned in the most critical moment by their Indian allies—unsupported by their brethren in New York—weakened by the timidity and desertion of the Canadians—worn down by a series of incessant efforts, and greatly reduced in their numbers by repeated battles, they were invested by an army nearly three times their number, without a possibility of retreat, or of replenishing their exhausted stock of provisions. A continual cannonade pervaded their camp, and rifle and grape shot fell in many parts of their lines. They nevertheless retained a great share of fortitude.

In the mean time the American army was hourly increasing. Volunteers came in from all quarters, eager to share in the glory of destroying or capturing those whom they considered as their most dangerous enemies. The 13th of October at length arrived. The day was spent in anxious expectation of its producing something of consequence. But as no prospect of assistance appeared, and their provisions were nearly expended, the hope of receiving any in due time for their relief, could not reasonably be further indulged. General Burgoyne thought proper in the evening, to take an account of the provisions left. It was found on enquiry, that they would amount to no more than a scanty subsistence for three days. In this state of distress, a council of war was called, and it was made so general, as to comprehend both the field officers and the captains. Their unanimous opinion was, that their present situation justified a capitulation on honourable terms. A messenger was therefore dispatched to begin this business. General Gates in the first instance demanded, that the royal army should surrender prisoners of war. He also proposed that the British should ground their arms. But general Burgoyne replied, "This article is inadmissible in every extremity; sooner than this army will consent to ground their arms in their encampment, they will rush on the enemy, determined to take no quarter." After various messages, a convention was settled, [53] by which it was substantially stipulated as follows:

The troops under general Burgoyne, to march out of their camp with the honours of war, and the artillery of the intrenchments to the verge of the river, where the arms and artillery are to be left. The arms to be piled by word of command from their own officers. A free passage to be granted to the army under lieutenant general Burgoyne to Great-Britain, upon condition of not serving again in North-America during the present contest, and the port of Boston to be assigned for the entry of the transports to receive the troops whenever general Howe shall so order. The army under lieutenant general Burgoyne to march to Massachusetts-Bay, by the easiest route, and to be quartered in, near, or as convenient as possible, to Boston. The troops to be provided with provision by general Gates' orders, at the same rate of rations as the troops of his own army. All officers to retain their carriages, bat-horses, and no baggage to be molested or searched. The officers are not, as far as circumstances will admit, to be separated from their men. The officers to be quartered according to their rank. All corps whatever of lieutenant general Burgoyne's army, to be included in the above articles. All Canadians, and persons belonging to the Canadian establishment, and other followers of the army, to be permitted to return to Canada—to be conducted to the first British post on Lake George, and to be supplied with provisions as the other troops, and to be bound by the same condition of not serving during the present contest. Passports to be granted to three officers, to carry despatches to Sir William Howe—Sir Guy Carleton, and to Great-Britain. The officers to be admitted on their parole, and to be permitted to wear their side arms.

Such were the embarrassments of the royal army, incapable of subsisting where it was, or of making its way to a better situation, that these terms were rather more favourable than they had a right to expect. On the other hand it would not have been prudent for the American general at the head of his army, which, though numerous, consisted mostly of militia or new levies, to have provoked the despair of even an inferior number of [54] brave disciplined regular troops. 1777 General Gates rightly judged that the best way to secure his advantages was to use them with moderation. Soon after the convention was signed, the Americans marched into their lines, and were kept there till the royal army had deposited their arms at the place appointed. The delicacy with which this business was conducted, reflected the highest honour on the American general. Nor did the politeness of Gates end here. Every circumstance was withheld, that could constitute a triumph in the American army. The captive general was received by his conqueror with respect and kindness. A number of the principal officers of both armies, met at general Gates' quarters, and for a while, seemed to forget in social and convivial pleasures, that they had been enemies. The conduct of general Burgoyne in this interview with general Gates was truly dignified, and the historian is at a loss whether to admire most, the magnanimity of the victorious, or the fortitude of the vanquished general.

The British troops partook liberally of the plenty that reigned in the American army. It was the more acceptable to them, as they were destitute of bread and flour, and had only as much meat left, as was sufficient for a days subsistance.

But the convention which has been mentioned, 5790 men were surrendered prisoners. The sick and wounded left in camp, when the British retreated to Saratoga, together with the numbers of the British, German and Canadian troops, who were killed, wounded or taken, and who had deserted in the preceding part of the expedition, were reckoned to be 4689. The whole royal force, exclusive of Indians, was probably about 10,000. The stores which the Americans acquired, were considerable. The captured artillery consisted of 35 brass field pieces. There were also 4647 muskets, and a variety of other useful and much wanted articles, which fell into their hands. The continentals in general Gates' army were 9093, the militia 4129, but of the former, 2103 were sick or on furlough, and 562 of the latter were in the same situation. The number of militia was constantly fluctuating.

1777

[55] The general exultation of the Americans, on receiving the agreeable intelligence of the convention of Saratoga, disarmed them of much of their resentment. The burnings and devastations which had taken place were sufficient to have inflamed their minds, but private feelings were in a great measure absorbed by a consideration of the many advantages, which the capture of so large an army promised to the new formed states.

In a short time after the convention was signed, general Gates moved forward to stop the devastations of the British on the North-River, but on hearing of the fate of Burgoyne, Vaughan and Wallace retired to New-York.

About the same time the British, which had been left in the rear of the royal army, destroyed their cannon, and abandoning Ticonderoga, retreated to Canada. The whole country, after experiencing for several months the confusions of war, was in a moment restored to perfect tranquility.

Great was the grief and dejection in Britain, on receiving the intelligence of the fate of Burgoyne. The expedition committed to him had been undertaken with the most confident hopes of success. The quality of the troops he commanded, was such, that from their bravery, directed by his zeal, talents and courage, it was presumed that all the northern parts of the United States would be subdued before the end of the campaign. The good fortune which for some time followed him justified these expectations, but the catastrophe proved the folly of planning distant expeditions, and of projecting remote conquests.

The consequences of these great events, vibrated round the world. The capture of Burgoyne was the hinge on which the revolution turned. While it encouraged the perseverance of the Americans by well grounded hopes of final success, it encreased the embarrassments of that ministry, which had so ineffectually laboured to compel their submission. Opposition to their measures gathered new strength, and formed a stumbling block in the road to conquest. This prevented Great-Britain from acting with that collected force which an union of sentiments [56] and councils would have enabled her to do. 1777 Hitherto the best informed Americans had doubts of success in establishing their independence, but henceforward their language was, "That whatever might be the event of their present struggle, they were forever lost to Great-Britain." Nor were they deceived. The eclat of capturing a large army of British and German regular troops, soon procured them powerful friends in Europe.

Immediately after the surrender of the troops, commanded by lieutenant general Burgoyne, they were marched to the vicinity of Boston. On their arrival they were quartered in the barracks on Winter and Prospect hills. The general court of Massachusetts passed proper resolutions for procuring suitable accommodations for the prisoners; but from the general unwillingness of the people to oblige them, and from the feebleness of that authority which the republican rulers had at that time over the property of their fellow citizens, it was impossible to provide immediately for so large a number of officers and soldiers, in such a manner as their convenience required, or as from the articles of convention they might reasonably expect. The officers remonstrated to general Burgoyne, that six or seven of them were crouded together in one room, without any regard to their respective ranks, in violation of the 7th article of the convention. General Burgoyne, on the 14th of November forwarded this account to general Gates, and added, "the public faith is broken." This letter being laid before Congress, gave an alarm. It corroborated an apprehension, previously entertained that the captured troops on their embarkation would make a junction with the British garrisons in America. The declaration of the general, that "the public faith was broken" while in the power of Congress, was considered by them as destroying the security which they before had in his personal honour, for in every event he might adduce his previous notice to justify his future conduct. They therefore resolved, "That the embarkation of lieutenant general Burgoyne, and the troops under his command, be postponed, till a distinct and explicit ratification of the convention of Saratoga be properly notified [57] by the court of Great-Britain to Congress." General Burgoyne explained the intention and construction of the passage objected to in his letter, and pledged himself, that his officers would join with him in signing any instrument that might be thought necessary for confirming the convention, but Congress would not recede from their resolution. They alledged, that it had been often asserted by their adversaries that "faith was not to be kept with rebels," and that therefore they would be deficient in attention to the interests of their constituents, if they did not require an authentic ratification of the convention by national authority, before they parted with the captured troops. They urged farther, that by the law of nations, a compact broken in one article, was no longer binding in any other. They made a distinction between the suspension and abrogation of the convention, and alledged that ground to suspect an intention to violate it, was a justifying reason for suspending its execution on their part, till it was properly ratified. The desired ratification if Great-Britain was seriously disposed to that measure, might have been obtained in a few months, and Congress uniformly

1777

declared themselves willing to carry it into full effect, as soon as they were secured of its observance by proper authority on the other side.

About eight months after certain royal commissioners, whose official functions shall be hereafter explained, made a requisition respecting these troops—offered to ratify the convention, and required permission for their embarkation. On enquiry it was found, that they had no authority to do any thing in the matter which would be obligatory on Great-Britain. Congress therefore resolved, "that no ratification of the convention, which may be tendered in consequence of powers, which only reach that case by construction and implication, or which may subject whatever is transacted relative to it, to the future approbation or disapprobation of the parliament of Great-Britain, can be accepted by Congress."

Till the capture of Burgoyne the powers of Europe were only spectators of the war between Great-Britain and her late colonies, but soon after that event they were [58] drawn in to be parties. In every period of the controversy, the claims of the Americans were patronised by sundry respectable foreigners. The letters, addresses, and other public acts of Congress, were admired by many who had no personal interest in the contest. Liberty is so evidently the undoubted right of mankind, that even they who never possessed it feel the propriety of contending for it, and whenever a people take up arms either to defend or to recover it, they are sure of meeting with encouragement or good wishes from the friends of humanity in every part of the world.

From the operation of these principles, the Americans had the esteem and good wishes of multitudes in all parts of Europe. They were reputed to be ill used, and were represented as a resolute and brave people, determined to resist oppression. Being both pitied and applauded, generous and sympathetic sentiments were excited in their favour. These circumstances would have operated in every case, but in the present, the cause of the Americans was patronised from additional motives. An universal jealousy prevailed against Great-Britain. Her navy had long tyranised over the nations of Europe, and demanded as a matter of right that the ships of all other powers should strike their sails to her, as mistress of the ocean. From her eagerness to prevent supplies going to her rebellious colonists, as

1777

she called the Americans, the vessels of foreign powers had for some time past been subjected to searches and other interruptions, when steering towards America, in a manner that could not but be impatiently born by independent nations. That pride and insolence which brought on the American war, had long disgusted her neighbours, and made them rejoice at her misfortunes, and especially at the prospect of dismembering her over-grown empire.

The Alliance between France and the United States. The Campaign of 1778.

[59] SOON AFTER INTELLIGENCE OF THE CAPTURE of Burgoyne's   1778
army reached Europe, the court of France concluded at Paris, treaties
of alliance and commerce with the United States. The circumstances
which led to this great event, deserve to be particularly unfolded.
The colonists having taken up arms, uninfluenced by the enemies of
Great-Britain, conducted their opposition for several months after
they had raised troops, and emitted money, without any reference
to foreign powers. They knew it to be the interest of Europe, to
promote a separation between Great-Britain and her colonies, but
as they began the contest with no other view than to obtain a redress
of grievances, they neither wished in the first period of their opposition
to involve Great-Britain in a war, nor to procure aid to themselves
by paying court to her enemies. The policy of Great-Britain in

attempting to deprive the Americans of arms, was the first event which made it necessary for them to seek foreign connexions. At the time she was urging military preparations to compel their submission, she forbad the exportation of arms, and solicited the commercial powers of Europe, to co-operate with her by adopting a similar prohibition. To frustrate the views of Great-Britain Congress, besides recommending the domestic manufacture of the materials for military stores, appointed a secret committee with powers to procure on their account arms and ammunition, and also employed agents in foreign countries for the same purpose. The evident advantage which France might derive from the continuance of the dispute and the countenance which individuals of that country daily gave to the Americans, encouraged Congress to send a political and commercial agent to that kingdom, with instructions to solicit its friendship, and to procure military stores. Silas Deane, being chosen for this purpose, sailed for France early in 1776, and was soon after his arrival at Paris instructed to sound count de Vergennes, the French minister for [60] foreign affairs, on the subject of the American controversy. As the public mind, for reasons which have been mentioned, closed against Great-Britain, it opened towards other nations.

1778

On the 11th of June 1776, Congress appointed a committee, to prepare a plan of a treaty to be proposed to foreign powers. The discussion of this novel subject engaged their attention till the latter end of September. While Congress was deliberating thereon, Mr. Deane was soliciting a supply of arms, ammunition and soldiers cloathing, for their service. A sufficiency for lading three vessels was soon procured. What agency the government of France had in furnishing these supplies, or whether they were sold or given as presents, are questions which have been often asked, but not satisfactorily answered, for the business was so conducted that the transaction might be made to assume a variety of complexions, as circumstances might render expedient.

It was most evidently the interest of France to encourage the Americans in their opposition to Great Britain, and it was true policy to do this by degrees and in a private manner, lest Great-Britain might take the alarm. Individuals are sometimes influenced by considerations of friendship and generosity, but interest is the pole

star by which nations are universally governed. It is certain that
Great-Britain was amused with declarations of the most pacific
dispositions on the part of France, at the time the Americans were
liberally supplied with the means of defence, and it is equally certain,
that this was the true line of policy for promoting that dismemberment
of the British empire which France had an interest in accomplishing.

Congress knew, that a diminution of the overgrown power of
Britain, could not but be desirable to France. Sore with the loss of
her possessions on the continent of North-America by the peace of
Paris in the year 1763, and also by the capture of many thousands
of her sailors in 1755, antecedent to a declaration of war, she must
have been something more than human, not to have rejoiced at an
opportunity of depressing an antient and formidable [61] rival. Besides 1778
the increasing naval superiority of Great-Britain, her vast resources,
not only in her antient dominions, but in colonies growing daily in
numbers and wealth, added to the haughtiness of her flag, made her
the object both of terror and envy. It was the interest of Congress
to apply to the court of France, and it was the interest of France to
listen to their application.

Congress having agreed on the plan of the treaty, which they
intended to propose to his Most Christian Majesty, proceeded to elect
commissioners to solicit its acceptance. Dr. Franklin, Silas Deane,
and Thomas Jefferson were chosen. The latter declining to serve,
Arthur Lee, who was then in London, and had been very serviceable
to his country in a variety of ways, was elected in his room. It was
resolved, that no member should be at liberty to divulge any thing
more of these transactions than "that Congress had taken such steps
as they judged necessary for obtaining foreign alliances." The secret
committee were directed to make an effectual lodgement in France
of ten thousand pounds sterling, subject to the order of these
commissioners. Dr. Franklin, who was employed as agent in the
business, and afterwards as minister plenipotentiary at the court of
France, was in possession of a greater proportion of foreign fame,
than any other native of America. By the dint of superior abilities,
and with but few advantages in early life, he had attained the highest
eminence among men of learning, and in many instances extended
the empire of science. His genius was vast and comprehensive, and

with equal ease investigate the mysteries of philosophy and the labyrinths of politics. His fame as a philosopher had reached as far as human nature is polished or refined. His philanthropy knew no bounds. The prosperity and happiness of the human race were objects which at all times had attracted his attention. Disgusted with great Britain, and glowing with the most ardent love for the liberties of his oppressed native country, he left London, where he had resided some years in the character of agent for several of the colonies, and early in 1775 returned to Philadelphia, [62] and immediately afterwards was elected by the legislature of Pennsylvania, to share in the opposition to Great-Britain as a member of Congress. Shortly after his appointment to solicit the interests of Congress in France, he sailed for that country. He was no sooner landed than universally carressed. His fame had smoothed the way for his reception in a public character. Doctor Franklin, Silas Deane, and Arthur Lee, having rendezvoused at Paris, soon after opened their business in a private audience with count de Vergennes. The Congress could not have applied to the court of France under more favourable circumstances. The throne was filled by a prince in the flower of his age, and animated with the desire of rendering his reign illustrious. Count de Vergennes was not less remarkable for extensive political knowledge, than for true greatness of mind. He had grown old in the habits of government, and was convinced that conquests are neither the surest nor the shortest way to substantial fame. He knew full well that no success in war, however brilliant, could so effectually promote the security of France, as the emancipation of the colonies of her ancient rival. He had the superior wisdom to discern, that there were no present advantages to be obtained by unequal terms, that would compensate for those lasting benefits which were likely to flow from a kind and generous beginning. Instead of grasping at too much, or taking any advantages of the humble situation of the invaded colonies, he aimed at nothing more than by kind and generous terms to a distressed country, to perpetuate the separation which had already taken place between the component parts of an empire, from the union of which his sovereign had much to fear.

Truly difficult was the line of conduct, which the real interest of the nation required of the ministers of His Most Christian Majesty.

An haughty reserve would have discouraged the Americans. An open reception, or even a legal countenance of their deputies might have alarmed the rulers of Great-Britain, and disposed them to a compromise with their colonies, or have brought on an immediate rupture between France and England. A middle [63] line as preferable to either, was therefore pursued. Whilst the French government prohibited, threatened and even punished the Americans; private persons encouraged, supplied, and supported them. Prudence, as well as policy required, that France should not be over-hasty in openly espousing their cause. She was by no means fit for war. From the state of her navy, and the condition of her foreign trade, she was vulnerable on every side. Her trading people dreaded the thoughts of a war with Great-Britain, as they would thereby be exposed to great losses. These considerations were strengthened from another quarter. The peace of Europe was supposed to be unstable from a prevailing belief, that the speedy death of the elector of Bavaria was an event extremely probable. But the principle reason which induced a delay, was an opinion, that the dispute between the Mother Country and the colonies would be compromised. Within the 13 years immediately preceding, twice had the contested claims of the two countries brought matters to the verge of extremity. Twice had the guardian genius of both interposed, and reunited them in the bonds of love and affection. It was feared by the sagacious ministry of France, that the present rupture would terminate in the same manner. These wise observers of human nature apprehended, that their too early interference would favour a reconciliation, and that the reconciled parties would direct their united force against the French, as the disturbers of their domestic tranquility. It had not yet entered into the hearts of the French nation, that it was possible for the British American colonists, to join with their antient enemies against their late friends.

At this period Congress did not so much expect any direct aid from France, as the indirect relief of a war between that country and Great-Britain. To subserve this design, they resolved, that "their commissioners at the court of France should be furnished with warrants and commissions, and authorised to arm and fit for war in the French ports any number of vessels (not exceeding six) at the

1778

expence of the United States, to war upon British property, provided they were satisfied this measure would [64] not be disagreeable to the court of France." This resolution was carried into effect, and in the year 1777 marine officers, with American commissions, both sailed out of French ports, and carried prizes of British property into them. They could not procure their condemnation in the courts of France, nor sell them publicly, but they nevertheless found ways and means to turn them into money. The commanders of these vessels were sometimes punished by authority to please the English, but they were oftener caressed from another quarter to please the Americans.

While private agents on the part of the United States were endeavouring to embroil the two nations, the American commissioners were urging the ministers of His Most Christian Majesty to accept the treaty proposed by Congress. They received assurances of the good wishes of the court of France, but were from time to time informed, that the important transaction required farther consideration, and were enjoined to observe the most profound secrecy. Matters remained in this fluctuating state from December 1776, till December 1777. Private encouragement and public discountenance were alternated, but both varied according to the complexion of news from America. The defeat on Long-Island, the reduction of New-York, and the train of disastrous events in 1776, which have already been mentioned, sunk the credit of the Americans very low and abated much of the national ardor for their support. Their subsequent successes at Trenton and Princeton, effaced these impressions, and rekindled active zeal in their behalf. The capture of Burgoyne fixed these wavering politics. The success of the Americans in the campaign of 1777, placed them on high ground. Their enmity had proved itself formidable to Britain, and their friendship became desirable to France. Having helped themselves, they found it less difficult to obtain help from others. The same interest, which hitherto had directed the court of France to a temporising policy, now required decisive conduct. Previous delay had favoured the dismemberment of the empire, but farther procrastination bid fair to promote, at least such a federal alliance of the [65] disjointed parts of the British Empire as would be no less hostile to the interests of France than a re-union of its severed parts. The news of the capitulation of Saratoga reached France, very early in December, 1777. The American deputies took that opportunity to press for an acceptance of the treaty, which had been under consideration for the preceding twelve months. The capture of Burgoyne's army convinced the French, that the opposition of the Americans to Great Britain was not the work of a few men who had got power in their hands, but of the great body of the people, and was like to be finally successful. It was therefore determined to take them by the hand, and publicly to espouse their cause. The commissioners of Congress were informed by Mr. Gerard one of the secretaries of the King's council of State,

DEC. 16
1777

> that it was decided to acknowledge the independence of the United States and to make a treaty with them. That in the treaty no advantage would be taken of their situation to obtain terms which, otherwise, it would not be convenient for them to agree to. That his Most Christian Majesty desired the treaty once made should be durable, and their amity to subsist forever, which could not be expected, if each nation did not find an interest in its continuance, as well as in its commencement. It was therefore intended that the terms of the treaty should be such as the new formed states would be willing to agree to if they had been long since established, and in the fulness of strength and power; and such as they should approve of when that time should come. That his most Christian Majesty was fixed in his determination not only to acknowledge, but to support, their independence. That in doing this he might probably soon be engaged in a war, yet he should not expect any compensation from the United States on that account, nor was it pretended that he acted wholly for their sakes, since besides his real good will to them, it was manifestly the interest of France, that the power of England should be diminished, by the separation of the colonies from its government. The only condition he should require and rely on would be, that the United States in no peace to be [66] made, should give up their independence and return to the obedience of the British government.

1778

At any time previously to the 16th of December, 1777, when Mr. Gerard made the foregoing declaration, it was in the power of the British ministry to have ended the American war, and to have established an alliance with the United States, that would have been of great service to both; but from the same haughtiness which for some time had predominated in their councils, and blinded them to their interests, they neglected to improve the favourable opportunity.

Conformably to the preliminaries proposed by Mr. Gerard, his most Christian Majesty Lewis the 16th, on the 6th of February 1778, entered into treaties of amity and commerce, and of alliance with the United States, on the footing of the most perfect equality and reciprocity. By the latter of these, that illustrious monarch became the guarantee of their sovereignty, independence and commerce.

On a review of the conduct of the French ministry to the Americans, the former appear to have acted uniformly from a wise regard to national interest. Any line of conduct, different from that which they adopted, might have overset the measures which they wished to establish. Had they pretended to act from disinterested principles of generosity to the distressed, the known selfishness of human nature would have contradicted the extravagant pretension. By avowing the real motive of their conduct they furnished such a proof of candor as begat confidence.

The terms of reciprocity on which they contracted with the United States were no less recommended by wise policy than dictated by true magnanimity. As there was nothing exclusive in the treaty, an opening was left for Great Britain to close the war when she pleased, with all the advantages for future commerce that France had stipulated for herself. This judicious measure made the establishment of American independence the common cause of all the commercial powers of Europe, for the question then was, whether the trade of the United States [67] should by the subversion of their independence be again monopolised by Great Britain, or by the establishment of it, laid open on equal terms to all the world.

In national events the public attention is generally fixed on the movements of armies and fleets. Mankind never fail to do homage to the able general and expert admiral. To this they are justly entitled, but as great a tribute is due to the statesman who, from a more elevated station, determines on measures in which the general safety and welfare of empires are involved. This glory in a particular manner belongs to the Count de Vergennes, who, as his most Christian Majesty's minister for foreign affairs, conducted the conferences which terminated in these treaties. While the ministers of his Britanic

1778

Majesty were pleasing themselves with the flattering idea of permanent peace in Europe, they were not less surprised than provoked by hearing of the alliance, which had taken place between his most Christian Majesty, and the United States. This event though often foretold was disbelieved. The zeal of the British ministry to reduce the colonies to submission, blinded them to danger from every other quarter. Forgetting that interest governs public bodies perhaps more than private persons, they supposed that feebler motives would outweigh its all commanding influence. Intent on carrying into execution the object of their wishes, they fancied that because France and Spain had colonies of their own, they would refrain from aiding or abetting the revolted British colonists, from the fear of establishing a precedent, which at a future day might operate against themselves. Transported with indignation against their late fellow subjects, they were so infatuated with the American war, as to suppose that trifling evils, both distant and uncertain, would induce the court of France to neglect an opportunity of securing great and immediate advantages.

How far this interference of the court of France can be justified by the laws of nations, it is not the province of history to decide. Measures of this kind are not determined by abstract reasoning. The present feelings of a nation, and the probable consequences of loss or gain influence more than the decisions of speculative men. Suffice [68] it to mention, that the French exculpated themselves from the heavy charges brought against them, by this summary mode of reasoning, "We have found" said they

1778

> the late colonies of Great Britain in actual possession of Independence, and in the exercise of the prerogatives of sovereignty. It is not our business to enquire, whether they had, or had not, sufficient reason to withdraw themselves from the government of Great Britain, and to erect an independent one of their own. We are to conduct towards nations, agreeably to the political state in which we find them, without investigating how they acquired it. Observing them to be independent in fact, we were bound to suppose they were so of right, and had the same liberty to make treaties with them as with any other sovereign power.

They also alleged, that Great Britain could not complain of their interference, since she had set them the example only a few years before, in supporting the Corsicans in opposition to the court of France. They had besides many well founded complaints against the British, whose armed vessels had for months past harassed their commerce, on the idea of preventing an illicit trade with the revolted colonies.

The marquis de la Fayette, whose letters to France had a considerable share in reconciling the nation to patronise the United States, was among the first in the American army who received the welcome tidings of the treaty. In a transport of joy, mingled with an effusion of tears, he embraced general Washington exclaiming "The king my master has acknowledged your Independence, and entered into an alliance with you for its establishment." The heart-felt joy, which spread from breast to breast, exceeded description. The several brigades assembled by order of the commander in chief. Their chaplains offered up public thanks to Almighty God, and delivered discourses suitable to the occasion. A feu de joie was fired, and on a proper signal being given, the air resounded with "Long live the king of France," poured forth from the breast of every private in the army. The Americans, having in their own strength for three years weathered the storms of war, fancied the port of peace to be in full

1778

[69] view. Replete with the sanguine hopes of vigorous youth, they presumed that Britain, whose northern army had been reduced by their sole exertions, would not continue the unequal contest with the combined force of France and America. Overvaluing their own importance, and undervaluing the resources of their adversaries, they were tempted to indulge a dangerous confidence. That they might not be lulled into carelessness, Congress made an animated address to them, in which, after reviewing the leading features of the war, they informed them "They must yet expect a severe conflict; that though foreign alliances secured their independence, they could not secure their country from devastation." The alliance between France and America had not been concluded three days, before it

MARCH
13

was known to the British ministry, and in less than five weeks more, it was officially communicated to the court of London in a rescript, delivered by the French ambassador, to lord Weymouth. In this new situation of affairs, there were some in Great Britain who advocated the measure of peace with America, on the footing of Independence:

But the point of honor, which had before precipitated the nation into the war, predominated over the voice of prudence and interest. The king and parliament of Great Britain resolved to punish the French nation for treating with their subjects, which they termed "An unprovoked aggression on the honor of the crown, and essential interests of the kingdom." And at the same time a vain hope was indulged, that the alliance between France and the United States, which was supposed to have originated in passion, might be dissolved. The national prejudices against the French, had been so instilled into the minds of Englishmen, and of their American descendants, that it was supposed practicable, by negotiations and concessions, to detatch the United States from their new alliance, and re-unite them to the parent state. Eleven days after the treaty between France and America had been concluded, the British minister introduced FEB. 17 into the house of commons a project for conciliation, founded on the idea of obtaining a re-union of the new States with Great Britain. This consisted of two bills, with the following [70] titles, "A bill for declaring the intention of Great Britain, concerning the exercise of 1778 the right of imposing taxes within his Majesty's colonies, provinces and plantations, in North America," and a bill to "enable his Majesty to appoint commissioners with sufficient powers, to treat, consult and agree, upon the means of quieting the disorders now subsisting in certain of the colonies, plantations and provinces of North America." These bills were hurried through both houses of Parliament, and before they passed into acts, were copied and sent across the Atlantic, to lord and general Howe. On their arrival in America, they were sent by a flag to Congress at Yorktown. When they were received, Congress was uninformed of the treaty which their com- APRIL 21 missioners had lately concluded at Paris. For upwards of a year, they had not received one line of information from them on any subject whatever. One packet had in that time been received, but all the letters therein were taken out before it was put on board the vessel which brought it from France, and blank paper put in their stead. A committee of Congress was appointed to examine these bills, and report on them. Their report was brought in the day following, and was unanimously adopted. By this they rejected the proposals of Great Britain. The vigorous and firm language in which Congress expressed their rejection of these offers, considered in connection with the circumstance of their being wholly ignorant of the late treaty with France, exhibits the glowing serenity of fortitude. While the royal commissioners were industriously circulating these bills in a partial and secret manner, as if they suspected an intention of concealing them from the common people, Congress trusting to the good sense of their constituents, ordered them to be forthwith printed for the public information. Having directed the affairs of their country with an honest reference to its welfare, they had nothing to fear from the people knowing and judging for themselves. They submitted the whole to the public. Their act, after some general remarks on the bill, concluded as follows,

1778

[71] From all which it appears evident to your committee, that the said bills are intended to operate upon the hopes and fears of the good people of these states, so as to create divisions among them, and a defection from the common cause, now, by the blessing of Divine Providence, drawing near to a favourable issue. That they are the sequel of that insidious plan, which, from the days of the stamp-act, down to the present time, hath involved this country in contention and bloodshed. And that, as in other cases so in this, although circumstances may force them at times to recede from their unjustifiable claims, there can be no doubt but they will, as heretofore, upon the first favourable occasion, again display that lust of domination, which hath rent in twain the mighty empire of Britain.

Upon the whole matter, the committee beg leave to report it as their opinion, that as the Americans united in this arduous contest upon principles of common interest, for the defence of common rights and privileges, which union hath been cemented by common calamities, and by mutual good offices and affection, so the great cause for which they contend, and in which all mankind are interested, must derive its success from the continuance of that union. Wherefore any man or body of men, who should presume to make any separate or partial convention or agreement with commissioners under the crown of Great-Britain, or any of them, ought to be considered and treated as open and avowed enemies of these United States.

And further, your committee beg leave to report it as their opinion, that these United States cannot, with propriety, hold any conference with any commissioners on the part of Great-Britain, unless they shall, as a preliminary thereto, either withdraw their fleets and armies, or else, in positive and express terms, acknowledge the independence of the said states.

And in as much as it appears to be the design of the enemies of these states to lull them into a fatal security—to the end that they may act with a becoming weight and importance, it is the opinion of your committee, that the several states be called upon to use the most strenuous exertions [72] to have their respective quotas of continental troops in the field as soon as possible, and that all the militia of the said states be held in readiness, to act as occasion may require.

1778

The conciliatory bills were speedily followed by royal commissioners, deputed to solicit their reception. Gov. Johnstone, Lord Carlisle and Mr. Eden, appointed on this business attempted to open a negotiation on the subject. They requested General Washington, to furnish a passport for their secretary Dr. Ferguson, with a letter from them to Congress, but this was refused, and the refusal was unanimously approved by congress. They then forwarded in the usual channel of communication, a letter addressed "to his Excellency Henry Laurens, the president, and the other members of congress," in which they communicated a copy of their commission and of the acts of Parliament on which it was founded, and offered to concur in every satisfactory and just arrangement towards the following among other purposes.

JUNE 9

To consent to a cessation of hostilities, both by sea and land.

To restore free intercourse, to revive mutual affection, and renew the common benefits of naturalization, through the several parts of this empire.

To extend every freedom to trade that our respective interests can require.

To agree that no military forces shall be kept up in the different states of North-America, without the consent of the general congress or particular assemblies.

To concur in measures calculated to discharge the debts of America, and to raise the credit and value of the paper circulation.

To perpetuate our union by a reciprocal deputation of an agent or agents from the different states, who shall have the privilege of a seat and voice in the parliament of Great-Britain; or, if sent from Britain, in that case to have a seat and voice in the assemblies of the different states to which they may be deputed respectively, in order to attend the several interests of those by whom they are deputed.

1778

[73] In short, to establish the power of the respective legislatures in each particular state, to settle its revenue, in civil and military establishment, and to exercise a perfect freedom of legislation and internal government, so that the British states throughout North-America, acting with us in peace and war under one common sovereign, may have the irrevocable enjoyment of every privilege, that is short of a total separation of interests, or consistent with that union of force, on which the safety of our common religion and liberty depends.

A decided negative having been already given, previous to the arrival of the British commissioners, to the overtures contained in the conciliatory bills, and intelligence of the treaty with France having in the mean time arrived, there was no ground left for farther deliberation. President Laurens therefore, by order of Congress, returned the following answer.

JUN. 17

I have received the letter from your excellencies of the 9th instant, with the enclosures, and laid them before Congress. Nothing but an earnest desire to spare the farther effusion of human blood could have induced them to read a paper, containing expressions so disrespectful to his most Christian Majesty, the good and great ally of these states; or to consider propositions so derogatory to the honour of an independent nation.

The acts of the British parliament, the commission from your sovereign, and your letter, suppose the people of these states to be subjects of the crown of Great-Britain, and are founded on the idea of dependence, which is utterly inadmissible.

I am further directed to inform your excellencies, that Congress are inclined to peace, notwithstanding the unjust claims from which this war originated, and the savage manner in which it hath been conducted. They will, therefore, be ready to enter upon the consideration of a treaty of peace and commerce, not inconsistent with treaties already subsisting, when the King of Great-Britain shall demonstrate a sincere disposition for that purpose. The only solid proof of this disposition will be, an explicit acknowledgment of the independence of these states, or the withdrawing his fleets and armies.

[74] Though Congress could not, consistently with national honor, 1778
enter on a discussion of the terms proposed by the British commissioners, yet some individuals of their body ably proved the propriety
of rejecting them. Among these Gouverneur Morris, and W. H.
Drayton, with great force of argument and poignancy of wit, justified
the decisive measures adopted by their countrymen.

As the British plan for conciliation was wholly founded on the idea
of the States returning to their allegiance, it was no sooner known
than rejected. In addition to the sacred ties of plighted faith and
national engagements, the leaders in Congress and the legislative
assemblies of America, had tasted the sweets of power and were in
full possession of its blessings, with a fair prospect of retaining them
without any foreign control. The war having originated on the part
of Great-Britain from a lust of power, had in its progress compelled
the Americans in self defence to assume and exercise its highest
prerogatives. The passions of human nature which induced the
former to claim power, operated no less forcibly with the latter,
against the relinquishment of it. After the colonies had declared
themselves independent states, had repeatedly pledged their honor
to abide by that declaration[,] had under the smiles of heaven
maintained it for three campaigns without foreign aid, after the
greatest monarch in Europe, had entered into a treaty with them,
and guarantied their independence: After all this to expect popular
leaders in the enjoyment of power voluntarily to retire from the helm
of government to the languid indifference of private life, and while
they violated national faith, at the same time to depress their country
from the rank of sovereign states to that of dependent provinces,
was not more repugnant to universal experience, than to, the
governing principles of the human heart. The high spirited ardor of
citizens in the youthful vigor of honor and dignity, did not so much
as enquire whether greater political happiness might be expected
from closing with the proposals of Great-Britain, or by adhering to
their new allies. Honor forbad any balancing on the subject, nor were
its dictates disobeyed. Though peace was desirable and the offers of
Great [75] Britain so liberal, that if proposed in due time, they would
have been acceptable, yet for the Americans, after they had declared
themselves independent, and at their own solicitation obtained the

aid of France, to desert their new allies, and leave them exposed to British resentment incurred on their account, would have argued a total want of honor and gratitude. The folly of Great Britain in expecting such conduct from virtuous freemen, could only be exceeded by the baseness of America, had her citizens realised that expectation.

These offers of conciliation in a great measure originated in an opinion that the Congress was supported by a faction, and that the great body of the people was hostile to independence, and well disposed to re-unite with Great Britain. The latter of these assertions was true, till a certain period of the contest, but that period was elapsed. With their new situation, new opinions and attachments had taken place. The political revolution of the government was less extraordinary than that of the stile and manner of thinking in the United States. The independent American citizens saw with other eyes, and heard with other ears, than when they were in the condition of British subjects. That narrowness of sentiment, which prevailed in England towards France, no longer existed among the Americans. The British commissioners unapprised of this real change in the public mind, expected to keep a hold on the citizens of the United States, by that illiberality which they inherited from their forefathers. Presuming that the love of peace, and the ancient national antipathy to France, would counterbalance all other ties, they flattered themselves that by perseverance an impression favourable to Great Britain might yet be made on the mind of America. They therefore renewed their efforts to open a negociation with Congress, in a letter of the 11th of July. As they had been informed in answer to their preceding letter of the 10th of June, that an explicit acknowledgment of the independence of the United States, or a withdrawing of their fleets and armies must precede an entrance on the consideration of a treaty of peace, and as neither branch of this alternative had been [76] complied with, it was resolved by Congress that no answer should be given to their reiterated application.

In addition to his public exertions as a commissioner, Governor Johnstone endeavoured to obtain the objects on which he had been sent by opening a private correspondence with some of the members of Congress, and other Americans of influence. He in particular

1778

addressed himself by letter to Henry Laurens, Joseph Reed, and Robert Morris. His letter to Henry Laurens, was in these words.

DEAR SIR,

I beg to transfer to my friend Dr. Ferguson, the private civilities which my friends Mr. Manning, and Mr. Oswald, request in my behalf. He is a man of the utmost probity and of the highest esteem, in the republic of letters.

If you should follow the example of Britain, in the hour of her insolence and send us back without a hearing, I shall hope from private friendship, that I may be permitted to see the country, and the worthy characters she has exhibited to the world, upon making the request in any way you may point out.

The following answer was immediately written.

York Town, June 14th, 1778.

DEAR SIR,

Yesterday I was honoured with your favour of the 10th, and thank you for the transmission of those from my dear and worthy friends, Mr. Oswald, and Mr. Manning. Had Dr. Ferguson been the bearer of these papers, I should have shewn that gentleman every degree of respect and attention, that times and circumstances admit of.

It is sir, for Great Britain to determine, whether, her commissioners shall return unheard by the representatives of the United States, or revive a friendship with the citizens at large, and remain among us as long as they please.

You are undoubtedly acquainted with the only terms upon which Congress can treat for accomplishing this good end, terms from which, although writing in a private [77] character, I may venture to assert with great assurance, they never will recede, even admitting the continuance of hostile attempts, and that from the rage of war, the good people of these States, shall be driven to commence a treaty west-ward of yonder mountains. And permit me to add, Sir, as my humble opinion the true interest of Great Britain, in the present advance of our contest, will be found in confirming our independence.

Congress in no hour have been haughty, but to suppose that their minds are less firm in the present than they were, when, destitute of all foreign aid, even without expectation of an alliance—when, upon a

1778

day of general public fasting and humiliation in their house of worship, and in presence of God, they resolved "to hold no conference or treaty with any commissioners on the part of Great-Britain unless they shall, as a preliminary thereto, either withdraw their fleets and armies, or in positive and express terms acknowledge the independence of these States," would be irrational.

At a proper time, Sir, I shall think myself highly honoured by a personal attention paid by contributing to render every part of these states agreeable to you; but until the basis of mutual confidence shall be established, I believe sir, neither former private friendship, nor any other consideration, can influence Congress to consent that even Governor Johnstone, a gentleman who has been so deservedly esteemed in America shall see the country. I have but one voice, and that shall be against it. But let me intreat you my dear sir, do not hence conclude that I am deficient in affection to my old friends, through whose kindness I have obtained the honor of the present correspondence, or that I am not with very great personal respect and esteem,

    Sir,

        Your most obedient,

            And most humble servant,

        (Signed) HENRY LAURENS

Philadelphia.

                        The Honorable Geo. Johnstone, Esq.

1776   [78] In a letter to Joseph Reed of April the 11th, governor Johnstone said,

The man who can be instrumental in bringing us all to act once more in harmony, and to unite together the various powers which this contest has drawn forth, will deserve more from the king and people, from patriotism, humanity, and all the tender ties that are affected by the quarrel and reconciliation, than ever was yet bestowed on human kind.

On the 16th of June he wrote to Robert Morris,

I believe the men who have conducted the affairs of America incapable of being influenced by improper motives, but in all such transactions there is risk, and I think, that whoever ventures should be secured, at the same time that honor and emolument should naturally follow the fortune of those, who have steered the vessel in the storm, and brought her safely to port. I think Washington and the President have a right to every favour, that grateful nations can bestow, if they could once more unite our interest, and spare the miseries and devastations of war. JUNE 21

To Joseph Reed, private information was communicated, that it had been intended by gov. Johnstone, to offer him, that in case of his exerting his abilities to promote a re-union of the two countries, if consistent with his principles and judgment, ten thousand pounds sterling, and any office in the colonies in his Majesty's gift. To which Mr. Reed replied, "I am not worth purchasing, but such as I am, the king of Great Britain is not rich enough to do it." Congress ordered all letters, received by members of Congress from any of the British JULY 9 commissioners, or their agents, or from any subject of the king of Great Britain, of a public nature, to be laid before them. The above letters and information being communicated, Congress resolved "That the same cannot but be considered, as direct attempts to corrupt their integrity, and that it is incompatible with the honor of Congress, to hold any manner of correspondence or intercourse with the said George Johnstone Esquire, especially to negociate with him upon affairs in which the cause of liberty is interested." Their determination, with the reasons thereof, were expressed [79] in the form of a declaration, a copy of which was signed by the President, and sent 1778 by a flag to the commissioners at New-York. This was answered by governor Johnstone, by an angry publication, in which he denied or explained away, what had been alleged against him. Lord Carlisle, Sir Henry Clinton and Mr. Eden, denied their having any knowledge of the matter charged on governor Johnstone.

The commissioners failing in their attempts to negociate with Congress had no resource left, but to persuade the inhabitants to adopt a line of conduct, counter to that of their representatives. To this purpose they published a manifesto and proclamation, addressed to Congress, the assemblies, and all others the free inhabitants of the colonies, in which they observed,

The policy, as well as the benevolence of Great-Britain, have thus far checked the extremes of war, when they tended to distress a people still considered as our fellow-subjects, and to desolate a country shortly to become a source of mutual advantage: But when that country professes the unnatural design not only of estranging herself from us, but of mortgaging herself and her resources to our enemies, the whole contest is changed; and the question is, how far Great-Britain may, by every means in her power, destroy or render useless a connection contrived for her ruin, and for the aggrandizement of France. Under such circumstances the laws of self-preservation must direct the conduct of Great-Britain; and if the British colonies are to become an accession to France, will direct her to render that accession of as little avail as possible to her enemy.

Congress upon being informed of the design of the commissioners to circulate these papers declared, that the agents employed to distribute the manifestoes and proclamation of the commissioners, were not entitled to protection from a flag. They also recommended to the several states to secure and keep them in close custody, but that they might not appear to hood-wink their constituents, they ordered the manifestoes and proclamation to be printed in the newspapers. The proposals of the commissioners were not more favourably received by the people [80] than they had been by Congress. In some places the flags containing them were not received, but ordered instantly to depart, in others they were received, and forwarded to Congress, as the only proper tribunal to take cognizance of them. In no one place, not immediately commanded by the British army, was there any attempt to accept, or even to deliberate, on the propriety of closing with the offers of Britain.

1778

To deter the British from executing their threats of laying waste the country, Congress published to the world a resolution and manifesto in which they concluded with these words.

OCTOBER
30

We, therefore, the Congress of the United States of America, do solemnly declare and proclaim, that if our enemies presume to execute their threats, or persist in their present career of barbarity, we will take such exemplary vengeance as shall deter others from a like conduct. We appeal to that God who searcheth the hearts of men, for the rectitude of our intentions; and in his holy presence we declare, that as we are not moved by any light and hasty suggestions of anger and revenge, so through every possible change of fortune we will adhere to this our determination.

This was the last effort of Great Britain, in the way of negotiation, to regain her colonies. It originated in folly, and ignorance of the real state of affairs in America. She had begun with *wrong* measures, and had now got into *wrong* time. Her concessions, on this occasion, were an implied justification of the resistance of the colonists. By offering to concede all that they at first asked for, she virtually acknowledged herself to have been the aggressor in an unjust war. Nothing could be more favourable to the cementing of the friendship of the new allies, than this unsuccessful negociation. The states had an opportunity of evincing the sincerity of their engagements, and France abundant reason to believe that by preventing their being conquered, her favourite scheme of lessening the power of Great Britain, would be secured beyond the reach of accident.

[81] After the termination of the campaign of 1777, the British 1778 army retired to winter quarters in Philadelphia, and the American army to Valley-Forge. The former enjoyed all the conveniences which an opulent city afforded, while the latter not half cloathed, and more than once on the point of starving, were enduring the severity of a cold winter in a hutted camp. It was well for them that the British made no attempt to disturb them, while in this destitute condition.

The winter and spring passed away without any more remarkable events in either army, than a few successful excursions of parties from Philadelphia to the neighbouring country, for the purpose of bringing in supplies, or destroying property. In one of these, a party of the British proceeded to Bordenton, and there burned four store-houses full of useful commodities. Before they returned to Philadelphia, they burned two frigates, nine ships, six privateer sloops, twenty three brigs, with a number of sloops and schooners.

Soon after, an excursion from Newport was made by 500 British and Hessians, under the command of lieut. col. Campbell. These having landed in the night, marched next morning in two bodies, MAY 25 the one for Warren, the other for the head of Kickemuet river. They destroyed about 70 flat bottomed boats, and burned a quantity of pitch, tar and plank. They also set fire to the meeting house at Warren, and seven dwelling houses. At Bristol they burned the church and 22 houses. Several other houses were plundered, and women were stripped of their shoe-buckles, gold rings and handkerchiefs.

APR. 13

JULY 9

1778

A French squadron, consisting of 12 ships of the line and 4 frigates, commanded by count D'Estaing, sailed from Toulon for America, in about two months after the treaty had been agreed upon between the United States and the king of France. After a passage of 87 days, the count arrived at the entrance of the Delaware. From an apprehension of something of this kind, and from the prospect of greater security, it was resolved in Great Britain, forthwith to evacuate Philadelphia and to concentrate [82] the royal force in the city and harbour of New-York. The commissioners brought out the orders for this movement, but knew nothing of the matter. It had an unfriendly influence on their proposed negotiations, but it was indispensibly necessary; for if the French fleet had blocked up the Delaware, and the Americans besieged Philadelphia, the escape of the British from either, would have been scarcely possible.

JUN. 18

JUN. 24

The royal army passed over the Delaware into New-Jersey. Gen. Washington, having penetrated into their design of evacuating Philadelphia, had previously detatched Gen. Maxwell's brigade, to co-operate with the Jersey militia, in obstructing their progress, till time would be given for his army to overtake them. The British were incumbered with an enormous baggage, which, together with the impediments thrown in their way, greatly retarded their march. The American army having, in pursuit of the British, crossed the Delaware, six hundred men were immediately detatched under col. Morgan, to reinforce Gen. Maxwell. Washington halted his troops, when they had marched to the vicinity of Princeton. The general officers in the American army, being asked by the commander in chief, "Will it be adviseable to hazard a general action?" answered in the negative, but recommended a detatchment of 1500 men, to be immediately sent, to act as occasion might serve, on the enemy's left flank and rear. This was immediately forwarded under General Scott. When Sir Henry Clinton had advanced to Allen-Town, he determined instead of keeping the direct course towards Staten-Island, to draw towards the sea coast and to push on towards Sandy-Hook. Gen. Washington on receiving intelligence that Sir Henry was proceeding in that direction towards Monmouth court-house, dispatched 1000 men under Gen. Wayne, and sent the Marquis de la Fayette to take command of the whole advanced corps, with orders to seize the first fair opportunity of attacking the enemy's rear. Gen. Lee who having been lately exchanged had joined the army, was offered this command, but he declined it, as he was in principle against [83] hazarding an attack. The whole army followed at a proper distance, for supporting the advanced corps, and reached Cranberry the next morning. Sir Henry Clinton sensible of the approach of the Americans, placed his grenadiers, light-infantry and chaseurs in his rear, and his baggage in his front. Gen. Washington increased his advanced corps with two brigades, and sent Gen. Lee, who now wished for the command, to take charge of the whole, and followed with the main army to give it support. On the next morning orders were sent to Lee, to move on and attack, unless there should be powerful reasons to the contrary. When Washington had marched about five miles to support the advanced corps, he found the whole of it retreating by Lee's orders, and without having made any opposition of consequence. Washington rode up to Lee and proposed certain questions to him, which implied censure. Lee answered with warmth and unsuitable language. The commander in chief ordered Col. Stewart's and Lieut. Col. Ramsay's battalions, to form on a piece of ground, which he judged suitable for giving a check to the advancing enemy. Lee was then asked if he would command on that ground, to which he consented, and was ordered to take proper measures for checking the enemy, to which he replied, "your orders shall be obeyed, and I will not be the first to leave the field." Washington then rode to the main army, which was formed with the utmost expedition. A warm cannonade immediately commenced, between the British and American artillery, and a heavy firing between the advanced troops of the British army, and the two battalions which Gen. Washington had halted. These stood their ground, till they were intermixed with a part of the British army. Lieut. Col. Ramsay the commander of one of them, was wounded and taken prisoner. Gen. Lee continued till the last on the field of battle, and brought off the rear of the retreating troops.

The check the British received, gave time to make a disposition of the left wing, and second line of the American army in the wood, and on the eminence to which Lee was retreating. On this, some cannon were placed [84] by lord Sterling, who commanded the left wing, which, with the co-operation of some parties of infantry, effectually stopped the advance of the British in that quarter. Gen. Greene took a very advantageous position, on the right of lord Sterling. The British attempted to turn the left flank of the Americans, but were repulsed. They also made a movement to the right, with as little success, for Greene with artillery disappointed their design. Wayne advanced with a body of troops, and kept up so severe and well directed a fire, that the British were soon compelled to give way. They retired and took the position, which Lee had before occupied. Washington resolved to attack them, and ordered Gen. Poor to move round upon their right, and Gen. Woodford to their left; but they could not get within reach, before it was dark. These remained on the ground, which they had been directed to occupy during the night, with an intention of attacking early next morning, and the main body lay on their arms in the field to be ready for supporting them. Gen. Washington reposed himself in his cloak, under a tree, in hopes of renewing the action the next day. But these hopes were frustrated: The British troops marched away in the night, in such silence, that Gen. Poor, though he lay very near them, knew nothing of their departure. They left behind them, four officers and about forty privates, all so badly wounded, that they could not be removed. Their other wounded were carried off. The British pursued their march without further interruption, and soon reached the neigh-bourhood of Sandy-Hook, without the loss of either their covering party or baggage. The American general declined all farther pursuit of the royal army, and soon after drew off his troops to the borders of the North river. The loss of the Americans, in killed and wounded, was about 250. The loss of the royal army, inclusive of prisoners, was about 350. Lt. col. Monckton, one of the British slain, on account of his singular merit, was universally lamented. Col. Bonner of Pennsylvania, and major Dickenson of Virginia, officers highly es-teemed by their country, fell in this engagement. The emotions of the mind, added to fatigue in a very hot [85] day, brought on such a fatal suppression of the vital powers, that some of the Americans, and 59 of the British, were found dead on the field of battle, without any marks of violence upon their bodies.

It is probable, that Washington intended to take no farther notice

JUN. 30

1778

of Lee's conduct in the day of action, but the latter could not brook the expressions used by the former at their first meeting, and wrote him two passionate letters. This occasioned his being arrested, and brought to trial. The charges exhibited against him were—

1st. For disobedience of orders, in not attacking the enemy on the 28th of June, agreeable to repeated instructions.

2dly. For misbehaviour before the enemy, on the same day, by making an unnecessary, disorderly and shameful retreat.

3dly, For disrespect to the commander in chief in two letters.

After a tedious hearing before a court-martial of which lord Sterling was president, Lee was found guilty and sentenced to be suspended from any command in the armies of the United States, for the term of one year, but the second charge was softened by the court martial, who in their award only found him guilty of misbehaviour before the enemy, by making an unnecessary and in some few instances a disorderly retreat. Many were displeased with this sentence. They argued

that by the tenor of Lee's orders, it was submitted to his discretion, whether to attack or not, and also, that the time and manner were to be determined by his own judgment. That at one time he intended to attack, but altered his opinion on apparently good grounds. That the propriety of an attack considering the superiority of the British cavalry, and the openness of the ground was very questionable. That though it might have distressed the enemy's rear in the first instance; it would probably have brought on a general action, before the advanced corps could have been supported by the main body, which was some miles in the rear.

If said they "Lee's judgment was against attacking the enemy, he could not be guilty of disobeying an order for that purpose, which was suspended on the condition of his own approbation of the measure." They also agreed [86] that a suspension from command, was not a sufficient punishment for his crimes, if really guilty. They therefore inferred a presumption of his innocence from the lenient sentence of his judges. Though there was a diversity of opinions relative to the first and second charges, all were agreed in pronouncing him guilty of disrespect to the commander in chief. The Americans

1778

had formerly idolised Gen. Lee, but some of them now went to the opposite extreme, and pronounced him treacherous or deficient in courage, though there was no foundation for either of these suspicions. His temper was violent, and his impatience of subordination had led him often to quarrel with those whom he was bound to respect and obey; but his courage and fidelity could not be questioned.

Soon after the battle of Monmouth, the American army took post at the White-Plains, a few miles beyond Kingsbridge and the British though only a few miles distant, did not molest them. They remained in this position from an early day in July, till a late one in the autumn, and then the Americans retired to Middle-Brook in Jersey, where they built themselves huts in the same manner as they had done at Valley-Forge.

Immediately on the departure of the British from Philadelphia, Congress, after an absence of nine months, returned to the former seat of their deliberations. Soon after their return, they were called AUG. 6 upon, to give a public audience to a Minister Plenipotentiary from the court of France. The person appointed to this office, was M. Gerard, the same who had been employed in the negotiations, antecedent to the treaty. The arrival and reception of a minister from France, made a strong impression on the minds of the Americans. They felt the weight and importance, to which they were risen among nations. That the same spot, which in less than a century, had been the residence of savages, should become the theatre on which, the representatives of a new, free and civilised nation, gave a public audience to a minister Plenipotentiary, from one of the oldest and most powerful kingdoms of Europe, afforded ample materials for philosophic contemplation. That in less than three years [87] from 1778 the day, on which an answer was refused by Great Britain to the united supplications of the colonists, praying for peace, liberty and safety, they should, as an independent people, be honored with the residence of a minister from the court of France, exceeded the expectation of the most sanguine Americans. The patriots of the new world revolved in their minds these transactions, with heart-felt satisfaction, while the devout were led to admire that Providence, which had, in so short a space, stationed the United States among the powers of the earth, and clothed them in robes of Sovereignty.

The British had but barely completed the removal of their fleet
and army, from the Delaware and Philadelphia to the harbour and
city of New-York, when they received intelligence, that a French
fleet was on the coast of America. This was commanded by count
D'Estaing, and consisted of twelve ships of the line and three frigates.
Among the former, one carried 90 guns, another 80 and six 74 guns
each. Their first object was the surprise of lord Howe's fleet in the
Delaware, but they arrived too late. In naval history, there are few
more narrow escapes than that of the British fleet, on this occasion.
It consisted only of six 64 gun ships, three of 50, and two of 40, with
some frigates and sloops. Most of these had been long on service,
and were in a bad condition. Their force, when compared with that
of the French fleet, was so greatly inferior, that had the latter reached
the mouth of the Delaware, in 75 days from its leaving Toulon, their
capture, in the ordinary course of events, would have been inevitable.
This stroke was providentially prevented, by the various hinderances
which retarded D'Estaing in his voyage to the term of 87 days, in the
last eleven of which, lord Howe's fleet, not only quitted the Delaware,
but reached the harbour of New-York. D'Estaing, disappointed in his
first scheme, pursued and appeared off Sandy-Hook. American pilots
of the first abilities, provided for the purpose, went on board his
fleet. Among them were persons, whose circumstances placed them
above the ordinary rank of pilots.

[88] The sight of the French fleet raised all the active passions of
their adversaries. Transported with indignation against the French,
for interfering in what they called a domestic quarrel, the British
displayed a spirit of zeal and barvery which could not be exceeded.
A thousand volunteers were dispatched from their transports to man
their fleet. The masters and mates of the merchantmen and traders
at New-York, took their stations at the guns with the common sailors.
Others put to sea in light vessels, to watch the motions of their
enemies. The officers and privates of the British army, contended
with so much eagerness to serve on board the men of war as marines,
that it became necessary to decide the point of honor by lot.

The French fleet came to anchor, and continued without the Hook
for eleven days. During this time the British had the mortification of
seeing the blockade of their fleet, and the capture of about 20 vessels

JULY 11

1778

under English colours. On the 22nd, the French fleet appeared under weigh. It was an anxious moment to the British. They supposed that Count D'Estaing would force his way into the harbour, and that an engagement would be the consequence. Every thing with them was at stake. Nothing less than destruction or victory would have ended the contest. If the first had been their lot, the vast fleet of transports and victuallers and the army must have fallen. The pilots on board the French fleet, declared it to be impossible to carry the large ships thereof over the bar, on account of their draught of water. D'Estaing on that account and by the advice of Gen. Washington, left the Hook and sailed for Newport. By his departure the British had a second escape for had he remained at the Hook but a few days longer, the fleet of admiral Byron must have fallen into his hands. That officer had been sent out to relieve lord Howe who had solicited to be recalled, and the fleet under his command had been sent to reinforce that which had been previously on the coast of America. Admiral Byron's squadron had met with bad weather, and was separated in different storms. It now arrived, scattered, broken, sickly, [89] dismasted or otherwise damaged. Within 8 days after the departure of the French fleet, the Renown, the Raisonable, the Centurion, and the Cornwall, arrived singly at Sandy-Hook.

JULY 22

1778

The next attempt of Count D'Estaing was against Rhode-Island, of which the British had been in possession since December, 1776. A combined attack against it was projected, and it was agreed that Gen. Sullivan should command the American land forces. Such was the eagerness of the people to co-operate with their new allies, and so confident were they of success, that some thousands of volunteers engaged in the service. The militia of Massachusetts was under the command of Gen. Hancock. The royal troops on the island, having been lately reinforced, were about 6000. Sullivan's force was about 10,000. Lord Howe followed Count D'Estaing, and came within sight of Rhode-Island, the day after the French fleet entered the harbour of New-Port. The British fleet exceeded the French in point of number, but was inferior with respect to effective force and weight of metal. On the appearance of lord Howe, the French admiral put out to sea with his whole fleet, to engage him. While the two commanders were exerting their naval skill to gain respectively the advantages of position, a strong gale of wind came on which afterwards increased to a tempest, and greatly damaged the ships on both sides. In this conflict of the elements, two capital French ships were dismasted. The Languedoc of 90 guns, D'Estaing's own ship, after losing all her masts and her rudder, was attacked by the Renown of 50 guns, commanded by Capt Dawson. The same evening the Preston of 50 guns, fell in with the Tonnant of 80 guns with only her mainmast standing, and attacked her with spirit, but night put an end to the engagement. Six sail of the French squadron came up in the night, which saved the disabled ships from any farther attack. There was no ship or vessel lost on either side. The British suffered less in the storm than their adversaries, yet enough to make it necessary for them to return to New-York, for the purpose of refitting. The French fleet came to anchor, on [90] the 20th, near to Rhode-Island, but 1778 sailed on the 22d, to Boston. Before they sailed, Gen. Greene and the Marquis de la Fayette went on board the Languedoc, to consult on measures proper to be pursued. They urged D'Estaing to return with his fleet into the harbour, but his principal officers were opposed to the measure, and protested against it. He had been instructed to go to Boston, if his fleet met with any misfortune. His officers insisted on his ceasing to prosecute the expedition against Rhode-Island, that he might conform to the orders of their common superiors. Upon the return of Gen. Greene and the Marquis de la Fayette, and their reporting the determination of Count D'Estaing, a protest was drawn up and sent to him, which was signed by John Sullivan, Nathaniel Greene, John Hancock, I. Glover, Ezekiel Cornel, William Whipple, John Tyler, Solomon Lovell, Jon. Fitconnell. In this they protested against the Count's taking the fleet to Boston, as derogatory to the honor of France, contrary to the intention of his most Christian Majesty, and the interest of his nation, and destructive in the highest degree to the welfare of the United States, and highly injurious to the alliance formed between the two nations. Had D'Estaing prosecuted his original plan within the harbour, either before or immediately after the pursuit of lord Howe, the reduction of the British post on Rhode-Island would have been probable, but his departure in the first instance to engage the British fleet, and in the second from Rhode-Island to Boston, frustrated the whole plan. Perhaps

Count D'Estaing, hoped by something brilliant to efface the impressions made by his late failure at New-York. Or he might have thought it imprudent to stake his whole fleet, within an harbour possessed by his enemies.

After his ships had suffered both from battle and the storm, the letter of his instructions—the importunity of his officers, and his anxiety to have his ships speedily refitted, might have weighed with him to sail directly for Boston. Whatever were the reasons which induced his adoption of that measure, the Americans were greatly dissatisfied. They complained that they had incurred [91] great expence and danger, under the prospect of the most effective co-operation—that depending thereon, they had risqued their lives on an island, where without naval protection, they were exposed to particular danger. That in this situation, they were first deserted, and afterwards totally abandoned, at a time, when by persevering in the original plan, they had well grounded hopes of speedy success. Under these apprehensions, the discontented militia went home in such crowds, that the regular army which remained, was in danger of being cut off from a retreat. In these embarrassing circumstances, General Sullivan extricated himself with judgment and ability. He began to send off his heavy artillery and baggage on the 26th, and retreated from his lines on the night of the 28th. It had been that day resolved in a council of war, to remove to the north end of the island—fortify their camp, secure a communication with the main, and hold the ground till it could be known whether the French fleet would return to their assistance. The Marquis de la Fayette by desire of his associates set off for Boston, to request the speedy return of the French fleet. To this Count D'Estaing would not consent, but he made a spirited offer to lead the troops under his command, and co-operate with the American land forces against Rhode-Island.

Sullivan retreated with great order, but he had not been five hours at the north end of the island, when his troops were fired upon by the British, who had pursued them on discovering their retreat. The pursuit was made by two parties and on two roads, to one was opposed Col. Henry B. Livingston, to the other John Laurens, aid de camp to Gen. Washington, and each of them had a command of light troops. In the first instance, these light troops were compelled by

1778

AUGUST

superior numbers to give way, but they kept up a retreating fire. On being reinforced they gave their pursuers a check, and at length repulsed them. By degrees the action became in some respects general, and near 1200 Americans were engaged. The loss on each side was between two and three hundred.

[92] Lord Howe's fleet with Sir Henry Clinton and about 4000 1778
troops on board, being seen off the coast, General Sullivan concluded immediately to evacuate Rhode-Island. As the centries of both armies were within 400 yards of each other, the greatest caution was necessary. To cover the design of retreating, the shew of resistance and continuance on the island was kept up. The retreat was made AUG. 30
in the night, and mostly completed by twelve o'clock. Towards the last of it the Marquis de la Fayette returned from Boston. He had rode thither from Rhode-Island, a distance of near 70 miles in 7 hours, and returned in six and a half. Anxious to partake in the engagement, his mortification was not little at being out of the way on the day before. He was in time to bring off the picquets, and other parties that covered the retreat of the American army. This he did in excellent order. Not a man was left behind, nor was the smallest article lost.

The bravery and good conduct which John Laurens displayed on this occasion, were excelled by his republican magnanimity, in declining a military commission which was conferred on him, by the representatives of his country. Congress resolved, that he should be presented with a continental commission, of Lieut. Colonel, in testimony of the sense which they entertained of his patriotic and spirited services, and of his brave conduct in several actions, particularly in that of Rhode-Island on the 29th of August.

On the next day he wrote to Congress a letter, expressing

his gratitude for the unexpected honor which they were pleased to confer on him, and of the satisfaction it would have afforded him, could he have accepted it without injuring the rights of the officers in the line of the army, and doing an evident injustice to his colleagues, in the family of the commander in chief. That having been a spectator of the convulsions occasioned in the army by disputes of rank, he held the tranquillity of it too dear, to be instrumental in disturbing it, and therefore intreated Congress to suppress their resolve, ordering him the commission of Lieut. Colonel, and to accept his sincere thanks for the intended honor.

1778

[93] With the abortive expedition to Rhode-Island, there was an end to the plans, which were in this first campaign projected by the allies of Congress, for a co-operation. The Americans had been intoxicated with hopes of the most decisive advantages, but in every instance they were disappointed. Lord Howe with an inferiority of force, not only preserved his own fleet, but counteracted and defeated all the views and attempts of Count D'Estaing. The French fleet gained no direct advantages for the Americans, yet their arrival was of great service to their cause. Besides deranging the plans of the British, it carried conviction to their minds, that his most Christian Majesty was seriously disposed to support them. The good will of their new allies was manifested to the Americans, and though it had failed in producing the effects expected from it, the failure was charged to winds, weather, and unavoidable incidents. Some censured Count D'Estaing, but while they attempted to console themselves, by throwing blame on him, they felt and acknowledged their obligation to the French nation, and were encouraged to persevere in the war, from the hope that better fortune would attend their future co-operation.

Sir Henry Clinton finding that the Americans had left Rhode-Island, returned to New-York, but directed Gen. Grey to proceed to Bedford and the neighbourhood, where several American privateers resorted. On reaching the place of their destination the General's party landed, and in a few hours destroyed about 70 sail of shipping, besides a number of small craft. They also burnt magazines, wharfs, stores, warehouses, vessels on the stocks, and a considerable number of dwelling houses. The buildings burned in Bedford, were estimated to be worth £20,000 sterling. The other articles destroyed were worth much more. The royal troops proceeded to Martha's vineyard. There they destroyed a few vessels, and made a requisition of the militia arms, the public money, 300 oxen and 2000 sheep, which was complied with.

SEPT. 5

A similar expedition under the command of Capt. Ferguson, was about the same time undertaken against Little [94] Egg-Harbour, at which place the Americans had a number of privateers and prizes, and also some salt-works. Several of the vessels got off but all that were found were destroyed. Previous to the embarkation of the British from Egg-Harbour for New-York, Capt. Ferguson with 250 men, surprised and put to death about fifty of a party of the Americans, who were posted in the vicinity. The attack being made in the night, little or no quarter was given.

The loss sustained by the British in these several excursions was trifling, but the advantage was considerable, from the supplies they procured, and the check which was given to the American privateers.

One of the most disastrous events, which occurred at this period of the campaign, was the surprise and massacre of an American regiment of light dragoons, commanded by Lieut. Col. Baylor. While employed in a detached situation, to intercept and watch a British foraging party, they took up their lodging in a barn near Taapan. The officer, who commanded the party which surprised them, was Major Gen. Grey. He acquired the name of the "No flint General" from his common practice of ordering the men, under his command, to take the flints out of their muskets, that they might be confined to the use of their bayonets. A party of militia, which had been stationed on the road, by which the British advanced, quitted their post, without giving any notice to Col. Baylor. This disorderly conduct was the occasion of the disaster which followed. Grey's men proceeded with such silence and address, that they cut off a serjeant's patrol without noise, and surrounded old Taapan without being discovered. They then rushed in upon Baylor's regiment, while they were in a profound sleep. Incapable of defence or resistance, cut off from every prospect of selling their lives dear, the surprised dragoons sued for quarters. Unmoved by their supplications, their adversaries applied the bayonet and continued its repeated thrusts, while objects could be found, in which any signs of life appeared. A few escaped, and others, after having received from five to eleven bayonet wounds in the trunk of [95] the body, were restored, in a course of time, to perfect health. Baylor himself was wounded, but not dangerously: He lost, in killed, wounded and taken, 67 privates out of 104. About 40 were made prisoners. These were indebted, for their lives, to the humanity of one of Grey's captains, who gave quarters to the whole fourth troop, though contrary to the orders of his superior officers. The circumstance of the attack being made in the night, when neither order nor discipline can be observed, may apologise in some degree, with men of a certain description, for this bloody scene. It cannot be maintained, that the laws of war require that quarters should be given in similar assaults, but the lovers of mankind must ever contend, that the laws of humanity are of superior obligation to those of war. The truly brave will spare when resistance ceases, and in every case where it can be done with safety. The perpetrators of such actions may justly be denominated the enemies of refined society. As far as their example avails, it tends to arrest the growing humanity of modern times, and to revive the barbarism of Gothic ages. On these principles, the massacre of Col. Baylor's regiment was the subject of much complaint. The particulars of it were ascertained, by the oaths of sundry credible witnesses, taken before Gov. Livingston of Jersey, and the whole was submitted to the judgment of the public.

1778   In the summer of this year, an expedition was undertaken against East-Florida. This was resolved upon, with the double view of protecting the State of Georgia from depredation, and of causing a diversion. Gen. Robert Howe, who conducted it, had under his command about 2000 men, a few hundred of which were continental troops, and the remainder militia of the States of South-Carolina and Georgia. They proceeded as far as St. Mary's river, and without any opposition of consequence. At this place, the British had erected a fort, which, in compliment to Tonyn, governor of the province, was called by his name. On the approach of Gen. Howe, they destroyed this fort, and after some slight skirmishing, retreated towards St. Augustine. The season was more fatal [96] to the Americans than any opposition they experienced from their enemies. Sickness and death raged to such a degree that an immediate retreat became necessary; but before this was effected, they lost nearly one fourth of their whole number.

The royal commissioners having failed in their attempts to induce the Americans to resume the character of British subjects, and the successive plans of co-operation between the new allies, having also failed, a solemn pause ensued. It would seem as if the commissioners indulged a hope, that the citizens of the United States, on finding a disappointment of their expectation from the French, would reconsider and accept the offers of Great-Britain. Full time was given, both for the circulation of their manifesto, and for observing its effects on the public mind, but no overtures were made to them from any quarter. The year was drawing near to a close, before any interesting expedition was undertaken. With this new aera, a new system was introduced. Hitherto the conquest of the states had been attempted by proceeding from north to south: But that order was henceforth inverted, and the southern states became the principal theatre, on which the British conducted their offensive operations. Georgia being one of the weakest states in the union, and at the same time abounding in provisions, was marked out as the first object of renewed warfare. Lieut. Colonel Campbell, an officer of known courage and ability embarked from New-York, for Savannah, with a force of about 2000 men, under the convoy of some ships of war commanded by commodore Hyde Parker. To make more sure of success in the enterprise, Major Gen. Prevost who commanded the royal forces in East-Florida, was directed to advance with them into the southern extremity of Georgia. The fleet that sailed from New-York, in about three weeks effected a landing near the mouth of the river Savannah. From the landing place a narrow causeway of six hundred yards in length, with a ditch on each side, led through a swamp. A body of the British light infantry moved forward along this causeway. On their advance they received a heavy fire from a small [97] party under Capt. Smith, posted for the purpose of impeding their passage. Capt. Cameron was killed, but the British made their way good, and compelled Capt. Smith to retreat. General Howe, the American officer to whom the defence of Georgia was committed, took his station on the main road, and posted his little army, consisting of about 600 continentals and a few hundred militia, between the landing-place and the town of Savannah, with the river on his left and a morass in front. This disposition announced great difficulties to be overcome, before the Americans could be dislodged. While Col. Campbell was making the necessary arrangements for this purpose, he received intelligence from a negro, of a private path through the swamp, on the right of the Americans, which lay in such

1778
NOV. 27

DEC. 23

a situation that, the British troops might march through it unobserved. Sir James Baird, with the light infantry, was directed to avail himself of this path, in order to turn the right wing of the Americans and attack their rear. As soon as it was supposed that Sir James Baird had cleared his passage, the British in front of the Americans, were directed to advance and engage. Howe, finding himself attacked in the rear as well as in the front, ordered an immediate retreat. The British pursued with great execution: Their victory was complete. Upwards of 100 of the Americans were killed. Thirty eight officers, 415 privates, 48 pieces of cannon, 23 mortars, the fort with its ammunition and stores, the shipping in the river, a large quantity of provisions with the capital of Georgia, were all, in the space of a few hours in the possession of the conquerors. The broken remains of the American army retreated up the river Savannah for several miles, and then took shelter by crossing into South-Carolina. Agreeably to instructions, Gen. Prevost had marched from East-Florida, about the same time that the embarkation took place from New-York. After encountering many difficulties, the king's troops from St. Augustine reached the inhabited parts of Georgia, and there heard the welcome tidings of the arrival and success of Col. Campbell. Savannah having fallen, the fort at Sunbury surrendered. Gen. Prevost marched to Savannah, and took the command of the combined [98] forces from New-York and St. Augustine. Previous to his arrival, a proclamation had been issued, to encourage the inhabitants to come in and submit to the conquerors, with promises of protection, on condition that with their arms they would support royal government.

1778

Lieut. Col. Campbell acted with great policy, in securing the submission of the inhabitants. He did more in a short time, and with comparatively a few men, towards the re-establishment of the British interest, than all the general officers who had preceded him. He not only extirpated military opposition, but subverted for some time every trace of republican government, and paved the way for the re-establishment of a royal legislature. Georgia soon after the reduction of its capital exhibited a singular spectacle. It was the only state of the union, in which after the declaration of independence, a legislative body was convened under the authority of the crown of Great Britain. The moderation and prudence of Lieut. Col. Campbell were more successful in reconciling the minds of the citizens to their former constitution, than, the severe measures which had been generally adopted by other British commanders.

The errors of the first years of the war forced on Congress some useful reforms, in the year 1778. The insufficiency of the provision, made for the support of the officers of their army, had induced the resignation of between two and three hundred of them, to the great injury of the service. From a conviction of the justice and policy of making commissions valuable, and from respect to the warm, but disinterested recommendations of Gen. Washington, Congress resolved "That half-pay should be allowed to their officers, for the term of seven years, after the expiration of their service." This was, afterwards, extended to the end of their lives. And finally, that was commuted for full pay, for five years. Resignations were afterwards rare, and the States reaped the benefit of experienced officers continuing in service, till the war was ended. APRIL, 1778

A system of more regular discipline was introduced into the American army, by the industry, abilities and judicious [99] regulations of Baron de Steuben a most excellent disciplinarian, who had served under the king of Prussia. A very important reform took place in the medical department, by appointing different officers, to discharge the directing and purveying business of the military hospitals, which had been before united in the same hands. Dr. Rush was principally instrumental, in effecting this beneficial alteration. Some regulations, which had been adopted for limiting the prices of commodities, being found not only impracticable, but injurious, were abolished.

A few detached events, which could not be introduced without interrupting the narrative of the great events of the campaign, shall close this chapter.

Cap. James Willing, in the service of the United States, arrived, with a few men from Fort-Pitt, at the Natches, a British settlement in West-Florida. He sent out parties, who, without any resistance, made the inhabitants prisoners. Articles of agreement were entered into, between them and Capt. Willing, by which they promised to observe a neutrality in the present contest, and in return it was engaged, that their property should be unmolested. FEB. 19

The Randolph, an American frigate of 36 guns and 305 men, commanded by Capt. Biddle, having sailed on a cruise from Charleston, fell in with the Yarmouth of 64 guns, and engaged her in the night. In about a quarter of an hour, the Randolph blew up. Four men only were saved, upon a piece of her wreck. These had subsisted for four days on nothing but rain water, which they sucked from a piece of blanket. On the 5th day, Cap. Vincent of the Yarmouth, though in chase of a ship, on discovering them, suspended the chase and took them on board. Capt. Biddle, who perished on board the Randolph, was universally lamented. He was in the prime of life, and had excited high expectations of future usefulness to his country, as a bold and skillful naval officer.

Major Talbot took the British schooner Pigot, of 8 twelve pounders, as she lay on the eastern side of Rhode-Island. [100] The Major, with a number of troops on board a small vessel, made directly for the Pigot in the night, and sustaining the fire of her marines, reserved his own till he had run his jibb-boom through her fore-shrouds. He then fired some cannon, and threw in a volley of musquetry, loaded with bullets and buck-shot, and immediately boarded her. The captain made a gallant resistance, but he was not seconded by his crew. Major Talbot soon gained undisturbed possession, and carried off his prize in safety. Congress, as a reward of his merit, presented him with the commission of Lieutenant Colonel.

Campaign of 1779.

THROUGHOUT THE YEAR 1779, the British seem to have aimed at little more, in the States to the northward of Carolina, than distress and depredation. Having publicly announced their resolution of making "The colonies of as little avail as possible to their new connections," they planned sundry expeditions, on this principle.

One of these consisting of both a naval and land force, was committed to Sir George Collyer and Gen. Mathews, who made a descent on Virginia. They sailed for Portsmouth, and on their arrival took possession of that defenceless town. The remains of Norfolk on the opposite side of the river, fell of course into their hands. The Americans burned some of their own vessels, but others were made prizes by the invaders. The British guards marched 18 miles in the night, and arriving at Suffolk by morning proceeded to the destruction

MAY 10

of vessels, naval stores, and of a large magazine of provisions, which had been deposited in that place. A similar destruction was carried on at Kemp's landing, Shepherds-gosport, Tanners creek, and other places in the vicinity. The frigates and armed vessels were employed on the same business [101] along the margin of the rivers. Three thousand hogsheads of tobacco were taken at Portsmouth. Every house in Suffolk was burnt except the church, and one dwelling house. The houses of several private gentlemen in the country, shared the same fate. Above 130 vessels were either destroyed or taken. All that were upon the stocks were burned, and every thing relative to the building or fitting of ships, was either carried off or destroyed. The fleet and army after demolishing fort Nelson, and setting fire to the store-houses, and other public buildings in the dockyard at Gosport, embarked from Virginia, and returned with their prizes and booty safe to New-York, in the same month in which they had left it. This expedition into Virginia distressed a number of its inhabitants, and enriched the British forces, but was of no real service to the royal cause. It was presumed that by involving the citizens in losses and distress, they would be brought to reflect on the advantages of submitting to a power, against which they had not the means of defending themselves: But the temper of the times was unfavourable to these views. Such was the high toned state of the American mind, that property had comparatively lost its value. It was fashionable to suffer in the cause of independence. Some hearty whigs gloried in their losses, with as much pride as others gloried in their possessions. The British supposing the Americans to be influenced, by the considerations which bias men in the languid scenes of tranquil life, and not reflecting on the sacrifices which enthusiastic patriotism is willing to make, proceeded in their schemes of distress: But the more extensively they carried on this mode of warfare, the more obstacles they created to the re-union of the empire. In about five weeks after the termination of the expedition to Virginia, a similar one was projected against the exposed margin of Connecticut. Gov. Tryon was appointed to the command of about 2600 land forces, employed on this business and he was supported by Gen. Garth. The transports which conveyed these troops, were covered by a suitable number of armed vessels, commanded by Sir George Collyer. They proceeded from New-York, [102] by the way of Hell-gate, and landed at East-Haven. The royal commanders made an address to the inhabitants, in which they invited them to return to their duty and allegiance, and promised protection to all who should remain peaceably in their usual place of residence, except the civil and military officers of the government. It also stated

JULY 5
1778

> that their property lay still within the grasp of that power, whose lenity had persisted in its mild and noble efforts, though branded with the most unworthy imputation. That the existence of a single house on their defenceless coast, ought to be a constant reproof of their ingratitude. That they who lay so much in the British power, afforded a striking monument of their mercy, and therefore ought to set the first example of returning to their allegiance.

One of the many addresses, from which the above extract is taken, was sent, by a flag to Col. Whiting of the militia near Fairfield. The Col. was allowed an hour for his answer, but he had scarcely time to read it before the town was in flames. He nevertheless returned the following answer "Connecticut, having nobly dared to take up arms against the cruel despotism of Great Britain, and the flames having preceded the answer to your flag, they will persist to oppose to the utmost, the power exerted against injured innocence". The British marched from their landing to New-Haven. The town on their entering it, was delivered up to promiscuous plunder, a few instances of protection excepted. The inhabitants were stripped of their household furniture and other moveable property. The harbour and water side was covered with feathers, which were discharged from opened beds. An aged citizen who labored under a natural inability of speech, had his tongue cut out by one of the royal army. After perpetrating every species of enormity, but that of burning houses, the invaders suddenly re-imbarked and proceeded by water to Fairfield. The militia of that place and the vicinity, posted themselves at the court-house green, and gave considerable annoyance to them, as they were advancing, but soon retreated to the height back of the town. On the approach of the British the town was [103] evacuated by most of its inhabitants. A few women remained with the view of saving their property. They imagined, that their sex would protect them. They also reposed confidence in an enemy who they knew had been formerly famed for humanity and politeness, but they bitterly repented their presumption. Parties of the royal army entered the deserted houses of the inhabitants, broke open desks, trunks, closets and chests, and took every thing of value that came in their way. They robbed the women of their buckles, rings, bonnets, aprons and handkerchiefs. They abused them with the foulest language, threatened their lives, and presented the bayonets to their breasts. A sucking infant was plundered of part of its clothing, while the bayonet was presented to the breast of its mother. Towards evening, they began to burn the houses, which they had previously plundered. The women begged Gen. Tryon to spare the town. Mr. Sayre, the episcopal minister, who had suffered for his attachment to the royal cause, joined the women in their requests, but their joint supplications were disregarded. They then begged, that a few houses might be spared for a general shelter. This was at first denied, but at length Tryon consented to save the buildings of Mr. Burr and of Mr. Elliot, and also said, that the houses for public worship should be spared. After his departure on the next morning with the main body, the rear guard consisting of German yaugers set fire to every thing which Tryon had spared, but on their departure the inhabitants extinguished the flames, and saved some of the houses. The militia were joined by numbers from the country which successively came in to their aid, but they were too few to make effectual opposition.

The British in this excursion, also burned East-Haven, and the greatest part of Green's farms, and the flourishing town of Norwalk. A considerable number of ships, either finished or on the stocks, with whale-boats and a large amount of stores and merchandise, were destroyed. Particular accounts of these devastations were, in a short time, transmitted by authority to Congress. By these it appeared that they were burnt at Norwalk [104] two houses of public worship, 80 dwelling houses, 87 barns, 22 stores, 17 shops, 4 mills and 5 vessels; And at Fairfield two houses of public worship, 15 dwelling houses, 11 barns and several stores. There were at the same time a number of certificates transmitted to Gen. Washington, in which sundry persons of veracity bore witness on oath to various acts of brutality, rapine and cruelty, committed on aged persons, women

1778

and prisoners. Congress, on receiving satisfactory attestation of the ravages of the British in this and other similar expeditions, resolved JULY 19 "To direct their marine committee to take the most effectual measures, to carry into execution their manifesto of October 30th 1778, by burning or destroying the towns belonging to the enemy in Great Britain or the West-Indies;" but their resolve was never carried into effect.

The older citizens of the United States, who had grown up with habits of love and attachment to the British nation, felt the keenest sensations of regret, when they contrasted the years 1759 and 1779. The former was their glory, when in the days of their youth, they were disposed to boast of the honors of their common country, but the latter filled them with distress, not only for what they suffered, but for the degradation of a country they revered as the natal soil of their forefathers. The one enobled the British name with the conquest of Crown-Point, Oswego, Montreal, Quebec and the whole province of Canada. The other was remarkable only, for the burning of magazines, store-houses, dock-yards, the towns of Fairfield, and Norwalk, and for the general distress of a defenceless peasantry.

The fires and destruction which accompanied this expedition, were severely censured by the Americans, and apologised for by the British in a very unsatisfactory manner. The latter in their vindication, alleged that the houses which they had burned gave shelter to the Americans, while they fired from them, and on other occassions concealed their retreat.

Tryon, who was a civil governor as well as a general, undertook the justification of the measure, on principles [105] of policy. "I 1779 should be very sorry" said he

if the destruction of these villages would be thought less reconcileable with humanity, than the love of my country, my duty to the king, and the laws of arms. The usurpers have professedly placed their hopes of severing the empire, in avoiding decisive actions—upon the waste of the British treasures, and upon the escape of their own property during the protracting of the war. Their power is supported by the general dread of their tyranny and threats, practiced to inspire a credulous mulitude, with a presumptuous confidence in our forbearance; I wish to detect this delusion.

These devastations were the subject of an elegant poem, written on the spot a few days after, by Col. Humphries.

While the British were proceeding in these desolating operations, Gen. Washington was called upon for continental troops, but he could spare very few. He durst not detach largely, as he apprehended that one design of the British in these movements was to draw off a proportion of his army from West-Point, to favour an intended attack on that important post. General Parsons, though closely connected with Connecticut, and though from his small force he was unable to make successful opposition to the invaders, yet instead of pressing General Washington for a large detachment of continental troops, wrote to him as follows, "The British may probably distress the country exceedingly, by the ravages they will commit, but I would rather see all the towns on the coast of my country in flames, than that the enemy should possess West-Point."

The inhabitants feared much more than they suffered. They expected that the whole margin of their country, 120 miles in extent, would suffer the fate of Fairfield and Norwalk. The season of the year added much to their difficulties, as the close attention of the farmers to their harvesting could not be omitted, without hazarding their subsistence. These fears were not of long duration. In about ten days after the landing of the British troops, an order was issued for their immediate return to New-York. This they effected, in a short time, [106] and with a loss so inconsiderable, that in the whole expedition, it did not exceed 150 men.

While the British were successfully making these desultory operations, the American army was incapable of covering the country. The former, having by means of their superior marine force, the command of the numerous rivers, bays and harbours of the United States, had it in their power to make descents, where they pleased, with an expedition that could not be equalled by the American land forces. Had Gen. Washington divided his army, conformably to the wishes of the invaded citizens, he would have subjected his whole force to be cut up in detail. It was therefore his uniform practice, to risque no more by way of covering the country than was consistent with the general safety.

His army was posted at some distance from British head quarters

1779

AUGUST

in New York, and on both sides of the North river. The van thereof consisting of 300 infantry and 150 cavalry, under the command of Col. Anthony Walton White, patroled constantly, for several months, in front of the British lines, and kept a constant watch on the Sound and on the North river. This corps had sundry skirmishes with parties of the British, and was particularly useful in checking their excursions, and in procuring and communicating intelligence of their movements.

About this time Gen. Putnam, who had been stationed with a respectable command at Reading in Connecticut, when on a visit to his out-post at Horse-Neck, was attacked by Gov. Tryon, with about 1500 men. Gen. Putnam had only a picket of 150 men, and two iron field pieces without horses or drag-ropes. He however planted his cannon on the high ground, near the meeting house, and by several fires retarded the advancing enemy, and continued to make opposition till he perceived the enemy's horse, supported by the infantry, were about to charge. Gen. Putnam after ordering the picket to provide for their safety, by retiring to a swamp inaccessible to horse, plunged down the precipice at the church. This is so steep as to have artificial stairs, composed [107] of nearly one hundred stone steps, for the accommodation of foot passengers. The dragoons stopped short, without venturing down the abrupt declivity, and before they got round the brow of the hill, Putnam was far enough beyond their reach; of the many balls that were fired at him, all missed except one, which went through his hat. He proceeded to Stamford, and having strengthened his picket with some militia, faced about and pursued Governor Tryon on his return. *1779*

The campaign of 1779, though barren of important events, was distinguished by one of the most gallant enterprises, which took place in the course of the war. This was the capture of Stoney-Point, on the North river. Gen. Wayne, who had the honor of conducting this enterprise, set out at the head of a strong detachment of the most active infantry in the American army at noon, and completed a march of about 14 miles, over bad roads, by eight o'clock in the evening. The detachment being then within a mile and a half of its object, was halted and formed into columns. The General, with a few of his officers, advanced and reconnoitred the works. At half past eleven, the whole moved forward to the attack. The van of the right, JULY 15 consisting of 150 volunteers under the command of Lieut. Col. Fleury, advanced with unloaded muskets, and fixed bayonets. These were preceded by 20 picked men, who were particularly instructed to remove the abbatis and other obstructions. The van of the left was led by Major Stewart, and advanced with unloaded muskets and fixed bayonets. It was also preceded by a similar forlorn hope. The General placed himself at the head of the right column, and gave the most pointed orders not to fire, but to depend solely on the bayonet. The two columns directed their attacks to opposite points of the works, while a detachment engaged the attention of the garrison, by a feint in their front. The approaches were more difficult than had been apprehended. The works were defended by a deep morass, which was also, at that time, overflowed by the tide. Neither the morass, the double row of abbatis, nor the strength of the works, damped the ardor [108] of the assailants. In the face of a most tremendous fire of musketry, and of cannon loaded with grape-shot, they forced their way, at the point of the bayonet, through every obstacle, until both columns met in the centre of the works, at nearly the same instant. Gen. Wayne as he passed the last abbatis, was wounded in the head by a musket ball, but nevertheless insisted on being carried forward, adding as a reason for it, ["] that if he died he wished it might be in the fort." Lieutenants Gibbons and Knox, who led the forlorn hope, escaped unhurt, although the first lost 17 men out of 20, and the last nearly as many. The killed and wounded of the Americans amounted to 98. The killed of the garrison were 63, and the number of their prisoners 543. Two flags, two standards, 15 pieces of ordnance, and a considerable quantity of military stores, fell into the hands of the conquerors. The vigor and spirit, with which this enterprise was conducted, was matter of triumph to the Americans. Congress gave their thanks to Gen. Washington "For the vigilance, wisdom and magnanimity with which he had conducted the military operations of the States, and which were among many other signal instances manifested in his orders for the above enterprise." They also gave thanks to Gen. Wayne, and ordered a medal, emblematical of the action, to be struck and one of gold to be presented to him. They directed a silver one to be presented to Lieut. Col. Fleury, and also to Major Stewart. At the same time, they passed general

resolutions in honor of the officers and men, but particularly desig-
nating Lieut. Col. Fleury, Major Stewart, Lieutenants Gibbons and
Knox. To the two latter and also to Mr. Archer, the General's
volunteer aid-de-camp, they gave the rank of Captain. The clemency
shewn to the vanquished, was universally applauded. The customs
of war, and the recent barbarities at Fairfield and Norwalk, would
have been an apology for the conquerors, had they put the whole
garrison to the sword, but the assailants, no less generous than brave,
ceased to destroy as soon as their adversaries ceased to resist. Upon
the capture of Stoney-Point, the victors turned its artillery [109]
against Verplank's-Point, and fired upon it with such effect, that the   1779
shipping in its vicinity cut their cables and fell down the river. As
soon as the news of these events reached New-York, preparations
were instantly made to relieve the latter post and to recover the
former. It by no means accorded with the cautious prudence of Gen.
Washington, to risque an engagement for either or for both of them.
He therefore removed the cannon and stores, destroyed the works,
and evacuated the captured post. Sir Henry Clinton regained possession of Stoney-Point, on the third day after its capture, and placed
in it a strong garrison.

The successful enterprise of the Americans at Stoney-Point, was
speedily followed by another, which equalled it in boldness of design.
This was the surprise of the British garrison at Powles-Hook, opposite
to New-York, which was effected by Major Lee with about 350 men.   JULY 19
Major Sutherland the commandant, with a number of Hessians got   1779
off safe to a small block-house on the left of the fort, but about 30 of
his men were killed and 160 taken prisoners. The loss of the Americans
was inconsiderable. Major Lee in conformity to the orders he had
received, made an immediate retreat, without waiting to destroy
either the barracks or the artillery. Congress honored him with their
thanks, and ordered a medal of gold, emblematical of the affair to
be struck, and presented to him as a reward "for his prudence,
address and bravery." They also passed resolutions applauding his
humanity, and expressing their high sense of the good conduct of
his troops, and at the same time, ordered a considerable donative in
money, to be distributed among them.

These advantages were more than counterbalanced, by an unsuccessful attempt, made by the state of Massachusetts, on a British post at Penobscot. Col. Macleane by the direction of Sir Henry Clinton, landed with a detachment of 650 men from Halifax, on the banks of Penobscot river, in the eastern confines of New-England, and proceeded soon after to construct a fort in a well chosen situation. This occasioned an alarm at Boston. To [110] counteract the establishment of the post, vigorous measures were resolved upon. That armed vessels, transports and sailors, might be secured for an expedition, which was immediately projected for this purpose, an embargo for 40 days was laid by the state of Massachusetts, on all their shipping. A considerable armament consisting of 18 armed vessels besides transports, was fitted out with extraordinary expedition, and put under the command of Com. Saltonstal. The largest vessel in this fleet, was the Warren of 32 guns, 18 and 12 pounders. The others varied from 24 to 12 guns. A body of land forces commanded by Gen. Lovel, embarked on this expedition. On the 25th of July, the American fleet consisting of 37 sail appeared off Penobscot. Col. Macleane had four days before gained information, of what was intended against him. This induced him to redouble his exertions in strengthening his fort, which was in an unfinished state. Two of the bastions were untouched. The remaining two were in no part above 4 or 5 feet high. The ditch was only about 3 feet deep. There was no platform laid, nor any artillery mounted. The American general on his landing, summoned the colonel to surrender, which being refused, he proceeded to erect a battery at the distance of 750 yards. A cannonading commenced, and was kept up for about a fortnight, but without any considerable effect. While the besiegers were making preparation for an assault, which they had in immediate contemplation, Sir George Collyer appeared full in view, with a squadron for the relief of the garrison. He had sailed from Sandy-Hook, on hearing of the intended attack on Col. Macleane's party, and in about 11 days arrived in the river Penobscot. His marine force consisted of the Raisonable of 64 guns and five frigates. The Americans at first made a shew of resistance, but they intended no more than to give the transports time to move up the river, that the troops might have an opportunity of landing, and making their escape. The superior force and weight of metal of the Raisonable was irresistible, and the escape of the Americans was impracticable. A general flight on the one side, and a general [111] chase on the other took place. Sir George destroyed and took 17 or 18 armed vessels. The American soldiers and sailors had to return a great part of their way by land, and to explore their route through thick woods.

1779

While the war languished as to great objects in the country where it originated, it was raging on a new element, and involving distant countries in its wide spreading flame. Hostilities between the fleets of France and Great-Britain, were carrying on in both the Indies and in the European seas, as well as on the coast of America. His most Catholic Majesty was also, about this time, induced to take a decided part with France against Great-Britain.

To the surprise of many, the Marquis D'Almodovar the Spanish ambassador delivered a manifesto to lord Viscount Weymouth, amounting to a declaration of war against Great-Britain. This event had often been predicted by the minority in the British parliament, but disbelieved by the ministry. The latter reasoned "that Spain could have no interest in joining their adversaries. That she had colonies of her own, and could not set so bad an example to them, as to give any countenance to the Americans. It was also said that Spain was naturally attached to Great-Britain, and unable to enter into war". They were so far imposed upon by their eagerness to effect the conquest of the United-States, as to believe that to be true which they wished to be so. The event proved that the politics of sovereign powers, are not reducible to fixed principles. Sometimes one interest clashes with another, and it is not always the case that the strongest preponderates. Whether the influence of the French counsels, or the prospect of recovering Gibralter, Jamaica and the two Floridas, or the pressure of recent injuries determined the court of Spain to adopt this measure it is impossible with certainty to decide, but circumstances make it probable, that the hope of regaining Gibraltar and Jamaica, was the principal inducement.

JUN. 16

The situation of Great Britain, was at this time truly distressing. She was weakened and distracted in a domestic contest, in which victory produced no advantages, [112] but defeat all its natural effects. In the midst of this wasting contest, in which her ability to reduce her revolted colonies, though without foreign aid was doubtful, she was suddenly involved in a new and much more dangerous war with one of the greatest powers in Europe. At this very time while she was engaged in this double warfare, against old friends and old enemies, his most Catholic Majesty added his force to that of her numerous foes.

In this situation a direliction of the American war was recommended by some leading characters in the nation, but every proposition of that kind was over-ruled, and assurances from both houses of Parliament, were given to his Majesty "to support him in carrying on the war against all his enemies".

From these events which only affected the United-States as far as they increased the embarrassments of Great Britain, I return to relate the transactions which took place within their own limits. In the year 1779, though the war was carried on for little more than distress or depredation in the northern states, the re-establishment of British government was seriously attempted in Carolina and Georgia. After the reduction of Savannah, a great part of the state of Georgia was restored to the King's peace. The royal army in that quarter was strengthened by a numerous re-inforcement from East Florida, and the whole was put under the command of Major Gen. Prevost. The force then in Georgia gave a serious alarm to the adjacent states. There were at that time but few continental troops in Georgia, or South Carolina, and scarce any in North-Carolina, as during the late tranquillity in the southern states, they had been detached to serve in the main army commanded by Gen. Washington. A body of militia was raised and sent forward by North Carolina to aid her neighbours. These joined the continental troops, but not till they had retreated out of Georgia, and taken post in South Carolina. Towards the close of the year 1778 Gen. Lincoln, at the request of the delegates of South Carolina, was appointed by Congress, to take the command of their southern army.

1779   [113] This consisted only of a few hundred continentals. To supply the deficiency of regular soldiers, a considerable body of militia was ordered to join him, but they added much more to his numbers than to his effective force.

They had not yet learned the implicit obedience necessary for military operations. Accustomed to activity on their farms, they could not bear the languor of an encampment. Having grown up in habits of freedom and independence, they reluctantly submitted to martial discipline. The royal army at Savannah being reinforced by the junction of the troops from St. Augustine, was in condition to extend their posts. Their first object was to take possession of Port-Royal, in South-Carolina. Major Gardiner with two hundred men being detached with this view, landed on the island, but Gen. Moultrie at the head of an equal number of Americans, in which there were only nine regular soldiers, attacked and drove him off it. This advantage was principally gained by two field pieces, which were well served by a party of Charleston militia artillery. The British lost almost all their officers. The Americans had eight men killed and 22 wounded. Among the former, was Lieut. Benjamin Wilkins an artillery officer of great merit, and a citizen of distinguished virtue, whose early fall deprived a numerous family of their chief support. He was the first officer of South-Carolina who lost his life in supporting its independence. This repulse restrained the British from attempting any immediate enterprise to the northward of Savannah, but they fixed posts at Ebenezer, and Augusta, and extended themselves over a great part of Georgia. They also endeavored to stengthen themselves by reinforcements from the tories, in the western settlements of Georgia and Carolina.

Emissaries were sent among the inhabitants of that description, to encourage them to a general insurrection. They were assured that if they embodied and added their force to that of the King's army in Georgia, they would have such a decided superiority as would make a speedy return to their homes practicable, on their own terms. Several hundreds of them accordingly rendezvoused, [114] and set off to join the royal forces at Augusta. Among those who called themselves loyalists, there were many of the most infamous characters. Their general complexion was that of a plundering banditti, more solicitous for booty, than for the honor and interest of their royal master. At every period before the war, the western wilderness of these States which extended to the Mississippi, afforded an asylum for the idle or disorderly, who disrelished the restraints of civil society. While the war raged, the demands of militia duty and of taxes contributed much to the peopling of those remote settlements,

1779

by holding out prospects of exemption from the control of government. Among these people the royal emissaries had successfully planted the standard of loyalty, and of that class was a great proportion of those, who in the upper country of the Carolinas and Georgia, called themselves the King's friends. They had no sooner embodied and begun their march to join the royal army at Augusta, than they commenced such a scene of plundering of the defenceless settlements through which they passed, as induced the orderly inhabitants to turn out to oppose them. Col. Pickens, with about 300 men of the latter character, immediately pursued and came up with them, near Kettle-creek. An action took place, which lasted three quarters of an hour. The tories were totally routed. About forty of them were killed, and in that number was their leader Col. Boyd, who had been secretly employed by British authority to collect and head them. By this action the British were disconcerted. The tories were dispersed. Some ran quite off. Others went to their homes, and cast themselves on the mercy of their country. These were tried by the laws of South Carolina for offending against an act called the sedition act, which had been passed since the revolution for the security of the new government. Seventy of them were condemned to die, but the sentence was only executed on five of their ringleaders.

As the British extended their posts on the Georgia side of Savannah river, Gen. Lincoln fixed encampments at Black-Swamp, and nearly opposite to Augusta on the Carolina [115] side. From these posts he

1779

formed a plan of crossing into Georgia, with the view of limiting the British to the low country, near the ocean. In the execution of this design, Gen. Ash with 1500 North-Carolina militia and a few regular troops, after crossing the river Savannah, took a position on Briar-

MAY 3

creek; but in a few days he was surprised by Lieut. Col. Prevost, who having made a circuitous march of about 50 miles, came unexpectedly on his rear with about 900 men. The militia were thrown into confusion, and fled at the first fire. One hundred and fifty of the Americans were killed, and 162 were taken. Few had any chance of escaping but by crossing the Savannah, in attempting which many were drowned. Of those who got off safe, a great part returned home. The number that rejoined the American camp did not exceed 450 men. The few continentals under Col. Elbert made a brave resistence, but the survivors of them, with their gallant leader, were at last compelled to surrender. This event deprived Gen. Lincoln of one fourth of his numbers, and opened a communication between the British, the Indians, and the tories of North and South-Carolina.

Unexperienced in the art of war, the Americans were subject to those reverses of fortune, which usually attend young soldiers. Unacquainted with military stratagems, deficient in discipline, and not thoroughly broken to habits of implicit obedience, they were often surprised, and had to learn by repeated misfortunes the necessity of subordination, and the advantages of watchfulness and discipline. Their numbers in the field, to those who are acquainted with European wars, must appear inconsiderable, but such is the difference of the state of society and of the population in the old and new world, that in America, a few hundreds decided objects of equal magnitude with those, which in Europe would have called into the field as many thousands. The prize contended for was nothing less than the Sovereignty of three millions of people, and of five hundred millions of acres of land, and yet from the remote situation of the invading powers, and the thin population of the invaded States, especially [116] in the southern extreme of the union, this momentous   1779 question was materially affected by the consequences of battles, in which only a few hundreds engaged.

The series of disasters which had followed the American arms since the landing of the British near Savannah, occasioned well founded apprehension for the safety of the adjacent States. The militia of South-Carolina was therefore put on a better footing, and a regiment of cavalry was raised. John Rutledge a Carolinian of the most distinguished abilities, was called to the chair of government by an almost unanimous vote, and in imitation of the ancient republic of Rome invested, in conjunction with his council, with dictatorial powers. By virtue of his authority, he convened a large body of the militia near the centre of the State, that they might be in constant readiness to march whithersoever public service required. The original plan of penetrating into Georgia was resumed. Part of the American force was stationed on the north side of the Savannah at Purrysburgh and Black-swamp, while Gen. Lincoln and the main army crossed into Georgia near Augusta. General Prevost availed himself of the critical moment, when the American army had ascended 150 miles towards the source of the Savannah, and crossed into Carolina over the same river near to its mouth, with about 2400 men. A considerable body of Indians, whose friendship the British had previously secured, were associated with the British on this expedition. The superior British force which crossed Savannah river, soon compelled General Moultrie, who was charged with the defence of South-Carolina, to retire. Lincoln on receiving information of these movements, detached 300 of his light troops to reinforce Moultrie, but proceeded with the main army towards the capital of Georgia. He was induced to pursue his original intention, from an idea that Gen. Prevost meant nothing more than to divert him by a feint on Carolina, and because his marching down on the south side of the river Savannah, would occasion very little additional delay in repairing to its defense. When Lincoln [117] found that Prevost was seriously pushing for Charleston, he re-crossed the Savannah and pursued him. The British proceeded in their march by the main road near the sea coast, with but little opposition, and in the mean time the Americans retreated before them towards Charleston. Gen. Moultrie, who ably conducted this retreat, had no cavalry to check the advancing foe. Instead of his receiving reinforcements from the inhabitants, as he marched through the country, he was abandoned by many of the militia who went to their homes. Their families and property lay directly in the route of the invading army. The abcence of the main army under Lincoln, the retreat of Moultrie, the plunderings and devastations of the invaders, and above all the dread of the Indian savages which accompanied the royal army, diffused a general panic among the inhabitants. The terror of each individual became a source of terror to another. From the influence of these causes, many were induced to apply for British protection. New converts to the royal standard endeavoured to ingratiate themselves with their protectors, by encouraging them to attempt the reduction of Charleston. Being in their power, they were more anxious to frame intelligence on the idea of what was agreeable, than of what was true. They represented the inhabitants as being generally tired of the war, and wishing for peace at all events. They also stated that Charleston was incapable of much resistance. These circumstances combined with the facility with which the British marched through the country, induced Gen. Prevost to extend his plan and push for Charleston. Had he designed it at first, and continued his march with the same rapidity with which it was begun, the town would probably have been carried by a coup-de-main, but he halted two or three days when advanced near half the distance. In that interval every preparation was made by the South-Carolinians, for the defence of their capital. All the houses in its suburbs were burnt. Lines and abbatis were, in a few days, carried across the peninsula between Ashley and Cooper rivers, and cannon were mounted at proper intervals on its whole extent. Though this visit [118] of the British, and especially an attack on the land side, was unexpected, yet in a few days great preparations were made, and a force of 3300 men assembled in Charleston for its defence.

1779

The main body and baggage of the British army, being left on the south side of Ashley river, an advanced detachment of 900 men, crossed the ferry and appeared before the town. In the mean time Lincoln was marching on as fast as possible, for the relief of Charleston, but as his arrival was doubtful and the crisis hazardous, to gain time was a matter of consequence. A whole day was therefore spent in the exchange of flags. Commissioners from the garrison were instructed "to propose a neutrality during the war between Great Britain and America, and that the question whether the state shall belong to Great Britain, or remain one of the United States, be determined by the treaty of peace between these powers". The British commanders refused this advantageous offer, alledging that they did not come in a legislative capacity, and insisted that as the inhabitants and others were in arms, they should surrender prisoners of war. This being refused the garrison prepared for an immediate assault, but this was not attempted. About this time Major Benjamin Huger commanding a party without the lines, was through mistake killed by his countrymen. This was a loss indeed. The liberality, generosity and public spirit, which distinguished him as a citizen, added to great political and military talents, rendered his untimely death the subject of universal regret. By his fall the country was deprived of one of its firmest and most useful friends, and the army lost one of its brightest ornaments. Prevost knowing by an intercepted letter,

MAY 11

that Lincoln was coming on in his rear, retreated from Charleston, and filed off with his whole force from the main to the islands near the sea, that he might avoid being between two fires. Both armies encamped in the vicinity of Charleston, watching each others motions till the 20th of June, when an attack was made with about 1200 Americans on six or 700 of the British, advantageously posted at Stono ferry. The latter had redoubts [119] with a line of communication, and field pieces in the intervals, and the whole was secured with an abbatis. By a preconcerted plan, a feint was to have been made from James Island, with a body of Charleston militia, at the moment when Gen. Lincoln began the attack from the main, but from mismanagement, they did not reach their place of destination till the action was over. The attack was continued for an hour and twenty minutes, and the assailants had the advantage, but the appearance of a reinforcement, to prevent which the feint from James Island was intended, made their retreat necessary. The loss of the Americans in killed and wounded was about 150. Among the former was Col. Roberts, an artillery officer of distinguished abilities. Having been bred to arms in his native country England, he had been particularly serviceable in diffusing military knowledge among the less informed American officers. In the short interval between his being wounded and his dying, he was visited on the field of battle by his son Capt. Roberts, of his own regiment. The expiring father presented his sword to his son, with an exhortation to behave worthy of it, and to use it in defence of liberty and his country. After a short conversation he desired him to return to his proper station, adding for reason "that there he might be useful, but to him he could be of no service."

Immediately after this attack, the American militia impatient of absence from their homes returned to their plantations, and about the same time the British left the islands adjacent to Charleston, retreating from one to another, till they arrived at Port-royal and Savannah. A considerable garrison was left at the former place under Col. Maitland, but the main body went to Savannah.

This incursion into South-Carolina contributed very little to the advancement of the royal cause, but added much to the wealth of the officers, soldiers and followers of the British army, and still more to the distresses of the inhabitants. The forces under the command of Gen. Prevost spread themselves over a considerable part of the richest settlements of the state, and where there are the fewest white inhabitants in proportion to the number of [120] slaves. There was much to attract, and but little to resist the invaders. Small parties visited almost every house, and unopposed took whatever they chose. They not only rifled the inhabitants of household furniture, but of wearing apparel, money, rings and other personal ornaments. Every place, in their line of march, experienced the effects of their rapacity.

1779

Soon after the affair at Stono, the continental forces under the command of Gen. Lincoln retired to Sheldon, a healthy situation in the vicinity of Beaufort. Both armies remained in their respective encampments, till the arrival of a French fleet on the coast, roused the whole country to immediate activity.

Count D'Estaing having repaired and victualled his fleet at Boston, sailed for the West-Indies, and on the same day Commodore Hotham with five men of war, a bomb vessel and some frigates, set out from New-York to convoy a number of transports with Gen. Grant, and 5000 men to the same theatre of naval operations.

NOV. 3, 1778

The British took St. Lucia, and Count D'Estaing took St. Vincents and Grenada. Soon after the reduction of the latter, the Count retired to Cape François. Having received instructions from the King his master to act in concert with the forces of the United States, and being strongly solicited by Gen. Lincoln, President Lownds, Gov. Rutledge, and Mr. Plombard Consul of France in Charleston, he sailed for the American continent with expectation of rendering essential service, in operating against the common enemy. He arrived on the coast of Georgia, with a fleet consisting of twenty sail of the line, two of fifty guns and eleven frigates. His appearance was so unexpected that the Experiment man of war, of 50 guns commanded by Sir James Wallace, and three frigates fell into his hands.

DEC. 30, 1778

JULY 1779

SEPT. 1

As soon as his arrival on the coast was known, Gen. Lincoln with the army under his command, marched for the vicinity of Savannah, and orders were given for the militia of Georgia and South-Carolina to rendezvous near the same place. The British were equally diligent in preparing for their defence. Great numbers were employed [121] both by day and night, in strengthening and extending their lines.

The American militia, flushed with the hope of speedily expelling the British from their southern possessions, turned out with an alacrity which far surpassed their exertions in the preceding campaign. D'Estaing before the arrival of Lincoln demanded the surrender of the town to the arms of France. Prevost in his answer declined surrendering on a general summons, and requested that specific terms should be proposed, to which he would give an answer. The Count replied that it was the part of the besieged to propose terms. Prevost then asked for a suspension of hostilities, for 24 hours, for preparing proper terms. This was inconsiderately granted. Before the 24 hours elapsed, Lieut. Col. Maitland with several hundred men who had been stationed at Beaufort, made their way good through many obstacles, and joined the royal army in Savannah. The garrison, encouraged by the arrival of so respectable a force, determined on resistance. The French and Americans, who formed a junction the evening after, were therefore reduced to the necessity of storming or besieging the garrison. The resolution of proceeding by siege being adopted, several days were consumed in preparing for it, and in the mean time the works of the garrison were hourly strengthened by the labour of several hundred negroes, directed by that able engineer Major Moncrief. The besiegers opened with nine mortars, thirty seven pieces of cannon from the land side, and fifteen from the water. Soon after the commencement of the cannonade, Prevost solicited for leave to send the women and children out of town, but this was refused. The combined army suspected that a desire of secreting the plunder, lately taken from the South-Carolinians, was covered under the veil of humanity. It was also presumed that a refusal would expedite a surrender. On a report from the engineers that a considerable time would be necessary to reduce the garrison by regular approaches, it was determined to make an assault. This measure was forced on Count D'Estaing by his marine officers, who had remonstrated against his continuing to risk so valuable [122] a fleet on a dangerous coast, in the hurricane season, and at so great a distance from the shore, that it might be surprised by a British fleet, completely repaired and fully manned. In a few days the lines of the besiegers might have been carried into the works of the besieged, but under these critical circumstances, no farther delay could be admitted. To

OCT. 4

1779

assault or raise the siege was the alternative. Prudence would have dictated the latter, but a sense of honor determined the besiegers to adopt the former. Two feints were made with the country militia, and a real attack on Spring-hill battery early in the morning, with OCT. 9 3500 French troops, 600 continentals, and 350 of the inhabitants of Charleston. These boldly marched up to the lines, under the command of D'Estaing and Lincoln, but a heavy and well directed fire from the batteries, and a cross fire from the gallies, threw the front of their columns into confusion. Two standards were nevertheless planted on the British redoubts. A retreat of the assailants was ordered, after they had stood the enemies fire for 55 minutes. Count D'Estaing and Count Pulaski were both wounded. The former slightly, but the latter mortally. Six hundred and thirty seven of the French, and upwards of 200 of the continentals and militia were killed or wounded. Gen. Prevost, Lieut. Col. Maitland, and Major Moncrief deservedly acquired great reputation by this successful defence. The force of the garrison was between 2 and 3000, of which about 150 were militia. The damage sustained by the besieged was trifling, as they fired from behind works, and few of the assailants fired at all. Immediately after this unsucessful assault, the militia, almost universally, went to their homes. Count D'Estaing reimbarked his troops and artillery, and left the continent.

While the siege of Savannah was pending, a remarkable enterprise was effected by Col. John White of the Georgia line. Capt. French had taken post with about 100 men near the river Ogechee, some time before the siege began. There were also at the same place forty sailors on board of five British vessels, four of which [123] were armed. All these men, together with the vessels and 130 stand of 1779 arms, were surrendered to Col. White, Capt. Elholm and four others, OCT. 1 one of which was the Colonel's servant. On the preceding night this small party kindled a number of fires in different places, and adopted the parade of a large encampment. By these and a variety of deceptive stratagems, Capt. French was fully impressed with an opinion, that nothing but an instant surrender, in conformity to a peremptory summons, could save his men from being cut to pieces by a superior force. He therefore gave up, without making any resistance.

This visit of the fleet of his most Christian Majesty to the coast of

America, though unsuccessful as to its main object, was not without utility to the United States. It disconcerted the measures already digested by the British commanders, and caused a considerable waste of time, before they could determine on a new plan of operations. It also occasioned the evacuation of Rhode-Island. But this was of no advantage to the United States. For of all the blunders committed by the British in the course of the American war, none was greater than their stationing near 6000 men, for two years and eight months, on that Island, where they were lost to every purpose of co-operation, and where they could render very little more service to the royal cause, than could have been obtained by a couple of frigates cruising in the vicinity.

The siege being raised, the continental troops retreated over the river Savannah. The vicissitudes of an autumnal atmosphere made a severe impression on the irritable fibres of men, exhausted with fatigue and dejected by defeat. In proportion to the towering hopes, with which the expedition was undertaken, was the depression of spirits subsequent to its failure. The Georgia exiles, who had assembled from all quarters to repossess themselves of their estates, were a second time obliged to flee from their country and possessions. The most gloomy apprehensions, respecting the Southern States, took possession of the minds of the people.

1779

[124] Thus ended the southern campaign of 1779, without any thing decisive on either side. After one year, in which the British had over-run the State of Georgia for 150 miles from the sea coast, and had penetrated as far as the lines of Charleston, they were reduced to their original limits in Savannah. All their schemes of cooperation with the tories had failed, and the spirits of that class of the inhabitants, by successive disappointments, were thoroughly broken.

The campaign of 1779 is remarkable for the feeble exertions of the Americans. Accidental causes, which had previously excited their activity, had in a great measure ceased to have influence. An enthusiasm for liberty made them comparatively disregard property, and brave all danger in the first years of the war. The successes of their arms near the beginning of 1777, and the hopes of capturing Burgoyne's army in the close of it, together with the brisk circulation of a large quantity of paper money in good credit, made that year both active and decisive. The flattering prospects inspired by the alliance with France in 1778 banished all fears of the success of the revolution, but the failure of every scheme of co-operation produced a despondency of mind unfavourable to great exertions. Instead of driving the British out of the country, as the Americans vainly presumed, the campaign of 1778 and 1779 terminated without any direct advantage from the French fleet sent to their aid. Expecting too much from their allies, and then failing in these expectations, they were less prepared to prosecute the war from their own resources, than they would have been had D'Estaing not touched on their coast. Their army was reduced in its numbers, and badly cloathed: In the first years of the war the mercantile character was lost in the military spirit of the times, but in the progress of it the inhabitants, cooling in their enthusiasm, gradually returned to their former habits of lucrative business. This made distinction between the army and the citizens, and was unfriendly to military exertions. While several foreign events tended to the embarrassment of Great-Britain, and indirectly to the establishment of independence, a variety [125] of internal causes relaxed the exertions of the Americans, and for a time made it doubtful, whether they would ultimately be independent citizens or conquered subjects. Among these, the daily depreciation of their bills of credit held a distinguished pre-eminence. This so materially affected every department as to merit a particular discussion. The subject, to prevent an interruption of the thread of the narrative, is treated of in a separate appendix.

1779

Of Continental Paper Currency.

IN THE MODERN MODE OF MAKING WAR, money is not less essential, than valour in the field, or wisdom in the cabinet. The deepest purse decides the fate of contending nations, as often as the longest sword. It early occurred to the founders of the American empire, that the established revenues of Great Britain, must eventually overbalance the sudden and impetuous sallies of men contending for freedom, on the spur of the occasion, and without the permanent means of defence; but how to remedy the evil, puzzled their wisest politicians. Gold and silver, as far as was known, had not a physical existence in the country, in any quantity equal to the demands of war, nor could they be procured from abroad, as the channels of commerce had been previously shut, by the voluntary association of Congress to suspend foreign trade. America having never been much taxed in any direct way, and being without established governments, and especially as she was contending against what was lately lawful authority, could not immediately proceed to taxation. Besides as the contest was on the subject of taxation, the laying on of taxes adequate to the exigencies of war, even though it had been practicable, would have been impolitic. The only plausible expedient in their power to adopt, was the emission of bills of credit representing specie, under a public engagement to be ultimately sunk by equal taxes, or exchanged for gold or silver. This practice had been familiar from the first settlement of the colonies, and under proper restrictions [126] had been found highly advantageous. Their resolution to raise an army in June 1775, was therefore followed by another to emit bills of credit, to the amount of two millions of dollars. To that sum on the 25th of the next month, it was resolved to add another million. For their redemption they pledged the confederated colonies, and directed each colony to find ways and means, to sink its proportion and quota, in four annual payments, the first to be made on or before the last of Nov. 1779. That time was fixed upon from an expectation, that previous to its arrival, the contest would be brought to a conclusion. On the 29th of November, 1775, an estimate having been made by Congress of the public expences already incurred, or likely to be incurred in carrying on their defence till the 10th of June, 1776, it was resolved to emit a farther sum of three millions of dollars, to be redeemed as the former by four annual payments, the first to be made on or before the last day of Novem. 1783. It was at the same time determined, that the quotas of bills to be redeemed by each colony, should be in a relative proportion to their respective numbers of inhabitants. This estimate was calculated to defray expences to the 10th of June, 1776, on the idea that an accommodation would take place before that time. Hitherto all arrangements, both for men and money were temporary, and founded on the supposed probability of a reconciliation. Early in 1776, Congress obtained information, that Great Britain had contracted for 16,000 foreign mercenaries, to be sent over for the purpose of subduing America. This enforced the necessity of extending their plan of defence, beyond the 10th of the next June. They therefore on the 17th of February 1776, ordered four millions of

1779

dollars to be emitted, and on the 9th of May and the 22d of July following, emitted ten millions more on the same security. Such was the animation of the times, that these several emissions amounting in the aggregate to 20 millions of dollars, circulated for several months without any depreciation, and commanded the resources of the country for public service, equally with the same sum of gold or [127] silver. The United States derived for a considerable time, as much benefit from this paper creation of their own, though without any established funds for its support or redemption, as would have resulted from a free gift of as many Mexican dollars. While the ministry of England were puzzling themselves for new taxes, and funds on which to raise their supplies, Congress raised theirs by resolutions, directing paper of no intrinsic value to be struck off, in form of promissory notes. But there was a point both in time and quantity, beyond which this congressional alchymy ceased to operate. That time was about 18 months from the date of their first emission, and that quantity about 20 millions of dollars.

1779

Independence being declared in the second year of the war, and the object for which arms were at first assumed being changed, it was obvious that more money must be procured, and equally so that if bills of credit were multiplied beyond a reasonable sum for circulation, they must necessarily depreciate. It was therefore on the 3d of October 1776 resolved to borrow five millions of dollars, and in the month following a lottery was set on foot for obtaining a farther sum on loan. The expences of the war were so great, that the money arising from both, though considerable, was far short of a sufficiency. The rulers of America thought it still premature to urge taxation. They therefore reiterated the expedient of farther emissions. The ease with which the means of procuring supplies were furnished by striking off bills of credit, and the readiness of the people to receive them, prompted Congress to multiply them beyond the limits of prudence. A diminution of their value was the unavoidable consequence. This at first was scarcely perceivable, but it daily increased. The zeal of the people nevertheless so far overbalanced the nice mercantile calculations of interest, that the campaigns of 1776 and 1777 were not affected by the depreciation of the paper currency. Congress foresaw that this could not long be the case. It was therefore on the 22d of November 1777 recommended to the several States, to raise by taxes the [128] sum of five millions of dollars, for the service of the year 1778.

1779

Previously to this it had been resolved to borrow larger sums, and for the encouragement of lenders, it was agreed to pay the interest which should accrue thereon by bills of exchange, payable in France, out of monies borrowed there for the use of the United States. This tax unfortunately failed in several of the States. From the impossibility of procuring a sufficiency of money either from loans or taxes, the old expedient of farther emissions was reiterated; but the value decreased as the quantity increased. Congress anxious to put a stop to the increase of their bills of credit, and to provide a fund for reducing what were issued, called upon the States on the 1st of January 1779, to pay into the continental treasury their respective quotas of fifteen millions of dollars for the service of that year, and of six millions annually from and after the year 1779, as a fund for reducing their early emissions and loans. Such had been the mistaken ideas, which originally prevailed of the duration of the contest, that though the war was raging, and the demands for money unabated, yet the period was arrived which had been originally fixed upon for the redemption of the first emissions of Congress.

In addition to these 15 millions called for on the 1st of January 1779, the States were on the 21st of May following called upon to furnish, for public service within the current year, their respective quotas of 45 millions of dollars. Congress wished to arrest the growing depreciation, and therefore called for taxes in large sums, proportioned to the demands of the public, and also to the diminished value of their bills. These requisitions, though nominally large, were by no means sufficient. From the fluctuating state of the money, it was impossible to make any certain calculations, for it was not two days of the same value. A sum which when demanded, would have purchased a sufficiency of the commodities wanted for the public service, was very inadequate, when the collection was made, and the money lodged in the treasury. The depreciation began at different periods in different [129] States; but in general about the middle of the year 1777, and progressively increased for three or four years. Towards the last of 1777, the depreciation was about two or three for one; in 1778 it advanced from two or three for one to five or six for one; in 1779, from five or six for one to 27 or 28 for one; in 1780 from 27 or 28 for one to 50 or 60 for one, in the first four or five months. Its circulation was afterwards partial, but where it passed it soon depreciated to 150 for one. In some few parts it continued in circulation for the first four or five months of 1781, but in this latter period many would not take it at any rate, and they who did, received it at a depreciation of several hundreds for one.

As there was a general clamor on account of the floods of money, which at successive periods had deluged the States, it was resolved in October 1779 that no farther sum should be issued on any account whatever than what, when added to the present sum in circulation, would in the whole be equal to 200 millions of dollars. It was at the same time resolved, that Congress should emit only such a part of the sum wanting to make up 200 millions, as should be absolutely necessary for the public exigencies, before adequate supplies could be otherwise obtained, relying for such supplies on the exertions of the several States. This was forcibly represented in a circular letter from Congress to their constituents, and the States were earnestly intreated to prevent that deluge of evils which would flow from their neglecting to furnish adequate supplies for the wants of the confederacy. The same circular letter stated the practicability of redeeming all the bills of Congress at par with gold and silver, and rejected with indignation the supposition that the States would ever tarnish their credit by violating public faith. These strong declarations in favour of the paper currency deceived many to repose confidence in it to their ruin. Subsequent events compelled Congress to adopt the very measure in 1780, which in the preceding year they had sincerely reprobated.

SEPT. 13, 1779

From the non-compliance of the States, Congress was obliged in a short time after the date of their circular letter to issue such a farther quantity, as when added to [130] previous emissions made the sum of 200 millions of dollars. Besides this immense sum, the paper emissions of the different States amounted to many millions; which mixed with the continental money, and added to its depreciation. What was of little value before now became of less. The whole was soon expended, and yet from its increased depreciation the immediate wants of the army were not supplied. The source which for five years had enabled Congress to keep an army in the field being exhausted, Gen. Washington was reduced for some time to the alternative of disbanding his troops, or of supplying them by a military force. He preferred the latter, and the inhabitants of New-York and New-Jersey, though they felt the injury, saw the necessity, and patiently submitted.

The States were next called upon to furnish in lieu of money determinate quantities of beef, pork, flour and other articles, for the use of the army. This was called a requisition for specific supplies or a tax in kind, and was found on experiment to be so difficult of execution, so inconvenient, partial and expensive, that it was speedily abandoned. About this time, Congress resolved upon another expedient. This was to issue a new species of paper money, under the guarantee of the several States. The old money was to be called in by taxes, and as soon as brought in to be burnt, and in lieu thereof, one dollar of the new was to be emitted for every twenty of the old, so that when the whole 200 millions were drawn in and cancelled, only ten millions of the new should be issued in their place, four tenths of which were to be subject to the order of Congress, and the remaining six tenths to the order of the several States. These new bills were to be redeemable in specie within six years, and to bear an interest at the rate of five per cent to be paid also in specie, at the redemption of the bills, or at the election of the owner annually in bills of exchange on the American commissioners in Europe, at four shillings and six pence for each dollar.

From the execution of these resolutions it was expected, that the old money would be cancelled—that the [131] currency would be reduced to a fixed standard—that the States would be supplied with 1779 the means of purchasing the specific supplies required of them, and that Congress would be furnished with efficient money, to provide for the exigencies of the war. That these good effects would have followed, even though the resolutions of Congress had been carried into execution, is very questionable, but from the partial compliances of the States the experiment was never fairly made, and the new paper answered very little purpose. It was hoped by varying the ground of credit, that Congress would gain a repetition of the advantages which resulted from their first paper expedient, but these hopes were of short duration. By this time much of the popular enthusiasm had spent itself, and confidence in public engagements was nearly expired. The event proved, that credit is of too delicate a nature to be sported with, and can only be maintained by honesty and punctuality. The several expedients proposed by Congress for raising supplies having failed, a crisis followed very interesting to the success of the revolution. The particulars of this shall be related among the public events of the year 1781, in which it took place. Some observations on that primary instrument of American Independence, the old continental bills of credit, shall for the present close this subject.

It would have been impossible to have carried on the war, without something in the form of money. There was spirit enough in America to bring to the field of battle as many of her sons, as would have outnumbered the armies of Britain, and to have risqued their fate on a general engagement; but this was the very thing they ought to avoid. Their principal hope lay in evacuating, retreating, and protracting to its utmost length a war of posts. The continued exertions, necessary for this species of defence, could not be expected from the impetuous sallies of militia. A regular permanent army became necessary. Though the enthusiasm of the times might have dispensed with present pay, yet without at least as much money, as would support them in the field, the most patriotic army must have dispersed.

1779   [132] The impossibility of the Americans procuring gold and silver even for that purpose, doubtless weighed with the British as an encouragement, to bring the controversy to the decision of the sword. What they knew could not be done by ordinary means, was accomplished by those which were extraordinary. Paper of no intrinsic value was made to answer all the purposes of gold and silver, and to support the expences of five campaigns. This was in some degree owing to a previous confidence, which had been begotten by honesty and fidelity, in discharging the engagements of government. From New-York to Georgia there never had been in matters relating to money, an instance of a breach of public faith. In the scarcity of gold and silver, many emergencies had imposed a necessity of emitting bills of credit. These had been uniformly and honestly redeemed.

The bills of Congress being thrown into circulation, on this favourable foundation of public confidence, were readily received. The enthusiasm of the people contributed to the same effect. That the endangered liberties of America ought to be defended, and that the credit of their paper was essentially necessary to a proper defence, were opinions engraven on the hearts of a great majority of the citizens. It was therefore a point of honor and considered as a part of duty, to take the bills freely at their full value. Private gain was then so little regarded, that the whig citizens were willing to run all the hazards incidental to bills of credit, rather than injure the cause of their country by under valuing its money. Every thing human has its limits. While the credit of the money was well supported by public confidence and patriotism, its value diminished from the increase of its quantity. Repeated emissions begat that natural depreciation, which results from an excess of quantity. This was helped on by various causes, which affected the *credit* of the money. The enemy very ingeniously counterfeited their bills, and industriously circulated their forgeries through the United States. Congress allowed to their public agents a commission on the amount of their purchases. Instead of exerting themselves to purchase at a low price, they had therefore [133] an interest in giving a high price for every thing. So strong was   1779 the force of prejudice, that the British mode of supplying armies by contract, could not for a long time obtain the approbation of Congress. While these causes operated, confidence in the public was abating, and at the same time, that fervor of patriotism which disregarded interest was daily declining. To prevent or retard the depreciation of their paper money, Congress attempted to prop its credit by means which wrecked private property, and injured the morals of the people without answering the end proposed. They recommended to the States to pass laws for regulating the prices of labour, manufacture and all sorts of commodities, and for confiscating and selling the estates of tories, and for investing the money arising from the sales thereof in loan-office certificates. As many of those who were disaffected to the revolution absolutely refused to take the bills of Congress even in the first stage of the war, when the real and nominal value was the same, with the view of counteracting their machinations, Congress early recommended to the States to pass laws for making the paper money a legal tender, at their nominal value in the discharge of *bona fide* debts, though contracted to be paid in gold or silver. With the same views, they farther recommended that laws should be passed by each of the States, ordaining that

> whosoever should ask or receive more, in their bills of credit for gold or silver or any species of money whatsoever, than the nominal sum thereof in Spanish dollars, or more in the said bills for any commodities whatsoever, than the same could be purchased from the same person in gold and silver, or offer to sell any commodities for gold or silver, and refuse to sell the same for the said bills, shall be deemed an enemy to the liberties of the United States, and forfeit the property so sold or offered for sale.

The laws which were passed by the States, for regulating the prices of labor and commodities, were found on experiment to be visionary and impracticable. They only operated on the patriotic few, who were disposed to sacrifice every thing in the cause of their country, and who implicitly obeyed every mandate [134] of their rulers. Others disregarded them, and either refused to part with their commodities, or demanded and obtained their own prices.

1779

These laws in the first instance, made an artificial scarcity, and had they not been repealed would soon have made a real one, for men never exert themselves unless they have the fruit of their exertions secured to them, and at their own disposal.

The confiscation and sale of the property of tories, for the most part brought but very little into the public treasury. The sales were generally made for credit, and by the progressive depreciation, what was dear at the time of the purchase, was very cheap at the time of payment. The most extensive mischief resulted in the progress, and towards the close of the war from the operation of the laws, which made the paper bills a tender, in the discharge of debts contracted payable in gold or silver. When this measure was first adopted little or no injustice resulted from it, for at that time the paper bills were equal, or nearly equal to gold or silver, of the same nominal sum. In the progress of the war, when depreciation took place, the case was materially altered. Laws which were originally innocent became eventually the occasion of much injustice.

The aged who had retired from the scenes of active business, to enjoy the fruits of their industry, found their substance melting away to a mere pittance, insufficient for their support. The widow who lived comfortably on the bequests of a deceased husband, experienced a frustration of all his well meant tenderness. The laws of the country interposed, and compelled her to receive a shilling, where a pound was her due. The blooming virgin who had grown up with an unquestionable title to a liberal patrimony, was legally stripped of every thing but her personal charms and virtues. The hapless orphan, instead of receiving from the hands of an executor, a competency to set out in business, was obliged to give a final discharge on the payment of 6d. in the pound. In many instances, the earnings of a long life of care and diligence were, in the space of a few years, reduced to a trifling sum. A few persons escaped [135] these affecting calamities, by secretly transferring their bonds, or by flying from the presence or neighbourhood of their debtors. The evils which resulted from the legal tender of these paper bills, were foreign from the intentions of Congress, and of the State legislatures. It is but justice to add farther, that a great proportion of them flowed from ignorance. Till the year 1780, when the bills fell to forty for one, it was designed by most of the rulers of America, and believed by a great majority of the people, that the whole sum in circulation would be appreciated by a reduction of its quantity, so as finally to be equal to gold or silver. In every department of government the Americans erred from ignorance, but in none so much, as in that which related to money.

1779

Such were the evils which resulted from paper money. On the other hand, it was the occasion of good to many. It was at all times the poor man's friend. While it was current, all kinds of labor very readily found their reward. In the first years of the war, none were idle from want of employment, and none were employed, without having it in their power to obtain ready payment for their services. To that class of people, whose daily labor was their support, the depreciation was no disadvantage. Expending their money as fast as they received it, they always got its full value. The reverse was the case with the rich, or those who were disposed to hoarding. No agrarian law ever had a more extensive operation, than continental money. That for which the Gracchi lost their lives in Rome, was peaceably effected in the United States, by the legal tender of these depreciating bills. The poor became rich, and the rich became poor. Money lenders, and they whose circumstances enabled them to give credit, were essentially injured. All that the money lost in its value was so much taken from their capital, but the active and industrious indemnified themselves, by conforming the price of their services to the present state of the depreciation. The experience of this time inculcated on youth two salutary lessons, the impolicy of depending on paternal acquisitions, and the necessity of their own exertions. They who [136] were in debt, and possessed property of any kind, could easily make the latter extinguish the former. Every thing that was useful when brought to market readily found a purchaser. A hog or two would pay for a slave; a few cattle for a comfortable house; and a good horse for an improved plantation. A small part of the productions of a farm would discharge the long outstanding accounts, due from its owner. The dreams of the golden age were realised to the poor man and the debtor, but unfortunately what these gained, was just so much taken from others.

1779

The evils of depreciation did not terminate with the war. They extend to the present hour. That the helpless part of the community were legislatively deprived of their property, was among the lesser evils, which resulted from the legal tender of the depreciated bills of credit. The iniquity of the laws estranged the minds of many of the citizens from the habits and love of justice.

The nature of obligations was so far changed, that he was reckoned the honest man, who from principle delayed to pay his debts. The mounds which government had erected, to secure the observance of honesty in the commercial intercourse of man with man, were broken down. Truth, honor, and justice were swept away by the overflowing deluge of legal iniquity, nor have they yet assumed their ancient and accustomed seats. Time and industry have already, in a great degree, repaired the losses of property, which the citizens sustained during the war, but both have hitherto failed in effacing the taint which was then communicated to their principles, nor can its total ablution be expected till a new generation arises, unpractised in the iniquities of their fathers.

___

Of Indians, and Expeditions into the Indian Country.

WHEN THE ENGLISH COLONIES were first planted in North America, the country was inhabited by numerous tribes of Indians, who principally supported [137] themselves by the spontaneous productions of nature. The arts and arms of Europeans soon gave them an ascendency over such untutored savages. Had the latter understood their interest, and been guided by a spirit of union, they would soon have expelled the invaders, and in that case they might now be flourishing in the possession of their ancient territories and independence. By degrees the old inhabitants were circumscribed within narrower limits, and by some strange fatality, their numbers have been constantly lessening. The names of several nations who in the last century boasted of several thousands, are now known only to those who are fond of curious researches. Many are totally extinct,

1779

and others can shew no more than a few straggling individuals, the remnants of their fallen greatness. That so many tribes should, in so short a time, lose both their country and their national existence, is an event scarcely to be paralleled in the history of the world. Spiritous liquors, the small pox, and an abridgment of territory, to a people whose mode of life needed an extensive range, evils which chiefly resulted from the neighbourhood of Europeans, were among the principal causes of their destruction. The reflections which may be excited by reviewing the havoc made among the native proprietors of this new world, is in some degree alleviated by its counterpart. While one set of inhabitants was insensibly dwindling away, another improving in the arts of civil and social life was growing in numbers, and gradually filling up their places. As the emigrants from Europe, and their dependents extended their possessions on the sea coast, the Aborigines retired from it. By this gradual advance of the one and retiring of the other, the former always presented an extensive frontier, to the incursions of the latter. The European emigrants from an avidity for land, the possession of which is the ultimate object of human avarice, were prone to encroach on the territories of the Indians, while the Indians from obvious principles of human nature, beheld with concern the descendants of the ancient proprietors circumscribed in their territory by the descendants of those strangers, whom their fathers had permitted [138] to reside among them. From these causes and especially from the licentious conduct of disorderly individuals of both Indians and white people, there were frequent interruptions of the peace in their contiguous settlements. In the war between France and England which commenced in 1755, both parties paid assiduous attention to the Aborigines. The former succeeded in securing the greatest number of adherents, but the superior success of the latter in the progress, and at the termination of the war, turned the current of Indian affections and interest in their favor. When the dispute between Great Britain and her colonies began to grow serious, the friendship of the Indians became a matter of consequence to both parties. Stretching for fifteen hundred miles along the whole north-western frontier of the colonies, they were to them desirable friends and formidable enemies. As terror was one of the engines by which Great Britain intended to enforce the submission

1779

of the colonies, nothing could be more conducive to the excitement of this passion, than the co-operation of Indians. Policy, not cruelty, led to the adoption of this expedient: But it was of that over-refined species which counteracts itself. In the competition for the friendship of the Indians, the British had advantages far superior to any which were possessed by the colonists. The expulsion of the French from Canada, an event which had only taken place about 13 years before, was still fresh in the memory of many of the savages, and had inspired them with high ideas of the martial superiority of British troops. The first steps taken by the Congress to oppose Great Britain, put it out of their power to gratify the Indians. Such was the effect of the non-importation agreement of 1774. While Great Britain had access to the principal Indian tribes through Canada on the north, and the two Floridas on the south, and was abundantly able to supply their many wants, the colonists had debarred themselves from importing the articles which were necessary for the Indian trade.

It was unfortunate for the colonies, that since the peace of Paris 1763, the transactions with the Indians [139] had been mostly carried on by superintendants appointed and paid by the King of Great Britain. These being under obligations to the crown, and expectants of further favours from it, generally used their influence with the Indians in behalf of the Mother Country, and against the colonies. They insinuated into the minds of the uninformed savages, that the King was their natural protector against the encroaching colonists, and that if the latter succeeded in their opposition to Great Britain, they would probably next aim at the extirpation of their red neighbours. By such representations, seconded with a profusion of presents, the attachment of the Indians was pre-engaged in support of the British interest.

The Americans were not unmindful of the Savages on their frontier. They appointed commissioners to explain to them the grounds of the dispute, and to cultivate their friendship by treaties and presents. They endeavoured to persuade the Indians that the quarrel was by no means relative to them, and that therefore they should take part with neither side.

For the greater convenience of managing the intercourse between the colonies and the Indians, the latter were divided into three departments, the northern, southern and middle, and commissioners were appointed for each. Congress also resolved to import and distribute among them a suitable assortment of goods, to the amount of £40,000 sterling, on account of the United States; but this was not executed. All the exertions of Congress were insufficient for the security of their western frontiers. In almost every period of the war, a great majority of the Indians took part with Great Britain against the Americans. South-Carolina was among the first of the States, which experienced the effects of British influence over the Indians. The Cherokees and Creeks inhabit lands, not far distant from the western settlements of Carolina and Georgia. The intercourse with these tribes had, for several years prior to the American war, been exclusively committed to John Stuart an officer of the crown, and devoted to the royal interest. His influence, which was great, was

wholly exerted in favor [140] of Great Britain. A plan was settled by him, in concert with the King's governors, and other royal servants, to land a royal armed force in Florida, and to proceed with it to the western frontier of the Southern States, and there in conjunction with the tories and Indians, to fall on the friends of Congress, at the same time that a fleet and army should invade them on the sea coast. The whole scheme was providentially discovered by the capture of Moses Kirkland, one of the principal agents to be employed in its execution, while he was on his way to Gen. Gage with despatches, detailing the particulars, and soliciting for the requisite aid to accomplish it. The possession of Kirkland, and of his papers, enabled the Americans to take such steps as in a great degree frustrated the views of the royal servants, yet so much was carried into effect, that the Cherokees began their massacres, at the very time the British fleet attacked the fort on Sullivan's Island. The undisturbed tranquillity, which took place in South-Carolina and the adjacent States, after the British had failed in their designs against them in the spring and summer of 1776, gave an opportunity for carrying war into the Indian country. This was done, not so much to punish what was past, as to prevent all future co-operation between the Indians and British in that quarter.

Virginia, North-Carolina, South-Carolina, and Georgia each sent about the same time a considerable force over the Alleghany mountains, which traversed the Indian settlements, burned their towns, and destroyed their fields of corn. Above 500 of the Cherokees were obliged, from the want of provisions, to take refuge in West-Florida, and were there fed at the expence of the British government. These unfortunate misled people sued for peace in the most submissive terms, and soon after assented to a treaty, by which they ceded a considerable part of their land to South-Carolina. The decision with which this expedition was conducted intimidated the Cherokees, for some years, from farther hostilities. Very different was the case of those Indians who were in the vicinity of the British posts, and contiguous to the frontier of the northern and middle States. The presents which they [141] continually received from England, the industry of the British agents, and the influence of a great number of American refugees who had taken shelter among them, operating on their native passion for rapine, excited them to frequent hostile excursions. Col. John Butler a Connecticut tory, and one Brandt a half Indian by blood, were the principal leaders of the Savages in these expeditions. The vast extent of frontier, and remote situation of the settlements, together with the exact knowledge which the refugees possessed of the country, made it practicable for even small marauding parties to do extensive mischief.

1779

A storm of Indian and tory vengeance burst with particular violence on Wyoming, a new and flourishing settlement on the eastern branch of Susquehannah. Unfortunately for the security of the inhabitants, the soil was claimed both by Connecticut and Pennsylvania. From the collision of contradictory claims, founded on royal charters, the laws of neither were steadily enforced. In this remote settlement, where government was feeble, the tories were under less control, and could easily assemble undiscovered. Nevertheless at one time 27 of them were taken, and sent to Hartford in Connecticut, but they were afterwards released. These and others of the same description, instigated by revenge against the Americans, from whom some of them had suffered banishment and loss of property, made a common cause with the Indians, and attacked the Wyoming settlement with their combined forces estimated at 1100 men, 900 of which were Indians. The whole was commanded by Col. John Butler, a Connecticut tory. One of the forts, which had been constructed for the

1778
JULY 1

security of the inhabitants, being very weak, surrendered to this party; but some of the garrison had previously retired to the principal fort at Kingston, called Forty-Fort. Col. John Butler next demanded the surrender of that. Col. Zebulon Butler a continental officer who commanded there, sent a message to him, proposing a conference at a bridge without the fort. This being agreed to, Col. Zebulon Butler, Dennison, and some other officers repaired to the [142] place appointed, and they were followed by the whole garrison, a few invalids excepted. None of the enemy appeared. The Wyoming people advanced, and supposed that the enemy were retiring. They continued to march on, till they were about three miles from the fort. They then saw a few of the enemy, with whom they exchanged some shot, but they presently found themselves ambuscaded and attacked by the whole body of Indians and tories. They fought gallantly, till they found that their retreat to the fort was cut off. Universal confusion then ensued. Of 417 who had marched out of the fort, about 360 were instantly slain. No quarters were given. Col. John Butler again demanded the surrender of Forty-Fort. This was agreed to under articles of capitulation, by which the effects of the people therein were to be secured to them. The garrison consisted of 30 men and 200 women. These were permitted to cross the Susquehannah, and retreat through the woods to Northampton county. The most of the other scattered settlers had previously retired, some through the woods to Northampton county, others down the river to Northumberland county. In this retreat, some women were delivered of children in the woods, and many suffered from want of provisions. Several of the settlers at Wyoming had erected good houses and barns, and made very considerable improvements. These and all the other houses in the vicinity, except about half a dozen, were destroyed. Their horses, cattle, sheep, and hogs were for the most part killed or driven away by the enemy.

The distresses of this settlement were uncommonly great. A large proportion of the male inhabitants were, in one day, slaughtered. In a single engagement, near 200 women were made widows, and a much greater number of children were left fatherless.

Soon after the destruction of the Wyoming settlement, an expedition was carried on against the Indians by Col. Butler of the

Pennsylvania troops. He and his party, having gained the head of the Delaware, marched down the river for two days, and then struck across the country to the [143] Susquehannah. They totally burnt or destroyed the Indian villages, both in that quarter and the other settlements, but the inhabitants escaped. The destruction was extended for several miles on both sides of the Susquehannah. The difficulties which Col. Butler's men encountered in this expedition, could not be undergone but by men who possessed a large share of hardiness, both of body and mind. They were obliged to carry their provisions on their backs, and thus loaded, frequently to wade through creeks and rivers. After the toil of a hard march, they were obliged to endure chilly nights and heavy rains, without even the means of keeping their arms dry. They completed their business in sixteen days. About four weeks after Col. Butler's return, some hundreds of Indians, a large body of tories, and about 50 regulars entered Cherry-Valley within the State of New-York. They made an unsuccessful attempt on fort Alden, but they killed and scalped thirty two of the inhabitants, mostly women and children, and also Col. Alden and ten soldiers.

An expedition which was to have taken place under Henry Hamilton Lt. Gov. of Detroit, fortunately for the Virginian back settlers, against whom it was principally directed fell through, in consequence of the spirited conduct of Col. Clarke. The object of the expedition was extensive and many Indians were engaged in it. Hamilton took post at St. Vincents in the winter, to have all things in readiness for invading the American settlements, as soon as the season of the year would permit. Clarke on hearing that Hamilton had weakened himself by sending away a considerable part of his Indians against the frontier settlers, formed the resolution of attacking him, as the best expedient for preventing the mischiefs which were designed against his country. After surmounting many difficulties he arrived with 130 men unexpectedly at St. Vincents.

The town immediately gave up to the Americans, and assisted them in taking the fort. The next day Hamilton, with the garrison, agreed to surrender prisoners of war on articles of capitulation. Clarke on hearing that a convoy of British goods and provisions was on its way from Detroit, [144] detached a party of sixty men which met them, and made prize of the whole. By this well conducted and spirited attack on Hamilton, his intended expedition was nipped in the bud. Col. Clarke transmitted to the council of Virginia letters and papers, relating to Lt. Gov. Hamilton, Philip De Jean justice of peace for Detroit, and William Lamothe captain of volunteers, whom he had made prisoners. The board reported that Hamilton had incited the Indians to perpetrate their accustomed cruelties on the defence-less inhabitants of the United States—had at the time of his captivity sent considerable detachments of Indians against the frontiers—had appointed a great council of them, to meet him and concert the operations of the ensuing campaign—had given standing rewards for scalps, and had treated American prisoners with cruelty. They also reported, that it appeared that De Jean was the willing and cordial instrument of Hamilton, and that Lamothe was captain of the volunteer scalping parties of Indians and tories, who went out from time to time, under general orders to spare neither men, women, nor children. They therefore considering them as fit objects, on which to begin the work of retaliation—advised the Governor to put them in irons—confine them in the dungeon of the public jail—debar them the use of pen, ink and paper, and exclude them from all converse, except with their keeper.

APR. 19

Col. Goose Van Schaick, with 55 men, marched from fort Schuyler to the Onandago settlements, and burned the whole, consisting of about 50 houses, together with a large quantity of provisions. Horses, and stock of every kind, were killed. The arms and ammunition of the Indians were either destroyed or brought off, and their settlements were laid waste. Twelve Indians were killed, and 34 made prisoners. This expedition was performed in less than six days, and without the loss of a single man.

In this manner, the savage part of the war was carried on in America. Waste and sometimes cruelty were inflicted and retorted, with infinite variety of scenes of horror and disgust. The selfish passions of human nature unrestrained by social ties, broke over all bounds of [145] decency or humanity. The American refugees, who had fled to the western wilderness, indulged their passion for rapine by assuming the colour and dress of Indians. At other times they acted as guides, and conducted these merciless ravagers into such

1779

settlements, as afforded the most valuable booty, and the fairest prospect of escape. The savages encouraged by British presents and agents, and led on by American refugees well acquainted with the country, and who cloaked the most consummate villainy under the specious name of loyalty, extended their depredations and murders far and near.

A particular detail of the devastation of property—of the distress of great numbers who escaped, only by fleeing to the woods, where they subsisted without covering on the spontaneous productions of the earth—and of the barbarous murders which were committed on persons of every age and sex, would be sufficient to freeze every breast with horror.

In sundry expeditions which had been carried on against the Indians, ample vengeance had been taken on some of them, but these partial successes produced no lasting benefit. The few who escaped, had it in their power to make thousands miserable. For the permanent security of the frontier inhabitants, it was resolved in the year 1779 to carry a decisive expedition into the Indian country. A considerable body of continental troops was selected for this purpose, and put under the command of Gen. Sullivan. The Indians who form the confederacy of the six nations, commonly called the Mohawks, were the objects of this expedition. They inhabit that immense and fertile tract of country, which lies between New-England, the middle States and the province of Canada. They had been advised by Congress, and they had promised, to observe a neutrality in the war, but they soon departed from this line of conduct. The Oneidas and a few others were friends to the Americans, but a great majority took part decidedly against them. Overcome by the presents and promises of Sir John Johnson and other British agents, and their own native appetite for depredation, they invaded the frontiers [146] carrying slaughter and devastation wherever they went. From the vicinity of their settlements, to the inhabited parts of the United States, they facilitated the inroads of the more remote Indians. Much was therefore expected from their expulsion. When Gen. Sullivan was on his way to the Indian country he was joined by the American Gen. Clinton with upwards of 1000 men. The latter made his way down the Susquehannah by a singular contrivance. The stream of water in

1779

that river was too low to float his batteaux. To remedy this inconvenience, he raised with great industry a dam across the mouth of the Lake Otsego, which is one of the sources of the river Susquehannah. The lake being constantly supplied by springs soon rose to the height of the dam. General Clinton having got his batteaux ready, opened a passage through the dam for the water to flow. This raised the river so high that he was enabled to embark all his troops and to float them down to Tioga. By this exertion they soon joined Sullivan. The Indians on hearing of the expedition projected against them, acted with firmness. They collected their strength, took possession of proper ground, and fortified it with judgment. Gen. Sullivan attacked them in their works. They stood a cannonade for more than two hours but then gave way. This engagement proved decisive: After the trenches were forced, the Indians fled without making any attempt to rally. They were pursued for some miles but without effect. The consternation occasioned among them by this defeat was so great, that they gave up all ideas of farther resistance. As the Americans advanced into their settlements, the Indians retreated before them, without throwing any obstructions in their way. Gen. Sullivan penetrated into the heart of the country inhabited by the Mohawks, and spread desolation every where. Many settlements in the form of towns were destroyed, besides detached habitations. All their fields of corn, and whatever was in a state of cultivation, underwent the same fate. Scarce any thing in the form of a house was left standing, nor was an Indian to be seen. To the surprise of the Americans, they found the lands about the Indian [147] towns well cultivated, and their houses both large and commodious. The quantity of corn destroyed was immense. Orchards in which were several hundred fruit trees were cut down, and of them many appeared to have been planted for a long series of years. Their gardens, which were enriched with great quantities of useful vegetables of different kinds, were laid waste. The Americans were so full of resentment against the Indians, for the many outrages they had suffered from them, and so bent on making the expedition decisive, that the officers and soldiers cheerfully agreed to remain till they had fully completed the destruction of the settlement. The supplies obtained in the country, lessened the inconvenience of short rations.

AUG. 29

1779

The ears of corn were so remarkably large, that many of them measured twenty two inches in length. Necessity suggested a novel expedient for pulverising the grains thereof. The soldiers perforated a few of their camp kettles with bayonets. The protrusions occasioned thereby formed a rough surface, and by rubbing the ears of corn thereon, a coarse meal was produced, which was easily converted into agreeable nourishment.

In about three months from his setting out, Sullivan reached Easton in Pennsylvania, and soon after rejoined the army.

The Indians, by this decisive expedition, being made to feel in the most sensible manner, those calamities they were wont to inflict on others, became cautious and timid. The sufferings they had undergone, and the dread of a repetition of them, in case of their provoking the resentment of the Americans, damped the ardor of their warriors from making incursions into the American settlements. The frontiers, though not restored to perfect tranquility, experienced an exemption from a great proportion of the calamities, in which they had been lately involved.

Though these good consequences resulted from this expedition, yet about the time of its commencement, and before its termination, several detached parties of Indians distressed different settlements in the United States. [148] A party of 60 Indians, and 27 white men, under Brandt attacked the Minisink settlement, and burnt 10 houses 12 barns, a fort and two mills, and carried off much plunder, together with several prisoners. The militia from Goshen and the vicinity, to the amount of 149, collected and pursued them, but with so little caution that they were surprised and defeated. About this time, Gen. Williamson and Col. Pickens, both of South-Carolina, entered the Indian country adjacent to the frontier of their State, burned and destroyed the corn of eight towns, and insisted upon the Indians removing immediately from their late habitations into more remote settlements.

In the same month, Col. Broadhead engaged in a successful expedition against the Mingo, Munsey, and Seneka Indians. He left Pittsburg with 605 men, and was gone about five weeks, in which time he penetrated about 200 miles from the fort, destroyed a number of Indian huts and about 500 acres of corn.

1779

JULY 23

AUG. 22

AUG. 11

The State of New-York continued to suffer in its frontier, from Indians and their tory associates. These burnt 50 houses, and 47 barns, the principal part of Canijohary, a fine settlement about 56 miles from Albany. They also destroyed 27 houses at Schoharie, and 20 at Normans creek. In about two months after, they made a second irruption, and attacked Stone Arabia, Canasioraga and Schoharie. At the same time, they laid waste a great extent of country about the Mohawk river, killed a number of the settlers, and made many prisoners.

AUG.
1780

OCTO.
1780

The Cherokee Indians, having forgot the consequences of provoking the Americans to invade their settlements in the year 1776, made an incursion into Ninety-Six district in South-Carolina, massacred some families, and burned several houses. Gen. Pickens collected a party of the militia, and penetrated into their country. This he accomplished in fourteen days, at the head of 394 horsemen. In that short space, he burned thirteen towns and villages, killed upwards of 40 Indians, and took a number of prisoners. Not one of his party was killed, and only two were wounded. None of the expeditions [149] against the Cherokees had been so rapid and decisive as this one. The Americans did not expend three rounds of ammunition, and yet only three Indians escaped after having been once seen. On this occasion, a new and successful mode of fighting them was introduced. The American militia rushed forwards on horse-back, and charged the Indians with drawn swords. The vanquished Cherokees again sued for peace, in the most submissive terms and obtained it, but not till they had promised, that instead of listening to the advice of the royalists, instigating them to war, they would deliver to the authority of the State of South-Carolina, all who should visit them on that errand.

1781

1779

Towards the end of the war, there was a barbarous and unprovoked massacre of some civilised Indians, who had been settled near the Muskingum. These under the influence of some pious missionaries of the Moravian persuasion, had been formed into some degree of civil and religious order. They abhorred war, and would take no part therein, giving for reason that "The Great Being did not make men to destroy men, but to love and assist each other." From a love of peace they advised those of their own colour, who were bent on war, to desist from it. They were also led from humanity, to inform the

1782

white people of their danger, when they knew that their settlements were about to be invaded. This provoked the hostile Indians to such a degree, that they carried these pacific people quite away from Muskingum to a bank of Sandusky creek. They finding corn dear and scarce in their new habitations, obtained liberty to come back in the fall of the same year to Muskingum, that they might collect the crops they had planted before their removal.

When the white people, at and near Monongahala, heard that a number of Indians were at the Moravian towns on the Muskingum, they gave out that their intentions were hostile. Without any further enquiry, 160 of them crossed the Ohio, and put to death these harmless, inoffensive people, though they made no resistance. In conformity to their religious principles, these Moravians patiently submitted to their hard fate, without attempting [150] to destroy their murderers. Upwards of ninety of this pacific set were killed by men, who while they called themselves Christians, were infinitely more deserving of the name of Savages than those whom they inhumanly murdered.

1779

Soon after this unprovoked massacre, a party of the Americans set out for Sandusky, to destroy the Indian towns in that part; but the Delawares, Wyandots, and other Indians opposed them. An engagement ensued, in which some of the white people were killed, and several were taken prisoners. Among the latter was Col. Crawford and his son in law. The Colonel was sacrificed to the manes of those Indians, who were massacred at the Moravian towns. The other prisoners were put to death with the tomahawk.

Throughout the American war, the desolation brought by the Indians on the frontier settlements of the United States, and on the Indians by the Americans, were sufficient to excite compassion in the most obdurate hearts.

Not only the men and warriors, but the women and children, and whole settlements were involved in the promiscuous desolations. Each was made a scourge to the other, and the unavoidable calamities of war were rendered doubly distressing, by the dispersion of families, the breaking up of settlements, and an addition of savage cruelties to the most extensive devastation of those things, which conduce to the comfort of human life.

Campaign of 1780 in the Southern States.

1780 [151] THE SUCCESSFUL DEFENCE OF SAVANNAH, together with the subsequent departure of Count D'Estaing from the coast of the United States, soon dissipated all apprehensions, previously entertained for the safety of New-York. These circumstances pointed out to Sir Henry Clinton, the propriety of renewing offensive operations. Having effected nothing of importance for the two preceding campaigns, he turned his attention southwardly, and regaled himself with flattering prospects of easy conquest, among the weaker States. The suitableness of the climate for winter operations, the richness of the country, and its distance from support, designated South-Carolina as a proper object of enterprize. No sooner therefore was the departure of the French fleet known and confirmed, than Sir Henry Clinton committed the command of the royal army in New-York to Lieut.

Gen. Kniphausen, and embarked for the southward, with four flank battalions, 12 regiments, and a corps British, Hessian and provincial, a powerful detachment of artillery, 250 cavalry, together with an ample supply of military stores and provisions. Vice Admiral Arbuthnot, with a suitable naval force, undertook to convey the troops to the place of their destination. The whole sailed from New-York. After a tedious and dangerous passage, in which part of their ordnance, most of their artillery, and all their cavalry horses were lost, the fleet arrived at Tybee in Georgia. In a few days, the transports with the army on board, sailed from Savannah for North-Edisto, and after a short passage, the troops made good their landing about 30 miles from Charleston, and took possession of John's Island and Stono ferry, and soon after of James Island, and Wappoo-cut. A bridge was thrown over the canal, and part of the royal army took post on the banks of Ashley river opposite to Charleston.

1779
DEC. 26

JAN. 31

FEB. 11

The assembly of the State was sitting when the British landed, but broke up after "delegating to Gov. Rutledge, and such of his council as he could conveniently consult, a power to do every thing necessary for the public good, [152] except the taking away the life of a citizen without a legal trial." The Governor immediately ordered the militia to rendezvous. Though the necessity was great, few obeyed the pressing call. A proclamation was issued by the Governor, under his extraordinary powers, requiring such of the militia as were regularly draughted, and all the inhabitants and owners of property in the town, to repair to the American standard and join the garrison immediately, under pain of confiscation. This severe though necessary measure produced very little effect. The country was much despirited by the late repulse at Savannah.

1780

The tedious passage from New-York to Tybee, gave the Americans time to fortify Charleston. This together with the losses which the royal army had sustained in the late tempestuous weather, induced Sir Henry Clinton, to dispatch an order to New-York for reinforcements of men and stores. He also directed Major General Prevost, to send on to him twelve hundred men from the garrison of Savannah. Brigadier General Patterson, at the head of this detachment, made his way good over the river Savannah, and through the intermediate country, and soon after joined Sir Henry Clinton near the banks of

Ashley river. The royal forces without delay proceeded to the siege. At Wappoo on James Island, they formed a depot, and erected fortifications both on that island and on the main, opposite to the southern and western extremities of Charleston. An advanced party crossed Ashley river, and soon after broke ground at the distance of 1100 yards from the American works. At successive periods, they erected five batteries on Charleston neck. The garrison was equally assiduous in preparing for its defence. The works which had been previously thrown up, were strengthened and extended. Lines and redoubts were continued across from Cooper to Ashley river. In front of the whole was a strong abbatis, and a wet ditch made by passing a canal from the heads of swamps, which run in opposite directions. Between the abbatis and the lines, deep holes were dug at short intervals. The lines were made particularly strong on the right and left, and so constructed as to rake the wet ditch in almost [153] its whole extent. To secure the center, a hornwork had been erected, which being closed during the siege formed a kind of citadel. Works were also thrown up on all sides of the town, where a landing was practicable. Though the lines were no more than field works, yet Sir Henry Clinton treated them with the respectful homage of three parallels. From the 3d to the 10th of April, the first parallel was completed, and immediately after the town was summoned to surrender. On the 12th, the batteries were opened, and from that day an almost incessant fire was kept up. About the time the batteries were opened a work was thrown up near Wando river, nine miles from town, and another at Lempriere's point, to preserve the communication with the country by water. A post was also ordered at a ferry over the Santee, to favour the coming in of reinforcements, or the retreat of the garrison when necessary. The British marine force consisting of one ship of fifty guns, two of forty four guns, four of thirty two, and the Sandwich armed ship, crossed the bar in front of Rebellion road and anchored in Five fathom hole. The American force opposed to this was the Bricole, which though pierced for forty four guns, did not mount half of that number, two of 32 guns, one of 28, two of 26, two of 20, and the brig Notre Dame of 16 guns. The first object of its commander Commodore Whipple, was to prevent Admiral Arbuthnot from crossing the bar, but on farther examination

MAR. 29

1780

MAR. 21

this was found to be impracticable. He therefore fell back to Fort Moultrie, and afterwards to Charleston. The crew and guns of all his vessels, except one, were put on shore to reinforce the batteries.

Admiral Arbuthnot weighed anchor at Five fathom hole, and with the advantage of a strong southerly wind, and flowing tide, passed Fort Moultrie without stopping to engage it, and anchored near the remains of Fort Johnson. Colonel Pinckney who commanded on Sullivan's Island, kept up a brisk and well directed fire on the ships in their passage, which did as great execution as could be expected. To prevent the royal armed vessels [154] from running into Cooper river, eleven vessels were sunk in the channel opposite to the exchange. The batteries of the besiegers soon obtained a superiority over those of the town. The former had 21 mortars and royals, the latter only two. The regular force in the garrison was much inferior to that of the besiegers, and but few of the militia could be persuaded to leave their plantations, and reinforce their brethren in the capital. A camp was formed at Monk's corner, to keep up the communication between the town and country, and the militia without the lines, were requested to rendezvous there: But this was surprised and routed by Lieutenant Colonel Tarleton. The British having now less to fear, extended themselves to the eastward of Cooper river. Two hundred and fifty horse, and 600 infantry were detached on this service, but nevertheless in the opinion of a council of war, the weak state of the garrison, made it improper to detach a number sufficient to attack that small force. About this time Sir Henry Clinton received a reinforcement of 3000 men from New-York. A second council of war held four days after the first, agreed that "a retreat would be attended with many distressing inconveniences, if not altogether impracticable," and advised, "that offers of capitulation before their affairs became more critical should be made to General Clinton, which might admit of the army's withdrawing, and afford security to the persons and property of the inhabitants." These terms being proposed, were instantly rejected, but the garrison adhered to them, in hopes that succours would arrive from the neighbouring States. The bare offer of capitulating, dispirited the garrison, but they continued to resist in expectation of favorable events. The British speedily completed the investiture of the town, both by land and

APRIL 9

1780

APR. 16
18

20

21

water. After Admiral Arbuthnot had passed Sullivan's Island, Colonel Pinckney, with 150 of the men under his command, were withdrawn from that post to Charleston. Soon after the fort on the island was surrendered without opposition to Captain Hudson of the royal navy. On the same day, the remains of the American cavalry which escaped from the [155] surprise at Monk's corner, on the 14th of April, were again surprised by Lieutenant Colonel Tarleton at Laneau's ferry on Santee, and the whole either killed, captured or dispersed. While every thing prospered with the British, Sir Henry Clinton began a correspondence with General Lincoln, and renewed his former offers to the garrison in case of their surrender. Lincoln was disposed to close with them, as far they respected his army, but some demur was made with a view of gaining better terms for the citizens, which it was hoped might be obtained on a conference. This was asked: But Clinton instead of granting it, answered "that hostilities should recommence at 8 o'clock." Nevertheless, neither party fired till nine. The garrison then recommenced hostilities. The besiegers immediately followed, and each cannonaded the other with unusual briskness. The British batteries of the third parallel opened on this occasion. Shells and carcases were thrown into almost all parts of the town, and several houses were burned. The cannon and mortars played on the garrison at a less distance than a hundred yards. The Hessian chasseurs were so near the American lines, that with their rifles they could easily strike any object that was visible on them. The British having crossed the wet ditch by sap, advanced within 25 yards of the American works, and were ready for making a general assault by land and water. All expectation of succour was at an end. The only hope left was that 9000 men, the flower of the British army, seconded by a naval force, might fail in storming extensive lines defended by less than 3000 men. Under these circumstances, the siege was protracted till the 11th. On that day a great number of the citizens addressed General Lincoln in a petition, expressing their acquiescence in the terms which Sir Henry Clinton had offered, and requesting his acceptance of them. On the reception of this petition, General Lincoln wrote to Sir Henry, and offered to accept the terms before proposed. The royal commanders wishing to avoid the extremity of a storm, and unwilling to press to unconditional submission an enemy, whose friendship they wished to conciliate, [156] returned a favourable answer. A capitulation was signed, and Major Gen. Leslie took possession of the town on the next day. The loss on both sides during the siege was nearly equal. Of the King's troops, 76 were killed, and 189 wounded. Of the Americans 89 were killed and 140 wounded. Upwards of 400 pieces of artillery were surrendered. By the articles of capitulation, the garrison was to march out of town, and to deposit their arms in front of the works, but the drums were not to beat a British march, nor the colors to be uncased. The continental troops and seamen were to keep their baggage, and remain prisoners of war till exchanged. The militia were to be permitted to return to their respective homes as prisoners on parole, and while they adhered to their parole, were not to be molested by the British troops in person or property. The inhabitants of all conditions to be considered as prisoners on parole, and to hold their property on the same terms with the militia. The officers of the army and navy to retain their servants swords, pistols and baggage un-searched. They were permitted to sell their horses, but not to remove them. A vessel was allowed to proceed to Philadelphia with Gen. Lincoln's dispatches unopened.

The numbers which surrendered prisoners of war, inclusive of the militia and every adult male inhabitant, was above 5000, but the proper garrison at the time of the surrender did not exceed 2500. The precise number of privates in the continental army was 1977, of which number 500 were in the hospitals. The captive officers were much more in proportion than the privates, and consisted of one Major General, 6 Brigadiers, 9 Colonels, 14 Lieut. Colonels, 15 Majors, 84 Captains, 84 Lieutenants, 32 second Lieutenants and Ensigns. The gentlemen of the country, who were mostly militia officers, from a sense of honor repaired to the defence of Charleston, though they could not bring with them privates equal to their respective com-mands. The regular regiments were fully officered, though greatly deficient in privates.

This was the first instance, in which the Americans had attempted to defend a town. The unsuccessful event [157] with its consequences, demonstrated the policy of sacrificing the towns of the Union, in preference to endangering the whole, by risquing too much for their defence.

Much censure was undeservedly cast on Gen. Lincoln, for attempting the defence of Charleston. Though the contrary plan was in general the best, he had particular reasons to justify his deviation from the example of the commander in chief of the American army. Charleston was the only considerable town in the southern extreme of the confederacy, and for its preservation, South-Carolina and the adjacent States seemed willing to make great exertions. The reinforcements, promised for its defence, were fully sufficient for that purpose. The Congress, and the States of North and South-Carolina gave Gen. Lincoln ground to expect an army of 9900 men to second his operations, but from a variety of causes this army, including the militia, was little more than one third of that number. As long as an evacuation was practicable, he had such assurances of support, that he could not attempt it with propriety. Before he could be ascertained of the futility of these assurances, the British had taken such a position, that in the opinion of good judges a retreat could not be successfully made.

Shortly after the surrender, the commander in chief adopted sundry measures to induce the inhabitants to return to their allegiance. It was stated to them in an hand bill, which though without a name seemed to flow from authority: "That the helping hand of every man was wanting to re-establish peace and good government— That the commander in chief wished not to draw them into danger, while any doubt could remain of his success, but as that was now certain, he trusted that one and all would heartily join, and give effect to necessary measures for that purpose." Those who had families were informed "That they would be permitted to remain at home, and form a militia for the maintenance of peace and good order, but from those who had no families it was expected that they would chearfully assist in driving their oppressors, and all the miseries of war, from their borders." To such it was promised "That when on service, they [158] would be allowed pay, ammunition and provisions, in the same manner as the King's troops." About the same time, Sir Henry Clinton in a proclamation declared

1780
MAY 22

That if any person should thenceforward appear in arms in order to prevent the establishment of his Majesty's government in that country, or should under any pretence or authority whatever, attempt to compel

482

any other person or persons so to do, or who should hinder the King's faithful subjects from joining his forces, or from performing those duties their allegiance required, such persons should be treated with the utmost severity, and their estates be immediately seized for confiscation. JUNE 1

In a few days after, Sir Henry Clinton and Admiral Arbuthnot, in the character of commissioners for restoring peace, offered to the inhabitants, with some exceptions, "Pardon for their past treasonable offences, and a re-instatement in the possession of all those rights and immunities which they heretofore had enjoyed under a free British government exempt from taxation, except by their own legislatures."

The capital having surrendered, the next object with the British was to secure the general submission of the whole body of the people.

To this end, they posted garrisons in different parts of the country to awe the inhabitants. They also marched with upwards of 2000 men towards North-Carolina. This caused an immediate retreat of some parties of Americans, who had advanced into the northern extremity of South-Carolina, with the expectation of relieving Charleston. One of these, consisting of about 300 continentals commanded by Col. Buford, was overtaken at Wachaws by Lt. Col. Tarleton and completely defeated. Five out of six of the whole were either killed or so badly wounded, as to be incapable of being moved from the field of battle; and this took place though they made such ineffectual opposition as only to kill 12 and wound five of the British. This great disproportion of the killed on the two sides, arose from the circumstance that Tarleton's party refused quarter to the Americans, after they had ceased to resist and laid down their arms.

[159] Sir Henry Clinton having left about 4000 men for the southern service, embarked early in June with the main army for New-York. On his departure the command devolved on Lieut. Gen. Cornwallis. The season of the year, the condition of the army, and the unsettled state of South-Carolina, impeded the immediate invasion of North-Carolina. Earl Cornwallis dispatched instructions to the principal loyalists in that state to attend to the harvest, prepare provisions, and remain quiet till the latter end of August or beginning of September. His Lordship committed the care of the frontier to Lord 1780

Rawdon, and repairing to Charleston, devoted his principal attention to the commercial and civil regulations of South-Carolina. In the mean time, the impossibility of fleeing with their families and effects, and the want of an army to which the militia of the States might repair, induced the people in the country, to abandon all schemes of farther resistance. At Beaufort, Camden, and Ninety-Six, they generally laid down their arms, and submitted either as prisoners or as subjects. Excepting the extremities of the state bordering on North-Carolina, the inhabitants who did not flee out of the country preferred submission to resistance. This was followed by an unusual calm, and the British believed that the state was thoroughly conquered. An opportunity was now given to make an experiment from which much was expected, and for the omission of which, Sir Henry Clinton's predecessor Sir William Howe, had been severely censured. It had been confidently asserted, that a majority of the Americans were well affected to the British government, and that under proper regulations, substantial service might be expected from them, in restoring the country to peace. At this crisis every biass in favor of Congress was removed. Their armies in the southern States were either captured or defeated. There was no regular force to the southward of Pennsylvania, which was sufficient to awe the friends of royal government. Every encouragement was held forth, to those of the inhabitants who would with arms support the old constitution. Confiscation and death were threatened as the consequence [160] of opposing its re-establishment. While there was no regular army within 400 miles to aid the friends of independence, the British were in force posted over all the country. The people were thus left to themselves, or rather strongly impelled to abandon an apparently sinking cause, and arrange themselves on the side of the conquerors. Under these favorable circumstances, the experiment was made, for supporting the British interest by the exertion of loyal inhabitants, unawed by American armies or republican demagogues. It soon appeared that the disguise which fear had imposed, subsisted no longer than the present danger, and that the minds of the people though overawed were actuated by an hostile spirit. In prosecuting the scheme for obtaining a military aid from the inhabitants, that tranquillity which previous successes had procured was disturbed,

1780

and that ascendency which arms had gained was interrupted. The inducement to submission with many, was a hope of obtaining a respite from the calamities of war, under the shelter of British protection. Such were not less astonished than confounded, on finding themselves virtually called upon to take arms in support of royal government. This was done in the following manner: After the inhabitants by the specious promises of protection and security, had generally submitted as subjects, or taken their parole as prisoners of war, a proclamation was issued by Sir Henry Clinton which set forth "That it was proper for all persons to take an active part in settling and securing his Majesty's government"—and in which it was declared

> That all the inhabitants of the province who were then prisoners on parole (those who were taken in Fort Moultrie and Charleston, and such as were in actual confinement excepted) should, from and after the 20th of June, be freed from their paroles, and restored to all the rights and duties belonging to citizens and inhabitants." And it was in the same proclamation farther declared that all persons under the description abovementioned, who should afterwards neglect to return to their allegiance, and to his Majesty's government, should be considered as enemies and rebels to the same, and treated [161] accordingly.

It was designed by this arbitrary change of the political condition of the inhabitants from prisoners to citizens, to bring them into a dilemma, which would force them to take an active part in settling and securing the royal government. It involved a majority in the necessity of either fleeing out of the country, or of becoming a British militia. With this proclamation the declension of British authority commenced, for though the inhabitants from motives of fear or convenience, had generally submitted, the greatest part of them retained an affection for their American brethren, and shuddered at the thought of taking arms against them. Among such it was said "if we must fight, let it be on the side of America, our friends and countrymen." A great number considering this proclamation as a discharge for their paroles, armed themselves in self defence, being induced thereto by the royal menaces, that they who did not return to their allegiance as British subjects, must expect to be treated as

1780

rebels. A greater number from being in the power of the British, exchanged their paroles as prisoners for the protection of subjects, but this was done in many cases, with a secret reservation of breaking the compulsory engagement, when a proper opportunity should present itself.

A party always attached to royal government, though they had conformed to the laws of the state, rejoiced in the ascendency of the royal arms, but their number was inconsiderable, in comparison with the multitude who were obliged by necessity, or induced by convenience, to accept of British protection.

The precautions taken to prevent the rising of the royalists in North-Carolina, did not answer the end. Several of the inhabitants of Tryon county, under the direction of Col. Moore took up arms, and were in a few days defeated by the whig militia, commanded by Gen. Rutherford. Col. Bryan another loyalist, though equally injudicious as to time, was successful. He reached the 71st regiment stationed in the Cheraws with about 800 men, assembled from the neighbourhood of the river Yadkin.

1780

[162] While the conquerors were endeavoring to strengthen the party for royal government, the Americans were not inattentive to their interests. Governor Rutledge who during the siege of Charleston had been requested by Gen. Lincoln to go out of town, was industriously and successfully negotiating with North-Carolina, Virginia and Congress, to obtain a force for checking the progress of the British arms. Representations to the same effect, had also been made in due time by Gen. Lincoln. Congress ordered a considerable detachment from their main army, to be marched to the Southward. North-Carolina also ordered a large body of militia to take the field. As the British advanced to the upper country of South-Carolina, a considerable number of determined whigs retreated before them, and took refuge in North-Carolina. In this class was Col. Sumter a distinguished partizan, who was well qualified for conducting military operations. A party of exiles from South-Carolina, made choice of him for their leader. At the head of this little band of freemen, he returned to his own state, and took the field against the victorious British, after the inhabitants had generally abandoned all ideas of farther resistance. This unexpected impediment to the extension of British conquests roused all the passions which disappointed ambition

can inspire. Previous successes had flattered the royal commanders with hopes of distinguished rank among the conquerors of America, but the renewal of hostilities obscured the pleasing prospect. Flushed with the victories they had gained in the first of the campaign, and believing every thing told them favorable to their wishes to be true, they conceived that they had little to fear on the south side of Virginia. When experience refuted these hopes, they were transported with indignation against the inhabitants, and confined several of them on suspicion of their being accessary to the recommencement of hostilities.

The first effort of renewed warfare was two months after the fall of Charleston, when 133 of Col. Sumter's corps attacked and routed a detachment of the royal forces and militia, which were posted in a lane at Williamson's [163] plantation. This was the first advantage gained over the British, since their landing in the beginning of the year. The steady persevering friends of America, who were very numerous in the North-western frontier of South-Carolina, turned out with great alacrity to join Col. Sumter, though opposition to the British government, had entirely ceased in every other part of the State. His troops in a few days amounted to 600 men. With this increase of strength, he made a spirited attack on a party of the British at Rocky Mount, but as he had no artillery, and they were secured under cover of earth filled in between logs, he could make no impression upon them, and was obliged to retreat. Sensible that the minds of men are influenced by enterprise and that to keep militia together it is necessary to employ them, this active partizan attacked another of the royal detachments, consisting of the Prince of Wales' regiment, and a large body of tories posted at the Hanging rock. The Prince of Wales' regiment was almost totally destroyed. From 273 it was reduced to 9. The loyalists, who were of that party which had advanced from North Carolina under Col. Bryan, were dispersed. The panic occasioned by the fall of Charleston daily abated. The whig militia on the extremities of the state formed themselves into parties, under leaders of their own choice, and sometimes attacked detachments of the British army, but more frequently those of their own countrymen, who as a royal militia were co-operating with the King's forces. While Sumter kept up the spirits of the people by a succession of gallant enterprizes, a

JULY 12

1780

respectable continental force was advancing through the middle States, for the relief of their southern brethren. With the hopes of relieving Charleston, orders were given for the Maryland and Delaware troops to march from Gen. Washington's head quarters to South-Carolina, but the Quarter-master-general was unable to put this detachment in motion as soon as was intended.

The manufacturers employed in providing for the army would neither go on with their business, nor deliver the articles they had completed, declaring they had suffered so much from the depreciation of the money, that they [164] would not part with their property without immediate payment. Under these embarrassing circumstances, the Southern States required an aid from the northern army, to be marched through the intermediate space of 800 miles. The Maryland and Delaware troops were with great exertions at length enabled to move. After marching through Jersey and Pennsylvania, they embarked at the Head of Elk and landed soon after at Petersburg, and thence proceeded through the country towards South-Carolina. This force was at first put under the command of Major Gen. Baron de Kalb, and afterwards of Gen. Gates. The success of the latter in the northern campaigns of 1776 and 1777, induced many to believe that his presence as commander of the southern army, would re-animate the friends of Independence. While Baron de Kalb commanded, a council of war had advised him to file off from the direct road to Camden, towards the well cultivated settlements in the vicinity of the Waxhaws: But Gen. Gates on taking the command did not conceive this movement to be necessary, supporting it to be most for the interest of the States that he should proceed immediately with his army, on the shortest road to the vicinity of the British encampments. This led through a barren country, in passing over which, the Americans severely felt the scarcity of provisions. Their murmurs became audible, and there were strong appearances of mutiny, but the officers who shared every calamity in common with the privates interposed, and conciliated them to a patient sufferance of their hard lot. They principally subsisted on lean cattle, picked up in the woods. The whole army was under the necessity of using green corn, and peaches in the place of bread. They were subsisted for several days on the latter alone. Dysenteries became common in consequence of this diet. The heat of the season, the unhealthiness of the climate, together with insufficient and unwholsome food, threatened destruction to the army. The common soliders, instead of desponding, began after some time to be merry with their misfortunes. They used "starvation" as a cant word, and vied with each other in burlesquing their [165] situation. The wit and humour displayed on the occasion contributed not a little to reconcile them to their sufferings. The American army, having made its way through a country of pine-barrens, sand-hills and swamps, reached Clermont, 13 miles from Camden. The next day, Gen. Stephens arrived with a large body of Virginia militia.

As the American army approached South-Carolina, lord Rawdon concentered his force at Camden. The retreat of the British from their out-posts, the advances of the American army, and the impolitic conduct of the conquerors towards their new subjects, concurred at this juncture to produce a general revolt in favor of Congress. The people were daily more dissatisfied with their situation. Tired of war, they had submitted to British government with the expectation of bettering their condition, but they soon found their mistake. The greatest address should have been practiced towards the inhabitants, in order to second the views of the Parent State in re-uniting the revolted colonies to her government. That the people might be induced to return to the condition of subjects, their minds and affections, as well as their armies, ought to have been conquered. This delicate task was rarely attempted. The officers, privates, and followers of the royal army, were generally more intent on amassing fortunes by plunder and rapine, than on promoting a re-union of the dissevered members of the empire. Instead of increasing the number of real friends to royal government, they disgusted those that they found. The high spirited citizens of Carolina, impatient of their rapine and insolence, rejoiced in the prospect of freeing their country from its oppressors. Motives of this kind, together with a prevailing attachment to the cause of Independence, induced many to break through all ties to join Gen. Gates, and more to wish him the completest success.

The similarity of language and appearance between the British and American armies, gave opportunities for imposing on the inhabitants.

Lieutenant Colonel Tarleton with a party, by assuming the name and dress of Americans, passed themselves near Black river, for [166] the advance of General Gates' army. Some of the neighbouring militia were eagerly collected by Mr. Bradley, to co-operate with their supposed friends, but after some time the veil being thrown aside, Bradley and his volunteers were carried to Camden, and confined there as prisoners.

General Gates on reaching the frontier of South-Carolina, issued a proclamation inviting the patriotic citizens "to join heartily in rescuing themselves and their country, from the oppression of a government imposed on them by the ruffian hand of conquest." He also gave

> assurances of forgiveness and perfect security, to such of the unfortunate citizens as had been induced by the terror of sanguinary puishment, the menace of confiscation, and the arbitrary measures of military domination, apparently to acquiesce under the British government, and to make a forced declaration of allegiance and support to a tyranny, which the indignant souls of citizens resolved on freedom, inwardly revolted at with horror and detestation,

excepting only from this amnesty, "those who in the hour of devastation, had exercised acts of barbarity and depredation on the persons and property of their fellow citizens." The army with which Gates advanced, was by the arrival of Stephens' militia, increased nearly to 4000 men, but of this large number, the whole regular force was only 900 infantry and 70 cavalry. On the approach of Gates, Earl Cornwallis hastened from Charleston to Camden, and arrived there on the 14th. The force which his Lordship found collected on his arrival, was 1700 infantry and 300 cavalry. This inferior number would have justified a retreat, but he chose rather to stake his fortune on the decision of a battle. On the night of the 15th, he marched from Camden with his whole force, intending, to attack the Americans in their camp at Clermont. In the same night Gates, after ordering his baggage to the Waxhaws, put his army in motion, with an intention of advancing to an eligible position, about 8 miles from Camden. The American army was ordered to march at 10 o'clock P.M. in the following order.

Colonel Armand's advance [167] cavalry. Colonel Porterfield's light 1780
infantry, on the right flank of Colonel Armand's in Indian-file, 200 yards
from the road. Major Armstrong's light infantry in the same order as
Colonel Porterfield's on the left flank of the legion advanced guard of
foot, composed of the advanced piquets, first brigade of Maryland, second
brigade of Maryland—division of North-Carolina, Virginia rear guard,
volunteer cavalry, upon flanks of the baggage equally divided.

The light infantry upon each flank were ordered to march up and
support the calvary, if it should be attacked by the British cavalry,
and Colonel Armand was directed in that case to stand the attack at
all events.

The advance of both armies met in the night and engaged. Some
of the cavalry of Armand's legion, being wounded in the first fire fell
back on others, who recoiled so suddenly, that the first Maryland
regiment was broken, and the whole line of the army was thrown
into confusion. This first impression struck deep, and dispirited the
militia. The American army soon recovered its order, and both they
and their adversaries kept their ground, and occasionally skirmished
through the night. Colonel Porterfield, a most excellent officer, on
whose abilities General Gates particularly depended, was wounded
in the early part of this night attack. In the morning a severe and
general engagement took place. At the first onset, the great body of
the Virginia militia, who formed the left wing of the army, on being
charged with fixed bayonets by the British infantry, threw down their
arms, and with the utmost precipitation fled from the field. A
considerable part of the North-Carolina militia followed the unworthy
example, but the continentals who formed the right wing of the
army, inferior as they were in numbers to the British, stood their
ground and maintained the conflict with great resolution. Never did
men acquit themselves better: for some time they had clearly the
advantage of their opponents, and were in possession of a considerable
body of prisoners: overpowered at last by numbers, and nearly
surrounded by the enemy, they were compelled reluctantly to leave
the ground. In justice [168] to the North-Carolina militia, it should
be remarked that part of the brigade commanded by Gen. Gregory
acquitted themselves well. They were formed immediately on the

left of the continentals, and kept the field while they had a cartridge to fire. Gen. Gregory himself was twice wounded by a bayonet in bringing off his men, and several of his brigade, who were made prisoners, had no wounds except from bayonets.* Two hundred and ninety American wounded prisoners were carried into Camden, after this action, of this number 206 were continentals, 82, were North-Carolina militia, and 2 were Virginia militia. The resistance made by each corps, may in some degree be estimated from the number of wounded. The Americans lost the whole of their artillery, eight field pieces, upwards of 200 waggons, and the greatest part of their baggage, almost all their officers were separated from their respective commands. Every corps was broken in action and dispersed. The fugitives who fled by the common road, were pursued above 20 miles by the horse of Tarleton's legion, and the way was covered with arms, baggage and waggons. Baron de Kalb, the second in command, a brave and experienced officer, was taken prisoner and died on the next day of his wounds. The baron who was a German by birth, had long been in the French service. He had travelled through the British provinces, about the time of the stamp act, and is said to have reported to his superiors on his return, "that the colonists were so firmly and universally attached to Great Britain, that nothing could shake their loyalty." The Congress resolved that a monument should be erected to his memory in Annapolis, with a very honorable inscription. General Rutherford of North-Carolina, was wounded and taken prisoner.

The royal army fought with great bravery, but the completeness of their victory was in a great degree owing to their superiority in cavalry, and the precipitate flight of the American militia. Their whole loss is supposed to have amounted to several hundreds. To add to the [169] distresses of the Americans, the defeat of Gates was immediately followed by the surprise and dispersion of Sumter's corps. While the former was advancing near to the British army, the latter who had previously taken post between Camden and Charleston, took a number of prisoners and captured sundry British stores,

1780

* This detail was furnished by Mr. Williamson, surgeon-general of the North-Carolina militia, who after the battle went into Camden with a flag.

together with their convoy. On hearing of the defeat of his superior officer, he began to retreat with his prisoners and stores. Tarleton with his legion, and a detachment of infantry, pursued with such celerity and address as to overtake and surprize this party at Fishing Creek. The British rode into their camp before they were prepared for defence. The retreating Americans, having been four days with little or no sleep, were more obedient to the calls of nature, than attentive to her first law self-preservation. Sumter had taken every prudent precaution to prevent a surprise, but his videttes were so overcome with fatigue, that they neglected their duty. With great difficulty he got a few to stand their ground for a short time, but the greater part of his corps fled to the river or the woods. He lost all his artillery, and his whole detachment was either killed, captured or dispersed. The prisoners he had lately taken were all retaken. On the 17th and 18th of Aug. about 150 of Gates' army rendezvoused at Charlotte. These had reason to apprehend that they would be immediately pursued and cut to pieces. There was no magazine of provisions in the town, and it was without any kind of defence. It was therefore concluded to retreat to Salisbury. A circumstantial detail of this, would be the picture of complicated wretchedness. There were more wounded men than could be conveniently carried off. The inhabitants hourly expecting the British to advance into their settlement, and generally intending to flee, could not attend to the accommodation of the suffering soldiers. Objects of distress occurred in every quarter. There were many who stood in need of kind assistance, but there were few who could give it to them. Several men were to be seen with but one arm, and some without any. Anxiety, pain and dejection, poverty, hurry and confusion, promiscuously marked the [170] gloomy scene. Under these circumstances the remains of that numerous army, which had lately caused such terror to the friends of Great-Britain, retreated to Salisbury and soon after to Hillsborough. General Gates had previously retired to this last place, and was there in concert with the government of North-Carolina, devising plans of defense, and for renewing military operations.

Though there was no army to oppose Lord Cornwallis, yet the season and bad health of his army, restrained him from pursuing his

1780

conquests. By the complete dispersion of the continental forces, the country was in his power. The present moment of triumph seemed therefore the most favorable conjuncture, for breaking the spirits of those who were attached to independence. To prevent their future co-operation with the armies of Congress, a severer policy was henceforward adopted.

Unfortunately for the inhabitants, this was taken up on grounds which involved thousands in distress, and not a few in the loss of life. The British conceived themselves in possession of the rights of sovereignty over a conquered country, and that therefore the efforts of the citizens, to assert their independence exposed them to the penal consequences of treason and rebellion. Influenced by these opinions, and transported with indignation against the inhabitants, they violated the rights which are held sacred between independent hostile nations. Orders were given by Lord Cornwallis "that all the inhabitants of the province, who had submitted, and who had taken part in this revolt, should be punished with the greatest rigor—that they should be imprisoned, and their whole property taken from them or destroyed." He also ordered in the most positive manner "that every militia man, who had born arms with the British, and afterwards joined the Americans, should be put to death." At Augusta, at Camden and elsewhere, several of the inhabitants were hanged in consequence of these orders. The men who suffered had been compelled by the necessities of their families, and the prospect of saving their property, to make an involuntary submission to the royal conquerors. Experience soon taught them the inefficacy of these submissions. This in [171] their opinion absolved them from the obligations of their engagements to support the royal cause, and left them at liberty to follow their inclinations. To treat men thus circumstanced, with the severity of punishment usually inflicted on deserters and traitors, might have a political tendency to discourage farther revolts, but the impartial world must regret that the unavoidable horrors of war, should be aggravated by such deliberate effusions of human blood.

Notwithstanding the decisive superiority of the British armies in South-Carolina, several of the most respectable citizens, though in the power of their conquerors, resisted every temptation to resume

1780

494

the character of subjects. To enforce a general submission, orders were given by lord Cornwallis immediately after his victory, to send out of South-Carolina a number of its principal citizens. Lieut. Gov. Gadsden, most of the civil and militia officers and some others, who had declined exchanging their paroles for the protection of British subjects, were taken up, put on board a vessel in the harbour, and sent to St. Augustine. General Moultrie remonstrated against the confinement and removal of these gentlemen, as contrary to their rights derived from the capitulation of Charleston. They at the same time challenged their adversaries to prove any conduct of theirs, which merited expulsion from their country and families. They received no farther satisfaction, than that the measure had been "adopted from motives of policy." To convince the inhabitants, that the conquerors were seriously resolved to remove from the country, all who refused to become subjects, an additional number of about thirty citizens of South-Carolina, who remained prisoners on parole, were sent off to the same place in less than three months. Gen. Rutherford and Col. Isaacs both of North-Carolina, who had been lately taken near Camden, were associated with them.

AUG. 27

To compel the re-establishment of British government, lord Cornwallis, in about four weeks after his victory, issued a proclamation for the sequestration of all estates belonging to the active friends of Independence. By [172] this he constituted

SEPT. 16

> John Cruden commissioner, with full power and authority, on the receipt of an order or warrant, to take into his possession the estates both real and personal (not included in the capitulation of Charleston) of those in the service or acting under the authority of the rebel Congress, and also the estates, both real and personal, of those persons who by an open avowal of rebellious principles, or by other notorious acts, manifested a wicked and desperate perseverance in opposing the re-establishment of his Majesty's just and lawful authority;

1780

and it was farther declared

> That any person or persons obstructing or impeding the said commissioner in the execution of his duty, by the concealment or removal of property or otherwise, should on conviction be punished as aiding and abetting rebellion.

An adherent to Independence was now considered as one who courted exile, poverty and ruin. Many yielded to the temptation, and became British subjects. The mischievous effects of slavery, in facilitating the conquest of the country, now became apparent. As the slaves had no interest at stake, the subjugation of the State was a matter of no consequence to them. Instead of aiding in its defence, they by a variety of means threw the weight of their little influence into the opposite scale.

Though numbers broke through all the ties which bound them to support the cause of America, illustrious sacrifices were made at the shrine of liberty. Several of the richest men in the state suffered their fortunes to remain in the power and possession of their conquerors, rather than stain their honor, by joining the enemies of their country. The patriotism of the ladies contributed much to this firmness. They crowded on board prison ships, and other places of confinement, to solace their suffering countrymen. While the conquerors were regaling themselves at concerts and assemblies, they could obtain very few of the fair sex to associate with them; but no sooner was an American officer introduced as a prisoner, than his company was sought for, and his person treated with every possible mark of attention and respect. On other occasions the ladies in a great measure [173] retired from the public eye, wept over the distresses of their country, and gave every proof of the warmest attachment to its suffering cause. Among the numbers who were banished from their families, and whose property was seized by the conquerors, many examples could be produced of ladies cheerfully parting with their sons, husbands and brothers, exhorting them to fortitude and perseverance; and repeatedly entreating them never to suffer family-attachments to interfere with the duty they owed to their country. When, in the progress of the war, they were also comprehended under a general sentence of banishment, with equal resolution they parted with their native country, and the many endearments of home—followed their husbands into prison-ships and distant lands, where they were reduced to the necessity of receiving charity.

Animated by such examples, as well as by a high sense of honor and the love of their country, a great proportion of the gentlemen of

1780

South-Carolina deliberately adhered to their first resolution, of risquing life and fortune in support of their liberties. Hitherto the royal forces in South-Carolina had been attended with almost uninterrupted success. Their standards overspread the country, penetrated into every quarter, and triumphed over all opposition.

The British ministry by this flattering posture of affairs, were once more intoxicated with the hope of subjugating America. New plans were formed, and great expectations indulged, of speedily re-uniting the dissevered members of the empire. It was now asserted with a confidence bordering on presumption, that such troops as fought at Camden, put under such a commander as Lord Cornwallis, would soon extirpate rebellion, so effectually as to leave no vestige of it in America. The British ministry and army by an impious confidence in their own wisdom and prowess, were duly prepared to give, in their approaching downfal, an useful lesson to the world.

The disaster of the army under General Gates, overspread at first the face of American affairs, with a dismal [174] gloom, but the day of prosperity to the United States, began as will appear in the sequel, from that moment to dawn. Their prospects brightened up, while those of their enemies were obscured by disgrace, broken by defeat, and at last covered with ruin. Elated with their victories, the conquerors grew more insolent and rapacious, while the real friends of independence became resolute and determined. 1780

We have seen Sumter penetrating into South-Carolina, and recommencing a military opposition to British government. Soon after that event, he was promoted by Governor Rutledge, to the rank of Brigadier General. About the same time Marion was promoted to the same rank, and in the northeastern extremities of the State, successfully prosecuted a similar plan. This valuable officer after the surrender of Charleston, retreated to North-Carolina. On the advance of General Gates, he obtained a command of sixteen men. With these he penetrated through the country, and took a position near the Santee. On the defeat of General Gates, he was compelled to abandon the State, but returned after an absence of a few days. For several weeks he had under his command only 70 men. At one time hardships and dangers reduced that number to 25, yet with this inconsiderable number he secured himself in the midst of surrounding foes. Various schemes were tried to detach the inhabitants from co-operating with him. Major Wemys burned scores of houses on Pedee, Lynch's creek and Black river, belonging to such as were supposed to do duty with Marion, or to be subservient to his views. This had an effect different from what was intended. Revenge and despair co-operated with patriotism, to make these ruined men keep the field. Having no houses to shelter them, the camps of their countrymen became their homes. For several months, Marion and his party were obliged to sleep in the open air, and to shelter themselves in the recesses of deep swamps. From these retreats they sallied out, whenever an opportunity of harrassing the enemy, or of serving their country presented itself.

1780   [175] Opposition to British government was not wholly confined to the parties commanded by Sumter and Marion. It was at no time altogether extinct in the extremities of the State. The disposition to revolt, which had been excited on the approach of General Gates, was not extinguished by his defeat. The spirit of the people was overawed, but not subdued. The severity with which revolters who fell into the hands of the British were treated, induced those who escaped to persevere and seek safety in swamps.

From the time of the general submission of the inhabitants in 1780, pains had been taken to encrease the royal force by the co-operation of the yeomanry of the country. The British persuaded the people to form a royal militia, by representing that every prospect of succeeding in their scheme of independence was annihilated, and that a farther opposition would only be a prolongation of their distresses, if not their utter ruin. Major Ferguson of the 71st regiment, was particularly active in this business. He visited the settlements of the disaffected to the American cause, and collected a corps of militia of that description, from which much active service was expected. He advanced to the northwestern settlements, to hold communication with the loyalists of both Carolinas. From his presence, together with assurances of an early movement of the royal army into North-Carolina, it was hoped that the friends of royal government would be roused to activity in the service of their King. In the mean time every preparation was made for urging offensive operations, as soon as the season and the state of the stores would permit.

That spirit of enterprize, which has already been mentioned as beginning to revive among the American militia about this time, prompted Col. Clarke to make an attempt on the British post at Augusta in Georgia; but in this he failed and was obliged to retreat. Major Ferguson with the hope of intercepting his party, kept near the mountains and at a considerable distance from support. These circumstances, together with the depredations of the loyalists, induced those hardy republicans, who reside on the west side of the Alleghany mountains, [176] to form an enterprize for reducing that distinguished partizan. This was done of their own motion, without any direction from the governments of America, or from the officers of the continental army.

  1780

There was, without any apparent design, a powerful combination of several detached commanders of several adjacent States, with their respective commands of militia. Col. Campbell of Virginia, Colonels Cleveland, Shelby, Sevier, and M'Dowel of North Carolina, together with Colonels Lacey, Hawthorn and Hill, of South-Carolina, all rendezvoused together, with a number of men amounting to 1600, though they were under no general command, and though they were not called upon to embody by any common authority, or indeed by any authority at all, but that of a general impulse on their own minds. They had so little of the mechanism of a regular army, that the Colonels of some of the States by common consent, commanded each day alternately. The hardships these volunteers underwent were very great. Some of them subsisted for weeks together, without tasting bread or salt, or spiritous liquors, and slept in the woods without blankets. The running stream quenched their thirst. At night the earth afforded them a bed, and the heavens, or at most the limbs of trees were their only covering. Ears of corn or pompions thrown into the fire, with occasional supplies of beef or venison, killed and roasted in the woods, were the chief articles of their provisions. They had neither commissaries, quarter-masters, nor stores of any kind. They selected about a thousand of their best men, and mounted them on their fleetest horses. These attacked Major Ferguson on the top of King's mountain, near the confines of North and South-Carolina. The Americans formed three parties. Col. Lacey of South-Carolina led one, which attacked on the west end. The two others were commanded by Cols. Campbell and Cleveland, one of which attacked on the east

  OCT. 7

end and the other in the centre. Ferguson with great boldness attacked the assailants with fixed bayonets, and compelled them successively to retire, but they only fell back a little way, and getting behind trees and rocks, renewed [177] their fire in almost every direction. The British being uncovered, were aimed at by the American marksmen, and many of them were slain. An unusual number of the killed were found to have been shot in the head. Riflemen took off riflemen with such exactness, that they killed each other when taking sight, so effectually that their eyes remained after they were dead, one shut and the other open, in the usual manner of marksmen when levelling at their object. Major Ferguson displayed as much bravery as was possible in his situation: But his encampment on the top of the mountain was not well chosen, as it gave the Americans an opportunity of covering themselves in their approaches. Had he pursued his march on charging and driving the first party of the militia which gave way, he might have got off with the most of his men, but his unconquerable spirit disdained either to flee or to surrender. After a severe conflict he received a mortal wound. No chance of escape being left, and all prospect of successful resistance being at an end, the contest was ended by the submission of the survivors. Upwards of 800 became prisoners, and 225 had been previously killed or wounded. Very few of the assailants fell, but in their number was Col. Williams a distinguished militia officer in Ninety-Six district, who had been very active in opposing the re-establishment of British government. Ten of the royal militia who had surrendered were hanged by their conquerors. They were provoked to this measure by the severity of the British, who had lately hanged several of the captured Americans, in South-Carolina and Georgia. They also alleged that the men who suffered were guilty of previous felonies, for which their lives were forfeited by the laws of the land. The fall of Ferguson was in itself a great loss to the royal cause. He possessed superior abilities as a partizan, and his spirit of enterprise was uncommon. To a distinguished capacity for planning great designs, he also added the practical abilities necessary to carry them into execution. The unexpected advantage which the Americans gained over him and his party, in a great degree frustrated a well concerted scheme for strengthening [178] the British army by the co-operation of the tory inhabitants, whom he had undertaken to discipline and prepare for active service. The total rout of the party, which had joined Major Ferguson, operated as a check on the future exertions of the loyalists. The same timid caution, which made them averse to joining their countrymen in opposing the claims of Great Britain, restrained them from risquing any more in support of the royal cause. Henceforward they waited to see how the scales were likely to incline, and reserved themselves till the British army, by its own unassisted efforts, should gain a decided superiority.

In a few weeks after the general action near Camden, Lord Cornwallis left a small force in that village, and marched with the main army towards Salisbury, intending to push forwards in that direction. While on his way thither, the North Carolina militia was very industrious and successful in annoying his detachments. Riflemen frequently penetrated near his camp, and from behind trees made sure of their objects. The late conquerors found their situation very uneasy, being exposed to unseen dangers if they attempted to make an excursion of only a few hundred yards from their main body. The defeat of Major Ferguson, added to these circumstances, gave a serious alarm to lord Cornwallis, and he soon after retreated to Winnsborough. As he retired, the militia took several of his waggons, and single men often rode up within gunshot of his army, discharged their pieces, and made their escape. The panic occasioned by the defeat of Gen. Gates had in a great measure worn off. The defeat of Major Ferguson and the consequent retreat of lord Cornwallis, encouraged the American militia to take the field, and the necessity of the times induced them to submit to stricter discipline. Sumter soon after the dispersion of his corps on the 18th of August, collected a band of volunteers, partly from new adventurers, and partly from those who had escaped on that day. With these, though for three months there was no continental army in the State, he constantly kept the field in support of American independence. He varied his position from [179] time to time about Evoree, Broad and Tyger rivers, and had frequent skirmishes with his adversaries. Having mounted his followers he infested the British parties with frequent incursions—beat up their quarters—intercepted their convoys, and so harrassed them with successive alarms, that their movements could not be made but with caution and difficulty. His spirit of enterprize was so particularly injurious to the British, that they laid sundry plans for destroying his force, but they all failed in the execution. He was attacked at Broad river by Major Wemys, commanding a corps of infantry and dragoons. In this action the British were defeated, and their commanding officer taken prisoner. Eight days after he was attacked at Black-Stocks, near Tyger river, by Lieut. Col. Tarleton. The attack was begun with 170 dragoons and 80 men of the 63d regiment. A considerable part of Sumter's force had been thrown into a large log barn, from the apertures of which they fired with security. Many of the 63d regiment were killed. Tarleton charged with his cavalry, but being unable to dislodge the Americans retreated, and Sumter was left in quiet possession of the field. The loss of the British in this action was considerable. Among their killed were three officers, Major Money, Lieut. Gibson and Cope. The Americans lost very few, but Gen. Sumter received a wound, which for several months interrupted his gallant enterprizes in behalf of his country. His zeal and activity in animating the militia, when they were discouraged by repeated defeats, and the bravery and good conduct he displayed in sundry attacks on the British detachments, procured him the applause of his countrymen, and the thanks of Congress.

For the three months which followed the defeat of the American army near Camden, Gen. Gates was industriously preparing to take the field. Having collected a force at Hillsbury he advanced to Salisbury, and very soon after to Charlotte. He had done every thing in his power to repair the injuries of his defeat, and was again in a condition to face the enemy; but from that [180] influence which popular opinion has over public affairs in a commonwealth, Congress resolved to supersede him, and to order a court of enquiry to be held on his conduct. This was founded on a former resolve, that whoever lost a post should be subject to a court of inquiry. The cases were no ways parallel, he had lost a battle but not a post. The only charge that could be exhibited against Gen. Gates was that he had been defeated. His enemies could accuse him of no military crime, unless that to be unsuccessful might be reckoned so. The public, sore with their losses, were desirous of a change, and Congress found

NOV. 1

NOV. 2

NOV.

1780

it necessary to gratify them, though at the expence of the feelings of one of their best, and till August 1780, one of their most successful officers. Virginia did not so soon forget Saratoga. When Gen. Gates was at Richmond on his way home from Carolina, the house of Burgesses of that State unanimously resolved

DEC. 28

> that a committee of four be appointed to wait on Gen. Gates, and assure him of their high regard and esteem, and that the remembrance of his former glorious services could not be obliterated by any reverse of fortune; but that ever mindful of his great merit, they would omit no opportunity of testifying to the world the gratitude which the country owed to him in his military character.

These events together with a few unimportant skirmishes not worthy of being particularly mentioned, closed the campaign of 1780 in the southern States. They afforded ample evidence of the folly of prosecuting the American war. Though British conquests had rapidly succeeded each other, yet no advantages accrued to the victors. The minds of the people were unsubdued, or rather more alienated from every idea of returning to their former allegiance. Such was their temper, that the expence of retaining them in subjection, would have exceeded all the profits of the conquest. British garrisons kept down open resistance in the vicinity of the places where they were established, but as soon as they were withdrawn, and the people left to themselves, a spirit of revolt hostile to Great-Britain always displayed itself, [181] and the standard of independence whensoever it was prudently raised, never wanted followers from the active and spirited part of the community.

CHAPTER XX

Campaign of 1780, in the Northern States.

WHILE THE WAR RAGED in South-Carolina, the campaign of 1780, in the northern States was barren of important events. At the close of the preceding campaign, the American northern army took post at Morristown and built themselves huts, agreeably to the practice which had been first introduced at Valley-Forge. This position was well calculated to cover the country from the excursions of the British, being only 20 miles from New-York.

Lord Sterling made an ineffectual attempt to surprise a party of the enemy on Staten-Island. While he was on the island, a number of persons from the Jersey side passed over and plundered the inhabitants, who had submitted to the British government. In these times of confusion, licentious persons fixed themselves near the lines, which divided the British from the Americans. Whensoever an opportunity offered, they were in the habit of going within the settlements of the opposite party, and under the pretence of distressing their enemies, committed the most shameful depredations. In the first months of the year 1780, while the royal army was weakened by the expedition against Charleston, the British were apprehensive for their safety in New-York. The rare circumstance which then existed of a connexion between the main and York island, by means of ice seemed to invite to the enterprise, but the force and equipments of the American army were unequal to it. Lieutenant General Kniphausen, who then commanded in New-York, apprehending such a design, embodied the inhabitants of the city as a militia for its defence. They very chearfully formed themselves into companies, and discovered great zeal in the service.

[182] An incursion was made into Jersey from New-York with 5000 men, commanded by Lieutenant General Kniphausen. They landed at Elizabeth-town, and proceeded to Connecticut farms. In this neighbourhood lived the Reverend Mr. James Caldwell, a Presbyterian clergyman of great activity, ability and influence, whose successful exertions in animating the Jersey militia to defend their rights, had rendered him particularly obnoxious to the British. When the royal forces were on their way into the country, a soldier came to his house in his absence and shot his wife Mrs. Caldwell instantly dead, by leveling his piece directly at her through the window of the room, in which she was sitting with her children. Her body at the request of an officer of the new levies, was moved to some distance, and then the house and every thing in it was reduced to ashes. The British burnt about 12 other houses, and also the Presbyterian church, and then proceeded to Springfield. As they advanced they were annoyed by Colonel Dayton with a few militia. On their approach to the bridge near the town, they were farther opposed by General Maxwell, who with a few continental troops was prepared to dispute its passage. They made a halt and soon after returned to Elizabeth town. Before they had retreated, the whole American army at Morristown marched to oppose them. While this royal detachment was in Jersey, Sir Henry Clinton returned with his victorious troops from Charleston to New-York. He ordered a reinforcement to Kniphausen, and the whole advanced a second time towards Springfield.

1780
JUNE 16

They were now opposed by General Greene, with a considerable body of continental troops. Colonel Angel with his regiment and a piece of artillery was posted to secure the bridge in front of the town. A severe action took place which lasted forty minutes. Superior numbers forced the Americans to retire. General Greene took post with his troops on a range of hills, in hopes of being attacked. Instead of this the British began to burn the town. Near fifty dwelling houses were reduced to ashes. The British then retreated, but were pursued by the enraged militia, till they entered Elizabethtown. [183] The next day they set out on their return to New-York. The loss of the Americans in the action was about 80, and that of the British was supposed to be considerably more. It is difficult to tell what was the precise object of this expedition. Perhaps the royal commanders hoped to get possession of Morristown, and to destroy the American stores. Perhaps they flattered themselves that the inhabitants were so dispirited by the recent loss of Charlestown, that they would submit without resistance; and that the soldiers of the continental army would desert to them: But if these were their views, they were disappointed in both. The firm opposition which was made by the Jersey farmers, contrasted with the conduct of the same people in the year 1776, made it evident that not only their aversion to Great-Britain, continued in full force; but that the practical habits of service and danger had improved the country militia, so as to bring them near to an equality with regular troops.

By such desultory operations, were hostilities carried on at this time in the northern States. Individuals were killed, houses were burnt, and much mischief done; but nothing was effected which tended either to reconcilement or subjugation.

The loyal Americans who had fled within the British lines, commonly called refugees, reduced a predatory war into system. On their petition to Sir Henry Clinton, they had been in the year 1779, permitted to set up a distinct government in New-York, under a jurisdiction called the honorable board of associated loyalists. They had something like a fleet of small privateers and cruisers, by the aid of which, they committed various depredations. A party of them who had formerly belonged to Massachusetts, went to Nantucket, broke open the warehouses, and carried off every thing that fell in their way. They also carried off two loaded brigs and two or three schooners. In a proclamation they left behind them, they observed "that they had been deprived of their property, and compelled to abandon their dwellings, friends and connections. And that they conceived themselves warranted by the laws of God and man, to wage [184] war against their persecutors, and to endeavour by every means in their power, to obtain compensation for their sufferings." These associated loyalists eagerly embraced every adventure, which gratified either their avarice or their revenge. Their enterprises were highly lucrative to themselves, and extremely distressing to the Americans. Their knowledge of the country and superior means of transportation, enabled them to make hasty descents and successful enterprises. A war of plunder in which the feelings of humanity were often suspended, and which tended to no valuable public purpose, was carried on in this shameful manner, from the double excitements of profit and revenge. The adjoining coasts of the continent, and especially the maritime parts of New-Jersey, became scenes of waste and havoc. 1780

The distress which the Americans suffered from the diminished value of their currency, though felt in the year 1778 and still more so in the year 1779, did not arrive to its highest pitch till the year 1780. Under the pressure of sufferings from this cause, the officers of the Jersey line addressed a memorial to their state legislature, setting forth "that four months pay of a private, would not procure for his family a single bushel of wheat, that the pay of a Colonel would not purchase oats for his horse; that a common laborer or express rider received four times as much as an American officer." They urged "that unless a speedy and ample remedy was provided, the total dissolution of their line was inevitable," and concluded with saying "that their pay should either be made up in Mexican dollars or in something equivalent." In addition to the insufficiency of their pay and support, other causes of discontent prevailed. The original idea of a continental army, to be raised, paid, subsisted and regulated upon an equal and uniform principle, had been in a great measure exchanged for State establishments. This mischievous measure partly originated from necessity, for State credit was not quite so much depreciated as continental. Congress not possessing the means of

1780

supporting their army, devolved the business on the component parts of the confederacy. Some States, from their [185] internal ability and local advantages, furnished their troops not only with cloathing, but with many conveniencies. Others supplied them with some necessaries, but on a more contracted scale. A few from their particular situation could do little or nothing at all. The officers and men in the routine of duty, mixed daily and compared circumstances. Those who fared worse than others, were dissatisfied with a service which made such injurious distinctions. From causes of this kind, superadded to a complication of wants and sufferings, a disposition to mutiny began to shew itself in the American army. This broke forth into full action among the soldiers, which were stationed at fort Schuyler. Thirty-one of the men of that garrison went off in a body. Being pursued sixteen of them were overtaken, and thirteen of the sixteen, were instantly killed. About the same time, two regiments of Connecticut troops mutinied and got under arms. They determined to return home, or to gain subsistence at the point of the bayonet. Their officers reasoned with them, and urged every argument, that could either interest their pride or their passions. They were reminded of their good conduct, of the important objects for which they were contending, but their answer was "our sufferings are too great and we want present relief." After much expostulation they were at length prevailed upon to go to their hutts. It is remarkable, that this mutinous disposition of the Connecticut troops, was in a great measure quelled by the Pennsylvania line, which in a few months, as shall hereafter be related, planned and executed a much more serious revolt, than that which they now suppressed. While the army was in this feverish state of discontent from their accumulated distresses, a printed paper addressed to the soldiers of the continental army, was circulated in the American camp. This was in the following words.

> The time is at length arrived, when all the artifices and falsehoods of the Congress and of your commanders, can no longer conceal from you the miseries of your situation. You are neither fed, cloathed nor paid. Your numbers are wasting away by sickness, famine and nakedness, and [186] rapidly so by the period of your stipulated services being expired. This is now the period to fly from slavery and fraud.

1780

I am happy in acquainting the old countrymen that the affairs of Ireland are fully settled, and that Great Britain and Ireland are united as well from interest as from affection. I need not tell you who are born in America, that you have been cheated and abused. You are both sensible that in order to procure your liberty you must quit your leaders, and join your real friends, who scorn to impose upon you, and who will receive you with open arms, kindly forgiving all your errors. You are told you are surrounded by a numerous militia. This is also false. Associate then together, make use of your firelocks, and join the British army, where you will be permitted to dispose of yourselves as you please.

About the same time or rather a little before, the news arrived of the reduction of Charleston, and the capture of the whole American southern army. Such was the firmness of the common soldiery, and so strong their attachment to the cause of their country, that though danger impelled, want urged, and British favor invited them to a change of sides, yet on the arrival of but a scanty supply of meat for their immediate subsistence, military duty was cheerfully performed, and no uncommon desertion took place.

So great were the necessities of the American army, that Gen. Washington was obliged to call on the magistrates of the adjacent counties for specified quantities of provisions, to be supplied in a given number of days. At other times he was compelled to send out detachments of his troops, to take provisions at the point of the bayonet from the citizens. This expedient at length failed, for the country in the vicinity of the army afforded no further supplies. These impressments were not only injurious to the morals and discipline of the army, but tended to alienate the affections of the people. Much of the support, which the American general had previously experienced from the inhabitants, proceeded from the difference of treatment they received from their own army, [187] compared with what they suffered from the British. The General, whom the inhabitants hitherto regarded as their protector, had now no alternative but to disband his troops, or to support them by force. The situation of Gen. Washington was eminently embarrassing. The army looked to him for provisions, the inhabitants for protection of their property. To supply the one, and not offend the other, seemed little less than an impossibility. To preserve order and subordination in an army of free republicans, even when well fed, paid and clothed, would have been a work of difficulty, but to retain them in service and restrain them with discipline, when destitute, not only of the comforts, but often of the necessaries of life, required address and abilities of such magnitude as are rarely found in human nature. In this choice of difficulties Gen. Washington not only kept his army together, but conducted with so much discretion, as to command the approbation both of the army and of the citizens.

So great a scarcity, in a country usually abounding with provisions, appears extraordinary, but various remote causes had concurred about this time to produce an unprecedented deficiency. The seasons both in 1779 and 1780 were unfavorable to the crops. The labors of the husbandmen, who were attached to the cause of independence, had been frequently interrupted by the calls for militia duty. Those who cared for neither side, or who from principles of religion held the unlawfulness of war, or who were secretly attached to the royal interest, had been very deficient in industry. Such sometimes reasoned that all labor on their farms, beyond a bare supply of their own necessities, was unavailing; but the principal cause of the sufferings of the army was the daily diminishing value of the continental bills of credit. The farmers found, that the longer they delayed the payment of taxes, the less quantity of country produce would discharge the stipulated sum. They also observed, that the longer they kept their grain on hand, the more of the paper currency was obtained in exchange for it. This either discouraged them from selling, or made them very tardy in coming to market. Many secreted

1780   their provisions [188] and denied their having any, while others who were contiguous to the British, secretly sold to them for gold or silver. The patriotism which at the commencement of the war had led so many to sacrifice property for the good of their country, had in a great degree subsided. Though they still retained their good wishes for the cause, yet these did not carry them so far as to induce a willingness to exchange the hard earned produce of their farms, for a paper currency of a daily diminishing value. For provisions carried to New-York, the farmers received real money, but for what was carried to the Americans, they only received paper. The value of the first was known, of the other daily varying, but in an unceasing progression from bad to worse. Laws were made against this intercourse, but they were executed in the manner laws uniformly have been in the evasion of which multitudes find an immediate interest.

In addition to these disasters from short crops, and depreciating money, disorder and confusion pervaded the departments for supplying the army. Systems for these purposes had been hastily adopted, and were very inadequate to the end proposed. To provide for an army under the best establishments, and with a full military chest, is a work of difficulty, and though guarded by the precautions which time and experience have suggested, opens a door to many frauds; but it was the hard case of the Americans to be called on to discharge this duty without sufficient knowledge of the business, and under ill digested systems, and with a paper currency that was not two days of the same value. Abuses crept in; frauds were practiced, and oeconomy was exiled.

To obviate these evils, Congress adopted the expedient of sending a committee of their own body to the camp of their main army. Mr. Schuyler of New-York, Mr. Peabody of New-Hampshire, and Mr. Mathews of South-Carolina, were appointed. They were furnished with ample powers and instructions to reform abuses—to alter preceding systems, and to establish new ones in their room. This committee proceeded to camp in May 1780, and thence wrote sundry letters to Congress [189] and the States, in which they confirmed the representations previously made of the distresses and disorders every where prevalent. In particular they stated

1780

that the army was unpaid for five months—that it seldom had more than six days provision in advance, and was on several occasions for sundry successive days without meat—that the army was destitute of forage—that the medical department had neither sugar, coffee, tea, chocolate, wine nor spiritous liquors of any kind—that every department of the army was without money, and had not even the shadow of credit left—that the patience of the soldiers, born down by the pressure of complicated sufferings, was on the point of being exhausted.

A tide of misfortunes from all quarters was at this time pouring in upon the United-States. There appeared not however, in their public bodies, the smallest disposition to purchase safety by concessions of any sort. They seemed to rise in the midst of their distresses, and to gain strength from the pressure of calamities. When Congress could neither command money nor credit for the subsistence of their army, the citizens of Philadelphia formed an association to procure a supply of necessary articles for their suffering soldiers. The sum of 300,000 dollars was subscribed in a few days, and converted into a bank, the principal design of which was to purchase provisions for the troops, in the most prompt and efficacious manner. The advantages of this institution were great, and particularly enhanced by the critical time in which it was instituted. The loss of Charleston, and the subsequent British victories in Carolina, produced effects directly the reverse of what were expected. It being the deliberate resolution of the Americans never to return to the government of Great-Britain, such unfavorable events as threatened the subversion of independence, operated as incentives to their exertions. The patriotic flame which had blazed forth in the beginning of the war was re-kindled. A willingness to do, and to suffer, in the cause of American liberty, was revived in the breasts of many. These dispositions were invigorated [190] by private assurances, that his most Christian Majesty would, in the course of the campaign, send a powerful armament to their aid. To excite the States to be in readiness for this event, Congress circulated among them an address of which the following is a part.

1780

> The crisis calls for exertion. Much is to be done in a little time, and every motive that can stimulate the mind of man presents itself to view. No period has occurred in this long and glorious struggle, in which indecision would be so destructive on the one hand, and on the other, no conjuncture has been more favorable to great and deciding efforts.

The powers of the committee of Congress in the American camp, were enlarged so far as to authorize them to frame and execute such plans as, in their opinion, would most effectually draw forth the resources of the country, in co-operating with the armament expected from France. In this character they wrote sundry letters to the States, stimulating them to vigorous exertions. It was agreed to make arrangements for bringing into the field 35,000 effective men, and to call on the States for specific supplies of every thing necessary for their support. To obtain the men it was proposed to complete the regular regiments by draughts from the militia, and to make up what they fell short of 35,000 effectives, by calling forth more of the militia. Every motive concurred to rouse the activity of the inhabitants. The States nearly exhausted with the war, ardently wished for its determination. An opportunity now offered for striking a decisive blow, that might at once, as they supposed, rid the country of its distresses. The only thing required on the part of the United States, was to bring into the field 35,000 men, and to make effectual arrangements for their support. The tardiness of deliberation in Congress was in a great measure done away, by the full powers given to their committee in camp. Accurate estimates were made of every article of supply, necessary for the ensuing campaign. These, and also the numbers of men wanted, were quotaed on the ten northern States in proportion to their abilities and numbers. In conformity to these requisitions, [191] vigorous resolutions were adopted for carrying them into effect. 1780 Where voluntary enlistments fell short of the proposed number, the deficiencies were, by the laws of several States, to be made up by draughts or lots from the militia. The towns in New-England and the counties in the middle States, were respectively called on for a specified number of men. Such was the zeal of the people in New-England, that neighbours would often club together, to engage one of their number to go into the army. Being without money, in conformity to the practice usual in the early stages of society, they paid for military duty with cattle. Twenty head were frequently given as a reward for eighteen months service. Maryland directed her Lieutenants of counties to class all the property in their respective counties, into as many equal classes as there were men wanted, and each class was by law obliged within ten days thereafter, to furnish an able bodied recruit to serve during the war, and in case of their neglecting or refusing so to do, the county Lieutenants were authorised to procure men at their expence, at any rate not exceeding 15 pounds in every hundred pounds worth of property, classed agreeably to the law. Virginia also classed her citizens, and called upon the respective classes for every fifteenth man for public service. Pennsylvania concentered the requisite power in her President Joseph Reed, and authorized him to draw forth the resources of the State, under certain limitations, and if necessary to declare martial law over the State. The legislative part of these complicated arrangements was speedily passed, but the execution though uncommonly vigorous lagged far behind. Few occasions could occur in which it might so fairly be tried, to what extent in conducting a war, a variety of wills might be brought to act in unison. The result of the experiment was, that however favorable republics may be to the liberty and happiness of the people in the time of peace, they will be greatly deficient in that vigor and dispatch, which military operations require, unless they imitate the policy of monarchies, by committing the executive departments of government to the direction of a single will.

1780   [192] While these preparations were making in America, the armament which had been promised by his most Christian Majesty was on its way. As soon as it was known in France, that a resolution was adopted, to send out troops to the United States, the young French nobility discovered the greatest zeal to be employed on that service. Court favor was scarcely ever solicited with more earnestness, than was the honor of serving under General Washington. The number of applicants was much greater than the service required. The disposition to support the American revolution, was not only prevalent in the court of France, but it animated the whole body of the nation. The winds and waves did not second the ardent wishes of the French troops. Though they sailed from France on the first of May 1780, they did not reach a port in the United States till the 10th of July following. On that day to the great joy of the Americans, M. de Ternay arrived at Rhode-Island, with a squadron of seven sail of the line, five frigates, and five smaller armed vessels. He likewise convoyed a fleet of transports with four old French regiments, besides the legion de Lauzun, and a battalion of artillery, amounting in the whole to 6000 men, all under the command of Lieutenant General Count de Rochambeau. To the French as soon as they landed possession was given of the forts and batteries on the island, and by their exertions, they were soon put in a high state of defence. In a

few days after their arrival, an address of congratulation from the
General Assembly of the State of Rhode-Island, was presented to
Count de Rochambeau, in which they expressed "their most grateful
sense of the magnanimous aid afforded to the United States, by their
illustrious friend and ally the Monarch of France, and also gave
assurances of every exertion in their power for the supply of the
French forces, with all manner of refreshments and necessaries for
rendering the service happy and agreeable." Rochambeau declared
in his answer, "that he only brought over the vanguard of a much
greater force which was destined for their aid; that he was ordered
by the King his master to assure them, that his whole power should
be [193] exerted for their support:" "The French troops" he said   1780
"were under the strictest discipline, and acting under the orders of
General Washington, would live with the Americans as brethren. He
returned their compliments by an assurance, that as brethren, not
only his own life, but the lives of all those under his command were
devoted to their service."

Gen. Washington recommended in public orders to the American
officers, as a symbol of friendship and affection for their allies, to
wear black and white cockades, the ground to be of the first colour,
and the relief of the second.

The French troops, united both in interest and affection with the
Americans, ardently longed for an opportunity to co-operate with
them against the common enemy. The continental army wished for
the same with equal ardor. One circumstance alone seemed unfavourable to this spirit of enterprise. This was the deficient clothing
of the Americans. Some whole lines, officers as well as men, were
shabby, and a great proportion of the privates were without shirts.
Such troops, brought along side even of allies fully clad in the elegance
of uniformity, must have been more or less than men to feel no
degradation on the contrast.

Admiral Arbuthnot had only four sail of the line at New-York, when
M. de Ternay arrived at Rhode-Island. This inferiority was in three
days reversed, by the arrival of Admiral Greaves with six sail of the
line. The British Admiral, having now a superiority, proceeded to
Rhode-Island. He soon discovered that the French were perfectly
secure from any attack by sea. Sir Henry Clinton, who had returned

in the preceding month with his victorious troops from Charleston, embarked about 8000 of his best men, and proceeded as far as Huntingdon-bay on Long-Island, with the apparent design of con-curring with the British fleet, in attacking the French force at Rhode-Island. When this movement took place, Gen. Washington set his army in motion, and proceeded to Peeks-kill. Had Sir Henry Clinton prosecuted what appeared to be his design, Gen. Washington intended to [194] have attacked New-York in his absence. Preparations were made for this purpose, but Sir Henry Clinton instantly turned about from Huntingdon-bay towards New-York.

In the mean time, the French fleet and army being blocked up at Rhode-Island, were incapacitated from cooperating with the Ameri-cans. Hopes were nevertheless indulged, that by the arrival of another fleet of his most Christian Majesty then in the West-Indies, under the command of Count de Guichen, the superiority would be so much in favor of the allies, as to enable them to prosecute their original intention, of attacking New-York. When the expectations of the Americans were raised to the highest pitch, and when they were in great forwardness of preparation to act in concert with their allies, intelligence arrived that Count de Guichen had sailed for France. This disappointment was extremely mortifying. The Americans had made uncommon exertions, on the idea of receiving such an aid from their allies, as would enable them to lay effectual siege to New-York, or to strike some decisive blow. Their towering expectations were in a moment levelled with the dust. Another campaign was anticipated, and new shades were added to the deep cloud, which for some time past had overshadowed American affairs.

The campaign of 1780, passed away in the northern States as has been related, in successive disappointments, and reiterated distresses. The country was exhausted, the continental currency expiring. The army for want of subsistence, kept inactive, and brooding over its calamities. While these disasters were openly menacing the ruin of the American cause, treachery was silently undermining it. A distin-guished officer engaged for a stipulated sum of money, to betray into the hands of the British an important post committed to his care. General Arnold who committed this foul crime was a native of Connecticut. That State, remarkable for the purity of its morals, for its republican principles and patriotism, was the birth place of a man to whom none of the other States have produced an equal. He had been among [195] the first to take up arms against Great-Britain, 1780 and to widen the breach between the Parent State and the colonies. His distinguished military talents had procured him every honor a greatful country could bestow. Poets and Painters had marked him as a suitable subject for the display of their respective abilities. He possessed an elevated seat in the hearts of his countrymen, and was in the full enjoyment of a substantial fame, for the purchase of which, the wealth of worlds would have been insufficient. His country had not only loaded him with honors, but forgiven him his crimes. Though in his accounts against the States there was much room to suspect fraud and imposition, yet the recollection of his gallantry and good conduct, in a great measure served as a cloak to cover the whole. He who had been prodigal of life in his country's cause was indulged in extraordinary demands for his services. The generosity of the States did not keep pace with the extravagance of their favorite officer. A sumptuous table and expensive equipage, unsupported by the resources of private fortune, unguarded by the virtues of oeconomy and good management, soon increased his debts beyond a possibility of his discharging them. His love of pleasure produced the love of money, and that extinguished all sensibility to the obligations of honor and duty. The calls of luxury were various and pressing, and demanded gratification though at the expence of fame and country. Contracts were made, speculations entered into, and partnerships instituted, which could not bear investigation. Oppression, extortion, misapplication of public money and property, furnished him with the farther means of gratifying his favorite passions. In these circumstances, a change of sides afforded the only hope of evading a scrutiny, and at the same time, held out a prospect of replenishing his exhausted coffers. The disposition of the American forces in the year 1780, afforded an opportunity of accomplishing this so much to the advantage of the British, that they could well afford a liberal reward for the beneficial treachery. The American army was stationed in the strong holds of the highlands [196] on both sides of the North-river. In this arrangement, Arnold solicited for the command of West-point. This has been called the Gibraltar of America. It was built after the loss of fort Montgomery, for the defence of the North river, and was deemed the most proper for commanding its navigation. Rocky ridges rising one behind another, rendered it incapable of being invested, by less than twenty thousand men. Though some even then entertained doubts of Arnold's fidelity, yet Gen. Washington in the unsuspecting spirit of a soldier, believing it to be impossible that honor should be wanting in a breast which he knew was the seat of valor, cheerfully granted his request, and intrusted him with the important post. Gen. Arnold thus invested with command, carried on a negociation with Sir Henry Clinton, by which it was agreed that the former should make a disposition of his forces, which would enable the latter to surprise West-point under such circumstances, that he would have the garrison so completely in his power, that the troops must either lay down their arms or be cut to pieces. The object of this negociation was the strongest post of the Americans, the thoroughfare of communication, between the eastern and southern State, and was the repository of their most valuable stores. The loss of it would have been severely felt.

The agent employed in this negociation on the part of Sir Henry Clinton, was Major André, adjutant general of the British army, a young officer of great hopes, and of uncommon merit. Nature had bestowed on him an elegant taste for literature and the fine arts, which by industrious cultivation he had greatly improved. He possessed many amiable qualities, and very great accomplishments. His fidelity together with his place and character, eminently fitted him for this business; but his high ideas of candor, and his abhorrence of duplicity, made him inexpert in practicing those arts of deception which it required. To favor the necessary communications, the Vulture sloop of war had been previously stationed in the North river, as near to Arnold's posts as was practicable, without exciting suspicion. Before this a written correspondence [197] between Arnold and André, had been for some time carried on, under the fictitious names of Gustavus and Anderson. A boat was sent at night from the shore to fetch Major André. On its return, Arnold met him at the beach, without the posts of either army. Their business was not finished till it was too near the dawn of day for André to return to the Vulture. Arnold told him he must be concealed till the next night. For that purpose, he was conducted within one of the American

1780

SEP. 21

posts, against his previous stipulation and knowledge, and continued with Arnold the following day. The boatmen refused to carry him back the next night, as the Vulture, from being exposed to the fire of some cannon brought up to annoy her, had changed her position. André's return to New-York by land, was then the only practicable mode of escape. To favor this he quitted his uniform which he had hitherto worn under a surtout, for a common coat, and was furnished with a horse, and under the name of John Anderson, with a passport "to go to the lines of White Plains or lower if he thought proper, he being on public business." He advanced alone and undisturbed a great part of the way. When he thought himself almost out of danger, he was stopt by three of the New-York militia, who were with others scouting between the out posts of the two armies. Major André instead of producing his pass, asked the man who stopt him "where he belonged to" who answered "to below" meaning New-York. He replied "so do I" and declared himself a British officer, and pressed that he might not be detained. He soon discovered his mistake. His captors proceeded to search him: Sundry papers were found in his possession. These were secreted in his boots, and were in Arnold's hand writing. They contained exact returns of the state of the forces, ordnance and defences at West-Point, with the artillery orders, critical remarks on the works, &c.

André offered his captors a purse of gold and a new valuable watch, if they would let him pass, and permanent provision and future promotion, if they would convey and accompany him to New-York. They nobly disdained [198] the proffered bribe, and delivered him a prisoner to Lieut. Col. Jameson, who commanded the scouting parties. In testimony of the high sense entertained of the virtuous and patriotic conduct of John Paulding, David Williams, and Isaac Van Vert, the captors of André, Congress resolved

1780

That each of them receive annually two hundred dollars in specie during life, and that the board of war be directed to procure for each of them a silver medal, on one side of which should be a shield with this inscription, *Fidelity*; and on the other, the following motto, *Vincit Amor Patriae*: and that the commander in chief be requested to present the same, with the thanks of Congress, for their fidelity and the eminent service they had rendered their country.

André when delivered to Jameson continued to call himself by the name of Anderson, and asked leave to send a letter to Arnold, to acquaint him with Anderson's detention. This was inconsiderately granted. Arnold on the receipt of this letter abandoned everything, and went on board the Vulture sloop of war. Lieut. Col. Jameson forwarded to Gen. Washington all the papers found on André, together with a letter giving an account of the whole affair, but the express, by taking a different route from the General, who was returning from a conference at Hartford with Count de Rochambeau, missed him. This caused such a delay as gave Arnold time to effect his escape. The same packet which detailed the particulars of André's capture, brought a letter from him, in which he avowed his name and character, and endeavoured to shew that he did not come under the description of a spy. The letter was expressed in terms of dignity without insolence, and of apology without meanness. He stated therein, that he held a correspondence with a person under the orders of his General. That his intention went no farther than meeting that person on neutral ground, for the purpose of intelligence, and that, against his stipulation, his intention, and without his knowledge beforehand, he was brought within the American posts, and had to concert his escape from them. Being taken on his return he was betrayed into the vile condition of an enemy in disguise. [199] His principal request was that "whatever his fate might be, a decency of treatment might be observed, which would mark, that though unfortunate he was branded with nothing that was dishonourable, and that he was involuntarily an imposter."

1780

General Washington referred the whole case of Major André to the examination and decision of a board, consisting of fourteen general officers. On his examination, he voluntarily confessed every thing that related to himself, and particularly that he did not come ashore under the protection of a flag. The board did not examine a single witness, but founded their report on his own confession. In this they stated the following facts:

> That Major André came on shore on the night of the 21st of September in a private and secret manner, and that he changed his dress within the American lines, and under a feigned name and disguised habit

passed their works, and was taken in a disguised habit when on his way
to New-York, and when taken, several papers were found in his
possession, which contained intelligence for the enemy.

From these facts they farther reported it as their opinion "That Major
André ought to be considered as a spy, and that agreeably to the
laws and usages of nations he ought to suffer death."

Sir Henry Clinton, Lieutenant General Robertson, and the late
American General Arnold, wrote pressing letters to General Washington, to prevent the decision of the board of general officers from
being carried into effect. General Arnold in particular urged, that
every thing done by Major André was done by his particular request,
and at a time when he was the acknowledged commanding officer in
the department. He contended "that he had a right to transact all
these matters for which though wrong, Major André ought not to
suffer." An interview also took place between General Robertson on
the part of the British, and General Greene, on the part of the
Americans. Everything was urged by the former, that ingenuity or
humanity could suggest for averting the proposed execution, Greene
made a proposition for delivering up André for Arnold; but finding
[200] this could not be acceded to by the British, without offending 1780
against every principle of policy, Robertson urged "that André went
on shore under the sanction of a flag, and that being then in Arnold's
power, he was not accountable for his subsequent actions, which
were said to be compulsory." To this it was replied that "he was
employed in the execution of measures very foreign from the objects
of flags of truce, and such as they were never meant to authorise or
countenance, and that Major André in the course of his examination
had candidly confessed, that it was impossible for him to suppose
that he came on shore under the sanction of a flag." As Greene and
Robertson differed so widely both in their statement of facts, and
the inferences they drew from them, the latter proposed to the
former, that the opinions of disinterested gentlemen might be taken
on the subject, and proposed Kniphausen and Rochambeau. Robertson also urged that André possessed a great share of Sir Henry
Clinton's esteem; and that he would be infinitely obliged if he should
be spared. He offered that in case André was permitted to return

with him to New-York, any person whatever, that might be named, should be set at liberty. All these arguments and entreaties having failed, Robertson presented a long letter from Arnold, in which he endeavoured to exculpate André, by acknowledging himself the author of every part of his conduct, "and particularly insisted on his coming from the Vulture, under a flag which he had sent for that purpose." He declared that if André, suffered he should think himself bound in honour to retaliate. He also observed "that forty of the principal inhabitants of South-Carolina had justly forfeited their lives, which had hitherto been spared only through the clemency of Sir Henry Clinton, but who could no longer extend his mercy if Major André suffered: an event which would probably open a scene of bloodshed, at which humanity must revolt." He intreated Washington by his own honour, and for that of humanity not to suffer an unjust sentence to touch the life of André, but if that warning should be disregarded and André suffer, he called [201] Heaven and earth to witness, that he alone would be justly answerable for the torrents of blood that might be spilt in consequence."

Every exertion was made by the royal commanders to save André, but without effect. It was the general opinion of the American army that his life was forfeited, and that national dignity and sound policy required that the forfeiture should be exacted.

André though superior to the terrors of death, wished to die like a soldier. To obtain this favour, he wrote a letter to Gen. Washington, fraught with sentiments of military dignity. From an adherence to the usages of war, it was not thought proper to grant this request; but his delicacy was saved from the pain of receiving a negative answer. The guard which attended him in his confinement, marched with him to the place of execution. The way, over which he passed, was crouded on each side by anxious spectators. Their sensibility was strongly impressed by beholding a well dressed youth, in the bloom of life, of a peculiarly engaging person, mien and aspect, devoted to immediate execution. Major André walked with firmness, composure and dignity, between two officers of his guard, his arm being locked in theirs. Upon seeing the preparations at the fatal spot, he asked with some degree of concern "Must I die in this manner?"— He was told it was unavoidable—He replied, "I am reconciled to my fate, but not to the mode;" but soon subjoined, "It will be but a momentary pang." He ascended the cart with a pleading countenance, and with a degree of composure, which excited the admiration and melted the hearts of all the spectators. He was asked when the fatal moment was at hand, if he had anything to say; he answered nothing but to request "That you will witness to the world that I die like a brave man." The succeeding moments closed the affecting scene.

This execution was the subject of severe censures. Barbarity, cruelty and murder, were plentifully charged on the Americans, but the impartial of all nations allowed, that it was warranted by the usages of war. It cannot be condemned, without condemning the maxims of [202] self-preservation, which have uniformly guided the practice of hostile nations. The finer feelings of humanity would have been gratified, by dispensing with the rigid maxims of war in favour of so distinguished an officer, but these feelings must be controlled by a regard for the public safety. Such was the distressed state of the American army, and so abundant were their causes of complaint, that there was much to fear from the contagious nature of treachery. Could it have been reduced to a certainty that there were no more Arnolds in America, perhaps André's life might have been spared; but the necessity of discouraging farther plots, fixed his fate, and stamped it with the seal of political necessity. If conjectures in the boundless field of possible contingencies were to be indulged, it might be said that it was more consonant to extended humanity to take one life, than by ill timed lenity to lay a foundation, which probably would occasion not only the loss of many, but endanger the independence of a great country.

Though a regard to the public safety imposed a necessity for inflicting the rigors of martial law, yet the rare worth of this unfortunate officer made his unhappy case the subject of universal regret. Not only among the partisans of royal government, but among the firmest American republicans, the friendly tear of sympathy freely flowed, for the early fall of this amiable young man. Some condemned, others justified, but all regretted the fatal sentence which put a period to his valuable life.

This grand project terminated with no other alteration in respect of the British, than that of their exchanging one of their best officers for the worst man in the American army. Arnold was immediately made a Brigadier General, in the service of the King of Great Britain. The failure of the scheme respecting West-Point, made it necessary for him to dispel the cloud, which overshadowed his character, by the performance of some signal service for his new masters. The condition of the American army, afforded him a prospect of doing something of consequence. He flattered himself that by the [203] allurements of pay and promotion, he should be able to raise a numerous force, from among the distressed American soldiery. He therefore took methods for accomplishing this purpose, by obviating their scruples, and working on their passions. His first public measure was issuing an address, directed to the inhabitants of America, dated

OCT. 7,
1781

from New-York, five days after André's execution. In this he endeavoured to justify himself for deserting their cause. He said "that when he first engaged in it, he conceived the rights of his country to be in danger, and that duty and honor called him to her defence. A redress of grievances was his only aim and object. He however acquiesced in the declaration of independence, although he thought it precipitate. But the reasons that then were offered to justify that measure, no longer could exist, when Great Britain with the open arms of a parent, offered to embrace them as children and to grant the wished for redress. From the refusal of these proposals, and the ratification of the French alliance, all his ideas of the justice and policy of the war were totally changed, and from that time, he had become a professed loyalist.["] He acknowledged that "in these principles he had only retained his arms and command, for an opportunity to surrender them to Great Britain." This address was soon followed by another, inscribed to the officers and soldiers of the continental army. This was intended to induce them to follow his example, and engage in the royal service. He informed them, that he was authorised to raise a corps of cavalry and infantry, who were to be on the same footing with the other troops in the British service. To allure the private men, three guineas were offered to each, besides payment for their horses, arms and accoutrements. Rank in the British army was also held out to the American officers, who would recruit and bring in a certain number of men, proportioned to the different grades in military service. These offers were proposed to unpaid soldiers, who were suffering from the want of both food and cloathing, and to officers who were in a great degree obliged to support themselves from their own resources, while they were [204] spending the prime of their days, and risquing their lives in the unproductive service of Congress. Though they were urged at a time when the paper currency was at its lowest ebb of depreciation, and the wants and distresses of the American army were at their highest pitch, yet they did not produce the intended effect on a single sentinel or officer. Whether the circumstances of Arnold's case, added new shades to the crime of desertion, or whether their providential escape from the deep laid scheme against West-point, gave a higher tone to the firmness of the American soldiery, cannot be unfolded: But either from these or some other causes, desertion wholly ceased at this remarkable period of the war.

It is matter of reproach to the United States, that they brought into public view a man of Arnold's character, but it is to the honor of human nature, that a great revolution and an eight years war produced but one. In civil contests, for officers to change sides has not been unusual, but in the various events of the American war, and among the many regular officers it called to the field, nothing occurred that bore any resemblance to the conduct of Arnold. His singular case enforces the policy of conferring high trusts exclusively on men of clean hands, and of withholding all public confidence from those who are subjected to the dominion of pleasure.

A gallant enterprize of Major Talmadge about this time shall close this chapter. He crossed the sound to Long-Island with 80 men, made a circuitous march of 20 miles to Fort-George, and reduced it without any other loss than that of one private man wounded. He killed and wounded eight of the enemy, captured a Lt. Colonel, a Captain and 55 privates.

1781

NOV. 28

CHAPTER XXI

Foreign Affairs, connected with the American Revolution 1780, 1781.

[205] THAT SPARK WHICH WAS FIRST KINDLED at Boston, gradually expanded itself till sundry of the nations of Europe were involved in its wide spreading flame. France, Spain and Holland were in the years 1778, 1779 and 1780 successively drawn in for a share of the general calamity.

These events had so direct an influence on the American war, that a short recapitulation of them becomes necessary.

Soon after his most Catholic Majesty declared war against Great-Britain, expeditions were carried on by Don Galvez the Spanish governor of Louisiana, against the British settlements in West-Florida. These were easily reduced. The conquest of the whole province was completed in a few months by the reduction of Pensacola. The Spaniards were not so successful in their attempts against Gibraltar and Jamaica. They had blockaded the former of these places on the landside ever since July 1779, and soon after invested it as closely by sea, as the nature of the gut, and variety of wind and weather, would permit. Towards the close of the year the garrison was reduced to great straits. Vegetables were with difficulty to be got at any price, but bread, the great essential both of life and health, was most deficient. Governor Elliott who commanded in the garrison, made an experiment to ascertain what quantity of rice would suffice a single person, and lived for eight successive days, on thirty two ounces of that nutritious grain.

FEB. 8
1780

The critical situation of Gibraltar called for relief. A strong squadron was prepared for that purpose, and the command of it given to Sir George Rodney. He when on his way thither fell in with 15 sail of merchant men, under a slight convoy bound from St. Sebastian to Cadiz, and captured the whole. Several of the vessels were laden with provisions which being sent into Gibraltar [206] proved a seasonable supply. In eight days after, he engaged near Cape St. Vincent with a Spanish squadron of eleven sail of the line, commanded by Don Juan de Langara. Early in the action the Spanish ship San Domingo mounting 70 guns, and carrying 600 men blew up, and all on board perished. The action continued with great vigor on both sides for ten hours. The Spanish Admiral's ship the Phoenix of 80 guns, with three of 70, were carried into a British port. The San Julian of 70 guns was taken. A Lieutenant with 70 British seamen was put on board, but as she ran on shore, the victors became prisoners. Another ship of the same force was also taken, but afterwards totally lost. Four escaped, but two of them were greatly damaged. The Spanish Admiral did not strike till his ship was reduced to a mere wreck. Captain Macbride of the Bienfaiscent, to whom he struck, disdaining to convey infection even to an enemy, informed him that a malignant small pox prevailed on board the Bienfaiscent; and offered to permit the Spanish prisoners to stay on board the Phoenix, rather than by a removal to expose them to the small pox, trusting to the Admiral's honor, that no advantage would be taken of the circumstance. The proposal was chearfully embraced, and the conditions honorably observed. The consequence of this important victory was the immediate and complete relief of Gibraltar. This

JULY 18

being done, Rodney proceeded to the West-Indies. The Spaniards nevertheless persevered with steadiness, in their original design of reducing Gibraltar. They seemed to be entirely absorbed in that object. The garrison, after some time, began again to suffer the inconveniences which flow from deficient and unwholsome food: But in April 1781, complete relief was obtained through the intervention of a British fleet, commanded by Admiral Darby.

APR. 12, 1781

The Court of Spain, mortified at this repeated disappointment, determined to make greater exertions. Their works were carried on with more vigor than ever. Having on an experiment of 20 months found the inefficacy of a blockade, they resolved to try the effects of a bombardment. Their batteries were mounted with guns of the [207] heaviest metal, and with mortars of the largest dimensions. These disgorged torrents of fire on a narrow spot. It seemed as if not only the works, but the rock itself must have been overwhelmed. All distinction of parts was lost in flame and smoke. This dreadful cannonade continued day and night, almost incessantly for three weeks, in every 24 hours of which 100,000 lbs. of gunpowder were consumed, and between 4 and 5000 shot and shells went through the town. It then slackened, but was not intermitted for one whole day for upwards of a twelve month. The fatigues of the garrison were extreme, but the loss of men was less than might have been expected. For the first ten weeks of this unexampled bombardment, the whole number of killed and wounded was only about 300. The damage done to the works was trifling. The houses in town about 500 in number were mostly destroyed. Such of the inhabitants as were not buried in the ruins of their houses, or torn to pieces by the shells, fled to the remote parts of the rocks, but destruction followed them to places which had always been deemed secure. No scene could be more deplorable. Mothers and children clasped in each others arms, were so completely torn to pieces, that it seemed more like an annihilation, than a dispersion of their shattered fragments. Ladies of the greatest sensibility and most delicate constitutions deemed themselves happy to be admitted to a few hours of repose in the casemates, amidst the noise of a crouded soldiery, and the groans of the wounded.

At the first onset Gen. Elliot retorted on the besiegers a shower of fire, but foreseeing the difficulty of procuring supplies he soon retrenched, and received with comparative unconcern, the fury and violence of his adversaries. By the latter end of November, the besiegers had brought their works to that state of perfection which they intended. The care and ingenuity employed upon them were extraordinary. The best engineers of France and Spain had united their abilities, and both kingdoms were filled with sanguine expectations of speedy success. In this conjuncture, when all Europe was in suspence concerning [208] the fate of the garrison, and when from the prodigious efforts made for its reduction, many believed that it could not hold out much longer, a sally was projected and executed, which in about two hours destroyed those works which had required so much time, skill and labor to accomplish.

A body of 2000 chosen men, under the command of Brig. Gen. Ross, marched out about 2 o'clock in the morning, and at the same instant made a general attack on the whole exterior front of the lines of the besiegers. The Spaniards gave way on every side, and abandoned their works. The pioneers and artillery men spread their fire with such rapidity, that in a little time every thing combustible was in flames. The mortars and cannon were spiked, and their beds, platforms and carriages destroyed. The magazines blew up, one after another. The loss of the detachment, which accomplished all this destruction, was inconsiderable.

1781.
NOV. 27

This unexpected event disconcerted the besiegers, but they soon recovered from their alarm, and with a perseverance almost peculiar to their nation, determined to go on with the siege. Their subsequent exertions, and re-iterated defeats, shall be related in the order of time in which they took place.

While the Spaniards were urging the siege of Gibraltar, a scheme which had been previously concerted with the French was in a train of execution. This consisted of two parts: The object of the first, concerted between the French and Spaniards, was no less than the conquest of Jamaica. The object of the second, in which the French and the Americans were parties, was the reduction of New-York. In conformity to this plan, the monarchs of France and Spain early in the year 1780, assembled a force in the West-Indies, superior to that of the British. Their combined fleets amounted to thirty six sail of the line, and their land forces were in a correspondent proportion.

By acting in concert, they hoped to make rapid conquests in the West Indies.

Fortunately for the British interest, this great hostile force carried within itself the cause of its own overthrow. [209] The Spanish troops from being too much crouded on board their transports, were seized with a mortal and contagious distemper. This spread through the French fleet and land forces, as well as their own. With the hopes of arresting its progress, the Spaniards were landed in the French islands. By these disastrous events, the spirit of enterprise was damped. The combined fleets, having neither effected nor attempted any thing of consequence, desisted from the prosecution of the objects of the campaign. The failure of the first part of the plan, occasioned the failure of the second. Count de Guichen the commander of the French fleet, who was to have followed M. de Ternay, and to have co-operated with Gen. Washington, instead of coming to the American continent, sailed with a large convoy collected from the French islands, directly to France.

The abortive plans of the French and Spaniards, operated directly against the interest of the United States, but this was in a short time counterbalanced, by the increased embarrassments occasioned to Great Britain, by the armed neutrality of the northern powers, and by a rupture with Holland.

The naval superiority of Great Britain, had long been the subject of regret and of envy. As it was the interest, so it seemed to be the wish of European sovereigns, to avail themselves of the present favourable moment, to effect an humilitation of her maritime grandeur. That the flag of all nations must strike to British ships of war, could not be otherwise than mortifying to independent sovereigns. This haughty demand was not their only cause of complaint. The activity and number of British privateers had rendered them objects of terror, not only to the commercial shipping of their enemies, but to the many vessels belonging to other powers, that were employed in trading with them. Various litigations had taken place between the commanders of British, armed vessels, and those who were in the service of neutral powers, respecting the extent of that commerce, which was consistent with a strict and fair neutrality. The British insisted on the lawfulness of seizing supplies, which [210] were about to be carried to their enemies. Having been in the habit of commanding on the sea, they considered power and right to be synonimous terms. As other nations from a dread of provoking their vengeance, had submitted to their claim of dominion on the ocean, they fancied themselves invested with authority to controul the commerce of independent nations, when it interfered with their views. This haughtiness worked its own overthrow. The Empress of Russia took the lead in establishing a system of maritime laws, which subverted the claims of Great Britain. Her trading vessels had long been harrassed by British searches and seizures, on pretence of their carrying on a commerce inconsistent with neutrality. The present crisis favoured the re-establishment of the laws of nature, in place of the usurpations of Great Britain.

A declaration was published by the empress of Russia, addressed to the courts of London, Versailles and Madrid. In this it was observed FEB. 26, 1780

that her Imperial Majesty had given such convincing proofs of the strict regard she had for the rights of neutrality, and the liberty of commerce in general, that it might have been hoped her impartial conduct, would have entitled her subjects to the enjoyment of the advantages belonging to neutral nations. Experience had however proved the contrary; her subjects had been molested in their navigation, by the ships and privateers of the belligerent powers.

Her Majesty therefore declared

that she found it necessary to remove these vexations which had been offered to the commerce of Russia, but before she came to any serious measures, she thought it just and equitable, to expose to the world and particularly to the belligerent powers, the principles she had adopted for her conduct, which were as follows.

That neutral ships should enjoy a free navigation, even from port to port, and on the coasts of the belligerent powers. That all effects belonging to the belligerent powers, should be looked on as free on board such neutral ships, with an exception of places actually blocked up or besieged, and with a proviso that they do not carry to the enemy contraband articles.

These were [211] limited by an explanation, so as to "comprehend only warlike stores and ammunition," her imperial Majesty declared that "she was firmly resolved to maintain these principles, and that with the view of protecting the commerce and navigation of her subjects, she had given orders to fit out a considerable part of her naval force." This declaration was communicated to the States General, and the empress of Russia invited them to make a common cause with her, so far as such an union might serve to protect commerce and navigation. Similar communications and invitations were also made to the courts of Copenhagen, Stockholm and Lisbon. A civil answer was received from the court of Great-Britain, and a very cordial one from the court of France. On this occasion, it was said by his most Christian Majesty "that what her Imperial Majesty claimed from the belligerent powers, was nothing more than the rules prescribed to the French navy." The Kings of Sweden and Denmark, also formally acceded to the principles and measures proposed by the empress of Russia. The States General did the same. The queen of Portugal was the only sovereign who refused to concur. The powers engaged in this association resolved to support each other against any of the belligerent nations, who should violate the principles which had been laid down, in the declaration of the empress of Russia.

This combination assumed the name of the armed neutrality. By it a respectable guarantee was procured to a commerce, from which France and Spain procured a plentiful supply of articles, essentially conducive to a vigorous prosecution of the war. The usurped authority of Great Britain on the highway of nature received a fatal blow. Her embarrassments from this source were aggravated by the consideration, that they came from a power in whose friendship she had confided.

About the same time the enemies of Great Britain were increased by the addition of the States General. Though these two powers were bound to each other, by the obligations of treaties, the conduct of the latter had long been considered, rather as hostile than friendly. [212] Few Europeans had a greater prospect of advantage from American independence than the Hollanders. The conquest of the United States, would have regained to Great Britain a monopoly of their trade; but the establishment of their independence promised to other nations, an equal chance of participating therein. As commerce is the soul of the United Netherlands, to have neglected the present opportunity of extending it, would have been a deviation from their established maxims of policy. Former treaties framed in distant periods, when other views were predominant, opposed but a feeble barrier to the claims of present interest. The past generation found it to their advantage, to seek the friendship and protection of Great Britain. But they who were now on the stage of life, had similar inducements to seek for new channels of trade. Though this could not be done without thwarting the views of the court of London, their recollection of former favours was not sufficient to curb their immediate favorite passion. From the year 1777, Sir Joseph Yorke, the British minister at the Hague, had made sundry representations to their High Mightinesses of the clandestine commerce, carried on between their subjects and the Americans. He particularly stated that Mr. Van Graaf, the Governor of St. Eustatius, had permitted an illicit commerce with the Americans; and had at one time returned the salute of a vessel carrying their flag. Sir Joseph, therefore demanded a formal disavowal of this salute, and the dismission and immediate recall of Governor Van Graaf. This insolent demand was answered with a pusillanimous temporising reply. On the 12th of September 1778, a memorial was presented to the States General, from the merchants and others of Amsterdam, in which they complained that their lawful commerce was obstructed by the ships of his Britannic Majesty. On the 22d of July, 1779, Sir Joseph Yorke demanded of the States General, the succours which were stipulated in the treaty of 1678: But this was not complied with. Friendly declarations and unfriendly actions followed each other in alternate succession. At length a declaration was published by the King [213] of Great Britain, by which it was announced "that the subjects of the United Provinces, were henceforth to be considered upon the same footing with other martial powers, not privileged by treaty." Throughout the whole of this period, the Dutch by means of neutral ports, continued to supply the Americans and the English, to insult and intercept their navigation, but open hostilities were avoided by both. The former aimed principally at the gains of a lucrative commerce, the latter to remove all obstacles which stood in the way of their favourite scheme of conquering the Americans. The event which occasioned a formal declaration of war, was the capture of Henry Laurens. In the deranged state of the American finances, that gentleman had been deputed by Congress, to solicit a loan for their service in the United Netherlands; and also to negociate a treaty between them and the United States. On his way thither, he was

SEP. 3, 1780

taken by the Vestal frigate commanded by Captain Kepple. He had thrown his papers overboard; but great part of them were nevertheless recovered without having received much damage. His papers being

OCT. 6

delivered to the ministry, were carefully examined. Among them was found one purporting to be a plan of a treaty of amity and commerce, between the States of Holland and the United States of America. This had been originally drawn up in consequence of some conversation between William Lee, whom Congress had appointed commissioner to the courts of Vienna and Berlin; and John de Neufville, merchant of Amsterdam, as a plan of a treaty destined to be concluded hereafter: But it had never been proposed either by Congress or the States of Holland, though it had received the approbation of the Pensionary Van Berkel, and of the city of Amsterdam. As this was not an official paper, and had never been read in Congress the original was given to Mr. Laurens as a paper that might be useful to him in his projected negociations. This unauthentic paper, which was in Mr. Laurens' possession by accident, and which was so nearly sunk in the ocean, proved the occasion of a national war. The court of Great Britain, was highly offended at it. [214] The paper itself and

NOV. 5
NOV. 10, 1780

some others, relating to the same subject were delivered to the Prince of Orange, who laid them before the States of Holland and West-Friesland.

Sir Joseph Yorke presented a memorial to the States General, in which he asserted

That the papers of Mr. Laurens, who stiled himself President of the pretended Congress, had furnished the discovery of a plot unexampled in all the annals of the republic. That it appeared by these papers, that the gentlemen of Amsterdam had been engaged in a clandestine correspondence with the American rebels, from the month of August 1778, and that instructions and full powers had been given by them for the conclusion of a treaty of indisputable amity with those rebels, who were the subjects of a sovereign, to whom the republic was united by the closest engagements.

He therefore, in the name of his master, demanded "A formal disavowal of this irregular conduct, and a prompt satisfaction proportioned to the offence, and an exemplary punishment of the Pensionary Van Berkel, and his accomplices, as disturbers of the public peace and violaters of the laws of nations.["] The States General disavowed the intended treaty of the city of Amsterdam, and engaged to prosecute the Pensionary according to the laws of the country; but this was not deemed satisfactory. Sir Joseph Yorke was ordered to withdraw from the Hague, and soon after a manifesto DEC. 20 against the Dutch was published in London. This was followed by an order of council "That general reprisals be granted against the ships, goods and subjects, of the States General." Whatever may be thought of the policy of this measure, its boldness must be admired. Great Britain, already at war with the United States of America, the monarchies of France and Spain, deliberately resolves on a war with Holland, and at a time when she might have avoided open hostilities. Her spirit was still farther evinced by the consideration that she was deserted by her friends, and without a single ally. Great must have been her resources to support so extensive a war against so many hostile sovereigns, but this very ability, by proving that her overgrown power was dangerous to [215] the peace of Europe, furnished an apology for their combination against her.

A war with Holland being resolved upon, the storm of British vengeance first burst on the Dutch Island of St. Eustatius. This though intrinsically of little value, had long been the seat of an extensive commerce. It was the grand freeport of the West-Indies, and as such was a general market and magazine to all nations. In consequence of its neutrality and situation, together with its unbounded freedom of trade, it reaped the richest harvests of commerce, during the seasons of warfare among its neighbours. It was in a particular manner, a convenient channel of supply to the Americans.

The Island is a natural fortification, and very capable of being made strong; but as its inhabitants were a motley mixture of transient persons, wholly intent on the gains of commerce, they were more solicitous to acquire property, than attentive to improve those means of security which the Island afforded.

Sir George Rodney and General Vaughan, with a large fleet and army, surrounded this Island, and demanded a surrender thereof and of its dependencies within an hour. Mr. de Graaf returned for answer "That being utterly incapable of making any defence against the force which invested the Island, he must of necessity surrender it, only recommending the town and its inhabitants to the known and usual clemency of British commanders."

The wealth accumulated in this barren spot was prodigious. The whole Island seemed to be one vast magazine. The store-houses were filled, and the beach covered with valuable commodities. These on a moderate calculation were estimated to be worth above three millions sterling. All this property, together with what was found on the Island, was indiscriminately seized and declared to be confiscated. This valuable booty was farther increased by new arrivals. The conquerors for some time kept up Dutch colors, which decoyed a number of French, Dutch and American vessels into their hands. Above 150 merchant vessels, most of which were richly laden, were captured. A Dutch frigate of 38 guns, and five [216] small armed vessels, shared the same fate. The neighbouring Islands of St. Martin and Saba were in like manner reduced. Just before the arrival of the British, 30 large ships, laden with West-India commodities, had sailed from Eustatius for Holland, under the convoy of a ship of sixty guns. Admiral Rodney despatched the Monarch and Panther, with the Sybil frigate in pursuit of this fleet. The whole of it was overtaken and captured.

The Dutch West-India company, many of the citizens of Amsterdam, and several Americans were great sufferers by the capture of this Island, and the confiscation of all property found therein, which immediately followed, but the British merchants were much more so. These confiding in the acknowledged neutrality of the island, and in acts of Parliament, had accumulated therein great quantities of West-India produce, as well as of European goods. They stated their hard case to Admiral Rodney and Gen. Vaughan, and contended that their connexion with the captured island was under the sanction of acts of Parliament, and that their commerce had been conducted according to the rules and maxims of trading nations. To applications of this kind it was answered, "That the island was Dutch, every thing in it was Dutch, was under the protection of the Dutch flag, and as Dutch it should be treated."

The severity with which the victors proceeded, drew on them pointed censures not only from the immediate sufferers, but from all Europe. It must be supposed that they were filled with resentment for the supplies which the Americans received through this channel, but there is also reason to suspect, that the love of gain was cloaked under the specious veil of national policy.

The horrors of an universal havoc of property were realised. The merchants and traders were ordered to give up their books of correspondence, their letters and also inventories of all their effects, inclusive of an exact account of all money and plate in their possession. The Jews were designated as objects of particular resentment. They were ordered to give up the keys of their stores, to leave their wealth and merchandize behind them, and to [217] depart the island without knowing the place of their destination. From a natural wish to be furnished with the means of supplying their wants, in the place of their future residence, they secreted in their wearing apparel, gold, silver and other articles of great value and small bulk. The policy of these unfortunate Hebrews did not avail them. The avarice of the conquerors, effectually counteracted their ingenuity. They were stripped, searched and despoiled of their money and jewels. In this state of wretchedness, many of the inhabitants were transported as outlaws and landed on St. Christopher's. The assembly of that island with great humanity, provided for them such articles as their situation required. The Jews were soon followed by the Americans, some of these though they had been banished from the United States, on account of their having taken part with Great Britain, were banished a second time by the conquering troops of the sovereign, in whose service they had prevously suffered. The French merchants and traders were next ordered off the island, and lastly the native Dutch were obliged to submit to the same sentence. Many opulent persons in consequence of these proceedings, were instantly reduced to extreme indigence.

In the mean time public sales were advertised, and persons of all nations invited to become purchasers. The island of St. Eustatius became a scene of constant auctions. There never was a better market for buyers. The immense quantities exposed for sale, reduced the price of many articles far below their original cost. Many of the commodities sold on this occasion, became in the hands of their new purchasers, as effectual supplies to the enemies of Great Britain, as they could have been in case the island had not been captured. The spirit of gain, which led the traders of St. Eustatius to sacrifice the interests of Great Britain, influenced the conquerors to do the same. The friends of humanity, who wish that war was exterminated from the world, or entered into only for the attainment of national justice, must be gratified when they are told, that this unexampled rapacity was one link in the great chain of causes which, as hereafter shall be explained [218], brought on the great event in the Chesapeak, which gave peace to contending nations. While Admiral Rodney and his officers were bewildered, in the sales of confiscated property at St. Eustatius, and especially while his fleet was weakened, by a large detachment sent off to convoy their booty to Great Britain, the French were silently executing a well digested scheme, which assured them a naval superiority on the American coast, to the total ruin of the British interest in the United States.

CHAPTER XXII

The revolt of the Pennsylvania line; of part of the Jersey troops; distresses of the American army; Arnold's invasion of Virginia.

THOUGH GENERAL ARNOLD'S ADDRESS to his countrymen produced no effect, in detaching the soldiery of America from the unproductive service of Congress, their steadiness could not be accounted for, from any melioration of their circumstances. They still remained without pay, and without such cloathing as the season required. They could not be induced to enter the British service, but their complicated distresses at length broke out into deliberate mutiny. This event which had been long expected, made its first threatening appearance in the Pennsylvania line. The common soldiers enlisted in that State, were for the most part natives of Ireland, but though not bound to America by the accidental tie of birth, they were inferior to none in discipline, courage, or attachment to the cause of independence. They had been but a few months before, the most active instruments in quelling a mutiny of the Connecticut troops, and had on all occasions done their duty to admiration. An ambiguity in the terms of their inlistment, furnished a pretext for their conduct. A great part of them were enlisted for three years or during the war, the three years were expired, and the men insisted that the choice of staying or going remained with them, while the officers contended that the choice was in the State.

[219] The mutiny was excited by the non-commissioned officers and privates, in the night of the 1st of January 1781, and soon became so universal in the line of that State as to defy all opposition. The whole, except three regiments, upon a signal for the purpose, turned out under arms without their officers, and declared for a redress of grievances. The officers in vain endeavoured to quell them. Several were wounded, and a captain was killed in attempting it. Gen. Wayne presented his pistols, as if about to fire on them; they held their bayonets to his breast and said "We love and respect you, but if you fire you are a dead man." "We are not going to the enemy, on the contrary, if they were now to come out, you should see us fight under your orders with as much alacrity as ever; but we will be no longer amused, we are determined on obtaining what is our just due." Deaf to arguments and entreaties, they to the number of 1300 moved off in a body from Morristown, and proceeded in good order with their arms and six field pieces to Princeton. They elected temporary officers from their own body, and appointed a Serjeant Major, who had formerly deserted from the British army, to be their commander. Gen. Wayne forwarded provisions after them, to prevent their plundering the country for their subsistence. They invaded no man's property, farther than their immediate necessities made unavoidable. This was readily submitted to by the inhabitants, who had long been used to exactions of the same kind, levied for similar purposes by their lawful rulers. They professed that they had no object in view, but to obtain what was justly due to them, nor were their actions inconsistent with that profession.

Congress sent a committee of their body, consisting of General Sullivan, Mr. Mathews, Mr. Atlee and Dr. Witherspoon, to procure an accommodation. The revolters were resolute in refusing any terms, of which a redress of their grievances was not the foundation.

Every thing asked of their country, they might at any time after the 6th of January, have obtained from the British, by passing over into New-York. This they [220] refused. Their sufferings had exhausted their patience but not their patriotism. Sir Henry Clinton, by confidential messengers, offered to take them under the protection of the British government—to pardon all their past offences—to have the pay due them from Congress faithfully made up, without any expectation of military service in return, although it would be received if voluntarily offered. It was recommended to them to move behind the South river, and it was promised, that a detachment of British troops should be in readiness for their protection as soon as desired. In the mean time, the troops passed over from New-York to Staten-Island, and the necessary arrangements were made for moving them into New-Jersey, whensoever they might be wanted. The royal commander was not less disappointed than surprised to find that the faithful, though revolting soldiers, disdained his offers. The messengers of Sir Henry Clinton were seized and delivered to Gen. Wayne. President Reed and General Potter were appointed, by the council of Pennsylvania, to accommodate matters with the revolters. They met them at Princeton, and agreed to dismiss all whose terms of enlistment were completed, and admitted the oath of each solider to be evidence in his own case. A board of officers tried and condemned the British spies, and they were instantly executed. President Reed offered a purse of 100 guineas to the mutineers, as a reward of their fidelity, in delivering up the spies; but they refused to accept it, saying "That what they had done was only a duty they owed their country, and that they neither desired nor would receive any reward but the approbation of that country, for which they had so often fought and bled."

By these healing measures the revolt was completely quelled; but the complaints of the soldiers being founded in justice, were first redressed. Those whose time of service was expired obtained their discharges, and others had their arrears of pay in a great measure made up to them. A general amnesty closed the business. On this occasion, the commander in chief stated in a circular letter to the four eastern states, the well founded complaints [221] of his army; and the impossibility of keeping them together, under the pressure

JAN. 17

of such a variety of sufferings. General Knox was requested to be the bearer of these dispatches; and to urge the States to an immediate exertion for the relief of the soldiers. He visited Massachusetts, New-Hampshire, Connecticut and Rhode-Island; and with great earnestness and equal success described the wants of the army. Massachusetts gave 24 silver dollars to each man of her line; and also furnished them with some cloathing. Other States about the same time made similar advances.

JANUARY
1781

The spirit of mutiny proved contagious. About 160 of the Jersey troops followed the example of the Pennsylvania line; but they did not conduct with equal spirit, nor with equal prudence. They committed sundry acts of outrage against particular officers, while they affected to be submissive to others. Major General Howe, with a considerable force, was ordered to take methods for reducing them to obedience. Convinced that there was no medium between dignity and servility, but coercion, and that no other remedy could be applied without the deepest wound to the service, he determined to proceed against them with decision. General Howe marched from Kingwood about midnight; and by the dawning of the next day, had his men in four different positions, to prevent the revolters from making their escape. Every avenue being secured, Colonel Barber of the Jersey line was sent to them, with orders immediately to parade without arms; and to march to a particular spot of ground. Some hesitation appearing among them, Colonel Sproat was directed to advance, and only five minutes were given to the mutineers to comply with the orders which had been sent them. This had its effect, and they to a man marched without arms to the appointed ground. The Jersey officers gave a list of the leaders of the revolt, upon which General Howe desired them to select three of the greatest offenders. A field court martial was presently held upon these three, and they were unanimously sentenced to death. Two of them were executed on the spot, and the executioners were selected from [222] among the most active in the mutiny. The men were divided into platoons, and made public concessions to their officers, and promised by future good conduct, to atone for past offences.

These mutinies alarmed the States, but did not produce permanent relief to the army. Their wants with respect to provisions were only partially supplied, and by expedients from one short time to another. The most usual was ordering an officer to seize on provisions wherever found. This differed from robbing only in its being done by authority for the public service, and in the officer being always directed to give the proprietor a certificate, of the quantity and quality of what was taken from him. At first some reliance was placed on these certificates as vouchers to support a future demand on the United States; but they soon became so common as to be of little value. Recourse was so frequently had to coercion, both legislative and military, that the people not only lost confidence in public credit but became impatient under all exertions of authority, for forcing their property from them. That an army should be kept together under such circumstances, so far exceeds credibility as to make it necessary to produce some evidence of the fact. The American General Clinton in a letter to General Washington dated at Albany, April 16th 1781, wrote as follows.

> There is not now (independent of fort Schuyler) three days provision in the whole department for the troops in case of an alarm, nor any prospect of procuring any. The recruits of the new levies, I cannot receive, because I have nothing to give them. The Canadian families, I have been obliged to deprive of their scanty pittance, contrary to every principle of humanity. The quartermaster's department is totally useless, the public armory has been shut up for near three weeks, and a total suspension of every military operation has ensued.

Soon after this General Washington was obliged to apply 9000 dollars, sent by the State of Massachusetts for the payment of her troops to the use of the quartermaster's department, to enable him to transport provisions from the adjacent States. Before he consented [223] to adopt this expedient, he had consumed every ounce of provision, which had been kept as a reserve in the garrison of West-Point; and had strained impress by military force, to so great an extent, that there was reason to apprehend the inhabitants, irritated by such frequent calls, would proceed to dangerous insurrections. Fort Schuyler, West-Point, and the posts up the North river, were on the point of being abandoned by their starving garrisons. At this period of the war, there was little or no circulating medium, either in the form of paper or specie, and in the neighbourhood of the American army there was a real want of necessary provisions. The deficiency of the former occasioned many inconveniences, and an unequal distribution of the burdens of the war; but the insufficiency of the latter, had well nigh dissolved the army, and laid the country in every direction open to British excursions.

These events were not unforeseen by the rulers of America. From the progressive depreciation of their bills of credit, it had for some time past occurred, that the period could not be far distant, when they would cease to circulate. This crisis which had been ardently wished for by the enemies, and dreaded by the friends of American independence, took place in 1781; but without realising the hopes of the one, or the fears of the other. New resources were providentially opened, and the war was carried on with the same vigor as before. A great deal of gold and silver was about this time introduced into the United States, by a beneficial trade with the French and Spanish West-India islands, and by means of the French army in Rhode-Island. Pathetic representations were made to the ministers of his most Christian Majesty by General Washington, Dr. Franklin, and particularly by Lieutenant Colonel John Laurens, who was sent to the court of Versailles as a special minister on this occasion. The King of France gave the United States a subsidy of six millions of livres, and became their security for ten millions more, borrowed for their use in the United Netherlands. A regular system of finance was also about this time adopted. All matters relative to [224] the treasury the supplies of the army and the accounts, were put under the direction of Robert Morris, who arranged the whole with judgment and oeconomy. The issuing of paper money by the authority of government was discontinued, and the public engagements were made payable in coin. The introduction of so much gold and silver, together with these judicious domestic regulations, aided by the bank, which had been erected the preceding year in Philadelphia, extricated Congress from much of their embarrassment, and put it in their power to feed, cloath and move their army.

About the same time the old continental money, by common consent, ceased to have currency. Like an aged man expiring by the decays of nature, without a sigh or a groan, it fell asleep in the hands of its last possessors. By the scale of depreciation the war was carried on five years, for little more than a million of pounds sterling, and 200 millions of paper dollars were made redeemable by five millions of silver ones. In other countries, such measures would probably have produced popular insurrections, but in the United States they were submitted to without any tumults. Public faith was violated, but in the opinion of most men public good was promoted. The evils consequent on depreciation had taken place, and the redemption of the bills of credit at their nominal value as originally promised, instead of remedying the distresses of the sufferers would in many cases have increased them, by subjecting their small remains of property to exorbitant taxation. The money had in a great measure got out of the hands of the original proprietors, and was in the possession of others, who had obtained it at a rate of value not exceeding what was fixed upon it by the scale of depreciation.

Nothing could afford a stronger proof that the resistence of America to Great Britain was grounded in the hearts of the people, than these events. To receive paper bills of credit issued without any funds, and to give property in exchange for them, as equal to gold or silver, demonstrated the zeal and enthusiasm with which the war was begun; but to consent to the extinction of [225] the same after a currency of five years, without any adequate provision made for their future redemption, was more than would have been born by any people, who conceived that their rulers had separate interests or views from themselves. The demise of one king and the coronation of a lawful successor have often excited greater commotions in royal governments, than took place in the United States on the sudden extinction of their whole current money. The people saw the necessity which compelled their rulers to act in the manner they had done, and being well convinced that the good of the country was their object, quietly submitted to measures, which under other circumstances, would scarcely have been expiated by the lives and fortunes of their authors.

While the Americans were suffering the complicated calamities which introduced the year 1781, their adversaries were carrying on the most extensive plan of operation, which had ever been attempted since the war. It had often been objected to the British commanders, that they had not conducted the war in the manner most likely to effect the subjugation of the revolted provinces. Military critics in particular, found fault with them for keeping a large army idle at New-York, which they said if properly applied, would have been sufficient to make successful impressions, at one and the same time, on several of the States. The British seem to have calculated the campaign of 1781, with a view to make an experiment of the comparative merit of this mode of conducting military operations. The war raged in that year, not only in the vicinity of British head quarters at New-York, but in Georgia, South-Carolina, North-Carolina, and in Virginia. The latter State from its peculiar situation, and from the modes of building, planting and living, which had been adopted by the inhabitants, is particularly exposed, and lies at the mercy of whatever army is master of the Chesapeak. These circumstances, together with the pre-eminent rank which Virginia held in the confederacy, pointed out the propriety of making that State the object of particular attention. To favour [226] lord Cornwallis' designs in the southern States, Major Gen. Leslie, with about 2000 men, had been detached from New-York to the Chesapeak, in the latter end of 1780; but subsequent events induced his lordship to order him from Virginia to Charleston, with the view of his more effectually co-operating with the army under his own immediate command. Soon after the departure of General Leslie, Virginia was again invaded by another party from New-York. This was commanded by Gen. Arnold, now a Brigadier in the royal army. His force consisted of about 1600 men, and was supported by such a number of armed vessels as enabled him to commit extensive ravages, on the unprotected coasts of that well watered country. The invaders landed about 15 miles below Richmond, and in two days marched into the town, where they destroyed large quantities of tobacco, salt, rum, sail-cloth and other merchandize. Successive excursions were made to several other places, in which the royal army committed similar devastations.

JAN. 5, 1781

JAN. 20 In about a fortnight, they marched into Portsmouth and began to fortify it. The loss they sustained from the feeble opposition of the dispersed inhabitants was inconsiderable. The havoc made by General Arnold, and the apprehension of a design to fix a permanent post in Virginia, induced General Washington to detach the Marquis de la Fayette, with 1200 of the American infantry, to that State, and also to urge the French in Rhode-Island to co-operate with him in attempting to capture Arnold and his party. The French commanders eagerly closed with the proposal. Since they had landed in the United States, no proper opportunity of gratifying their passion for military fame, had yet presented itself. They rejoiced at that which now offered, and indulged a cheerful hope of rendering essential service to their allies, by cutting off the retreat of Arnold's party. With this view, their fleet with 1500 additional men on board, sailed from Rhode-Island for Virginia. D'Estouches, who since the death of de Ternay on the preceding December had commanded the French fleet, previous to the sailing of his whole naval force, dispatched the Eveillé, a sixty [227] four gun ship, and two frigates, with orders to destroy the British ships and frigates in the Chesapeak. These took or destroyed ten vessels, and captured the Romulus of 44 guns. Arbuthnot with a British fleet sailed from Gardiner's-bay in pursuit of D'Estouches. The former overtook and engaged the latter off the capes of Virginia. The British had the advantage of more guns than the French, but the latter were much more strongly manned than the former. The contest between the fleets thus nearly balanced, ended without the loss of a ship on either side; but the British obtained the fruits of victory so far as to frustrate the whole scheme of their adversaries. The fleet of his most Christian Majesty returned to Rhode-Island, without effecting the object of the expedition. Thus was Arnold saved from imminent danger of falling into the hands of his exasperated countrymen. The day before the French fleet returned to Newport, a convoy arrived in the Chesapeak from New-York, with Major Gen. Philips and about 2000 men. This distinguished officer, who having been taken at Saratoga had been lately exchanged, was appointed to be commander of the royal forces in Virginia. Philips and Arnold soon made a junction, and carried every thing before them. They successively defeated those bodies of militia which came in their way. The whole country was open to their excursions. On their embarkation from Portsmouth, a detachment visited York-town, but the main body proceeded to Williamsburgh. On the 22d of April they reached Chickapowing. A party proceeded up that river 10 or 12 miles, and destroyed much property. On the 24th they landed at City-point, and soon after they marched for Petersburgh. About one

MARCH 8

FEB. 9

MARCH 25
10
16

MARCH 25

APRIL 22

24

mile from the town they were opposed by a small force commanded by Baron Steuben; but this after making a gallant resistance was compelled to retreat.

At Petersburgh they destroyed 4000 hogsheads of tobacco, a ship and a number of small vessels. Within three days one party marched to Chesterfield courthouse, and burned a range of barracks, and 300 barrels of flour. On the same day, another party under the command [228] of Gen. Arnold marched to Osborne's. About four miles above that place, a small marine force was drawn up to oppose him. Gen. Arnold sent a flag to treat with the commander of this fleet, but he declared that he would defend it to the last extremity. Upon this refusal, Arnold advanced with some artillery, and fired upon him with decisive effect from the banks of the river. Two ships and ten small vessels loaded with tobacco, cordage, flour, &c. were captured. Four ships, five brigantines and a number of small vessels were burnt or sunk. The quantity of tobacco taken or destroyed in this fleet, exceeded 2000 hogsheads, and the whole was effected without the loss of a single man, on the side of the British. The royal forces then marched up the fork till they arrived at Manchester. There they destroyed 1200 hogsheads of tobacco; returning thence they made great havoc at Warmic. They destroyed the ships on the stocks, and in the river, and a large range of rope walks. A magazine of 500 barrels of flour, within a number of warehouses, and of tan houses, all filled with their respective commodities, were also consumed in one general conflagration. On the 9th of May they returned to Petersburgh, having in the course of the preceding three weeks, destroyed property to an immense amount. With this expedition, Major Gen. Philips terminated a life, which in all his previous operations had been full of glory. At early periods of his military career, on different occasions of a preceding war, he had gained the full approbation of Prince Ferdinand, under whom he had served in Germany. As an officer he was universally admired. Though much of the devastations committed by the troops under his command, may be vindicated on the principles of those who hold that the rights and laws of war, are of equal obligation with the rights and laws of humanity; yet the friends of his fame, have reason to regret that he did not die three weeks sooner.

APRIL 27

30

Campaign of 1781. Operations in the two Carolinas and Georgia.

[229] THE SUCCESSES WHICH, with a few checks, followed the   1781
British arms since they had reduced Savannah and Charleston,
encouraged them to pursue their object by advancing from south to
north. A vigorous invasion of North-Carolina was therefore projected,
for the business of the winter which followed Gen. Gates' defeat.
The Americans were sensible of the necessity of reinforcing, and
supporting their southern army, but were destitute of the means of
doing it. Their northern army would not admit of being farther
weakened, nor was there time to march over the intervening distance
of seven hundred miles, but if men could have been procured and
time allowed for marching them to South-Carolina, money for
defraying the unavoidable expences of their transportation, could
not be commanded, either in the latter end of 1780, or the first

months of 1781. Though Congress was unable to forward either men or money, for the relief of the Southern States, they did what was equivalent. They sent them a general, whose head was a council, and whose military talents were equal to a reinforcement. The nomination of an officer for this important trust, was left to Gen. Washington. He mentioned General Greene, adding for reason "that he was an officer in whose abilities and integrity, from a long and intimate experience, he had the most entire confidence."

The army after its defeat and dispersion on the 16th of August 1780, rendezvoused at Hillsborough. In the latter end of the year they advanced to Charlotte-Town. At this place Gen. Gates transferred the command to Gen. Greene. The manly resignation of the one, was equalled by the delicate disinterestedness of the other. Expressions of civility, and acts of friendship and attention were reciprocally exchanged. Greene upon all occasions, was the vindicator of Gates' reputation. In his letters and conversation, he uniformly maintained that his predecessor, had failed in no part of his military duty, and [230] that he had deserved success, though he could not command it. Within a few hours after Greene took charge of the army a report was made of a gallant enterprize of Lieut. Col. Washington. Being out on a foraging excursion, he had penetrated within 13 miles of Camden, to Clermont the seat of Lieut. Col. Rigely of the British militia. This was fortified by a block house, and encompassed by an abbatis, and was defended by upwards of one hundred of the inhabitants, who had submitted to the British government. Lieut. Col. Washington advanced with his cavalry, and planted the trunk of a pine tree, so as to resemble a field piece. The lucky moment was seized and a peremptory demand of an immediate surrender was made, when the garrison was impressed with the expectation of an immediate cannonade in case of their refusal. The whole surrendered at discretion, without a shot on either side. This fortunate incident, through the superstition to which most men are more or less subject, was viewed by the army as a presage of success under their new commander.

When Gen. Greene took the command, he found the troops had made a practice of going home without permission, staying several days or weeks, and then returning to camp. Determined to enforce strict discipline, he gave out that he would make an example of the

1781

first deserter of the kind he caught. One such being soon taken, was accordingly shot, at the head of the army, drawn up to be spectators of the punishment. This had the desired effect, and put a stop to the dangerous practice.

The whole southern army at this time consisted of about 2000 men, more than half of which were militia. The regulars had been for a long time without pay, and were very deficient in cloathing. All sources of supply from Charleston were in possession of the British, and no imported article could be obtained from a distance less than 200 miles. The procuring of provisions for this small force was a matter of difficulty. The paper currency was depreciated so far, as to be wholly unequal to the purchase of even such supplies as the country afforded. Hard money had not a physical existence in any [231] hands accessible to the Americans. The only resource left for 1781 supplying the army was by the arbitrary mode of impress. To seize on the property of the inhabitants, and at the same time to preserve their kind affections, was a difficult business and of delicate execution, but of the utmost moment, as it furnished the army with provisions without impairing the disposition of the inhabitants to co-operate with it in recovering the country. This grand object called for the united efforts of both. Such was the situation of the country, that it was almost equally dangerous for the American army to go forward or stand still. In the first case every thing was hazarded; in the last the confidence of the people would be lost, and with it all prospect of being supported by them. The impatience of the suffering exiles and others, led them to urge the adoption of rash measures. The mode of opposition they preferred was the least likely to effect their ultimate wishes. The nature of the country thinly inhabited, abounding with swamps, and covered with woods—the inconsiderable force of the American army, the number of the disaffected, and the want of magazines, weighed with Gen. Greene to prefer a partizan war. By close application to his new profession, he had acquired a scientific knowledge of the principles and maxims for conducting wars in Europe but considered them as often inapplicable to America. When they were adapted to his circumstances he used them, but oftener deviated from them, and followed his own practical judgement, founded on a comprehensive view of his real situation.

With an inconsiderable army, miserably provided, Gen. Greene took the field against a superior British regular force, which had marched in triumph 200 miles from the sea coast, and was flushed with successive victories through a whole campaign. Soon after he took the command, he divided his force and sent Gen. Morgan with a respectable detachment to the western extremity of South-Carolina, and about the same time marched with the main body to Hick's-creek, on the north side of the Pedee, opposite to Cheraw-Hill.

1781

[232] After the general submission of the militia in the year 1780, a revolution took place highly favourable to the interest of America. The residence of the British army, instead of increasing the real friends to royal government, diminished their number, and added new vigor to the opposite party. The British had a post in Ninety six for thirteen months, during which time the country was filled with rapine, violence and murder. Applications were daily made for redress, yet in that whole period, there was not a single instance wherein punishment was inflicted, either on the soldiery or on the tories. The people soon found that there was no security for their lives, liberties or property, under the military government of British officers, careless of their civil rights. The peaceable citizens were reduced to that uncommon distress, in which they had more to fear from oppression, than resistance. They therefore most ardently wished for an American force. Under these favourable circumstances General Greene detached General Morgan, to take a position in that district. The appearance of this force, a sincere attachment to the cause of independence, and the impolitic conduct of the British, induced several persons to resume their arms, and to act in concert with the continental troops.

When this irruption was made into the district of Ninety six, lord Cornwallis was far advanced in his preparations for the invasion of North-Carolina. To leave General Morgan in his rear, was contrary to military policy. In order therefore to drive him from this station, and to deter the inhabitants from joining him, Lieutenant Colonel Tarleton was ordered to proceed with about 1100 men and "push him to the utmost." He had two field pieces, and a superiority of infantry in the proportion of five to four, and of cavalry in the proportion of three to one. Besides this inequality of force, two thirds of the troops under General Morgan were militia. With these fair prospects of success, Tarleton engaged Morgan at the Cowpens, with the expectation of driving him out of South-Carolina. The latter drew up his men in two lines. The whole of the southern militia, with 190 from [233] North-Carolina, were put under the command of Colonel Pickens. These formed the first line, and were advanced a few hundred yards before the second, with orders to form on the right of the second, when forced to retire. The second line consisted of the light infantry, and a corps of Virginia militia riflemen. Lieutenant Colonel Washington, with his cavalry and about 45 militia men, mounted and equipped with swords, were drawn up at some distance in the rear of the whole. The open wood in which they were formed, was neither secured in front, flank or rear. On the side of the British, the light legion infantry and fusileers, though worn down with extreme fatigue, were ordered to form in line. Before this order was executed, the line, though far from being complete, was led to the attack by Tarleton himself. They advanced with a shout and poured in an incessant fire of musquetry. Colonel Pickens directed the men under his command to restrain their fire, till the British were within forty or fifty yards. This order though executed with great firmness was not sufficient to repel their advancing foes. The militia fell back. The British advanced and engaged the second line, which after an obstinate conflict was compelled to retreat to the cavalry. In this crisis Lieutenant Colonel Washington made a successful charge on Captain Ogilvie, who with about forty dragoons, was cutting down the militia, and forced them to retreat in confusion. Lieutenant Colonel Howard, almost at the same moment rallied the continental troops and charged with fixed bayonets. The example was instantly followed by the militia. Nothing could exceed the astonishment and confusion of the British occasioned by these unexpected charges. Their advance fell back on their rear, and communicated a panic to the whole. Two hundred and fifty horse which had not been engaged fled with precipitation. The pieces of artillery were seized by the Americans, and the greatest confusion took place among the infantry. While they were in this state of disorder, Lieutenant Colonel Howard called to them, to "lay down their arms," and promised them good quarter. Some hundreds accepted the offer [234] and surrendered. The first battalion of the 71st, and two British light infantry companies, laid down their arms to the American militia. A party which had been left some distance in the rear to guard the baggage, was the only body of infantry that escaped. The officer of that detachment on hearing of Tarleton's defeat, destroyed a great part of the baggage, and retreated to lord Cornwallis. Upwards of 300 of the British were killed or wounded, and above 500 prisoners were taken. Eight hundred muskets, two field pieces, 35 baggage waggons, and 100 dragoon horses fell into the hands of the conquerors. The Americans had only 12 men killed and 60 wounded.

General Morgan's good conduct on this memorable day, was honoured by Congress with a gold medal. They also presented medals of silver to Lieutenant Colonels Washington and Howard, a sword to colonel Pickens, a brevet majority to Edward Giles the General's aid de camp, and a Captaincy to Baron Glassbeck. Lieutenant Colonel Tarleton hitherto triumphant in a variety of skirmishes, on this occasion lost his laurels, though he was supported by the 7th regiment, one battalion of the 71st, and two companies of light infantry; and his repulse did more essential injury to the British interest, than was equivalent to all the preceding advantages he had gained. It was the first link in a chain of causes which finally drew down ruin, both in North and South Carolina on the royal interest. That impetuosity of Tarleton which had acquired him great reputation, when on former occasions he had surprised an incautious enemy, or attacked a panic struck militia, was at this time the occasion of his ruin. Impatient of delay he engaged with fatigued troops, and led them on to action, before they were properly formed, and before the reserve had taken its ground. He was also guilty of a great oversight in not bringing up a column of cavalry to support and improve the advantages he had gained when the Americans retreated.

Lord Cornwallis though preparing to extend his conquests north-wardly was not inattentive to the security of South-Carolina. Besides the force at Charleston, he left [235] a considerable body of troops under the command of lord Rawdon. These were principally stationed at Camden, from which central situation they might easily be drawn forth to defend the frontiers or to suppress insurrections. To facilitate the intended operations against North-Carolina, Major Craig, with a detachment of about 300 men from Charleston, and a small marine force took possession of Wilmington. While these arrangements were making, the year 1781 commenced with the fairest prospects to the friends of British government. The arrival of General Leslie in Charleston, with his late command in Virginia gave Earl Cornwallis a decided superiority, and enabled him to attempt the reduction of North-Carolina, with a force sufficient to bear down all probable opposition. Arnold was before him in Virginia, while South-Carolina in his rear, was considered as completely subdued. His lordship had much to hope and little to fear. His admirers flattered him with the expectation, that his victory at Camden would prove but the dawn of his glory; and that the events of the approaching campaign would immortalize his name as the conqueror, at least of the southern States. Whilst lord Cornwallis was indulging these pleasing prospects, he received intelligence, no less unwelcome than unexpected, that Tarleton his favourite officer, in whom he placed the greatest confidence, instead of driving Morgan out of the country, was completely defeated by him. This surprised and mortified, but did not discourage his lordship. He hoped by vigorous exertions soon to obtain reparation for the late disastrous event, and even to recover what he had lost. With the expectation of retaking the prisoners captured at the Cowpens, and to obliterate the impression made by the issue of the late action at that place, his lordship instantly determined on the pursuit of General Morgan, who had moved off towards Virginia with his prisoners. The movements of the royal army in consequence of this determination induced General Greene immediately to retreat from Hick's creek, lest the British by crossing the upper sources of the Pedee, should get between him and the detachment, [236] which was incumbered with the prisoners. In this critical situation General Greene left the main army, under the command of General Huger, and rode 150 miles through the country, to join the detachment under General Morgan, that he might be in front of lord Cornwallis, and direct the motions of both divisions of his army, so as to form a speedy junction between them. Immediately after the action, on the 17th of January, Morgan sent on his prisoners under a proper guard, and having made every arrangement in his power for their security retreated with expedition. Nevertheless the British gained ground upon him. Morgan intended to cross the

1781

mountains with his detachment and prisoners, that he might more effectually secure the latter: But Greene on his arrival ordered the prisoners to Charlotteville, and directed the troops to Guildford court-house, to which place he had also ordered General Huger to proceed with the main army.

In this retreat the Americans underwent hardships almost incredible. Many of them performed this march without shoes over frozen ground, which so gashed their naked feet, that their blood marked every step of their progress. They were sometimes without meat, often without flour, and always without spiritous liquors. Their march led them through a barren country, which scarcely afforded necessaries for a few straggling inhabitants. In this severe season, also with very little cloathing, they were daily reduced to the necessity of fording deep creeks, and of remaining wet without any change of cloaths, till the heat of their bodies and occasional fires in the woods dried their tattered rags. To all these difficulties they submitted without the loss of a single centinal by desertion. Lord Cornwallis reduced the quantity of his own baggage, and the example was followed by the officers under his command. Every thing which was not necessary in action, or to the existence of the troops, was destroyed. No waggons were reserved except those loaded with hospital stores, salt and ammunition, and four empty ones for the use of the sick. The royal army, encouraged by the example of his lordship, [237] submitted to every hardship with cheerfulness. They beheld, without murmuring, their most valuable baggage destroyed['] their spiritous liquors staved, when they were entering on hard service, and under circumstances which precluded every prospect of supply.

1781

The British had urged the pursuit with so much rapidity, that they reached the Catawba on the evening of the same day on which their fleeing adversaries had crossed it. Before the next morning a heavy fall of rain made that river impassable. The Americans, confident of the justice of their cause, considered this event as an interposition of providence in their favour. It is certain that if the rising of the river had taken place a few hours earlier, Gen. Morgan with his whole detachment and 500 prisoners would have scarcely had any chance of escape. When the fresh had subsided so far as to leave the river fordable, a large proportion of the King's troops received orders to be in readiness to march at one o'clock in the morning. Feints had FEB. 1 been made of passing at several different fords, but the real attempt was made at a ford near M'Cowans, the north banks of which were defended by a small guard of militia commanded by Gen. Davidson. The British marched through the river upwards of 500 yards wide and about three feet deep, sustaining a constant fire from the militia on the opposite bank without returning it till they had made good their passage. The light infantry and grenadier companies as soon as they reached the land dispersed the Americans. Gen. Davidson the brave leader of the latter was killed at the first onset. The militia throughout the neighbouring settlements were dispirited, and but few of them could be persuaded to take or keep the field. A small party which collected about ten miles from the ford was attacked, and dispersed by Lt. Col. Tarleton. All the fords were abandoned, and the whole royal army crossed over without any farther opposition. The passage of the Catawba being effected, the Americans continued to flee and the British to pursue. The former by expeditious movements crossed the Yadkin, partly in flats, and partly by fording on the second and third days of February, and secured their boats on [238] the north side. Though the British were close in their rear, yet 1781 the want of boats and the rapid rising of the river from preceding rains made their crossing impossible. This second hair breadth escape was considered by the Americans as a farther evidence that their cause was favoured by Heaven. That they in two successive instances should effect their passage, while their pursuers only a few miles in their rear could not follow, impressed the religious people of that settlement with such sentiments of devotion as added fresh vigor to their exertions in behalf of American independence.

The British having failed in their first scheme of passing the Yadkin, were obliged to cross at the upper fords; but before this was completed, the two divisions of the American army made a junction at Guildford court-house. Though this had taken place, their combined numbers were so much inferior to the British, that Gen. Greene could not FEB. 7 with any propriety risque an action. He therefore called a council of officers, who unanimously concurred in opinion that he ought to retire over the Dan, and to avoid an engagement till he was reinforced.

Lord Cornwallis knowing the inferiority of the American force conceived hopes, by getting between General Greene and Virginia, to cut off his retreat, intercept his supplies and reinforcements, and oblige him to fight under many disadvantages. With this view, his lordship kept the upper country where only the rivers are fordable— supposing that his adversaries, from the want of a sufficient number of flats, could not make good their passage in the deep water below, or in case of their attempting it, he expected to overtake and force them to action before they could cross. In this expectation he was deceived. Gen. Greene by good management eluded his lordship. The British urged their pursuit with so much rapidity, that the American light troops were on the 14th compelled to retire upwards

FEB
of 40 miles. By the most indefatigable exertions Gen. Greene had that day transported his army, artillery and baggage, over the river Dan into Virginia. So rapid was the pursuit, and so narrow the escape,

1781
that the van of the pursuing British [239] just arrived as the rear of the Americans had crossed. The hardships and difficulties, which the royal army had undergone in this march, were exceeded by the mortification that all their toils and exertions were to no purpose. They conceived it next to impossible that General Greene could escape, without receiving a decisive blow. They therefore cheerfully submitted to difficulties, of which they who reside in cultivated countries can form no adequate ideas. After surmounting incredible hardships, when they fancied themselves within grasp of their object, they discovered that all their hopes were blasted.

The continental army being driven out of North-Carolina, Earl Cornwallis thought the opportunity favourable for assembling the loyalists. With this view he left the Dan, and proceeded to Hillsborough. On his arrival there, he erected the King's standard, and published a proclamation, inviting all loyal subjects to repair to it with their arms and ten days provision, and assuring them of his readiness to concur with them in effectual measures for suppressing the remains of rebellion, and for the reestablishment of good order and constitutional government. Soon after the King's standard was erected at Hillsborough, some hundreds of the inhabitants rode in to the British camp. They seemed to be very desirous of peace, but averse to any co-operation for procuring it. They acknowledged the continentals were chased out of the province, but expressed their apprehensions that they would soon return, and on the whole declined to take any decided part in a cause which yet appeared dangerous. Notwithstanding the indifference or timidity of the loyalists near Hillsborough, lord Cornwallis hoped for substantial aid from the inhabitants between Haw and Deep river. He therefore detached Lieut. Col. Tarleton with 450 men, to give countenance to the friends of royal government in that district. Greene being informed that many of the inhabitants had joined his lordship, and that they were repairing in great numbers to make their submission, was apprehensive that unless some spirited measure was immediately taken, the whole country would be lost to the Americans. He therefore concluded, [240] at every hazard, to recross the Dan. This was done by the light troops, and these on the next day were followed by the main body accompanied with a brigade of Virginia militia. Immediately after the return of the Americans to North-Carolina, some of their light troops, commanded by Gen. Pickens and Lieut. Colonel Lee, were detached in pursuit of Tarleton, who had been sent to encourage the insurrection of the loyalists. Three hundred and fifty of these tories commanded by Col. Pyles, when on their way to join the British, fell in with this light American party, and mistook them for the royal detachment sent for their support. The Americans attacked them, laboring under this mistake, to great advantage, and cut them down as they were crying out "God save the King" and making protestations of their loyalty. Natives of the British colonies, who were of this character, more rarely found mercy than European soldiers. They were considered by the whig Americans as being cowards, who not only wanted spirit to defend their constitutional rights, but who unnaturally co-operated with strangers in fixing the chains of foreign domination on themselves and countrymen. Many of them on this occasion suffered the extremity of military vengeance. Tarleton was refreshing his legion, about a mile from this scene of slaughter. Upon hearing the alarm, he re-crossed the Haw and returned to Hillsborough. On his retreat he cut down several of the royalists, as they were advancing to join the British army, mistaking them for the rebel militia of the country. These events, together with the return of the American army, overset all the schemes of lord

1781
FEB. 21

Cornwallis. The tide of public sentiment was no longer in his favour. The recruiting service in behalf of the royal army was entirely stopped. The absence of the American army, for one fortnight longer, might have turned the scale. The advocates for royal government being discouraged by these adverse accidents, and being also generally deficient in that ardent zeal which characterised the patriots, could not be induced to act with confidence. They were so dispersed over a large extent of a thinly [241] settled country, that it was difficult to bring them to unite in any common plan. They had no superintending Congress to give system or concert to their schemes. While each little district pursued separate measures, all were obliged to submit to the American governments. Numbers of them, who were on their way to join lord Cornwallis, struck with terror at the unexpected return of the American army, and with the unhappy fate of their brethren, went home to wait events. Their policy was of that timid kind, which disposed them to be more attentive to personal safety, than to the success of either army.

1781

Though Gen. Greene had recrossed, his plan was not to venture upon an immediate action, but to keep alive the courage of his party—to depress that of the loyalists, and to harass the foragers and detachments of the British, till reinforcements should arrive. While Greene was unequal even to defensive operations, he lay seven days within ten miles of Cornwallis' camp, but took a new position every night, and kept it a profound secret where the next was to be. By such frequent movements lord Cornwallis, could not gain intelligence of his situation in time to profit by it. He maneuvered in this manner, to avoid an action for three weeks, during which time he was often obliged to ask bread from the common soldiers, having none of his own. By the end of that period, two brigades of militia from North-Carolina, and one from Virginia, together with 400 regulars raised for 18 months, joined his army, and gave him a superiority of numbers. He therefore determined no longer to avoid an engagement. Lord Cornwallis having long sought for this, no longer delay took place on either side. The American army consisted of about 4400 men, of which more than one half were militia. The British of about 2400, chiefly troops grown veteran in victories. The former was drawn up in three lines. The front composed of North-Carolina militia, the

MARCH 15, 1781

second of Virginia militia, the third and last of continental troops commanded by Gen. Huger and Col. Williams. After a brisk cannonade in front, the British advanced in three columns. The Hessians on the right, the guards in the [242] center, and Lieut. Col. Webster's brigade on the left, and attacked the front line. This gave way when their adversaries were at the distance of 140 yards, and was occasioned by the misconduct of a colonel, who on the advance of the enemy, called out to an officer at some distance "that he would be surrounded." The alarm was sufficient: Without enquiring into the probability of what had been injudiciously suggested, the militia precipitately quitted the field: As one good officer may sometimes mend the face of affairs, so the misconduct of a bad one may injure a whole army. Untrained men when on the field are similar to each other. The difference of their conduct depends much on incidental circumstances, and on none more than the manner of their being led on, and the quality of the officers by whom they are commanded.

The Virginia militia stood their ground, and kept up their fire till they were ordered to retreat. Gen. Stevens their commander, had posted 40 riflemen at equal distances, twenty paces in the rear of his brigade, with orders to shoot every man who should leave his post. That brave officer though wounded through the thigh did not quit the field. The continental troops were last engaged, and maintained the conflict with great spirit for an hour and a half. At length the discipline of veteran troops gained the day. They broke the second Maryland brigade, turned the American left flank, and got in rear of the Virginia brigade. They appeared to be gaining Greene's right, which would have encircled the whole of the continental troops, a retreat was therefore ordered. This was made in good order, and no farther than over the reedy fork, a distance of about three miles. Greene halted there and drew up till he had collected most of the stragglers, and then retired to Speedwell's iron works, ten miles distant from Guildford. The Americans lost 4 pieces of artillery and two ammunition waggons. The victory cost the British dear. Their killed and wounded amounted to several hundreds. The guards lost Colonel Stuart and three Captains, besides subalterns. Colonel Webster, an officer of distinguished [243] merit died of his wounds, to the great regret of the whole royal army. Generals O'Hara and

Howard, and Lieutenant Colonel Tarleton, were wounded. About 300 of the continentals, and one hundred of the Virginia militia were killed or wounded. Among the former was Major Anderson of the Maryland line a most valuable officer, of the latter were Generals Huger and Stevens. The early retreat of the North-Carolinians saved them from much loss. The American army sustained a great diminution, by the numerous fugitives who instead of rejoining the camp went to their homes. Lord Cornwallis suffered so much that he was in no condition to improve the advantage he had gained. The British had only the name, the Americans, all the good consequences of a victory. General Greene retreated, and lord Cornwallis kept the field, but notwithstanding the British interest in North-Carolina was from that day ruined. Soon after this action, lord Cornwallis issued a proclamation setting forth his complete victory, and calling on all loyal subjects to stand forth, and take an active part in restoring order and good government, and offering a pardon and protection to all rebels, murderers excepted, who would surrender themselves on or before the 20th of April. On the next day after this proclamation was issued, his lordship left his hospital and 75 wounded men, with the numerous loyalists in the vicinity, and began a march towards Wilmington, which had the appearance of a retreat. Major Craig who for the purposes of cooperating with his lordship, had been stationed at Wilmington, was not able to open a water communication with the British army while they were in the upper country. The distance, the narrowness of Cape Fear river, the commanding elevation of its banks, and the hostile sentiments of the inhabitants on each side of it forbad the attempt. The destitute condition of the British army, made it necessary to go to these supplies, which for these reasons could not be brought to them.

MAR. 18

General Greene no sooner received information of this movement of lord Cornwallis, than he put his army in motion to follow him. As he had no means of [244] providing for the wounded, of his own, and the British forces, he wrote a letter to the neighbouring inhabitants of the Quaker persuasion, in which he mentioned his being brought up a Quaker, and urged them to take care of the wounded on both sides. His recommendations prevailed, and the Quakers supplied the hospitals with every comfort in their power.

1781

The Americans continued the pursuit of Cornwallis till they had arrived at Ramsay's mill on Deep river, but for good reasons desisted from following him any farther. MARCH 28

Lord Cornwallis halted and refreshed his army for about three weeks at Wilmington, and then marched across the country to Petersburg in Virginia. Before it was known that his lordship had determined on this movement, the bold resolution of returning to South-Carolina, was formed by Gen. Greene. This animated the friends of Congress in that quarter. Had the American army followed his lordship, the southern States would have conceived themselves conquered; for their hopes and fears prevailed just as the armies marched north or south. Though lord Cornwallis marched through North-Carolina to Virginia, yet as the American army returned to South-Carolina, the people considered that movement of his lordship in the light of a retreat.

While the two armies were in North-Carolina, the whig inhabitants of South-Carolina were animated by the gallant exertions of Sumter and Marion. These distinguished partisans, while surrounded with enemies, kept the field. Though the continental army was driven into Virginia, they did not despair of the commonwealth. Having mounted their followers, their motions were rapid, and their attacks unexpected. With their light troops they intercepted the British convoys of provisions, infested their out posts, beat up their quarters, and harassed their detachments with such frequent alarms, that they were obliged to be always on their guard. In the western extremity of the State, Sumter was powerfully supported by Cols. Niel, Lacey, Hill, Winn, [245] Bratton, Brandon and others, each of whom held militia commissions, and had many friends. In the north eastern extremity, Marion received in like manner great assistance from the active exertions of Cols. Peter Horry, and Hugh Horry, Lt. Col. John Baxter, Col. James Postell, Major John Postell, and Major John James. 1781

The inhabitants, either as affection or vicinity induced them, arranged themselves under some of the militia officers and performed many gallant enterprises. These singly were of too little consequence to merit a particular relation, but in general they displayed the determined spirit of the people and embarrassed the British. One in which Major John Postell commanded may serve as an illustration of the spirit of the times, and particularly of the indifference for property which then prevailed. Capt. James de Peyster of the royal army, with 25 grenadiers, having taken post in the house of the Major's father, the Major posted his small command of 21 militia men, in such positions as commanded its doors, and demanded their surrender. This being refused, he set fire to an outhouse, and was proceeding to burn that in which they were posted, and nothing but the immediate submission of the whole party restrained him from sacrificing his father's valuable property, to gain an advantage to his country.

While lord Cornwallis was preparing to invade Virginia, Gen. Greene determined to re-commence offensive military operations in the southern extreme of the confederacy, in preference to pursuing his lordship into Virginia. Gen. Sumter, who had warmly urged this measure, was about this time authorised to raise a State brigade, to be in service for eighteen months. He had also prepared the militia to co-operate with the returning continentals. With these forces an offensive war was recommenced in South-Carolina, and prosecuted with spirit and success.

Before Greene set out on his march for Carolina, he sent orders to General Pickens, to prevent supplies from going to the British garrisons at Ninety-Six and Augusta, and also detached Lieutenant Colonel Lee to advance [246] before the continental troops. The latter in eight days penetrated through the intermediate country to General Marion's quarters upon the Santee. The main army, in a few more days, completed their march from Deep river to Camden. The British had erected a chain of posts from the capital to the extreme districts of the State, which had regular communications with each other. Lord Cornwallis being gone to Virginia, these became objects of enterprize to the Americans. While Gen. Greene was marching with his main force against Camden, fort Watson, which lay between Camden and Charleston, was invested by Gen. Marion and Lieut. Col. Lee. The besiegers speedily erected a work which overlooked the fort, though that was built on an Indian mount upwards of 30 feet high, from which they fired into it with such execution that the besieged durst not shew themselves. Under these circumstances the garrison, consisting of 114 men, surrendered by capitulation.

1781

APRIL 23

Camden, before which the main American army was encamped, is a village situated on a plain, covered on the south and east sides by the Wateree and a creek, the western and northern by six redoubts. It was defended by lord Rawdon with about 900 men. The American army, consisting only of about an equal number of continentals, and between two and three hundred militia, was unequal to the task of carrying this post by storm, or of completely investing it. Gen. Greene therefore took a good position about a mile distant, in expectation of alluring the garrison out of their lines. Lord Rawdon armed his whole force, and with great spirit sallied on the 25th. An engagement ensued. Victory for some time evidently inclined to the Americans, but in the progress of the action, the premature retreat of two companies eventually occasioned the defeat of the whole American army. Greene with his usual firmness, instantly took measures to prevent lord Rawdon from improving the success he had obtained. He retreated with such order that most of his wounded and all his artillery, together with a number of prisoners, were carried off. The British retired to Camden, and the Americans encamped [247] about five miles from their former position. Their loss was between two and three hundred. Soon after this action Gen. Greene, knowing that the British garrison could not subsist long in Camden without fresh supplies from Charleston or the country, took such positions as were most likely to prevent their getting any.

APRIL 25

1781

MAY 7

Lord Rawdon received a reinforcement of 4 or 500 men by the arrival of Col. Watson from Pedee. With this increase of strength, he attempted on the next day to compel Gen. Greene to another action, but found it to be impracticable. Failing in this design, he returned to Camden and burned the jail, mills, many private houses and a great deal of his own baggage. He then evacuated the post, and retired to the southward of Santee. His lordship discovered as much prudence in evacuating Camden, as he had shewn bravery in its defence. The fall of fort Watson broke the chain of communication with Charleston, and the position of the American army, in a great measure intercepted supplies from the adjacent country. The British in South-Carolina, now cut off from all communication with lord Cornwallis, would have hazarded the capital, by keeping large detachments in their distant out-posts. They therefore resolved to contract their limits by retiring within the Santee. This measure animated the friends of Congress in the extremities of the State, and disposed them to co-operate with the American army. While Greene lay in the neighbourhood of Camden, he hung in one day eight soldiers, who had deserted from his army. This had such effect afterwards that there was no desertion for three months. On the day after the evacuation of Camden the post at Orangeburg, consisting of 70 British militia and 12 regulars, surrendered to Gen. Sumter. On the next day fort Motte capitulated. This was situated above the fork on the south side of the Congaree. The British had built their works round Mrs. Motte's dwelling house. She with great cheerfulness furnished the Americans with materials for firing her own house. These being thrown by them on its roof soon kindled into flame. The firing of the house, [248] which was in the center of the British works, compelled the garrison, consisting of 165 men, to surrender at discretion.

MAY 11

MAY 12

1781

In two days more the British evacuated their post at Nelson's ferry, and destroyed a great part of their stores. On the day following, fort Granby, garrisoned by 352 men mostly royal militia, surrendered to Lieut. Col. Lee: Very advantageous terms were given them, from an apprehension that lord Rawdon was marching to their relief.

MAY 14

MAY 15

Their baggage was secured, in which was included an immense quantity of plunder. The American militia were much disgusted at the terms allowed the garrison, and discovered a disposition to break the capitulation and kill the prisoners; but Greene restrained them, by declaring in the most peremptory manner that he would instantly put to death any one, who should offer violence to those who by surrendering were under his protection.

General Marion with a party of militia, marched about this time to Georgetown, and began regular approaches against the British post in that place. On the first night after his men had broken ground, their adversaries evacuated their works, and retreated to Charleston; shortly after one Manson, an inhabitant of South-Carolina, who had joined the British, appeared in an armed vessel, and demanded permission to land his men in the town. This being refused, he sent a few of them ashore and set fire to it. Upwards of forty houses were speedily reduced to ashes.

In the rapid manner just related, the British lost six posts, and abandoned all the northeastern extremities of South-Carolina. They still retained possession of Augusta and Ninety-six, in addition to their posts near the sea coast. Immediately after the surrender of fort Granby, Lieutenant Colonel Lee began his march for Augusta, and in four days completed it.

The British post at Silver-Bluff, with a field piece and considerable stores, surrendered to a detachment of Lee's legion commanded by Captain Rudolph. Lee on his arrival at Augusta joined Pickens, who with a body of militia had for some time past taken post in the vicinity. [249] They jointly carried on their approaches against fort Cornwallis at Augusta, in which Colonel Brown commanded. Two batteries were erected within 30 yards of the parapet, which overlooked the fort. From these eminences the American riflemen shot into the inside of the works with success: The garrison buried themselves in a great measure under ground, and obstinately refused to capitulate, till the necessity was so pressing that every man who attempted to fire on the besiegers, was immediately shot down. At length when farther resistance would have been madness, the fort with about 300 men surrendered, on honorable terms of capitulation. The Americans during the siege had about forty men killed and wounded. After the surrender, Lieutenant Colonel Grierson of the British militia, was shot by the Americans. A reward of 100 guineas was offered, but in vain, for the perpetrator of the perfidious deed. Lieutenant Colonel Brown, would probably have shared the same fate, had not his conquerors furnished him with an escort to the royal garrison in Savannah. Individuals whose passions were inflamed by injuries, and exasperated, with personal animosity, were eager to gratify revenge in violation of the laws of war. Murders had produced murders. Plundering, assassinations, and house burnings, had become common. Zeal for the King or the Congress were the ostensible motives of action; but in several of both sides, the love of plunder, private pique, and a savageness of disposition, led to actions which were disgraceful to human nature. Such was the state of parties in the vicinity of Savannah river, and such the exasperation of whigs against tories, and of tories against whigs; and so much had they suffered from and inflicted on each other, that the laws of war, and the precepts of humanity afforded but a feeble security for the

MAY 21

1781

JUNE 5

observance of capitulations on either side. The American officers exerted themselves to procure to their prisoners that safety which many of the inhabitants, influenced by a remembrance of the sufferings of themselves, and of their friends, were unwilling to allow them.

1781

[250] While operations were carrying on against the small posts, Greene proceeded with his main army and laid siege to Ninety-six, in which Lieutenant Colonel Cruger, with upwards of 500 men was advantageously posted. On the left of the besiegers was a work, erected in the form of a star. On the right was a strong blockade fort, with two block houses in it. The town was also picquetted in with strong picquets, and surrounded with a ditch, and a bank, near the height of a common parapet. The besiegers were more numerous than the besieged, but the disparity was not great.

MAY 25

The siege was prosecuted with indefatigable industry. The garrison defended themselves with spirit and address. On the morning after the siege began, a party sallied from the garrison, and drove the advance of the besiegers from their works. The next night, two strong block batteries were erected at the distance of 350 yards. Another battery 20 feet high, was erected within 220 yards, and soon after a fourth one was erected within 100 yards of the main fort, and lastly, a rifle battery was erected 30 feet high, within 30 yards of the ditch; from all of which the besiegers fired into the British works. The abbatis was turned, and a mine and two trenches were so far extended, as to be within six feet of the ditch. At that interesting moment, intelligence was conveyed into the garrison, that lord Rawdon was near at hand, with about 2000 men for their relief. These had arrived in Charleston from Ireland after the siege began, and were marched for Ninety-six, on the seventh day after they landed. In these circumstances, Gen. Greene had no alternative but to raise the siege,

JUNE 18

or attempt the reduction of the place by assault. The latter was attempted. Though the assailants displayed great resolution, they failed of success. On this General Greene raised the siege, and retreated over Saluda. His loss in the assault and previous conflicts was about 150 men. Lieutenant Colonel Cruger deservedly gained great reputation by this successful defence. He was particularly indebted to Major Greene, who had bravely and judiciously defended that redoubt, for the reduction of which, the [251] greatest exertions had been made. Truly distressing was the situation of the American army. When they were nearly masters of the whole country, they were compelled to seek safety by retreating to its remotest extremity. In this gloomy situation Greene was advised to retire with his remaining force to Virginia. To suggestions of this kind he nobly replied. "I will recover South-Carolina or die in the attempt." This distinguished officer whose genius was most vigorous in those perilous extremities, when feeble minds abandon themselves to despair, adopted the only expedient now left him, that of avoiding an engagement till the British force should be divided. Lord Rawdon who by rapid marches was near Ninety-six, at the time of the assault, pursued the Americans as far as the Enoree river; but without overtaking them. Desisting from this fruitless pursuit he drew off a part of his force from Ninety-six, and fixed a detachment at the Congaree. General Greene on hearing that the British force was divided, faced about to give them battle. Lord Rawdon no less surprised than alarmed at this unexpected movement of his lately retreating foe, abandoned the Congaree in two days after he had reached it, and marched to Orangeburgh. General Greene in his turn pursued and offered him battle. His lordship would not venture out, and his adversary was too weak to attack him in his encampment, with any prospect of success.

Reasons similar to those which induced the British to evacuate Camden, weighed with them about this time, to withdraw their troops from Ninety-six. While the American army lay near Orangeburgh, Lieutenant Colonel Cruger, having evacuated the post he had gallantly defended, was marching with the troops of that garrison, through the forks of Edisto, to join lord Rawdon at Orangeburgh. General Greene being unable to prevent their junction, and still less so to stand before their combined force, retired to the high hills of Santee. The evacuation of Camden having been effected by striking at the posts below it, the same manoeuvre was now attempted to induce the British to leave Orangeburgh. With this view Generals Sumter and Marion, with their brigades, and the [252] legion cavalry, were detached to Monk's corner and Dorchester. They moved down different roads, and commenced separate and successful attacks, on convoys and detachments in the vicinity of Charleston. In this manner was the war carried on. While the British kept their forces compact, they could not cover the country, and the American General had the prudence to avoid fighting. When they divided their army, their detachments were attacked and defeated. While they were in the upper country, light parties of Americans annoyed their small posts in the lower settlements. The people soon found that the late conquerors were not able to afford them their promised protection. The spirit of revolt became general, and the royal interest daily declined.

The British having evacuated all their posts to the northward of Santee and Congaree, and to the westward of Edisto, conceived themselves able to hold all that fertile country, which is in a great measure enclosed by these rivers. They therefore once more resumed their station, near the junction of the Wateree and Congaree. This induced Gen. Greene to concert farther measures for forcing them down towards Charleston. He therefore crossed the Wateree and Congaree, and collected his whole force on the south side of the latter, intending to act offensively. On his approach the British retired about 40 miles nearer Charleston, and took post at the Eutaw springs. Gen. Greene advanced with 2000 men, to attack them in their encampment at this place. His force was drawn up in two lines: The first was composed of militia, and the second of continental troops. As the Americans advanced they fell in with two parties of the British, three or four miles a head of their main army. These being briskly attacked soon retired. The militia continued to pursue and fire, till the action became general, and till they were obliged to give way. They were well supported by the continental troops. In the hottest of the action Col. O. Williams, and Lieut. Col. Campbel with the Maryland and Virginia continentals charged with trailed arms. Nothing could surpass the intrepidity of both officers and men on this occasion.

1781 They rushed on [253] in good order through a heavy cannonade, and a shower of musketry, with such unshaken resolution, that they bore down all before them. Lieut. Col. Campbel, while bravely leading his men on to that successful charge, received a mortal wound. After he had fallen he enquired who gave way, and being informed that the British were fleeing in all quarters, replied "I die contented," and immediately expired. The British were vigorously pursued, and upwards of 500 of them were taken prisoners. On their retreat they took post in a strong brick house, and in a picquetted garden: From these advantageous positions they renewed the action. Four six pounders were ordered up before the house, from under cover of which the British were firing. The Americans were compelled to leave these pieces and retire, but they left a strong picquet on the field of battle, and only retreated to the nearest water in their rear. In the evening of the next day, Lieut. Col. Stuart who commanded the British on this occasion, left seventy of his wounded men and a thousand stand of arms, and moved from the Eutaws towards Charleston. The loss of the British inclusive of prisoners, was upwards of 1100 men; that of the Americans above 500, in which number were sixty officers.

Congress honored Gen. Greene for his good conduct in this action, with a British standard and a golden medal. They also voted their thanks to the different corps and their commanders.

Soon after this engagement, the Americans retired to their former position on the high hills of Santee, and the British took post in the vicinity of Monks-Corner. In the close of the year Gen. Greene moved down into the lower country, and about the same time the British abandoned their outposts, and retired with their whole force to the quarter house on Charleston-neck. The defence of the country was given up, and the conquerors, who had lately carried their arms to the extremities of the State, seldom aimed at any thing more than to secure themselves in the vicinity of the capital. The crops, which had been planted in the spring of the year under [254] British auspices, and with the expectation of affording them supplies, fell into the hands of the Americans and administered to them a seasonable relief. The battle of Eutaw may be considered as closing the national war in South-Carolina. A few excursions were afterwards made by the British, and sundry small enterprizes were executed, but nothing of more general consequence than the loss of property, and of individual lives. Thus ended the campaign of 1781, in South-Carolina. At its commencement the British were in force over all the State; at its close they durst not, but with great precaution, venture 20 miles from Charleston. History affords but few instances of

1781

commanders, who have achieved so much with equal means, as was done by Gen. Greene in the short space of a twelve month. He opened the campaign with gloomy prospects, but closed it with glory. His unpaid and half naked army had to contend with veteran soldiers, supplied with every thing that the wealth of Britain or the plunder of Carolina could procure. Under all these disadvantages, he compelled superior numbers to retire from the extremity of the State, and confine themselves in the capital and its vicinity. Had not his mind been of the firmest texture he would have been discouraged, but his enemies found him as formidable on the evening of a defeat, as on the morning after a victory.

Campaign of 1781. Operations in Virginia: Cornwallis captured: New-London destroyed.

IT HAS ALREADY BEEN MENTIONED that lord Cornwallis, soon after the battle of Guildford, marched to Wilmington in North-Carolina. When he had completed that march, various plans of operation were presented to his view. It was said in favour of his proceeding southwardly, that the country between Wilmington and Camden was barren and of difficult passage—that an embarkation for Charleston would be both tedious and disgraceful [255]—that a junction with the royal forces in Virginia, and the prosecution of solid operations in that quarter, would be the most effectual plan for effecting and securing the submission of the more southern States. Other arguments of apparently equal force urged his return to South-Carolina. Previous to his departure for Virginia, he had received information that Gen. Greene had begun his march for Camden, and

1781

he had reason from past experience to fear that if he did not follow him, the inhabitants by a second revolt, would give the American army a superiority over the small force left under lord Rawdon. Though his lordship was very apprehensive of danger from that quarter, he hoped either that lord Rawdon would be able to stand his ground, or that Gen. Greene would follow the royal army to Virginia, or in the most unfavourable event he flattered himself, that by the conquest of Virginia, the recovery of South-Carolina would be at any time practicable. His lordship having too much pride to turn back, and prefering the extensive scale of operations which Virginia presented, to the narrow one of preserving past conquests,

APR. 25

determined to leave Carolina to its fate. Before the end of April, he therefore proceeded on his march, from Wilmington towards Virginia. To favour the passage of the many rivers, with which the country is intersected, two boats were mounted on carriages and taken along with his army. The King's troops proceeded several days without opposition, and almost without intelligence. The Americans made an attempt at Swift-creek and afterwards at Fishing-creek to stop their progress, but without any effect. The British took the shortest road to Halifax, and on their arrival there defeated several parties of the Americans and took some stores, with very little loss on their side. The Roanoke, the Meherrin, and the Nottaway rivers were successively crossed by the royal army, and with little or no opposition

MAY 20

from the dispersed inhabitants. In less than a month the march from Wilmington to Petersburg was completed. The latter had been fixed upon as the place of rendezvous, in a private correspondence with

1781

Gen. Philips. By this [256] combination of the royal force previously employed in Virginia, with the troops which had marched from Wilmington, lord Cornwallis was at the head of a very powerful army. This junction was scarcely completed, when lord Cornwallis received lord Rawdon's report of the advantage he had gained over Gen. Greene, on the 25th of the preceding month. About the same time he received information that three British regiments had sailed from Cork for Charleston.

These two events eased his mind of all anxiety for South-Carolina, and inspired him with brilliant hopes of a glorious campaign. He considered himself as having already subdued both the Carolinas, and as being in a fair way to increase his military fame, by the addition of Virginia to the list of his conquests. By the late combination of the royal forces under Philips and Cornwallis, and by the recent arrival of a reinforcement of 1500 men directly from New-York, Virginia became the principal theatre of operations for the remainder of the campaign. The formidable force, thus collected in one body, called for the vigorous exertions of the friends of independence. The defensive operations, in opposition to it, were principally entrusted to the Marquis de la Fayette. Early in the year he had been detached from the main American army on an expedition, the object of which was a co-operation with the French fleet in capturing Gen. Arnold. On the failure of this, the Marquis marched back as far as the head of Elk. There he received an order to return to Virginia to oppose the British forces, which had become more formidable by the arrival of a considerable reinforcement, under Gen. Phillips. He proceeded without delay to Richmond, and arrived there the day before the British reached Manchester, on the opposite side of James river. Thus was the capital of Virginia, at that time filled with almost all the military stores of the State, saved from imminent danger. So great was the superiority of numbers on the side of the British, that the Marquis had before him a labor of the greatest difficulty, and was pressed with many embarrassments. In the first moments of the rising [257] tempest, and till he could provide against its utmost rage, he began to retire with his little army, which consisted only of about 1000 regulars, 2000 militia, and 60 dragoons. 1781

Lord Cornwallis advanced from Petersburg to James river which he crossed at Westown, and thence marching through Hanover county crossed the South Anna or Pamunkey river. The Marquis followed his motions, but at a guarded distance. The superiority of the British army, especially of their cavalry, which they easily supplied with good horses from the stables and pastures of private gentlemen in Virginia, enabled them to traverse the country in all directions. Two distant expeditions were therefore undertaken. The one was to Charlotteville, with the view of capturing the Governor and Assembly of the State. The other to Point of Fork to destroy stores. Lt. Col. Tarleton to whom the first was committed, succeeded so far as to disperse the Assembly, capture seven of its members, and to destroy a great quantity of stores at and near Charlotteville. The other expedition which was committed to Lt. Col. Simcoe, was only in part successful, for the Americans had previously removed the most of their stores from Point of Fork. In the course of these marches and counter marches, immense quantities of property were destroyed and sundry unimportant skirmishes took place. The British made many partial conquests, but these were seldom of longer duration than their encampments. The young Marquis, with a degree of prudence that would have done honor to an older soldier, acted so cautiously on the defensive and made so judicious a choice of posts, and shewed so much vigor and design in his movements, as to prevent any advantage being taken of his weakness. In his circumstances, not to be destroyed, was triumph. He effected a junction at Racoonford with Gen. Wayne, who was at the head of 800 Pennsylvanians. While this junction was forming the British got between the American army and its stores, which had been removed from Richmond, to Albemarle old court house. The possession of these

1781

was an object [258] with both armies. The Marquis by forced marches got within a few miles of the British army, when they were two days march from Albemarle old court house. The British general considered himself as sure of his adversary for he knew that the stores were his object; and he conceived it impracticable for the Marquis to get between him and the shore; but by a road in passing which he might be attacked to advantage. The Marquis had the address to extricate himself from this difficulty, by opening in the night a nearer road to Albemarle old court house which had been long disused and was

JUNE 18

much embarrassed. To the surprize of lord Cornwallis, the Marquis fixed himself the next day between the British army and the American stores. Lord Cornwallis, finding his schemes frustrated fell back to Richmond. About this time the Marquis' army was reinforced by Steuben's troops, and by militia from the parts adjacent. He followed lord Cornwallis, and had the address to impress him with an idea that the American army was much greater than it really was. His

JUNE 26

lordship therefore retreated to Williamsburg. The day after the main body of the British army arrived there, their rear was attacked by an American light corps under Col. Butler and sustained a considerable loss.

About the time lord Cornwallis reached Williamsburg he received intelligence from New-York, setting forth the danger to which the royal army in that city was exposed from a combined attack, that was said to be threatened by the French and Americans. Sir Henry Clinton therefore required a detachment from Earl Cornwallis, if he was not engaged in any important enterprise, and recommended to him a healthy station, with an ample defensive force, till the danger of New-York was dispersed. Lord Cornwallis thinking it expedient to comply with this requisition, and judging that his command after-wards would not be adequate to maintain his present position at Williamsburg, determined to retire to Portsmouth. For the execution of this project, it was necessary to cross James river. The Marquis de la Fayette, conceiving this to be a favourable opportunity for acting [259] offensively, advanced on the British. Gen. Wayne relying on the information of a countryman, that the main body of the British had crossed James river, pushed forwards with about 800 light troops to harass their rear. Contrary to his expectations, he found the whole British army drawn up ready to oppose him. He instantly conceived that the best mode of extricating himself from his perilous situation would be, to assume a bold countenance, and engage his adversaries before he attempted to retreat. He therefore pressed on for some time, and urged an attack with spirit before he fell back. Lord Cornwallis, perhaps suspecting an ambuscade, did not pursue. By this bold manoeuvre Wayne got off but with little loss.

In the course of these various movements, the British were joined by few of the inhabitants, and scarcely by any of the natives. The Virginians for the most part either joined the Americans, or what was much more common, kept out of the way of the British. To purchase safety by submission was the policy of very few, and these were for the most part natives of Britain. After Earl Cornwallis had crossed James river, he marched for Portsmouth. He had previously taken the necessary steps for complying with the requisition of Sir Henry Clinton, to send a part of his command to New-York. But before they sailed, an express arrived from Sir Henry Clinton with a letter, expressing his preference of Williamsburgh to Portsmouth for the residence of the army, and his desire that Old-Point-Comfort or

1781

JULY 6

577

Hampton road should be secured as a station for line of battle ships. The commander in chief, at the same time, allowed his lordship to detain any part or the whole of the forces under his command, for completing this service. On examination, Hampton road was not approved of as a station for the navy. It being a principal object of the campaign to fix on a strong permanent post or place of arms in the Chesapeak for the security of both the army and navy, and Portsmouth and Hampton road having both been pronounced unfit for that purpose, York-Town and Gloucester Points were considered as most likely to accord with the views of the royal commanders.

Portsmouth was therefore evacuated, and its garrison [260] transferred to York-Town. Lord Cornwallis availed himself of Sir Henry Clinton's permission to retain the whole force under his command, and impressed with the necessity of establishing a strong place of arms in the Chesapeak, applied himself with industry to fortify his new posts, so as to render them tenable by his present army, amounting to 7000 men, against any force that he supposed likely to be brought against them.

At this period the officers of the British navy expected that their fleet in the West-Indies would join them, and that solid operations in Virginia would in a short time re-commence with increased vigor.

While they were indulging these hopes Count de Grasse with a French fleet of 28 sail of the line from the West-Indies entered the Chesapeak, and about the same time intelligence arrived, that the French and American armies which had been lately stationed in the more northern States, were advancing towards Virginia. Count de Grasse, without loss of time, blocked up York river with three large ships and some frigates, and moored the principal part of his fleet in Lynhaven-bay. Three thousand two hundred French troops, brought in this fleet from the West-Indies, commanded by the Marquis de St. Simon, were disembarked and soon after formed a junction with the continental troops under the Marquis de la Fayette, and the whole took post at Williamsburg. An attack on this force was intended, but before all the arrangements subservient to its execution were fixed upon, letters of an early date in September were received by lord Cornwallis from Sir Henry Clinton, announcing that he would do his utmost to reinforce the royal army in Chesapeak, or make every diversion in his power, and that Admiral Digby was hourly expected on the coast. On the receipt of this intelligence Earl Cornwallis, not thinking himself justified in hazarding an engagement, abandoned the resolution of attacking the combined force of Fayette and St. Simon. It is the province of history to relate what has happened, and not to indulge conjectures in the boundless field of contingencies; otherwise it might be added that Earl Cornwallis, by this change [261] of opinion, lost a favourable opportunity of extri- 1781 cating himself from a combination of hostile force, which by farther concentration soon became irresistible. On the other hand if an attack had been made, and that had proved unsuccessful, he would have been charged with rashness in not waiting for the promised co-operation. On the same uncertain ground of conjecturing what ought to have been done, it might be said that the knowledge Earl Cornwallis had of public affairs would have justified him in abandoning York-Town, in order to return to South-Carolina. It seems as though this would have been his wisest plan; but either from an opinion that his instructions to stand his ground were positive, or that effectual relief was probable, his lordship thought proper to risque every thing on the issue of a siege. An attempt was made to burn or dislodge the French ships in the river, but none to evacuate his posts at this early period, when that measure was practicable.

Admiral Greaves with 20 sail of the line, made an effort for the relief of lord Cornwallis, but without effecting his purpose. When he appeared off the capes of Virginia, M. de Grasse went out to meet him, and an indecisive engagement took place. The British were SEP. 7 willing to renew the action; but de Grasse for good reasons declined it. His chief object in coming out of the capes was to cover a French fleet of eight line of battle ships, which was expected from Rhode-Island. In conformity to a preconcerted plan, Count de Barras commander of this fleet, had sailed for the Chesapeak, about the time de Grasse sailed from the West-Indies for the same place. To avoid the British fleet, he had taken a circuit by Bermuda. For fear that the British fleet might intercept him on his approach to the capes of Virginia; de Grasse came out to be at hand for his protection. While Greaves and de Grasse were manoeuvering near the mouth of the Chesapeak, Count de Barras passed the former in the night, and

got within the capes of Virginia. This gave the fleet of his most
Christian Majesty a decided superiority. Admiral Greaves soon took
his departure, and M. de Grasse re-entered the Chesapeak. All this
time [262] conformably to the well digested plan of the campaign,
the French and the American forces were marching through the
middle states on their way to York-town. To understand their proper
connexion, the great events shortly to be described, it is necessary
to go back and trace the remote causes which brought on this grand
combination of fleets and armies which put a period to the war.

The fall of Charleston in May 1780, and the complete rout of the
American southern army in August following, together with the
increasing inability of the Americans to carry on the war, gave a
serious alarm to the friends of independence. In this low ebb of their
affairs, a pathetic statement of their distresses was made to their
illustrious ally the King of France. To give greater efficacy to their
solicitations, Congress appointed Lieutenant Colonel John Laurens
their special minister, and directed him after repairing to the court
of Versailles, to urge the necessity of speedy and effectual succour,
and in particular to solicit for a loan of money, and the cooperation
of a French fleet, in attempting some important enterprise against
the common enemy. His great abilities as an officer, had been often
displayed; but on this occasion, the superior talents of the statesman
and negotiator were called forth into action. Animated as he was
with the ardor of the warmest patriotism, and feeling most sensibly
for the distresses of his country, his whole soul was exerted to
interest the court of France in giving a vigorous aid to their allies.
His engaging manners and insinuating address, procured a favourable
reception to his representations. He won the hearts of those who
were at the helm of public affairs, and inflamed them with zeal to
assist a country whose cause was so ably pleaded, and whose sufferings
were so pathetically represented. At this crisis his most Christian
Majesty gave his American allies, a subsidy of six millions of livres,
and became their security for ten millions more borrowed for their
use in the United Netherlands. A naval co-operation was promised
and a conjunct expedition against their common foes was projected.

[263] The American war was now so far involved in the consequences of naval operations, that a superior French fleet, seemed to

be the only hinge on which it was likely soon to take a favourable turn. The British army being parcelled in the different sea ports of the United States, any division of it blocked up by a French fleet, could not long resist the superior combined force, which might be brought to operate against it. The Marquis de Castries who directed the marine of France, with great precision calculated the naval force, which the British could concentre on the coast of the United States, and disposed his own in such a manner as ensured him a superiority. In conformity to these principles, and in subserviency to the design of the campaign, M. de Grasse sailed in March 1781, from Brest with 25 sail of the line, several thousand land forces, and a large convoy amounting to more than 200 ships. A small part of this force was destined for the East-Indies, but M. de Grasse with the greater part sailed for Martinique. The British fleet then in the West-Indies, had been previously weakened by the departure of a squadron for the protection of the ships, which were employed in carrying to England the booty which had been taken at St. Eustatius. The British Admirals Hood and Drake, were detached to intercept the outward bound French fleet commanded by M. de Grasse, but a junction between his force and eight ships of the line and one of 50 guns, which were previously at Martinique and St. Domingo, was nevertheless effected. By this combination of fresh ships from Europe, with the French fleet previously in the West-Indies, they had a decided superiority. M. de Grasse having finished his business in the West-Indies, sailed in the beginning of August with a prodigious convoy. After seeing this out of danger he directed his course for the Chesapeak, and arrived there as has been related on the thirtieth of the same month. Five days before his arrival in the Chesapeak, the French fleet in Rhode-Island sailed for the same place. These fleets notwithstanding their original distance from the scene of action and from each other, coincided in their operations in an extraordinary manner, [264] far beyond the reach of military calculation. They all tended to one object and at one and the same time, and that object was neither known nor suspected by the British, till the proper season for counter-action was elapsed. This co-incidence of favourable circumstances, extended to the marches of the French and American land forces. The plan of operations had been so well digested, and was so faithfully

1781

581

executed by the different commanders, that Gen. Washington and Count Rochambeau, had passed the British head quarters in New-York, and were considerably advanced in their way to York-town, before Count de Grasse had reached the American coast. This was effected in the following manner, Monsr. de Barras appointed to the command of the French squadron at Newport, arrived at Boston with dispatches for Count de Rochambeau. An interview soon after took place at Weathersfield, between Gen. Washington, Knox and du Portail on the part of the Americans, and Count de Rochambeau and the Chavalier Chastelleux, on the part of the French. At this interview, an eventual plan of the whole campaign was fixed. This was to lay siege to New-York in concert with a French fleet, which was to arrive on the coast in the month of August. It was agreed that the French troops should march towards the North-river. Letters were addressed by Gen. Washington to the executive officers of New-Hampshire, Massachusetts, Connecticut and New-Jersey, requiring them to fill up their battalions, and to have their quotas 6200 militia in readiness, within a week of the time they might be called for. Conformably to these outlines of the campaign, the French troops marched from Rhode-Island in June, and early in the following month joined the American army. About the time this junction took place, Gen. Washington marched his army from their winter encampment near Peeks-kill, to the vicinity of Kingsbridge. General Lincoln fell down the North-river with a detachment in boats, and took possession of the ground where fort Independence formerly stood. An attack was made upon him but was soon discontinued. The British about this time, retired with almost the whole of their force to [265] York-Island. Gen. Washington hoped to be able to commence operations against New-York, about the middle, or at farthest the latter end of July. Flat bottomed boats sufficient to transport 5000 men were built near Albany, and brought down Hudson's river to the neighbourhood of the American army before New-York. Ovens were erected opposite to Staten-Island, for the use of the French troops. Every movement was made which was introductory to the commencement of the siege. It was not a little mortifying to Gen. Washington, to find himself on the 2d of August to be only a few hundreds stronger, than he was on the day his army first moved from their winter quarters. To have fixed on a plan of operations, with a foreign officer at the head of a

MAY 6

1781

respectable force: To have brought that force from a considerable distance, in confident expectation of reinforcements sufficiently large to commence effective operations against the common enemy, and at the same time to have engagements in behalf of the state violated in direct opposition to their own interest, and in a manner derogatory to his personal honour, was enough to have excited storms and tempests, in any mind less calm than that of Gen. Washington. He bore this hard trial with his usual magnanimity, and contented himself with repeating his requisitions to the states, and at the same time urged them by every tie, to enable him to fulfil engagements entered into on their account, with the commander of the French troops.

That tardiness of the states, which at other times had brought them near the brink of ruin, was now the accidental cause of real service. Had they sent forward their recruits for the regular army, and their quotas of militia as was expected, the siege of New-York would have commenced, in the latter end of July, or early in August. While the season was wasting away in expectation of these reinforcements, lord Cornwallis as has been mentioned, fixed himself near the capes of Virginia. His situation there, the arrival of a reinforcement of 3000 Germans from Europe to New-York, the superior strength of that garrison, the failure of the states in filling up their [266] battalions and embodying their milita, and especially recent intelligence from Count de Grasse, that his destination was fixed to the Chesapeak, concurred about the middle of August, to make a total change of the plan of the campaign.

1781

AUG. 15

The appearance of an intention to attack New-York was nevertheless kept up. While this deception was played off, the allied army crossed the North-river, and passed on by the way of Philadelphia, through the intermediate country, to York-town. An attempt to reduce the British force in Virginia promised success with more expedition, and to secure an object of nearly equal importance as the reduction of New-York. No one can undertake to say what would have been the consequence, if the allied forces had persevered in their original plan; but it is evident from the event, that no success could have been greater, or more conducive to the establishment of their schemes, than what resulted from their operations in Virginia.

24

While the attack of New-York was in serious contemplation, a letter from General Washington detailing the particulars of the intended operations of the campaign, being intercepted, fell into the hands of Sir Henry Clinton. After the plan was changed, the royal commander was so much under the impression of the intelligence contained in the intercepted letter, that he believed every movement towards Virginia to be a feint, calculated to draw off his attention from the defence of New-York. Under the influence of this opinion he bent his whole force to strengthen that post, and suffered the French and American armies to pass him without any molestation. When the best opportunity of striking at them was elapsed, then for the first time he was brought to believe that the allies had fixed on Virginia, for the theatre of their combined operations. As truth may be made to answer the purposes of deception, so no feint of attacking New-York, could have been more successful than the real intention.

AUG. 24
1781

In the latter end of August the American army began their march to Virginia, from the neighbourhood of [267] New-York. Gen. Washington had advanced as far as Chester, before he received the news of the arrival of the fleet, commanded by Monsr. de Grasse. The French troops marched at the same time, and for the same place. In the course of this summer they passed through all the extensive settlements which lie between Newport and York-Town. It seldom, if ever happened before, that an army led through a foreign country, at so great a distance from their own, among a people of different principles, customs, language, and religion, behaved with so much regularity. In their march to York-Town they had to pass through 500 miles of a country abounding in fruit, and at a time when the most delicious productions of nature, growing on and near the public highways, presented both opportunity and temptation to gratify their appetites. Yet so complete was their discipline, that in this long march, scarce an instance could be produced of a peach or an apple being taken, without the consent of the inhabitants. Gen. Washington

SEP. 14

and Count Rochambeau reached Williamsburg on the 14th of September. They with Generals Chastelleux, Du Portail, and Knox proceeded to visit Count de Grasse on board his ship the Ville de Paris, and agreed on a plan of operations.

The Count afterwards wrote to Washington, that in case a British fleet appeared, "he conceived that he ought to go out and meet them

at sea, instead of risquing an engagement in a confined situation."
This alarmed the General. He sent the Marquis de la Fayette, with a
letter to dissuade him from the dangerous measure. This letter and
the persuasions of the Marquis had the desired effect.

The combined forces proceeded on their way to York-town, partly
by land, and partly down the Chesapeak. The whole, together with
a body of Virginia militia, under the command of General Nelson,
amounting in the aggregate to 12,000 men, rendezvoused at Williamsburg on the 25th of September, and in five days after, moved down
to the investiture of York-town. The French fleet at the same time
moved to the mouth of York-river, [268] and took a position which   1781
was calculated to prevent lord Cornwallis, either from retreating, or
receiving succour by water. Previously to the march from Williamsburg to York-town, Washington gave out in general orders as follows.
"If the enemy should be tempted to meet the army on its march,
the General particularly enjoins the troops to place their principal
reliance on the bayonet, that they may prove the vanity of the boast,
which the British make of their peculiar prowess, in deciding battles
with that weapon."

The combined army halted in the evening, about two miles from
York-town, and lay on their arms all night. On the next day Colonel
Scammell, an officer of uncommon merit, and of the most amiable
manners, in approaching the outer works of the British, was mortally
wounded and taken prisoner. About this time Earl Cornwallis received
a letter from Sir Henry Clinton, announcing the arrival of Admiral
Digby with three ships of the line from Europe, and the determination
of the General and flag officers in New-York to embark 5000 men in
a fleet, which would probably sail on the 5th of October—that this
fleet consisted of 23 sail of the line, and that joint exertions of the
navy and army would be made for his relief. On the night after the
receipt of this intelligence, Earl Cornwallis quitted his outward
position, and retired to one more inward.

The works erected for the security of York-town on the right, were
redoubts and batteries, with a line of stockade in the rear. A marshy
ravine lay in front of the right, over which was placed a large redoubt.
The morass extended along the center, which was defended by a line
of stockade, and by batteries: On the left of the center was a hornwork

with a ditch, a row of fraize and an abbatis. Two redoubts were advanced before the left. The combined forces advanced and took possession of the ground from which the British had retired. About this time the legion cavalry and mounted infantry, passed over the river to Gloucester, General de Choisy invested the British post on that side so fully, as to cut off all communication between it and the country. In the mean time the royal [269] army was straining every nerve to strengthen their works and their artillery was constantly employed in impeding the operations of the combined army. On the 9th and 10th of October, the French and Americans opened their batteries. They kept up a brisk and well directed fire from heavy cannon, from mortars and howitzers. The shells of the besiegers reached the ships in the harbour, the Charon of 44 guns and a transport ship were burned. On the 10th a messenger arrived with a dispatch from Sir Henry Clinton to Earl Cornwallis, dated on the 30th of September, which stated various circumstances tending to lessen the probability of relief being obtained, by a direct movement from New-York. Earl Cornwallis was at this juncture advised to evacuate York-town, and after passing over to Gloucester, to force his way into the country. Whether this movement would have been successful, no one can with certainty pronounce, but it could not have produced any consequences more injurious to the royal interest, than those which resulted from declining the attempt. On the other hand had this movement been made, and the royal army been defeated or captured in the interior country, and in the mean time had Sir Henry Clinton with the promised relief, reached York-town, the precipitancy of the noble Earl, would have been perhaps more the subject of censure, than his resolution of standing his ground and resisting to the last extremity. From this uncertain ground of conjectures, I proceed to relate real events. The besiegers commenced their second parallel 200 yards from the works of the besieged. Two redoubts which were advanced on the left of the British, greatly impeded the progress of the combined armies. It was therefore proposed to carry them by storm. To excite a spirit of emulation, the reduction of the one was committed to the French, of the other to the Americans. The assailants marched to the assault with unloaded arms; having passed the abbatis and palisades, they attacked on all sides, and carried the redoubt in a few minutes with the loss of 8

killed and 28 wounded, Lieutenant Colonel Laurens personally took
the commanding officer prisoner. His humanity and [270] that of his
associates, so overcame their resentments that they spared the
British, though they were charged when they went to the assault, to
remember New-London (the recent massacres at which place shall
be hereafter related) and to retaliate by putting the men in the
redoubt to the sword. Being asked why they had disobeyed orders
by bringing them off as prisoners, they answered, "We could not put
them to death, when they begged for their lives." About five of the
British were killed and the rest were captured. Colonel Hamilton
who conducted the enterprise, in his report to the Marquis de la
Fayette mentioned to the honour of his detachment, "that incapable
of imitating examples of barbarity, and forgetting recent provocations,
they spared every man who ceased to resist."

The French were equally successful on their part. They carried
the redoubt assigned to them with rapidity, but lost a considerable
number of men. These two redoubts were included in the second
parallel, and facilitated the subsequent operations of the besiegers.
The British could not with propriety risque repeated sallies. One was
projected at this time consisting of 400 men, commanded by Lieutenant Colonel Abercrombie. He proceeded so far as to force two
redoubts, and to spike eleven pieces of cannon. Though the officers
and soldiers displayed great bravery in this enterprise, yet their
success produced no essential advantage. The cannon were soon
unspiked and rendered fit for service.

By this time the batteries of the besiegers were covered with nearly
a hundred pieces of heavy ordnance, and the works of the besieged
were so damaged, that they could scarcely shew a single gun. Lord
Cornwallis had now no hope left but from offering terms of capitulation or attempting an escape. He determined on the latter. This
though less practicable than when first proposed, was not altogether
hopeless. Boats were prepared to receive the troops in the night, and
to transport them to Gloucester-Point. After one whole embarkation
had crossed, a violent storm of wind and rain dispersed the boats
employed on this business, and frustrated the whole scheme. The
royal army, thus weakened by division, was exposed to increased
danger.

[271] Orders were sent to those who had passed, to re-cross the

river to York-Town. With the failure of this scheme the last hope of the British army expired. Longer resistance could answer no good purpose, and might occasion the loss of many valuable lives. Lord Cornwallis therefore wrote a letter to Gen. Washington, requesting a cessation of arms for 24 hours, and that commissioners might be appointed to digest terms of capitulation. It is remarkable while Lieut. Col. Laurens, the officer employed by Gen. Washington on this occasion, was drawing up these articles, that his father was closely confined in the tower of London, of which Earl Cornwallis was Constable. By this singular combination of circumstances, his lordship became a prisoner, to the son of his own prisoner.

OCT. 19

The posts of York and Gloucester were surrendered by a capitulation, the principal articles of which were as follows: The troops to be prisoners of war to Congress, and the naval force to France. The officers to retain their side arms and private property of every kind; but all property, obviously belonging to the inhabitants of the United States, to be subject to be reclaimed. The soldiers to be kept in Virginia, Maryland and Pennsylvania, and to be supplied with the same rations, as are allowed to soldiers in the service of Congress. A proportion of the officers to march into the country with the prisoners; the rest to be allowed to proceed on parole to Europe, to New-York, or to any other American maritime post in possession of the British. The honor of marching out with colors flying, which had been refused to Gen. Lincoln on his giving up Charleston, was now refused to Earl Cornwallis; and General Lincoln was appointed to receive the submission of the royal army at York-Town, precisely in the same way his own had been conducted, about 18 months before. Lord Cornwallis endeavoured to obtain permission for the British and German troops to return to their respective countries, under no other restrictions than an engagement not to serve against France or America. He also tried to obtain an indemnity for those of the inhabitants who had joined them; but he was obliged to recede from

1781

the former, [272] and also to consent that the loyalists in his camp should be given up, to the unconditional mercy of their countrymen. His lordship nevertheless obtained permission for the Bonetta sloop of war to pass unexamined to New-York. This gave an opportunity of screening such of them, as were most obnoxious to the Americans.

The regular troops of France and America, employed in this siege, consisted of about 7000 of the former, and 5500 of the latter; and they were assisted by about 4000 militia. On the part of the combined army about 300 were killed or wounded. On the part of the British about 500; and 70 were taken in the redoubts, which were carried by assault on the 14th of October. The troops of every kind that surrendered prisoners of war exceeded 7000 men, but so great was the number of sick and wounded, that there were only 3800 capable of bearing arms. The French and American engineers and artillery, merited and received the highest applause. Brigadiers General Du Portail and Knox were both promoted to the rank of Major Generals, on account of their meritorious services. Lieut. Col. Gorion and Captain Rochefontaine of the corps of engineers, respectively received brevets, the former to the rank of a Colonel, and the latter to the rank of a Major.

Congress honored Gen. Washington, Count de Rochambeau, Count de Grasse and the officers of the different corps, and the men under them, with thanks for their services in the reduction of lord Cornwallis. The whole project was conceived with profound wisdom, and the incidents of it had been combined with singular propriety. It is not therefore wonderful, that from the remarkable coincidence in all its parts, it was crowned with unvaried success.

A British fleet and an army of 7000 men, destined for the relief of lord Cornwallis, arrived off the Chesapeak on the 24th of October; but on receiving advice of his lordship's surrender, they returned to Sandy-hook and New-York. Such was the fate of that General, from whose gallantry and previous successes the speedy [273] conquests of the southern States had been so confidently expected. No event during the war bid fairer for oversetting the independence of at least a part of the confederacy, than his complete victory at Camden; but by the consequences of that action, his lordship became the occasion of rendering that a revolution, which from his previous success was in danger of terminating in a rebellion. The loss of his army may be considered as the closing scene of the continental war in North America.

The troops under the command of lord Cornwallis had spread waste and ruin over the face of all the country for four hundred

1781

miles on the sea coast, and for two hundred miles to the west-ward. Their marches from Charleston to Camden, from Camden to the river Dan, from the Dan through North-Carolina to Wilmington, from Wilmington to Petersburg, and from Petersburg through many parts of Virginia, till they finally settled in York-Town, made a route of more than eleven hundred miles. Every place through which they passed in these various marches, experienced the effects of their rapacity. Their numbers enabled them to go whithersoever they pleased, their rage for plunder disposed them to take whatever they had the means of removing, and their animosity to the Americans led them often to the wanton destruction of what they could neither use nor carry off. By their means thousands had been involved in distress. The reduction of such an army occasioned unusual transports of joy, in the breasts of the whole body of the people. Well authenticated testimony asserts that the nerves of some were so agitated, as to produce convulsions, and that at least one man expired under the tide of pleasure which flowed in upon him, when informed of his lordship's surrender*. The people throughout the United States displayed a social triumph and exultation, which no private prosperity is ever able fully to inspire. General Washington, on the day after the surrender, ordered "that those who were [274] under arrest

1781 should be pardoned and set at liberty." His orders closed as follows, "divine service shall be performed to morrow in the different brigades and divisions. The commander in chief recommends, that all the troops that are not upon duty do assist at it with a serious deportment, and that sensibility of heart, which the recollection of the surprising and particular interposition of providence in our favour claims."

SEPT. 6 Congress on receiving the official account of the great events, which had taken place at York-town, resolved to go in procession to church and return public thanks to Almighty God for the advantages they had gained. They also issued a proclamation for "religiously observing through the United States the 13th of December as a day of thanksgiving and prayer." The singularly interesting event of captivating a

---

* The door keeper of Congress an aged man died suddenly, immediately after hearing of the capture of lord Cornwallis' army. This death was universally ascribed to a violent emotion of political joy.

---

second royal army, produced strong emotions, which broke out in all the variety of ways with which the most rapturous joy usually displays itself.

While the combined armies were advancing to the siege of York-town, an excursion was made from New-York, which was attended with no small loss to the Americans. Gen. Arnold who had lately returned from Virginia, was appointed to conduct an expedition, the object of which, was the town of New-London in his native country. The troops employed therein, were landed in two detachments on each side of the harbour. The one was commanded by Lieut. Col. Eyre and the other by General Arnold. The latter met with little opposition, fort Trumbull and a redoubt which was intended to cover the harbour, not being tenable were evacuated, and the men crossed the river to fort Griswold on Groton hill. This was furiously attacked by Lieut. Col. Eyre: The garrison defended themselves with great resolution, but after a severe conflict of forty minutes, the fort was carried by the assailants. The Americans had not more than six or seven men killed, when the British carried their lines, but a severe execution took place afterwards, though resistance had ceased. An officer of the conquering troops enquired on his entering the fort who commanded. Col. Ledyard answered. [275] "I did, but you do now." And presented him his sword. The Col. was immediately run through the body and killed. Between 30 and 40 were wounded, and about 40 were carried off prisoners. On the side of the British 48 were killed and 145 wounded: Among the latter was Major Montgomery, and among the former was Colonel Eyre. About 15 vessels loaded with the effects of the inhabitants, retreated up the river, and four others remained in the harbour unhurt, but all excepting these were burned by the communication of fire from the burning stores. Sixty dwelling houses and 84 stores were reduced to ashes[;] the loss which the Americans sustained by the destruction of naval stores, of provisions and merchandise, was immense. Gen. Arnold having completed the object of the expedition, returned in eight days to New-York. The Americans lost many valuable men, and much of their possessions by this incursion, but the cause for which they contended was uninjured. Expeditions which seemed to have no higher object than the destruction of property, alienated their

SEPT. 6

1781

affections still farther from British government. They were not so extensive as to answer the ends of conquest, and the momentary impression resulting from them, produced no lasting intimidation. On the other hand, they excited a spirit of revenge against the authors of such accumulated distresses.

The year 1781 terminated, in all parts of the United States, in favour of the Americans. It began with weakness in Carolina, mutiny in New-Jersey, and devastation in Virginia; nevertheless in its close, the British were confined to their strong holds in or near New-York, Charleston and Savannah, and their whole army in Virginia was captured. They in the course of the year had acquired much plunder by which individuals were enriched, but their nation was in no respect benefited. The whole campaign passed away on their part without one valuable conquest, or the acquisition of any post or place, from which higher purposes were answered, than destroying public stores or distressing individuals, and enriching the officers and privates of their army and navy. The important services rendered by France to the Americans, [276] cemented the union of the two nations with additional ties. The orderly inoffensive behaviour of the French troops in the United States, contrasted with the havoc of property made by the British in their marches and excursions, was silently turning the current of popular esteem in favour of the former, and working a revolution in the minds of the inhabitants, greatly conducive to the establishment of that which had taken place in the government. The property of the inhabitants of Rhode-Island, received no damage of any account from the French troops, during their eleven months residence among them. The soldiers were rather a guard than a nuisance: The citizens met with no interruption when prosecuting their lawful business, either by night or day, and were treated with every mark of attention and respect. While the progress of the British army, in a circuitous march of 1100 miles from Charleston to Yorktown, was marked with rapine and desolation; the march of the French troops from Rhode-Island to the same place, a distance nearly equal in a right line, was productive of no inconvenience to the intermediate inhabitants. They were welcome guests wherever they came, for they took nothing by fraud or force, but punctually paid for all they wanted with hard money. In a contest

1781

where the good will of the people had so powerful an influence on its final issue, such opposite modes of conduct could not fail of producing their natural effects. The moderation and justice of the French, met with its reward in the general good will of the people, but the violence and rapine of the British, contributed among other things, to work the final overthrow of all their schemes in America.

On the last day of this year Henry Laurens was released from his long confinement in the tower of London. He had been committed there, as already related, on the 6th of October 1780, "On suspicion of high treason," after being examined in the presence of lord Stormont, lord George Germaine, lord Hillsborough, Mr. Chamberlain, Mr. Justice Addington, and others. The commitment was accompanied with a warrant to the Lieutenant [277] of the tower to receive and confine him. Their lordships orders were "To confine him a close prisoner; to be locked up every night; to be in the custody of two warders; not to suffer him to be out of their sight one moment, day nor night; to allow him no liberty of speaking to any person, nor to permit any person to speak to him; to deprive him of the use of pen and ink; to suffer no letter to be brought to him, nor any to go from him." Mr. Laurens was then fifty five years old, and severely afflicted with the gout and other infirmities. In this situation he was conducted to apartments in the tower, and was shut up in two small rooms which together made about twenty feet square, with a warder for his constant companion, and a fixed bayonet under his window, without any friend to converse with and without any prospect or even the means of correspondence. Being debarred the use of pen and ink, he procured pencils, which proved an useful substitute. After a month's confinement, he was permitted to walk out on limited ground, but a warder with a sword in his hand followed close behind. This indulgence was occasionally taken for about three weeks, when lord George Gordon, who was also a prisoner in the tower, unluckily met and asked Mr. Laurens to walk with him. Mr. Laurens declined the offer and instantly returned to his apartment. Governor Gore caught at this transgression of orders, and locked him up for 37 days, though the attending warder exculpated him from all blame. At the end of that time the Governor relented so far, as to permit his prisoner to walk on the parade before the door, but this honor, as

1781
DEC. 31

coming from him, was refused. General Vernon, on hearing of what had passed, gave orders that Mr. Laurens should be permitted to walk out, and this exercise was in consequence thereof resumed, after an intermission of two months and a half.

About this time an old friend and mercantile correspondent, having solicited the Secretaries of State for Mr. Laurens' enlargement on parole, and having offered his whole fortune as security for his good conduct, sent him the following message: "Their lordships say, if you will [278] point out any thing for the benefit of Great Britain, in the present dispute with the Colonies, you shall be enlarged." This proposition filled him with indignation, and provoked a sharp reply, part of which was in the following words: "I perceive from the message you sent me, that if I were a rascal I might presently get out of the tower, but I am not. You have pledged your word and fortune for my integrity. I will never dishonour you nor myself. I can foresee what will come to pass, happen to me what may. I fear no possible consequences."

The same friend soon after visited Mr. Laurens, and being left alone with him, addressed him as follows, "I converse with you this morning, not particularly as your friend, but as the friend of Great Britain. I have certain propositions to make, for obtaining your liberty, which I advise you should take time to consider." Mr. Laurens desired to know what they were, and added "That an honest man required no time to give an answer, in a case where his honor was concerned;" ["]If," said he, "the Secretaries of State will enlarge me upon parole, I will strictly conform to my engagement to do nothing directly or indirectly to the hurt of this kingdom. I will return to America, or remain in any part of England which may be assigned, and surrender myself when demanded." It was answered "No, Sir, you must stay in London among your friends: The ministers will often have occasion to send for and consult you: You can write two or three lines to the ministers, and barely say you are sorry for what is past: A pardon will be granted: Every man has been wrong, at some time or other of his life, and should not be ashamed to acknowledge it." Mr. Laurens replied "I will never subscribe to my own infamy, and to the dishonour of my children." He was then told of long and painful confinement, and hints were thrown out of the possible consequences of his refusal: To which he replied "I am afraid of no consequences but such as would flow from dishonourable acts."

In about a week after this interview, Major General James Grant, who had long been acquainted with Mr. [279] Laurens, and had served with him near twenty years before, on an expedition against the Cherokee Indians, visited him in the tower, and talked much of the inconveniences of his situation, and then addressed him thus, "Colonel Laurens, I have brought paper and pencil to take down any propositions you have to make to administration, and I will deliver them myself." Mr. Laurens replied, "I have pencil and paper, but not one proposition, beyond repeating a request to be enlarged on parole. I had well weighed what consequences might follow before I entered into the present dispute. I took the path of justice and honour, and no personal evils can cause me to shrink." MAR. 14 1781

About this time Lieutenant Colonel John Laurens, the eldest son of Henry Laurens arrived in France, as the special minister of Congress. The father was requested to write to the son to withdraw himself from the court of France, and assurances were given that it would operate in his favour. To these requests he replied, "my son is of age, and has a will of his own; if I should write to him in the terms you request, it would have no effect: He would only conclude, that confinement and persuasion had softened me. I know him to be a man of honour: He loves me dearly, and would lay down his life to save mine; but I am sure he would not sacrifice his honour to save my life, and I applaud him."

Mr. Laurens penciled an address to the secretaries of State for the use of pen and ink, to draw a bill of exchange on a merchant in London who was in his debt, for money to answer his immediate exigencies, and to request that his youngest son might be permitted to visit him, for the purpose of concerting a plan for his farther education and conduct in life. This was delivered to their lordships; but they, though they had made no provision for the support of their prisoner, returned no answer. Mr. Laurens was thus left to languish in confinement under many infirmities, and without the means of applying his own resources on the spot, for his immediate support. JUNE 29

[280] As soon as Mr. Laurens had completed a year in the tower,

he was called upon to pay £9 7ſ10 sterling to the two warders for attending on him. To which he replied, "I was sent to the tower by the secretaries of State without money (for aught they knew)—their lordships have never supplied me with any thing—It is now upwards of three months since I informed their lordships that the fund I had hitherto subsisted upon was nearly exhausted, and prayed for leave to draw a bill on Mr. John Nutt, who was in my debt, which they have been pleased to refuse by the most grating of all denials a total silence, and now a demand is made for £9 7ſ10. If their lordships will permit me to draw for money where it is due to me, I will continue to pay my own expences, but I will not pay the warders whom I never employed, and whose attendance I shall be glad to dispense with."

Three weeks after, the secretaries of State consented that Mr. Laurens should have the use of pen and ink, for the purpose of drawing a bill of exchange, but they were taken away the moment that business was done.

About this time Henry Laurens jun. wrote an humble request to lord Hillsborough for permission to see his father, which his lordship refused to grant. He had at first been permitted to visit his father, and converse with him for a short time; but these interviews were no longer permitted. They nevertheless occasionally met on the lines and saluted each other, but durst not exchange a single word, lest it might occasion a second confinement, similar to that to which lord George Gordon had been accessary.

As the year 1781 drew near a close, Mr. Laurens' sufferings in the tower became generally known, and excited compassion in his favour, and odium against the authors of his confinement. It had been also found by the inefficacy of many attempts, that no concessions could be obtained from him. It was therefore resolved to release him, but difficulties arose about the mode. Mr. Laurens would not consent to any act, which implied that he was a British subject, and he had been committed as such, on charge of high treason. Ministers to extricate themselves [281] from this difficulty, at length proposed to take bail for his appearance at the court of King's-Bench. When the words of the recognizance, "Our Sovereign Lord the King," were read to Mr. Laurens, he replied in open court "Not my Sovereign," and with this declaration he, with Mr. Oswald and Mr. Anderson as his securities, entered into an obligation for his appearance at the court of King's-Bench the next Easter term, and for not departing thence without leave of the court. Thus ended a long and a painful farce. Mr. Laurens was immediately released. When the time of his appearance at court drew near, he was not only discharged from all obligations to attend, but was requested by lord Shelburne to go to the continent, in subserviency to a scheme for making peace with America. Mr. Laurens, startled at the idea of being released without any equivalent, as he had uniformly held himself to be a prisoner of war, replied that "He durst not accept himself as a gift, and that as Congress had once offered Lieut. Gen. Burgoyne for him, he had no doubt of their now giving Lieut. Gen. Earl Cornwallis for the same purpose."

Of the treatment of prisoners, and of the distresses of the Inhabitants.

MANY CIRCUMSTANCES OCCURRED to make the American war particularly calamitous. It was originally a civil war in the estimation of both parties, and a rebellion to its termination, in the opinion of one of them. Unfortunately for mankind doubts have been entertained of the obligatory force of the law of nations in such cases. The refinement of modern ages has stripped war of half its horrors, but the systems of some illiberal men have tended to re-produce the barbarism of Gothic times, by withholding the benefits of that refinement from those who are effecting revolutions. An enlightened philanthropist embraces the whole human race and enquires, [282] not whether an object of distress is or is not an unit of an acknowledged nation. It is sufficient that he is a child of the same common parent, and capable of happiness or misery. The prevalence of such a temper

1781

would have greatly lessened the calamities of the American war, but while from contracted policy, unfortunate captives were considered as not entitled to the treatment of prisoners, they were often doomed without being guilty, to suffer the punishment due to criminals.

The first American prisoners were taken on the 17th of June 1775. These were thrown indiscriminately into the jail at Boston, without any consideration of their rank. Gen. Washington wrote to Gen. Gage on this subject, to which the latter answered by asserting that the prisoners had been treated with care and kindness, though indiscriminately "as he acknowledged no rank that was not derived from the King." To which Gen. Washington replied "You affect, Sir, to despise all rank not derived from the same source with your own; I cannot conceive one more honorable, than that which flows from the uncorrupted choice of a brave and free people, the purest source and original fountain of all power." AUG 11, 1775

Gen. Carleton during his command conducted towards the American prisoners with a degree of humanity, that reflected the greatest honor on his character. Before he commenced his operations on the lake in 1776, he shipped off those of them who were officers for New-England, but previously supplied them with every thing requisite to make their voyage comfortable. The other prisoners, amounting to 800, were sent home by a flag after exacting an oath from them, not to serve during the war unless exchanged. Many of these being almost naked were comfortably cloathed by his orders, previously to their being sent off.

The capture of Gen. Lee proved calamitous to several individuals. Six Hessian field officers were offered in exchange for him, but this was refused. It was said by the British, that Lee was a deserter from their service, and as such could not expect the indulgences usually given to prisoners of war. The Americans replied, that as [283] he had resigned his British commission previously to his accepting one from the Americans, he could not be considered as a deserter. He was nevertheless confined, watched, and guarded. Congress thereupon resolved, that Gen. Washington be directed to inform Gen. Howe, that should the proffered exchange of Gen. Lee for six field officers not be accepted, and the treatment of him as above mentioned be continued, the principles of retaliation should occasion five of the 1781 said Hessian field officers, together with Lt. Col. Archibald Campbell to be detained, in order that the said treatment which Gen. Lee received, should be exactly inflicted on their persons. The Campbell thus designated as the subject of retaliation, was a humane man, and a meritorious officer, who had been captured by some of the Massachusett's privateers near Boston, to which, from the want of information, he was proceeding soon after the British had evacuated it. The above act of Congress was forwarded to Massachusetts with a request that they would detain Lt. Col. Campbell and keep him in safe custody till the further order of Congress. The council of Massachusett's exceeded this request, and sent him to Concord jail, where he was lodged in a gloomy dungeon of twelve or thirteen feet square. The attendance of a single servant on his person was denied him, and every visit from a friend refused.

The prisoners captured by Sir William Howe in 1776, amounted to many hundreds. The officers were admitted to parole, and had some waste houses assigned to them as quarters; but the privates were shut up in the coldest season of the year in churches, sugar houses, and such like large open buildings. The severity of the weather, and the rigor of their treatment, occasioned the death of many hundreds of these unfortunate men. The filth of the places of their confinement, in consequence of fluxes which prevailed among them, was both offensive and dangerous. Seven dead bodies have been seen in one building, at one time, and all lying in a situation shocking to humanity. The provisions served out to them were deficient in quantity, and of an unwholsome quality. These suffering prisoners were [284] generally

1781

pressed to enter into the British service, but hundreds submitted to death, rather than procure a melioration of their circumstances by enlisting with the enemies of their country. After Gen. Washington's successes at Trenton and Princeton, the American prisoners fared somewhat better. Those who survived were ordered to be sent out for exchange, but some of them fell down dead in the streets, while attempting to walk to the vessels. Others were so emaciated that their appearance was horrible. A speedy death closed the scene with many.

DEC. 1,
1777

The American board of war, after conferring with Mr. Boudinot the commissary-general of prisoners, and examining evidences produced by him, reported among other things,

That there were 900 privates and 300 officers of the American army, prisoners in the city of New-York, and about 500 privates and 50 officers prisoners in Philadelphia. That since the beginning of October all these prisoners, both officers and privates, had been confined in prison ships or the Provost: That from the best evidence the subject could admit of, the general allowance of prisoners, at most did not exceed four ounces of meat per day, and often so damaged as not to be eatable: That it had been a common practice with the British, on a prisoner's being first captured, to keep him three, four or five days without a morsel of meat, and then to tempt him to enlist to save his life: That there were numerous instances of prisoners of war, perishing in all the agonies of hunger.

About this time there was a meeting of merchants in London, for the purpose of raising a sum of money to relieve the distresses of the American prisoners, then in England. The sum subscribed for that purpose amounted in two months to £4647 15s. Thus while human nature was dishonoured by the cruelties of some of the British in America, there was a laudable display of the benevolence of others of the same nation in Europe. The American sailors, when captured by the British, suffered more than even the soldiers, which fell into their hands. The former were confined on board prison ships. [285] They were there crouded together in such numbers, and their accommodations were so wretched, that diseases broke out and swept them off in a manner, that was sufficient to excite compassion in breasts of the least sensibility. It has been asserted, on as good evidence as the case will admit, that in the last six years of the war upwards of eleven thousand persons died on board the Jersey, one of these prison ships, which was stationed in east river near New-York. On many of these, the rights of sepulture were never, or but very imperfectly conferred. For some time after the war was ended, their bones lay whitening in the sun, on the shores of Long Island.

The operations of treason laws added to the calamities of the war. Individuals on both sides, while they were doing no more than they supposed to be their duty, were involved in the penal consequences of capital crimes. The Americans in conformity to the usual policy of nations, demanded the allegiance of all who resided among them, but several of these preferred the late royal government and were disposed, when opportunity offered, to support it. While they acted in conformity to these sentiments, the laws enacted for the security

DEC. 24, 1777

1781

of the new government, condemned them to death. Hard is the lot of a people involved in civil war; for in such circumstances the lives of individuals may not only be legally forfeited, but justly taken from those, who have acted solely from a sense of duty. It is to be wished that some more rational mode than war might be adopted for deciding national contentions; but of all wars, those which are called civil are most to be dreaded. They are attended with the bitterest resentments, and produce the greatest quantity of human woes. In the American war, the distresses of the country were aggravated, from the circumstance that every man was obliged, some way or other, to be in the public service. In Europe, where military operations are carried on by armies hired and paid for the purpose, the common people partake but little of the calamities of war: but in America, where the whole people were enrolled as a militia, and where both sides endeavoured to strengthen themselves by oaths and [286] by laws, denouncing the penalties of treason on those who aided or abetted the opposite party, the sufferings of individuals were renewed, as often as fortune varied her standard. Each side claimed the co-operation of the inhabitants, and was ready to punish when it was withheld. Where either party had a decided superiority the common people were comparatively undisturbed; but the intermediate space between the contending armies, was subject to the alternate ravages of both.

1781

In the first institution of the American governments, the boundaries of authority were not properly fixed; Committees exercised legislative, executive and judicial powers. It is not to be doubted, that in many instances these were improperly used, and that private resentments were often covered under the specious veil of patriotism. The sufferers in passing over to the royalists, carried with them a keen remembrance of the vengeance of committees, and when opportunity presented, were tempted to retaliate. From the nature of the case, the original offenders were less frequently the objects of retaliation, than those who were entirely innocent. One instance of severity begat another, and they continued to encrease in a proportion that doubled the evils of common war. From one unadvised step, individuals were often involved in the loss of all their property. Some from present appearances, apprehending that the British would finally conquer, repaired to their standard. Their return after the partial storm which intimidated them to submission, had blown over, was always difficult and often impossible. From this single error in judgement, such were often obliged to seek safety by continuing to support the interest of those to whom, in an hour of temptation, they had devoted themselves. The embarrassments on both sides were often so great, that many in the humbler walks of life, could not tell what course was best to pursue. It was happy for those who having made up their minds on the nature of the contest, invariably followed the dictates of their consciences, for in every instance they enjoyed self-approbation. Though they could not be deprived of this reward, they were not always successful in saving [287] their property. 1781 They who varied with the times, in like manner often missed their object, for to such it frequently happened that they were plundered by both, and lost the esteem of all. A few saved their credit and their property; but of these, there was not one for every hundred of those, who were materially injured either in the one or the other. The American whigs were exasperated against those of their fellow citizens who joined their enemies, with a resentment which was far more bitter, than that which they harboured against their European adversaries. Feeling that the whole strength of the states was scarcely sufficient to protect them against the British, they could not brook the desertion of their countrymen to invading foreigners. They seldom would give them credit for acting from principle, but generally supposed them to be influenced either by cowardice or interest, and were therefore inclined to proceed against them with rigor. They were filled with indignation at the idea of fighting for the property of such as had deserted their country, and were therefore clamorous, that it should be seized for public service. The royalists raised the cry of persecution and loudly complained that merely for supporting the government, under which they were born, and to which they owed a natural allegiance, they were doomed to suffer all the penalties due to capital offenders. Those of them who acted from principle felt no consciousness of guilt, and could not look but with abhorrence upon a government, which inflicted such severe punishments on what they deemed a laudable line of conduct. Humanity would shudder at a particular recital of the calamities which the whigs inflicted on the tories, and the tories on the whigs. It is particularly remarkable that on both sides, they for the most part consoled themselves with the belief, that they were acting or suffering in a good cause. Though the rules of moral right and wrong never vary, political innocence and guilt, changes so much with circumstances, that the innocence of the sufferer, and of the party that punishes, are often compatible. The distresses of the American prisoners in the southern states, prevailed particularly towards the close of the war. Colonel [288] Campbell, who reduced Savannah, though he had personally suffered from the Americans, treated all who fell into his hands with humanity. Those who were taken at Savannah and at Ashe's defeat, suffered very much from his successors in South Carolina. The American prisoners with a few exceptions, had but little to complain of till after Gates' defeat. Soon after that event, sundry of them, though entitled to the benefits of the capitulation of Charleston, were separated from their families and sent into exile; others in violation of the same solemn agreement were crouded into prison ships, and deprived of the use of their property. When a general exchange of prisoners was effected, the wives and children of those inhabitants who adhered to the Americans, were exiled from their homes to Virginia and Philadelphia. Upwards of one thousand persons were thrown upon the charity of their fellow citizens in the more northern states. This severe treatment was the occasion of retaliating on the families of those who had taken part with the British. In the first months of the year 1781, the British were in force in the remotest settlements of South-Carolina, but as their limits were contracted in the course of the year, the male inhabitants who joined them, thought proper to retire with the royal army towards the capital. In retaliation for the expulsion of the wives and children of the whig Americans from the state, Governor Rutledge ordered the brigadiers of militia, to send within the British lines, the families of such of the inhabitants as adhered to their interest. In consequence of this order, and more especially in consequence of the one which occasioned it, several hundreds of helpless women and children were reduced to great distress.

The refugees who had fled to New-York, were formed into an association under Sir Henry Clinton, for the purposes of retaliating on the Americans, and for reimbursing the losses they had sustained from their countrymen. The depredations they committed in their several excursions would fill a volume, and would answer little purpose but to excite compassion and horror. Towards the close of

the war, they began to retaliate on a bolder [289] scale. Captain
Joshua Huddy who commanded a small party of Americans at a block   1781
house, in Monmouth County New-Jersey was, after a gallant resistance, taken prisoner by a party of these refugees. He was brought to
New-York and there kept in close custody fifteen days, and then told   APR. 2
"that he was ordered to be hanged." Four days after, he was sent out
with a party of refugees, and hanged on the highths of Middleton.
The following label was affixed to his breast "We the refugees having
long with grief beheld the cruel murders of our brethren, and finding
nothing but such measures daily carrying into execution; we therefore
determine not to suffer without taking vengeance for the numerous
cruelties, and thus begin, and have made use of Capt. Huddy as the
first object to present to your view, and further determine to hang
man for man, while there is a refugee existing: Up goes Huddy for
Philip White." The Philip White in retaliation for whom Huddy was
hanged, had been taken by a party of the Jersey militia, and was
killed in attempting to make his escape.

Gen. Washington resolved on retaliation for this deliberate murder,
but instead of immediately executing a British officer he wrote to Sir
Henry Clinton, that unless the murderers of Huddy were given up,
he should be under the necessity of retaliating. The former being
refused, Capt. Asgill was designated by lot for that purpose. In the
mean time the British instituted a court martial for the trial of Capt.
Lippencutt, who was supposed to be the principal agent, in executing
Capt. Huddy. It appeared in the course of this trial that Gov. Franklin,
the President of the board of associated loyalists, gave Lippencutt
verbal orders for what he did, and that he had been designated as a
proper subject for retaliation, having been, as the refugees stated, a
persecutor of the loyalists, and particularly as having been instrumental in hanging Stephen Edwards, who had been one of that
description. The court having considered the whole matter gave their
opinion

That as what Lippencutt did was not the effect of malice or ill will, but
proceeded from a conviction that it was his duty to obey the orders
[290] of the board of directors of associated loyalists, and as he did not
doubt their having full authority to give such orders, he was not guilty
of the murder laid to his charge, and therefore they acquitted him.

Sir Guy Carleton, who a little before this time had been appointed commander in chief of the British army, in a letter to Gen. Washington, accompanying the tryal of Lippencutt, declared "that notwithstanding the acquittal of Lippencutt, he reprobated the measure, and gave assurances of prosecuting a farther enquiry." Sir Guy Carleton about the same time, broke up the board of associated loyalists, which prevented a repetition of similar excesses. The war also drawing near a close, the motives for retaliation as tending to prevent other murders, in a great measure ceased. In the mean time Gen. Washington received a letter from the Count de Vergenes interceding for Capt. Asgill, which was also accompanied with a very pathetic one, from his mother Mrs. Asgill to the Count. Copies of these several letters were forwarded to Congress, and soon after they resolved, "that the commander in chief be directed to set Capt. Asgill at liberty." The lovers of humanity rejoined that the necessity for retaliation was superseded, by the known humanity of the new commander in chief, and still more by the well founded prospect of a speedy peace. Asgill who had received every indulgence, and who had been treated with all possible politeness, was released and permitted to go into New-York.

NOV. 7,
1782

Campaign of 1782. Foreign events and negotiations.
Peace 1782.

AFTER THE CAPTURE OF LORD CORNWALLIS, General Washington, with the greatest part of his force returned to the vicinity of
New-York. He was in no condition to attempt the reduction of that
post, and the royal army had good reasons for not urging hostilities
without their lines. An obstruction of the communication between
town and country, some indecisive skirmishes [291] and praedatory
excursions, were the principal evidences of an existing state of war.   1782
This in a great measure was also the case in South-Carolina. From
December 1781, General Greene had possession of all the state except
Charleston and the vicinity. The British sometimes sallied out of
their lines for the acquisition of property and provisions, but never   AUG 27,
for the purposes of conquest. In opposing one of these near Combahee   1782
Lieutenant Colonel John Laurens, an accomplished officer of uncom-

mon merit, was mortally wounded. Nature had adorned him with a large proportion of her choicest gifts, and these were highly cultivated by an elegant, useful and practical education. His patriotism was of the most ardent kind. The moment he was of age, he broke off from the amusements of London, and on his arrival in America, instantly joined the army. Wherever the war raged most, there was he to be found. A dauntless bravery was the least of his virtues, and an excess of it his greatest foible. His various talents fitted him to shine in courts or camps, or popular assemblies. He had a heart to conceive, a head to contrive, a tongue to persuade, and a hand to execute schemes of the most extensive utility to his country, or rather to mankind, for his enlarged philanthropy knowing no bounds, embraced the whole human race. This excellent young man, who was the pride of his country, the idol of the army, and an ornament of human nature, lost his life in the 27th year of his age, in an unimportant skirmish with a foraging party, in the very last moments of the war.

At the commencement of the year 1782, the British had more extensive range in Georgia, than in any other of the United States, but of this they were soon abridged. From the unsuccessful issue of the assault on Savannah in 1779, that State had eminently suffered the desolations of war. Political hatred raged to such a degree that the blood of its citizens was daily shed by the hands of each other, contending under the names of whigs and tories. A few of the friends of the revolution kept together in the western settlements, and exercised the powers of independent government. The whole [292] extent between these and the capital, was subject to the alternate ravages of both parties. After the surrender of lord Cornwallis, General Greene being reinforced by the Pennsylvania line, was enabled to detach General Wayne with a part of the southern army to Georgia. General Clarke who commanded in Savannah, on hearing of their advance, sent orders to his officers in the out posts, to burn as far as they could, all the provisions in the country, and then to retire within the lines at the capital. The country being evacuated by the British, the Governor came with his council from Augusta to Ebenezer, and re-established government in the vicinity of the sea coast.

MAY 21, 1782

Colonel Brown at the head of a considerable force marched out of the garrison of Savannah, with the apparent intention of attacking the Americans. General Wayne by a bold manoeuvre got in his rear, attacked him at 12 o'clock at night, and routed his whole party. A large number of Creek Indians, headed by a number of their chiefs and a British officer, made a furious attack on Wayne's infantry in the night. For a few minutes they possessed themselves of his field pieces, but they were soon recovered. In the mean time Colonel White with a party of the cavalry came up, and pressed hard upon them. Both sides engaged in close quarters. The Indians displayed uncommon bravery, but were at length completely routed. Shortly after this affair, a period was put to the calamities of war, in that ravaged state. In about three months after the capture of lord Cornwallis was known in Great-Britain, the parliament resolved to abandon all offensive operations in America. In consequence thereof, every idea of conquest being given up, arrangements were made for withdrawing the royal forces from Georgia and South-Carolina. Peace   JULY 11 was restored to Georgia, after it had been upwards of three years in possession of the British, and had been ravaged nearly from one extreme to the other. It is computed that the state lost by the war, one thousand of its citizens, besides four thousand slaves. In about five months after the British left Georgia, [293] they in like manner   1782 withdrew their force, from South-Carolina. The inhabitants of Charleston, who had remained therein, while it was possessed by the British, felt themselves happy in being delivered from the severities of a garrison life. The exiled citizens collected from all quarters and took possession of their estates. Thus in less than three years from the landing of the British in South-Carolina, they withdrew all their forces from it. In that time the citizens had suffered an accumulation of evils. There was scarcely an inhabitant however obscure in character, or remote in situation, whether he remained firm to one party or changed with the times, who did not partake of the general distress.

In modern Europe the revolutions of public affairs seldom disturb the humble obscurity of private life, but the American revolution involved the interest of every family, and deeply affected the fortunes and happiness of almost every individual in the United States. South-Carolina lost a great number of its citizens, and upwards of 20,000 of its slaves. Property was sported with by both parties. Besides those who fell in battle or died of diseases brought on by the war, many were inhumanly murdered by private assassinations. The country abounded with widows and orphans. The severities of a military life co-operating with the climate, destroyed the healths and lives of many hundreds of the invading army. Excepting those who enriched themselves by plunder, and a few successful speculators, no private advantage was gained by individuals on either side, but an experimental conviction of the folly and madness of war.

Though in the year 1782 the United States afforded few great events, the reverse was the case with the other powers involved in the consequences of the American war.

FEB. 5

Minorca after a tedious siege surrendered to the Duke de Crillon in the service of his most Catholic Majesty. About the same time the settlements of Demarara and Essequibo, which in the preceding year had been taken by the British, were taken from them by the French. The gallant Marquis de Bouille added to the splendor of his former fame by reducing St. Eustatia and St. Kitts, the former [294] at the

1782

close of the year 1781, and the latter early in the year 1782. The islands of Nevis and Monserrat followed the fortune of St. Kitts. The French at this period seemed to be established in the West Indies, on a firm foundation. Their islands were full of excellent troops, and their marine force was truly respectable. The exertions of Spain were also uncommonly great. The strength of these two monarchies had never before been so conspicuously displayed, in that quarter of the globe. Their combined navies amounted to threescore ships of the line, and these were attended with a prodigious multitude of frigates and armed vessels. With this immense force they entertained hopes of wresting from his Britannic Majesty a great part of his West-India islands.

In the mean time, the British ministry prepared a strong squadron, for the protection of their possessions in that quarter. This was commanded by Admiral Rodney and amounted, after a junction with Sir Samuel Hood's squadron, and the arrival of three ships from Great Britain, to 36 sail of the line.

It was the design of Count de Grasse, who commanded the French fleet at Martinque amounting to 34 sail of the line, to proceed to Hispaniola and join the Spanish Admiral Don Solano, who with sixteen ships of the line and a considerable land force was waiting for his arrival, and to make in concert with him an attack on Jamaica.

The British admiral wished to prevent this junction, or at least to force an engagement before it was effected. Admiral Rodney came up with Count de Grasse, soon after he had set out to join the Spanish fleet at Hispaniola. Partial engagements took place on the three first days, after they came near to each other. In these, two of the French ships were so badly damaged, that they were obliged to quit the fleet. On the next day a general engagement took place: This began at seven in the morning, and continued till past six in the evening. There was no apparent superiority on either side till between twelve and one o'clock, when Admiral Rodney broke the French line of battle, by bearing down upon their centre, and [295] penetrating through it. The land forces, destined for the expedition against Jamaica, amounting to 5500 men, were distributed on board the French fleet. Their ships were therefore so crouded, that the slaughter on board was prodigious. The battle was fought on both sides with equal spirit, but with a very unequal issue. The French for near a century, had not in any naval engagement been so completely worsted. Their fleet was little less than ruined. Upwards of 400 men were killed on board one of their ships, and the whole number of their killed and wounded amounted to several thousands, while the loss of the British did not much exceed 1100 men. The French lost in this action, and the subsequent pursuit, eight ships of the line. On board the captured ships, was the whole train of artillery, with the battering cannon and travelling carriages, intended for the expedition against Jamaica. One of them was the Ville de Paris, so called from the city of Paris, having built her at its own expence, and made a present of her to the King. She had cost four millions of livres, and was esteemed the most magnificent ship in France; she carried 110 guns and had on board 1300 men. This was truly an unfortunate day to Count de Grasse. Though his behaviour throughout the whole action was firm and intrepid, and his resistance continued till he and two more were the only men left standing upon the upper deck, he was at last obliged to strike. It was no small addition to his misfortunes that he was on the point of forming a junction, which would have set him above all danger. Had this taken place, the whole

APR. 8

APR. 12

1782

British naval power in the West-Indies, on principles of ordinary calculation, would have been insufficient to have prevented him from carrying into effect, schemes of the most extensive consequence.

The ships of the defeated fleet fled in a variety of directions. Twenty three or twenty four sail made the best of their way to Cape François. This was all that remained in a body of that fleet, which was lately so formidable. By this signal victory, the designs of France and Spain were frustrated. No farther enterprises were [296] undertaken against the fleets or possessions of Great Britain in the West-Indies, and such measures only were embraced, as seemed requisite for the purposes of safety. When the news of Admiral Rodney's victory reached Great Britain, a general joy was diffused over the nation. Before there had been much despondency. Their losses in the Chesapeak and in the West-Indies, together with the increasing number of their enemies, had depressed the spirits of the great body of the people; but the advantages gained on the 12th of April, placed them on high ground, either for ending or prosecuting the war. It was fortunate for the Americans, that this success of the British was posterior to their loss in Virginia. It so elevated the spirits of Britain, and so depressed the hopes of France, that had it taken place prior to the surrender of lord Cornwallis, that event would have been less influential in disposing the nation to peace. As the catastrophe of York-Town closed the national war in North-America, so the defeat of de Grasse, in a great measure, put a period to hostilities in the West-Indies.

Other decisive events soon followed, which disposed another of the belligerent powers to a pacification. Gibraltar though successively relieved, still continued to be besieged. The reduction of Minorca inspired the Spanish nation with fresh motives to perseverance. The Duke de Crillon, who had been recently successful in the siege of Minorca, was appointed to conduct the siege of Gibraltar, and it was resolved to employ the whole strength of the Spanish monarchy in seconding his operations. No means were neglected, nor expence spared, that promised to forward the views of the besiegers. From the failure of all plans, hitherto adopted for effecting the reduction of Gibraltar, it was resolved to adopt new ones. Among the various projects for this purpose, one which had been formed by the Chevalier

D'Arcon, was deemed the most worthy of trial. This was to construct such floating batteries as could neither be sunk nor fired. With this view their bottoms were made of the thickest timber, and their sides of wood and cork long soaked in water, with a large layer of wet sand between.

[297] To prevent the effects of red hot balls, a number of pipes were contrived to carry water through every part of them, and pumps were provided to keep these constantly supplied with water. The people on board were to be sheltered from the fall of bombs by a cover of rope netting, which was made sloping and overlaid with wet hides. 1782

These floating batteries, ten in number, were made out of the hulls of large vessels, cut down for the purpose, and carried from 28 to ten guns each, and were seconded by 80 large boats mounted with guns of heavy metal, and also by a multitude of frigates, ships of force, and some hundreds of small craft.

General Elliott the intrepid defender of Gibraltar, was not ignorant that inventions of a peculiar kind were prepared against him, but knew nothing of their construction. He nevertheless provided for every circumstance of danger that could be foreseen or imagined. The 13th day of Sept. was fixed upon by the besiegers for making a grand attack, when the new invented machines, with all the united powers of gunpowder and artillery in their highest state of improvement, were to be called into action. The combined fleets of France and Spain in the bay of Gibraltar amounted to 48 sail of the line. Their batteries were covered with 154 pieces of heavy brass cannon. The numbers employed by land and sea against the fortress were estimated at one hundred thousand men. With this force and by the fire of 300 cannon, mortars, and howitzers, from the adjacent isthmus, it was intended to attack every part of the British works at one and the same instant. The surrounding hills were covered with people assembled to behold the spectacle. The canonade and bombardment was tremendous. The showers of shot and shells from the land batteries, and the ships of the besiegers, and from the various works of the garrison, exhibited a most dreadful scene. Four hundred pieces of the heaviest artillery were playing at the same moment. The whole Peninsula seemed to be overwhelmed in the torrents of fire, which were incessantly poured upon it. The Spanish floating batteries for some time answered [298] the expectations of their framers. The heaviest shells often rebounded from their tops, while thirty two pound shot, made no visible impression upon their hulls. For some hours, the attack and defence were so equally supported, as scarcely to admit any appearance of superiority on either side. The construction of the battering ships was so well calculated, for withstanding the combined force of fire and artillery, that they seemed for some time to bid defiance to the powers of the heaviest ordnance. In the afternoon the effects of hot shot became visible. At first there was only an appearance of smoke, but in the course of the night, after the fire of the garrison had continued about 15 hours, two of the floating batteries were in flames, and several more were visibly beginning to kindle. The endeavors of the besiegers were now exclusively directed to bring off the men from the burning vessels, but in this they were interrupted. Captain Curtis who lay ready with 12 gun boats, advanced and fired upon them with such order and expedition, as to throw them into confusion before they had finished their business. They fled with their boats, and abandoned to their fate great numbers of their people. The opening of day light disclosed a most dreadful spectacle. Many were seen in the midst of the flames crying out for help, while others were floating upon pieces of timber, exposed to equal danger from the opposite element. The generous humanity of the victors equalled their valor, and was the more honorable, as the exertions of it exposed them to no less danger than those of active hostility. In endeavoring to save the lives of his enemies, Capt. Curtis nearly lost his own. While for the most benevolent purpose, he was along side the floating batteries one of them blew up, and some heavy pieces of timber fell into his boat, and pierced through its bottom. By similar perilous exertions, near 400 men were saved from inevitable destruction. The exercise of humanity to an enemy, under such circumstances of immediate action, and impending danger, conferred more true honor than could be acquired by the most splendid series of victories. It in some degree obscured the impression made to the disadvantage [299] of human nature, by the madness of mankind in destroying each other by wasteful wars. The floating batteries were all consumed. The violence of their explosion was such, as to burst open doors, and windows at a great distance. Soon after the destruction of the floating batteries, lord Howe with 35 ships of the line, brought to the brave garrison an ample supply of every thing wanted, either for their support or their defence. This complete relief of Gibraltar, was the third decisive event in the course of a twelve month, which favoured the re-establishment of a general peace.

The capture of the British army in Virginia—the defeat of Count de Grasse, and the destruction of the Spanish floating batteries, inculcated on Great Britain, France and Spain, the policy of sheathing the sword, and stopping the effusion of human blood. Each nation found on a review of past events, that though their losses were great, their gains were little or nothing. By urging the American war, Great Britain had encreased her national debt one hundred millions of pounds sterling, and wasted the lives of at least 50,000 of her subjects. To add to her mortification she had brought all this on herself, by pursuing an object the attainment of which seemed to be daily less probable, and the benefits of which, even though it could have been attained, were very problematical. While Great Britain, France and Spain were successively brought to think favourably of peace, the United States of America had the consolation of a public acknowl- edgment of their independence, by a second power of Europe. This was effected in a great measure by the address of John Adams. On the capture of Henry Laurens, he had been commissioned to be the minister plenipotentiary of Congress, to the States General of the United Provinces, and was also empowered to negociate a loan of money among the Hollanders. Soon after his arrival he presented to their High Mightinesses a memorial, in which he informed them that the United States of America, had thought fit to send him a com- mission with full power and instructions, to confer with them concerning a treaty of amity and commerce, and [300] that they had appointed him to be their Minister Plenipotentiary to reside near them. Similar information, was the same time communicated to the Statholder the Prince of Orange.

About a year after the presentation of this memorial, it was resolved "that the said Mr. Adams was agreeable to their High Mightinesses, and that he should be acknowledged in quality of Minister Plenipo-

JAN. 1, 1781

APR. 19, 1781

APR. 22, 1782

tentiary." Before this was obtained much pains had been taken and much ingenuity had been exerted, to convince the rulers and people of the States General, that they had an interest in connecting themselves with the United States. These representations, together with some recent successes in their contests on the sea with Great Britain, and their evident commercial interest, encouraged them to venture on being the second power of Europe, to acknowledge American Independence.

Mr. Adams having gained this point, proceeded on the negociation of a treaty of amity and commerce between the two countries. This was a few months concluded, to the reciprocal satisfaction of both parties. The same success which attended Mr. Adams in these negociations, continued to follow him in obtaining a loan of money, which was a most seasonable supply to his almost exhausted country.

OCT. 8

Mr. Jay had for nearly three years past exerted equal abilities, and equal industry with Mr. Adams, in endeavouring to negociate a treaty between the United States and his most Catholic Majesty, but his exertions were not crowned with equal success.

To gain the friendship of the Spaniards, Congress passed sundry resolutions, favouring the wishes of his most Catholic Majesty to re-annex the two Floridas to his dominions. Mr. Jay was instructed to contend for the right of the United States to the free navigation of the river Mississippi, and if an express acknowledgement of it could not be obtained, he was restrained from acceding to any stipulation, by which it should be relinquished. But in February 1781, when lord Cornwallis was making rapid progress in overrunning the southern States, and [301] when the mutiny of the Pennsylvania line and other unfavourable circumstances depressed the spirits of the Americans, Congress, on the recommendation of Virginia, directed him to recede from his instructions, so far as they insist on the free navigation of that part of the river Mississippi, which lies below the thirty first degree of North Latitude, and on a free port or ports below the same; provided such cession should be unalterably insisted on by Spain, and provided the free navigation of the said river above the said degree of North Latitude should be acknowledged and guarantied by his Catholic Majesty, in common with his own subjects.

1782

These propositions were made to the ministers of his most Catholic

P. 22,
31

Majesty, but not accepted. Mr. Jay in his own name informed them "That if the acceptance of this offer should, together with the proposed alliance, be postponed to a general peace, the United States would cease to consider themselves bound by any propositions or offers he might then make in their behalf."

Spain having delayed to accept of these terms, which originated more in necessity than in policy, till the crisis of American independence was past, Congress apprehensive that their offered relinquishment of the free navigation of the Mississippi should at that late hour be accepted, instructed their minister "To forbear making any overtures to the court of Spain, or entering into any stipulations, in consequence of any which he had previously made." The ministers of his most Catholic Majesty, from indecision and tardiness of deliberation, let slip an opportunity of gaining a favourite point, which from the increasing numbers of the western settlements of the United States, seems to be removed at a daily increasing distance. Humiliating offers, made and rejected in the hour of distress, will not readily be renewed in the day of prosperity. AUG. 7, 1782

It was expected not only by the sanguine Americans, but by many in England, that the capture of lord Cornwallis would instantly dispose the nation to peace; but whatever might have been the wish or the interest of the [302] people, the American war was too much the favourite of ministry to be relinquished, without a struggle for its continuance. 1782

Just after intelligence arrived of the capitulation of York-Town, the King of Great Britain, in his speech to Parliament, declared "That he should not answer the trust committed to the sovereign of a free people, if he consented to sacrifice either to his own desire of peace, or to their temporary ease and relief, those essential rights and permanent interests, upon the maintenance and preservation of which the future strength and security of the country must forever depend." The determined language of this speech, pointing to the continuance of the American war, was echoed back by a majority of both Lords and Commons. NOV. 27, 1781

In a few days after, it was moved in the house of commons that a resolution should be adopted declaring it to be their opinion "That all farther attempts to reduce the Americans to obedience by force DEC. 12

would be ineffectual, and injurious to the true interests of Great Britain." Though the debate on this subject was continued till two o'clock in the morning, and though the opposition received additional strength, yet the question was not carried. The same ground of argument was soon gone over again, and the American war underwent, for the fourth time since the beginning of the session, a full discussion; but no resolution, disapproving its farther prosecution, could yet obtain the assent of a majority of the members. The advocates for peace becoming daily more numerous, it was moved by Gen. Conway "That an humble address be presented to his Majesty, that he will be pleased to give directions to his ministers not to pursue any longer the impracticable object of reducing his Majesty's revolted colonies by force to their allegiance, by a war on the continent of America." This brought forth a repetition of the former arguments on the subject, and engaged the attention of the house till two o'clock in the morning. On a division, the motion for the address was lost by a single vote. In the course of these debates, while the minority were gaining ground, the ministry were giving [303] up one point after another. They at first consented that the war should not be carried on to the same extent as formerly—then that there should be no internal continental war—next that there should be no other war than what was necessary for the defence of the posts already in their possession—and last of all, none but against the French in America.

The ministry as well as the nation began to be sensible of the impolicy of continental operations, but hoped that they might gain their point, by prosecuting hostilities at sea. Every opposition was therefore made by them against the total direliction of a war, on the success of which they had so repeatedly pledged themselves, and on the continuance of which they held their places. General Conway in five days after, brought forward another motion expressed in different words, but to the same effect with that which he had lost by a single vote. This caused a long debate which lasted till two o'clock in the morning. It was then moved to adjourn the debate till the 13th of March. There appeared for the adjournment 215, and against it 234.

The original motion, and an address to the king formed upon the resolution were then carried without a division, and the address was ordered to be presented by the whole house.

To this his majesty answered, "that in pursuance of their advice, he would take such measures as should appear to him the most conducive to the restoration of harmony, between Great Britain and the revolted colonies." The thanks of the house were voted for this answer. But the guarded language thereof, not inconsistent with farther hostilities against America; together with other suspicious circumstances, induced General Conway to move another resolution, expressed in the most decisive language. This was to the following effect. "That the house would consider as enemies to his majesty and the country, all those who should advise or by any means attempt the further prosecution of offensive war, on the continent of North-America, for the purpose of reducing the colonies to obedience by force." This motion [304] after a feeble opposition was 1782 carried without a division, and put a period to all that chicanery by which ministers meant to distinguish between a prosecution of offensive war in North-America, and a total direliction of it. This resolution and the preceding address, to which it had reference, may be considered as the closing scene of the American war. As it was made a parliamentary war, by an address from parliament for its prosecution in February 1775[, i]t now was no longer so, by an address from the most numerous house of the same parliament in February 1782, for its discontinuance. A change of ministry was the consequence of this total change of that political system which, for seven years, had directed the affairs of Great Britain. A new administration was formed under the auspices of the Marquis of Rockingham, and was composed of characters who opposed the American war. It has been said that the new minister stipulated with the court JULY 1 before he entered into office, that there should be peace with the Americans, and that the acknowledgement of their independence should not be a bar to the attainment of it. Soon after the Marquis of Rockingham, on whom Great Britain relied with a well placed confidence, for extrication from surrounding embarrassments departed this life, and his much lamented death, for some time obscured the agreeable prospects which had lately begun to dawn on the nation. On the decease of the noble Marquis, Earl Shelburne was appointed his successor. To remove constitutional impediments to negociate with the late British colonies, an act of parliament was passed, granting to the crown powers for negotiating or concluding a general or particular peace or truce with the whole, or with any part of the colonies, and for setting aside all former laws, whose operations where in controvention to that purpose.

Sir Guy Carleton, who was lately appointed to the command of the royal army in North-America, was instructed to use his endeavours for carrying into effect the wishes of Great-Britain, for an accommodation with the Americans. He therefore dispatched a letter to General Washington, informing him of the late proceedings of [305] parliament, and of the dispositions so favourable to America, which were prevalent in Great Britain, and at the same time solicited a passport for his secretary, Mr. Morgan to pay a visit to Congress. His request was refused. The application for it, with its concomitant circumstances were considered as introductory to a scheme for opening negotiations with Congress or the states, without the concurrence of their allies. This caused no small alarm and gave rise to sundry resolutions, by which several states declared, that a proposition from the enemy to all or any of the United States for peace or truce, separate from their allies was inadmissible. Congress not long after resolved "that they would not enter into the discussion of any overtures for pacification, but in confidence and in concert with his most Christian Majesty, and as a proof of this, they recommended to the several States to pass laws, that no subject of his Britannic Majesty coming directly or indirectly from any part of the British dominions, be admitted into any of the United States during the war." This decisive conduct extinguished all hopes that Great Britain might have entertained, of making a separate peace with America. Two of the first sovereigns of Europe, the Empress of Russia, and the Emperor of Germany, were the mediators in accomplishing the great work of peace. Such was the state of the contending parties, that the intercession of powerful mediators was no longer necessary. The disposition of Great Britain, to recognize the independence of the United States, had removed the principal difficulty, which had hitherto obstructed a general pacification. It would be curious to trace the successive steps by which the nation was brought to this measure, so irreconcilable to their former declarations. Various auxiliary causes might be called in to account for this great change of the public mind of Great Britain, but the sum of the whole must be resolved into this simple proposition, "That it was unavoidable." A state of perpetual war was inconsistent with the interest of a commercial nation. Even the longer continuance of hostilities was forbidden by every principle of wise policy.

[306] The avowed object of the alliance between France and America, and the steady adherence of both parties to enter into no negotiations without the concurrence of each other, reduced Great Britain to the alternative of continuing a hopeless unproductive war, or of negotiating under the idea of recognizing American independence. This great change of the public mind in Great Britain, favourable to American independence, took place between November 1781, and March 1782. In that interval Mr. Laurens was released from his confinement in the tower. Before and after his release, he had frequent opportunities of demonstrating to persons in power, that from his personal knowledge of the sentiments of Congress, and of their instructions to their ministers, every hope of peace, without the acknowledgement of independence was illusory. Seven years experience had proved to the nation that the conquest of the American States was impracticable; they now received equal conviction, that the recognition of their independence, was an indispensible preliminary to the termination of a war, from the continuance of which, neither profit nor honor was to be acquired. The pride of Great Britain for a long time resisted, but that usurping passion was obliged to yield to the superior influence of interest. The feelings of the great body of the people were no longer to be controuled, by the honor of ministers, or romantic ideas of national dignity. At the close of the war, a revolution was effected in the sentiments of the inhabitants of Great Britain, not less remarkable than what in the beginning of it, took place among the citizens of America.

Independence which was neither thought of nor wished for by the latter in the year 1774, and 1775, became in the year 1776 their favorite object. A recognition of this, which throughout the war, had been with few exceptions the object of abhorrence to the British nation, became in the year 1782, a popular measure in Great Britain, as the means of putting an end to a ruinous war.

The commissioners for negotiating peace on the part of the United

States, were John Adams, Benjamin Franklin, John Jay, and Henry Laurens. On the part of Great Britain, Mr. Fitzherbert, and Mr. Oswald. Provisional [307] articles of peace, between Great Britain and the United States were agreed upon by these gentlemen, which were to be inserted in a future treaty of peace, to be finally concluded between the parties, when that between Great Britain and France took place. By these the independence of the states was acknowledged in its fullest extent. Very ample boundaries were allowed them, which comprehended the fertile and extensive countries on both sides of the Ohio, and on the east side of the Mississippi, in which was the residence of upwards of twenty nations of Indians, and particularly of the five nations, who had long been the friends and allies of Great Britain. An unlimited right of fishery on the banks of Newfoundland, and on other places where both nations had heretofore been accustomed to fish, was likewise confirmed to the Americans. From the necessity of the case, the loyalists were sacrificed, nothing further than a simple recommendation for restitution, being stipulated in their favour. Five days after these provisional articles were signed, the British parliament met. They underwent a severe parliamentary discussion. It was said by the opposition that independence being recognized, every thing ceded by Great Britain required an equivalent; but that while they gave up the many posts they held in the United States, an immense extent of north and western territory, a participation in the fur trade, and in the fisheries, nothing was stipulated in return.

It must be acknowledged, that the ministers of Congress procured for their countrymen better terms than they had reason to expect; but from a combination of circumstances, it was scarcely possible to end the war without similar concessions on the part of Great Britain. By the alliance between France and America, there could be no peace without independence. That once granted, most of the other articles followed of course. It is true the boundaries agreed upon, were more extensive than the States, when colonies had claimed, yet the surplus ceded could have been of little or no use to Great Britain, and might if retained have given an occasion to a future war.

[308] The case of the loyalists was undoubtedly a hard one, but unavoidable, from the complex constitution of the United States.

The American ministers engaged as far as they were authorised, and Congress did all that they constitutionally could; but this was no more than simply to recommend their case to the several States, for the purpose of making them restitution. To have insisted on more, under such circumstances, would have been equivalent to saying that there should be no peace. It is true much more was expected from the recommendations of Congress, than resulted from them; but this was not the consequence of deception, but of misunderstanding the principles of the confederation. In conformity to the letter and spirit of the treaty, Congress urged in strong terms the propriety of making restitution to the loyalists, but to procure it was beyond their power. In the animation produced by the war, when the Americans conceived their liberties to be in danger, and that their only safety consisted in obeying their foederal head, they yielded a more unreserved obedience to the recommendations of Congress, than is usually paid to the decrees of the most arbitrary sovereigns. But the case was widely different, when at the close of the war, a measure was recommended, in direct opposition to their prejudices. It was the general opinion of the Americans, that the continuance of the war, and the asperity with which it had been carried on, was more owing to the machinations of their own countrymen, who had taken part with royal government, than to their British enemies. It is certain that the former had been most active in predatory excursions, and most forward in scenes of blood and murder. Their knowledge of the country enabled them to do mischief, which would never have occurred to European soldiers. Many powerful passions of human nature operated against making restitution to men, who were thus considered as the authors of so great a share of the general distress.

There were doubtless among the loyalists many worthy characters—friends to peace, and lovers of justice: To such, restitution was undoubtedly due, and to many [309] such it was made; but it is one of the many calamities incident to war, that the innocent, from the impossibility of discrimination, are often involved in the same distress with the guilty. The return of the loyalists to their former places of residence, was as much disrelished by the whig citizens of America, as the proposal for reimbursing their confiscated property. In sundry

1782

places committees were formed, which in an arbitrary manner, opposed their peaceable residence. The sober and dispassionate citizens exerted themselves in checking these irregular measures; but such was the violence of party spirit, and so relaxed were the sinews of government, that in opposition to legal authority, and the private interference of the judicious and moderate, many indecent outrages were committed on the persons and property of the returning loyalists. Nor were these all the sufferings of those Americans who had attached themselves to the royal cause. Being compelled to depart their native country, many of them were obliged to take up their abodes in the inhospitable wilds of Nova Scotia, or on the barren shores of the Bahama Islands. Parliamentary relief was extended to them, but this was obtained with difficulty, and distributed with a partial hand. Some who invented plausible tales of loyalty and distress received much more than they ever possessed; but others, less artful, were not half reimbursed for their actual losses. The bulk of the sufferings, subsequent to the peace among the Americans, fell to the share of the merchants, and others, who owed money in England. From the operations of the war remittances were impossible. In the mean time payments were made in America by a depreciating paper, under the sanction of a law which made it a legal tender. The unhappy persons, who in this manner suffered payment, could not apply it to the extinguishment of their foreign debts. If they retained in their hands the paper which was paid to them, it daily decreased in value: If they invested it in public securities, from the deficiency of funds, their situation was no better: If they purchased land, such was the superabundance of territory ceded by the peace, that it fell greatly [310] in value. Under all these embarrassments, the American debtor was by treaty bound to make payments in specie of all his *bona fide* debts, due in Great Britain. The British merchant was materially injured by being kept for many years out of his capital, and the American was often ruined by being ultimately held to pay in specie, what he received in paper. Enough was suffered on both sides to make the inhabitants, as well in Great Britain as in America, deprecate war as one of the greatest evils incident to humanity.

1782

The State of parties; the advantages and disadvantages of the Revolution; its influence on the minds and morals of the Citizens.

PREVIOUS TO THE AMERICAN REVOLUTION, the inhabitants of the British colonies were universally loyal. That three millions of such subjects should break through all former attachments, and unanimously adopt new ones, could not reasonably be expected. The revolution had its enemies, as well as its friends, in every period of the war. Country religion, local policy, as well as private views, operated in disposing the inhabitants to take different sides. The New-England provinces being mostly settled by one sort of people, were nearly of one sentiment. The influence of placemen in Boston, together with the connexions which they had formed by marriages, had attached sundry influential characters in that capital to the British interest, but these were but as the dust in the balance, when compared with the numerous independent whig yeomanry of the country. The same and other causes produced a large number in New-York, who were attached to royal government. That city had long been head quarters of the British army in America, and many intermarriages, and other connexions, had been made between British officers, and some of their first families. The practice of entailing estates had prevailed in [311] New-York to a much greater extent, than in any of the other provinces. The governors thereof had long been in the habit of indulging their favorites with extravagant grants of land. This had introduced the distinction of landlord and tenant. There was therefore in New-York an aristocratic party, respectable for numbers, wealth and influence, which had much to fear from independence. The city was also divided into parties by the influence of two ancient and numerous families, the Livingstones and Delanceys. These having been long accustomed to oppose each other at elections, could rarely be brought to unite, in any political measures. In this controversy, one almost universally took part with America, the other with Great Britain.

The Irish in America, with a few exceptions were attached to independence. They had fled from oppression in their native country, and could not brook the idea that it should follow them. Their national prepossessions in favour of liberty, were strengthened by their religious opinions. They were Presbyterians, and people of that denomination, for reasons hereafter to be explained, were mostly whigs. The Scotch on the other hand, though they had formerly sacrificed much to liberty in their own country, were generally disposed to support the claims of Great-Britain. Their nation for some years past had experienced a large proportion of royal favour. A very absurd association was made by many, between the cause of John Wilkes and the cause of America. The former had rendered himself so universally odious to the Scotch, that many of them were prejudiced against a cause, which was so ridiculously, but generally associated, with that of a man who had grossly insulted their whole nation. The illiberal reflections cast by some Americans on the whole body of the Scotch, as favourers of arbitrary power, restrained high spirited individuals of that nation, from joining a people who suspected their love of liberty. Such of them as adhered to the cause of independence, were ready in their attachment. The army and the

Congress ranked among their best officers, and most valuable members, some individuals of that nation.

[312] Such of the Germans, in America, as possessed the means of information, were generally determined whigs, but many of them were too little informed, to be able to chuse their side on proper ground. They, especially such of them as resided in the interior country, were from their not understanding the English language, far behind most of the other inhabitants, in a knowledge of the merits of the dispute. Their disaffection was rather passive than active: A considerable part of it arose from principles of religion, for some of their sects deny the lawfulness of war. No people have prospered more in America than the Germans. None have surpassed, and but few have equalled them, in industry and other republican virtues.

The great body of tories in the southern states, was among the settlers on their western frontier. Many of these were disorderly persons, who had fled from the old settlements, to avoid the restraints of civil government. Their numbers were encreased by a set of men called regulators. The expence and difficulty of obtaining the decision of courts, against horse-thieves and other criminals, had induced sundry persons, about the year 1770, to take the execution of the laws into their own hands, in some of the remote settlements, both of North and South-Carolina. In punishing crimes, forms as well as substance, must be regarded. From not attending to the former, some of these regulators, though perhaps aiming at nothing but what they thought right, committed many offences both against law and justice. By their violent proceedings regular government was prostrated. This drew on them the vengeance of royal governors. The regulators having suffered from their hands, were slow to oppose an established government, whose power to punish they had recently experienced. Apprehending that the measures of Congress were like their own regulating schemes, and fearing that they would terminate in the same disagreeable consequences, they and their adherents were generally opposed to the revolution.

Religion also divided the inhabitants of America. The presbyterians and independents, were almost universally [313] attached to the measures of Congress. Their religious societies are governed on the republican plan.

From independence they had much to hope, but from Great Britain if finally successful, they had reason to fear the establishment of a church hierarchy. Most of the episcopal ministers of the northern provinces, were pensioners on the bounty of the British government. The greatest part of their clergy, and many of their laity in these provinces, were therefore disposed to support a connexion with Great Britain. The episcopal clergy in these southern provinces being under no such bias, were often among the warmest whigs. Some of them foreseeing the downfall of religious establishments from the success of the Americans, were less active, but in general where their church was able to support itself, their clergy and laity, zealously espoused the cause of independence. Great pains were taken to persuade them, that those who had been called dissenters, were aiming to abolish the episcopal establishment, to make way for their own exaltation, but the good sense of the people, restrained them from giving any credit to the unfounded suggestion. Religious controversy was happily kept out of view: The well informed of all denominations were convinced, that the contest was for their civil rights, and therefore did not suffer any other considerations to interfere, or disturb their union.

The quakers with a few exceptions were averse to independence. In Pennsylvania they were numerous, and had power in their hands. Revolutions in government are rarely patronised by any body of men, who foresee that a diminution of their own importance, is likely to result from the change. Quakers from religious principles were averse to war, and therefore could not be friendly to a revolution, which could only be effected by the sword. Several individuals separated from them on account of their principles, and following the impulse of their inclinations, joined their countrymen in arms. The services America received from two of their society, Generals Greene and Mifflin, made some amends for the embarrassment, [314] which the disaffection of the great body of their people occasioned to the exertions of the active friends of independence.

The age and temperament of individuals had often an influence in fixing their political character. Old men were seldom warm whigs. They could not relish the great changes which were daily taking place. Attached to ancient forms and habits, they could not readily

1782

accommodate themselves to new systems. Few of the very rich were active in forwarding the revolution. This was remarkably the case in the eastern and middle States; but the reverse took place in the southern extreme of the confederacy. There were in no part of America, more determined whigs than the opulent slaveholders in Virginia, the Carolinas and Georgia. The active and spirited part of the community, who felt themselves possessed of talents, that would raise them to eminence in a free government, longed for the establishment of independent constitutions: But those who were in possession or expectation of royal favour, or of promotion from Great Britain, wished that the connexion between the Parent State and the colonies, might be preserved. The young, the ardent, the ambitious and the enterprising were mostly whigs, but the phlegmatic, the timid, the interested and those who wanted decision were, in general, favourers of Great Britain, or at least only the lukewarm inactive friends of independence. The whigs received a great reinforcement from the operation of continental money. In the year 1775, 1776, and in the first months of 1777, while the bills of Congress were in good credit, the effects of them were the same, as if a foreign power had made the United States a present of twenty million of silver dollars. The circulation of so large a sum of money, and the employment given to great numbers in providing for the American army, increased the numbers and invigorated the zeal of the friends to the revolution: on the same principles, the American war was patronised in England, by the many contractors and agents for transporting and supplying the British army. In both cases the inconveniences of interrupted commerce [315] were lessened by the employment which war and a domestic circulation of money substituted in its room. The convulsions of war afforded excellent shelter for desperate debtors. The spirit of the times revolted against dragging to jails for debt, men who were active and zealous in defending their country, and on the other hand, those who owed more than they were worth, by going within the British lines, and giving themselves the merit of suffering on the score of loyalty, not only put their creditors to defiance, but sometimes obtained promotion or other special marks of royal favour.

The American revolution, on the one hand, brought forth great vices; but on the other hand, it called forth many virtues, and gave

1782

occasion for the display of abilities which, but for that event, would have been lost to the world. When the war began, the Americans were a mass of husbandmen, merchants, mechanics and fishermen; but the necessities of the country gave a spring to the active powers of the inhabitants, and set them on thinking, speaking and acting, in a line far beyond that to which they had been accustomed. The difference between nations is not so much owing to nature, as to education and circumstances. While the Americans were guided by the leading strings of the mother country, they had no scope nor encouragement for exertion. All the departments of government were established and executed for them, but not by them. In the years 1775 and 1776 the country, being suddenly thrown into a situation that needed the abilities of all its sons, these generally took their places, each according to the bent of his inclination. As they severally pursued their objects with ardor, a vast expansion of the human mind speedily followed. This displayed itself in a variety of ways. It was found that the talents for great stations did not differ in kind, but only in degree, from those which were necessary for the proper discharge of the ordinary business of civil society. In the bustle that was occasioned by the war, few instances could be produced of any persons who made a figure, or who rendered essential services, but from among those who had given specimens of similar talents [316] in their respective professions. Those who from indolence or dissipation, had been of little service to the community in time of peace, were found equally unserviceable in war. A few young men were exceptions to this general rule. Some of these, who had indulged in youthful follies, broke off from their vicious courses, and on the pressing call of their country became useful servants of the public: but the great bulk of those, who were the active instruments of carrying on the revolution, were self-made, industrious men. These who by their own exertions, had established or laid a foundation for establishing personal independence, were most generally trusted, and most successfully employed in establishing that of their country. In these times of action, classical education was found of less service than good natural parts, guided by common sense and sound judgement.

Several names could be mentioned of individuals who, without the knowledge of any other language than their mother tongue, wrote not only accurately, but elegantly, on public business. It seemed as if the war not only required, but created talents. Men whose minds were warmed with the love of liberty, and whose abilities were improved by daily exercise, and sharpened with a laudable ambition to serve their distressed country, spoke, wrote, and acted, with an energy far surpassing all expectations which could be reasonably founded on their previous acquirements.

The Americans knew but little of one another, previous to the revolution. Trade and business had brought the inhabitants of their seaports acquainted with each other, but the bulk of the people in the interior country were unacquainted with their fellow citizens. A continental army, and Congress composed of men from all the States, by freely mixing together, were assimilated into one mass. Individuals of both, mingling with the citizens, disseminated principles of union among them. Local prejudices abated. By frequent collision asperities were worn off, and a foundation was laid for the establishment of a nation, out of discordant materials. Intermarriages between men and women of different States [317] were much more common than before the war, and became an additional cement to the union. Unreasonable jealousies had existed between the inhabitants of the eastern and of the southern States; but on becoming better acquainted with each other, these in a great measure subsided. A wiser policy prevailed. Men of liberal minds led the way in discouraging local distinctions, and the great body of the people, as soon as reason got the better of prejudice, found that their best interests would be most effectually promoted by such practices and sentiments as were favourable to union. Religious bigotry had broken in upon the peace of various sects, before the American war. This was kept up by partial establishments, and by a dread that the church of England through the power of the mother country, would be made to triumph over all other denominations. These apprehensions were done away by the revolution. The different sects, having nothing to fear from each other, dismissed all religious controversy. A proposal for introducing bishops into America before the war, had kindled a flame among the dissenters; but the revolution was no sooner accomplished, than a scheme for that purpose was perfected, with the consent and

1782

approbation of all those sects who had previously opposed it. Pulpits which had formerly been shut to worthy men, because their heads had not been consecrated by the imposition of the hands of a Bishop or of a Presbytery, have since the establishment of independence, been reciprocally opened to each other, whensoever the public convenience required it. The world will soon see the result of an experiment in politics, and be able to determine whether the happiness of society is increased by religious establishments, or diminished by the want of them.

Though schools and colleges were generally shut up during the war, yet many of the arts and sciences were promoted by it. The geography of the United States before the revolution was but little known; but the marches of armies, and the operations of war, gave birth to many geographical enquiries and discoveries, which otherwise would not have been made. A passionate fondness [318] for studies of this kind, and the growing importance of the country, excited one of its sons, the Rev. Mr. Morse, to travel through every State of the Union, and amass a fund of topographical knowledge, far exceeding any thing heretofore communicated to the public. The necessities of the States led to the study of Tactics, Fortification, Gunnery, and a variety of other arts connected with war, and diffused a knowledge of them among a peaceable people, who would otherwise have had no inducement to study them.

1782

The abilities of ingenious men were directed to make farther improvements in the art of destroying an enemy. Among these, David Bushnell of Connecticut invented a machine for submarine navigation, which was found to answer the purpose of rowing horizontally, at any given depth under water, and of rising or sinking at pleasure. To this was attached a magazine of powder, and the whole was contrived in such a manner, as to make it practicable to blow up vessels by machinery under them. Mr. Bushnell also contrived sundry other curious machines for the annoyance of British shipping; but from accident they only succeeded in part. He destroyed one vessel in charge of Commodore Symonds, and a second one near the shore of Long-Island.

Surgery was one of the arts which was promoted by the war. From the want of hospitals and other aids, the medical men of America, had few opportunities of perfecting themselves in this art, the thorough knowledge of which can only be acquired by practice and observation. The melancholy events of battles, gave the American students an opportunity of seeing, and learning more in one day, than they could have acquired in years of peace. It was in the hospitals of the United States, that Dr. Rush first discovered the method of curing the lock jaw by bark and wine, added to other invigorating remedies, which has since been adopted with success in Europe, as well as in the United States.

The science of government, has been more generally diffused among the Americans by means of the revolution. The policy of Great Britain, in throwing [319] them out of her protection, induced   1782
a necessity of establishing independent constitutions. This led to reading and reasoning on the subject. The many errors that were at first committed by unexperienced statesmen, have been a practical comment on the folly of unbalanced constitutions, and injudicious laws. The discussions concerning the new constitution, gave birth to much reasoning on the subject of government, and particularly to a series of letters signed Publius, but really the work of Alexander Hamilton, in which much political knowledge and wisdom were displayed, and which will long remain a monument of the strength and acuteness of the human understanding in investigating truth.

When Great Britain first began her encroachments on the colonies, there were few natives of America who had distinguished themselves as speakers or writers, but the controversy between the two countries multiplied their number.

The stamp act, which was to have taken place in 1765, employed the pens and tongues of many of the colonists, and by repeated exercise improved their ability to serve their country. The duties imposed in 1767, called forth the pen of John Dickinson, who in a series of letters signed a Pennsylvania Farmer, may be said to have sown the seeds of the revolution. For being universally read by the colonists, they universally enlightened them on the dangerous consequences, likely to result from their being taxed by the parliament of Great Britain.

In establishing American independence, the pen and the press had merit equal to that of the sword. As the war was the people's war, and was carried on without funds, the exertions of the army would have been insufficient to effect the revolution, unless the great body of the people had been prepared for it, and also kept in a constant disposition to oppose Great Britain. To rouse and unite the inhabitants, and to persuade them to patience for several years, under present sufferings, with the hope of obtaining remote advantages for their posterity, was a work of difficulty: This was effected in a great measure by the tongues and pens of the well informed [320] citizens, and on it depended the success of military operations.

To enumerate the names of all those who were successful labourers in this arduous business, is impossible. The following list contains in nearly alphabetical order, the names of the most distinguished writers in favour of the rights of America.

John Adams, and Samuel Adams, of Boston; Bland, of Virginia; John Dickinson, of Pennsylvania; Daniel Dulany, of Annapolis; William Henry Drayton, of South-Carolina; Dr. Franklin, of Philadelphia; John Jay, and Alexander Hamilton, of New-York; Thomas Jefferson, and Arthur Lee of Virginia; Jonathan Hyman, of Connecticut; Governor Livingston, of New-Jersey; Dr. Mayhew, and James Otis, of Boston; Thomas Paine, Dr. Rush, Charles Thompson, and James Wilson, of Philadelphia; William Tennant, of South-Carolina; Josiah Quincy, and Dr. Warren, of Boston. These and many others laboured in enlightening their countrymen, on the subject of their political interests, and in animating them to a proper line of conduct, in defence of their liberties. To these individuals may be added, the great body of the clergy, especially in New-England. The printers of news-papers, had also much merit in the same way. Particularly Eedes and Gill, of Boston; Holt, of New-York; Bradford, of Philadelphia; and Timothy, of South-Carolina.

The early attention which had been paid to literature in New-England, was also eminently conducive to the success of the Americans in resisting Great Britain. The university of Cambridge was founded as early as 1636, and Yale college in 1700. It has been computed, that in the year the Boston port act was passed, there were in the four eastern colonies, upwards of two thousand graduates of their colleges dispersed through their several towns, who by their knowledge and abilities, were able to influence and direct the great body of the people to a proper line of conduct, for opposing the encroachments of Great Britain on their liberties. The colleges to the southward of New-England, except that of William and Mary in Virginia, were but [321] of modern date; but they had been of a standing sufficiently long, to have trained for public service, a considerable number of the youth of the country. The college of New-Jersey, which was incorporated about 28 years before the revolution, had in that time educated upwards of 300 persons, who, with a few exceptions, were active and useful friends of independence. From the influence which knowledge had in securing and preserving the liberties of America, the present generation may trace the wise policy of their fathers, in erecting schools and colleges. They may also learn that it is their duty to found more, and support all such institutions. Without the advantages derived from these lights of this new world, the United States would probably have fallen in their unequal contest with Great Britain. Union which was essential to the success of their resistance, could scarcely have taken place, in the measures adopted by an ignorant multitude. Much less could wisdom in council, unity in system, or perseverance in the prosecution of a long and self denying war, be expected from an uninformed people. It is a well known fact, that persons unfriendly to the revolution, were always most numerous in those parts of the United States, which had either never been illuminated, or but faintly warmed by the rays of science. The uninformed and the misinformed, constituted a great proportion of those Americans, who preferred the leading strings of the Parent State, though encroaching on their liberties, to a government of their own countrymen and fellow citizens.

As literature had in the first instance favoured the revolution, so in its turn, the revolution promoted literature. The study of eloquence and of the Belles lettres, was more successfully prosecuted in America, after the disputes between Great Britain and her colonies began to be serious, than it ever had been before. The various orations, addresses, letters, dissertations and other literary performances which the war made necessary, called forth abilities where they were, and excited the rising generation to study arts, which brought with them their own reward. Many incidents afforded materials for the favourites of the [322] muses, to display their talents. Even burlesquing royal proclamations, by parodies and doggerel poetry, had great effects on the minds of the people. A celebrated historian has remarked, that the song of Lillibullero forwarded the revolution of 1688 in England. It may be truly affirmed, that similar productions produced similar effects in America. Francis Hopkinson rendered essential service to his country, by turning the artillery of wit and ridicule on the enemy. Philip Freneau laboured successfully in the same way. Royal proclamations and other productions which issued from royal printing presses, were by the help of a warm imagination, arrayed in such dresses as rendered them truly ridiculous. Trumbull with a vein of original Hudibrastic humour, diverted his countrymen so much with the follies of their enemies, that for a time they forgot the calamities of war. Humphries twined the literary with the military laurel, by superadding the fame of an elegant poet, to that of an accomplished officer. Barlow increased the fame of his country and of the distinguished actors in the revolution, by the bold design of an epic poem ably executed, on the idea that Columbus foresaw in vision, the great scenes that were to be translated on the theatre of that new world, which he had discovered. Dwight struck out in the same line, and at an early period of life finished, an elegant work entitled the conquest of Canaan, on a plan which has rarely been attempted. The principles of their mother tongue, were first unfolded to the Americans since the revolution, by their countryman Webster. Pursuing an unbeaten track, he has made discoveries in the genius and construction of the English language, which had escaped the researches of preceding philologists. These and a group of other literary characters have been brought into view by the revolution. It is remarkable, that of these, Connecticut has produced an unusual proportion. In that truly republican state, every thing conspires to adorn human nature with its highest honours.

From the later periods of the revolution till the present time, schools, colleges, societies and institutions for promoting literature, arts, manufactures, agriculture, and [323] for extending human happiness, have been increased far beyond any thing that ever took place before the declaration of independence. Every state in the union, has done more or less in this way, but Pennsylvania has done the most. The following institutions have been very lately founded in that state, and most of them in the time of the war or since the peace. An university in the city of Philadelphia; a college of physicians in the same place; Dickinson college at Carlisle; Franklin college at Lancaster; the Protestant Episcopal academy in Philadelphia; academies at York-town, at Germantown, at Pittsburgh and Washington; and an academy in Philadelphia for young ladies; societies for promoting political enquiries; for the medical relief of the poor, under the title of the Philadelphia Dispensary; for promoting the abolition of slavery, and the relief of free negroes unlawfully held in bondage; for propagating the gospel among the Indians, under the direction of the United Brethren; for the encouragement of manufactures and the useful arts; for alleviating the miseries of prisons. Such have been some of the beneficial effects, which have resulted from that expansion of the human mind, which has been produced by the revolution, but these have not been without alloy.

To overset an established government unhinges many of those principles, which bind individuals to each other. A long time, and much prudence, will be necessary to reproduce a spirit of union and that reverence for government, without which society is a rope of sand. The right of the people to resist their rulers, when invading their liberties, forms the corner stone of the American republics. This principle, though just in itself, is not favourable to the tranquility of present establishments. The maxims and measures, which in the years 1774 and 1775 were successfully inculcated and adopted by American patriots, for oversetting the established government, will answer a similar purpose when recurrence is had to them by factious demagogues, for disturbing the freest governments that were ever devised.

[324] War never fails to injure the morals of the people engaged in it. The American war, in particular, had an unhappy influence of this kind. Being begun without funds or regular establishments, it could not be carried on without violating private rights; and in its progress, it involved a necessity for breaking solemn promises; and plighted public faith. The failure of national justice, which was in some degree unavoidable, increased the difficulties of performing private engagements, and weakened that sensibility to the obligations of public and private honor, which is a security for the punctual performance of contracts.

In consequence of the war, the institutions of religion have been deranged, the public worship of the Deity suspended, and a great number of the inhabitants deprived of the ordinary means of obtaining that religious knowledge, which tames the fierceness, and softens the rudeness of human passions and manners. Many of the temples dedicated to the service of the most High, were destroyed, and these from a deficiency of ability and inclination, are not yet rebuilt. The clergy were left to suffer, without proper support. The depreciation of the paper currency was particularly injurious to them. It reduced their salaries to a pittance, so insufficient for their maintenance, that several of them were obliged to lay down their profession, and engage in other pursuits. Public preaching, of which many of the inhabitants were thus deprived, seldom fails of rendering essential service to society, by civilising the multitude and forming them to union. No class of citizens have contributed more to the revolution than the clergy, and none have hitherto suffered more in consequence of it. From the diminution of their number, and the penury to which they have been subjected, civil government has lost many of the advantages it formerly derived from the public instructions of that useful order of men.

On the whole, the literary, political, and military talents of the citizens of the United States have been improved by the revolution, but their moral character is inferior to what it formerly was. So great is the change [325] for the worse, that the friends of public order are fondly called upon to exert their utmost abilities, in extirpating the vicious principles and habits, which have taken deep root during the late convulsions.

The discharge of the American army: the evacuation of ·1783
New-York: The resignation of General Washington:
Arrangements of Congress for the disposing of their
western territory, and paying their debts: The distresses
of the States after the peace: The inefficacy of the
articles of the Confederation: A Grand Convention for
amending the Government: The New Constitution:
General Washington appointed President: An address to
the people of the United States.

WHILE THE CITIZENS OF THE United States were anticipating the
blessings of peace, their army which had successfully stemmed the
tide of British victories, was unrewarded for its services. The States
which had been rescued by their exertions from slavery, were in no
condition to pay them their stipulated due. To dismiss officers and
soldiers, who had spent the prime of their days in serving their
country, without an equivalent for their labors, or even a sufficiency
to enable them to gain a decent living, was a hard but unavoidable
case. An attempt was made by anonymous and seditious publications   MARCH
to inflame the minds of the officers and soldiers, and induce them   10, 1783
to unite in redressing their own grievances, while they had arms in
their hands. As soon as General Washington was informed of the
nature of these papers, he requested the General and field officers,

with one officer from each company, and a proper representation from the staff of the army, to assemble on an early day. He rightly judged that it would be much easier to divert from a wrong to a right path, than to recal fatal and hasty steps, after they had once been taken. The period, previously to the meeting of the officers, was improved in preparing them for the adoption of moderate [326] measures. Gen. Washington sent for one officer after another, and enlarged in private, on the fatal consequences, and particularly on the loss of character to the whole army, which would result from intemperate resolutions. When the officers were convened the commander in chief addressed them in a speech well calculated to calm their mind. He also pledged himself to exert all his abilities and influence in their favor, and requested them to rely on the faith of their country, and conjured them "as they valued their honor—as they respected the rights of humanity, and as they regarded the military and national character of America, to express their utmost detestation of the man, who was attempting to open the floodgates of civil discord, and deluge their rising empire with blood." Gen. Washington then retired. The minds of those who had heard him were in such an irritable state, that nothing but their most ardent patriotism and his unbounded influence, prevented the proposal of rash resolutions which if adopted, would have sullied the glory of seven years service. No reply whatever was made to the General's Speech. The happy moment was seized, while the minds of the officers softened by the eloquence of their beloved commander, were in a yielding state, and a resolution was unanimously adopted by which they declared "that no circumstances of distress or danger, should induce a conduct that might tend to sully the reputation and glory they had acquired, that the army continued to have an unshaken confidence, in the justice of Congress and their country. That they viewed with abhorrence and rejected with disdain, the infamous propositions in the late anonymous address to the officers of the army.["] Too much praise cannot be given to Gen. Washington, for the patriotism and decision which marked his conduct, in the whole of this serious transaction. Perhaps in no instance did the United States receive from heaven a more signal deliverance, through the hands of the commander in chief.

CHAPTER XXVII

Soon after these events, Congress completed a resolution which MARCH 22 1783 had been for some time pending, that the officers of their army, who preferred a sum in gross to an annuity, [327] should be entitled to receive to the amount of five years full pay, in money or securities at six per cent. per annum, instead of the half pay for life, which had been previously promised to them.

To avoid the inconveniences of dismissing a great number of MAY 26 soldiers in a body, furloughs were freely granted to individuals, and after their dispersion they were not enjoined to return. By this arrangement a critical moment was got over. A great part of an unpaid army, was disbanded and dispersed over the States, without tumult or disorder. The privates generally betook themselves to labor, and crowned the merit of being good soldiers, by becoming good citizens. Several of the American officers, who had been bred mechanics resumed their trades. In old countries the disbanding a single regiment, even though fully paid, has often produced serious consequences, but in America where arms had been taken up for self defence, they were peaceably laid down as soon as they became unnecessary. As soldiers had been easily and speedily formed in 1775, out of farmers, planters, and mechanics, with equal ease and expedition in the year 1783, they dropped their adventitious character, and resumed their former occupations. About 80 of the Pennsylvania levies formed an exception to the prevailing peaceable disposition of the army. These in defiance of their officers, set out from Lancaster and marched to Philadelphia to seek a redress of their grievances, from the executive council of the state. The JUNE 20, 1783 mutineers in opposition to advice and intreaties, persisted in their march, till they arrived at Philadelphia. They were there joined by some other troops, who were quartered in the barracks. The whole amounting to upwards of 300 men, marched with fixed bayonets and drums, to the statehouse, in which Congress and the supreme executive council of Pennsylvania held their sessions. They placed guards at every door, and sent in a written message to the President and Council of the state, and threatened to let loose an enraged soldiery upon them, if they were not gratified as to their demand within 20 minutes. The situation of Congress, though they were [328] not the particular object of the soldiers resentment, was far from being agreeable. After being about three hours under duresse they retired, but previously resolved that the authority of the United States had been grossly insulted. Soon after they left Philadelphia, and fixed on Princeton as the place of their next meeting. General Washington immediately ordered a large detachment of his army, to march for Philadelphia. Previously to their arrival, the disturbances were quieted without bloodshed. Several of the mutineers were tried and condemned, two to suffer death, and four to receive corporal punishment, but they were all afterwards pardoned.

OCT. 18, 1783

Towards the close of the year, Congress issued a proclamation, in which the armies of the United States were applauded, "for having displayed in the progress of an arduous and difficult war, every military and patriotic virtue, and in which the thanks of their country were given them, for their long, eminent and faithful services." Congress then declared it to be their pleasure, "that such part of their foederal armies, as stood engaged to serve during the war, should from and after the third day of November next, be absolutely discharged from the said service." On the day preceding their dismission, General Washington issued his farewell orders, in the most endearing language. After giving them his advice respecting their future conduct, and bidding them an affectionate farewell, he concluded with these words,

NOV. 2

> May ample justice be done them here, and may the choicest of Heaven's favours, both here and hereafter, attend those, who under the divine auspices have secured innumerable blessings for others. With these wishes, and this benediction, the commander in chief is about to retire from service; the curtain of separation will soon be drawn, and the military scene, to him, will be closed forever.

With great exertions of the superintendant of finance; four months pay, in part of several years arrearages, were given to the army. This sum, though triffling, was all the immediate recompense the States were able to make to those brave men, who had conducted their country through an eight years war, to peace and independence.

[329] The evacuation of New-York, took place in about three weeks after the American army was discharged. For a twelvemonth preced-

ing, there had been an unrestrained communication between that city, though a British garrison, and the adjacent country. The bitterness of war passed away, and civilities were freely interchanged between those, who had lately fought for opportunities to destroy each other. General Washington and Governor Clinton, with their suites, made a public entry into the city of New-York, as soon as the royal army was withdrawn. The Lieutenant Governor, and members of the council, the officers of the American army, and the citizens, followed in an elegant procession. It was remarked that an unusual proportion of those who in 1776, had fled from New-York, were by death cut off from partaking in the general joy, which flowed in upon their fellow citizens, on returning to their ancient habitations. The ease and affluence which they enjoyed in the days of their prosperity, made the severities of exile inconvenient to all, and fatal to many, particularly to such as were advanced in life. Those who survived, both felt and expressed the overflowings of joy, on finding their sufferings and services rewarded with the recovery of their country; the expulsion of their enemies, and the establishment of their independence. In the evening there was a display of fireworks, which exceeded every thing of the kind before seen in the United States. They commenced by a dove's descending with an olive branch, and setting fire to a marron battery.

The hour now approached in which it became necessary for General Washington to take leave of his officers, who had been endeared to him by a long series of common sufferings and dangers. This was done in a solemn manner. The officers having previously assembled for the purpose, General Washington joined them, and calling for a glass of wine, thus addressed them, "with an Heart full of love and gratitude, I now take leave of you, I most devoutly wish that your latter days may be as prosperous and happy, as your former ones have been glorious and honourable." The officers came up successively, [330] and he took an affectionate leave of each of them. When this affecting scene was over, Washington left the room, and passed through the corps of light infantry, to the place of embarkation. The officers followed in a solemn mute procession, with dejected countenances. On his entering the barge to cross the north river, he turned towards the companions of his glory, and by waving his hat, bid them a silent adieu. Some of them answered this last signal of respect and affection with tears, and all of them hung upon the barge which conveyed him from their sight, till they could no longer distinguish in it the person of their beloved commander in chief.

A proposal was made to perpetuate the friendship of the officers, by forming themselves into a society, to be named after the famous Roman patriot Cincinnatus. The extreme jealousy of the new republics suspected danger to their liberties, from the union of the leaders of their late army, and especially from a part of their institution, which held out to their posterity, the honour of being admitted members of the same society. To obviate all grounds of fear, the general meeting of the society, recommended an alteration of their institution, which has been adopted by eight of the state societies. By this recommendation it was proposed to expunge every thing that was hereditary, and to retain little else than their original name, and a social charitable institution for perpetuating their personal friendships, and relieving the wants of their indigent brethren. General Washington on the approaching dissolution of the American army, by a circular letter to the Governors or Presidents of the individual states, gave his parting advice to his countrymen; and with all the charms of eloquence, inculcated the necessity of union, justice, subordination and of such principles and practices, as their new situation required.

The army being disbanded, the commander in chief proceeded to Annapolis, then the seat of Congress, to resign his commission. On his way thither, he delivered to the Comptroller in Philadelphia an account of the expenditure of all the public money he had ever received. [331] This was in his own hand writing, and every entry was made in a very particular manner. The whole sum, which in the course of the war had passed through his hands, amounted only to £14,479 18 9 sterling. Nothing was charged or retained as a reward for personal services, and actual disbursements had been managed with such oeconomy and fidelity, that they were all covered by the above moderate sum.

In every town and village, through which the General passed, he was met by public and private demonstrations of gratitude and joy. When he arrived at Annapolis, he informed Congress of his intention

1783

DEC. 19

to ask leave to resign the commission he had the honor to hold in their service, and desired to know their pleasure in what manner it would be most proper to be done. They resolved that it should be in a public audience. When the day fixed for that purpose arrived, a great number of distinguished personages attended the interesting scene. At a proper moment, General Washington addressed Thomas Mifflin the President, in the following words:

DEC. 23

Mr. President,

The great events on which my resignation depended, having at length taken place, I have now the honor of offering my sincere congratulations to Congress, and of presenting myself before them to surrender into their hands, the trust committed to me, and to claim the indulgence of retiring from the service of my country.

Happy in the confirmation of our independence and sovereignty, and pleased with the opportunity afforded the United States of becoming a respectable nation, I resign with satisfaction the appointment I accepted with diffidence; a diffidence in my abilities to accomplish so arduous a task, which however was superseded by a confidence in the rectitude of our cause, the support of the Supreme Power of the union, and the patronage of Heaven.

The successful termination of the war has verified the most sanguine expectations, and my gratitude for the interposition of Providence, and the assistance I have received from my countrymen, increases with every review of the momentous contest.

[332] While I repeat my obligations to the army in general, I should do injustice to my own feelings not to acknowledge, in this place, the peculiar services, and distinguished merits of the persons who have been attached to my person during the war: it was impossible the choice of confidential officers to compose my family should have been more fortunate; permit me, sir, to recommend in particular those who have continued in the service to the present moment, as worthy of the favourable notice and patronage of Congress.

1783

I consider it as an indispensible duty to close this last solemn act of my official life, by commending the interests of our dearest country to the protection of Almighty God, and those who have the superintendance of them, to His holy keeping.

Having now finished the work assigned me, I retire from the great theatre of action; and bidding an affectionate farewell to this august body, under whose orders I have long acted, I here offer my commission, and take my leave of all the employments of public life.

To this the President returned the following answer:

The United States in Congress assembled, receive with emotions too affecting for utterance, the solemn resignation of the authorities under which you have led their troops with success, through a perilous and doubtful war.

Called upon by your country to defend its invaded rights, you accepted the sacred charge before it had formed alliances, and whilst it was without friends or a government to support you.

You have conducted the great military contest with wisdom and fortitude, invariably regarding the rights of the civil power through all disasters and changes: you have by the love and confidence of your fellow citizens enabled them to display their martial genius, and transmit their fame to posterity; you have persevered, till these United States, aided by a magnanimous King and nation, have been enabled, under a just Providence, to close the war in freedom, safety and independence; on which happy event we sincerely join you in congratulations.

[333] Having defended the standard of liberty in this new world—having taught a lesson useful to those who inflict, and to those who feel oppression, you retire from the great theatre of action, with the blessing of your fellow citizens, but the glory of your virtues will not terminate with your military command, it will continue to animate remotest ages. We feel with you, our obligations to the army in general, and will particularly charge ourselves with the interest of those confidential officers, who have attended your person to this affecting moment.

We join you in commending the interests of our dearest country to the protection of Almighty God, beseeching Him to dispose the hearts and minds of its citizens, to improve the opportunity afforded them, of becoming a happy and respectable nation; and for YOU, we address to Him our earnest prayers, that a life so beloved may be fostered with all His care: That your days may be happy as they have been illustrious, and that He will finally give you that reward which this world cannot give.

The great scenes that crouded in upon the imagination of the General, and of the President, so affected them both, that they almost

1783

lost the power of utterance. The mingled emotions that agitated the minds of the spectators, on seeing the commander in chief of their armies, resigning all public employments, and his country acknowledging his services, and loading him with their blessings were beyond description. Immediately on resigning his commission, Mr. Washington, "hastened with ineffable delights," (to use his own words) to his seat at Mount Vernon, on the banks of the Potowmac in Virginia. Here the historian would wish to make a pause, while he described, the simple and heartfelt joy of neighbours and domestics, who welcomed him to his home. Let it not be deemed foreign to his present subject, to do homage to the feelings and character of the amiable partner of his conjugal happiness, upon this occasion. She deserved this tide of unparalelled female honour and felicity, for she loved her country, and bore with more than Roman—with christian patience and fortitude, the pains to which his [334] long absence, 1783 and the perils of his health and life had exposed her. Fain would the historian pursue the illustrious hero of the revolution, a little further, and attempt to describe his feelings upon his first review of the events of the war, from the quiet station which he now occupied. But this digression would lead him far from the objects of his history.

To pass suddenly from the toils of the first public commission in the United States, to the care of a farm; to exchange the instruments of war, for the implements of husbandry, and to become at once, the patron and example of ingenious and profitable agriculture, would to most men have been a difficult task. But to the elevated mind of the late commander in chief, of the armies of the United States, it was natural and delightful; and should these pages descend to posterity, and war continue ages hence to be the means of establishing national justice, let the commanders of armies learn from the example of General Washington, that the same which is acquired by the sword, without guilt or ambition, may be preserved without power, or splendor, in private life.

Though the war was over, much remained for Congress to do. The proper disposition of their unsettled western and northern frontier, became an object of serious attention. The eastern states had been settled uniformly in townships, but the middle and southern states by indiscriminate location. On a comparison of the merits of these different methods of settling a new country, Congress gave a decided preference to the former. Conformably to these principles, an ordinance was passed on the 20th of May 1785, for disposing of that part of the western territory, which bounds on Pennsylvania. Many settlers soon migrated to this country. Civil Government was established among them. A Governor and Judges were appointed and paid by Congress. They fixed their capital to which they gave the name of Marietta, at the conflux of the Muskingum and Ohio. In the first years of their settlement, Congress ordained that they should be governed as a colony of the United States, but engaged, that as soon as they had attained a population, equal to that of the smallest of the old states, they should be received [335] into the union on equal terms. By this liberal policy, the blessings of a free government, may be gradually extended to the remotest bounds of the United States.

These arrangements for promoting domestic tranquillity were accompanied by others, for forming commercial connexions with sovereigns of Europe. Towards the close of the war, Dr. Franklin had concluded a treaty between the United States, and the King of Sweden. He Mr. Adams and Mr. Jefferson were appointed joint commissioners for forming commercial treaties with foreign powers. They succeeded in their negotiation with the King of Prussia, and the Emperor of Morocco. Mr. Adams was also appointed Minister Plenipotentiary from the United States, to the Court of Great Britain; and was instructed to solicit a treaty between these two powers, but the Ministers of his Britannic Majesty, declined entering into any treaty with him. They assigned the inability of Congress, to compel the different states to observe general commercial regulations, as a reason for declining the proposed connexion. From mismanagement, the United States with respect to trade were in fact nearly as dependent on Great Britain, after the peace, as before the war. They had lost the privileges of British subjects with regard to some branches of commerce, but suffered most of the inconveniences of that political condition, in consequence of their inability to regulate their commerce by one will. In this deranged state of public affairs, Great Britain could expect little more from a treaty with the United States, than what her merchants already possessed. She continued to reap the benefits of an extensive trade with America, without a reciprocity of advantages. Mr. Adams finding his labours ineffectual, desired leave to return to America, which was granted.

To provide funds for paying their continental debt, engaged the attention of Congress, for some time before, and after the peace. The amount of this at the close of the war as nearly as could be calculated, was about forty millions of dollars. In prosecuting the necessary means for discharging it, the inefficacy of the articles of confederation soon became apparent. By these, Congress [336] though bound to pay, possessed no power of raising a revenue. Its constitutional authority extended no farther, than to make requisitions on the several states for their quotas, to be ascertained in a relative proportion to the value of their lands. A proposition was made to the several states near to the close of the war, to invest Congress with a power to levy an impost of five per cent, at the time and place of importation, on the value of all goods imported from foreign countries, till the whole of their public debt should be extinguished. Danger being now nearly over, selfish passions began to operate. Objections were made, to trusting the purse and the sword into the hands of the same body of men, and that too, for an indefinite period of time. To obviate these scruples, Congress on a reconsideration, proposed to limit the grant of a continental impost to 25 years, and to confine the application of its neat proceeds exclusively, to the discharge of existing debts. On these principles, a system of revenue for funding and ultimately paying the whole public debt was completed, and offered to the states for their ratification. By this, it was proposed to raise 2 millions and a half of dollars annually, to defray the interest of the continental debt. It was expected that the impost would bring in the first year one million of dollars, and increase every year afterwards. The states were respectively called upon to raise the balance, according to proportions assigned them, from some permanent established fund subject to the disposal of Congress. A proposition was also made, to change the federal rule of apportioning the public debt, from the value of land, to the more practicable one of numbers of inhabitants in the different states. The whole system was transmitted to the state legislatures, and accompanied by an animated address, enforcing the propriety of its immediate adoption. Some of the states adopted it in the whole; others only in part, and

APR. 18, 1783

some not at all. The states whose population was great, and whose lands were of an inferior quality, objected to changing the federal rule of apportionment, from the value of lands to numbers. Some of the states which from their having convenient ports, [337] were called importing states, found it to be more for their immediate advantage, to raise money by impost for their separate use, than for the benefit of the union. They who received foreign goods through neighbouring states, and which were called consuming states, complained that by the revolution they had only changed masters, for that instead of being taxed by Great Britain without their consent, they were virtually taxed in like manner by their sister states, who happened to be more favourably situated for importing foreign goods. From these jarring interests, and from the want of a disposition to support a supreme head, and to give up local advantages for the general benefit, the revenue system of Congress was never put in operation. Its failure was the source of many evils. No efficient funds being provided to pay the interest of the national debt, the public securities of the United States fell in their value to ten for one, and became an article of speculation. The war-worn soldier who received at the close of the contest only an obligation for the payment of his hard earned dues, was from necessity often obliged to transfer his rights for an insignificant sum. The monied man who had trusted his country in the hour of her distress, was deprived not only of his interest, on which he counted for his daily support, but of a great part of the value of his capital. The non-payment of public debts, sometimes inferred a necessity, and always furnished an apology, for not discharging private contracts. Confidence between man and man received a deadly wound. Public faith being first violated, private engagements lost much of their obligatory force. Gen. Washington who nobly refused any thing for himself, had eloquently though unsuccessfully pleaded the cause of the army, and other public creditors, in his circular letter to the governors before his resignation, and predicted the evils which followed from the rejection of the revenue system of Congress. His observations were as follows:

As to the second article which respects the performance of public justice, Congress have in their late address to the United States almost exhausted the subject. They have explained their ideas so fully, and have enforced the obligations [338] the states are under to render complete justice to all the public creditors, with so much dignity and energy, that in my opinion no real friend to the honor and independency of America, can hesitate a single moment respecting the propriety of complying with the just and honorable measures proposed. If their arguments do not produce conviction, I know of nothing that will have greater influence, especially when we recollect that the system referred to, being the result of the collected wisdom of the continent, must be esteemed, if not perfect, certainly the least objectionable of any that could be devised, and that if *it shall not be carried into immediate execution, a national bankruptcy with all its deplorable consequences will take place,* before any different plan can possibly be proposed or adopted. So pressing are the present circumstances, and such is the alternative now offered to the states.

Congress continued to send forth annual requisitions, for the sums wanted for the public service, and indulged the hope that the states would e'er long be convinced, of the necessity of adopting an efficient system of general revenue: But their requisitions as well as their system of revenue, were disregarded by some of the states, and but partially complied with by others. From this failure of public justice, a deluge of evils overflowed the United States. These were also encreased by an unfavorable balance of trade. The ravages of armies, and the interruption of a free communication, between Europe and America during the war, had multiplied the wants of the latter, to a degree which exceeded all previous calculations. An inundation of European manufactures, was therefore one of the first effects which followed the establishment of peace. These were purchased by the Americans far beyond their means of payment. Adventurers grasping at the profits of trading with the new formed states, exported to America goods to a great amount, exceeding what either prudence or policy could justify. The Americans soon found themselves involved in a debt, to the discharge of which their resources were unequal. In several instances, these debts were contracted on credit by persons to whom the United States were indebted. [339] These presuming on the justice of their country, had involved themselves in private engagements, hoping that what they received from the public would furnish them with the means of payment. Such were doubly distressed.

The sufferings of the inhabitants were increased in consequence of the obstructions of their trade. That intercourse with the West-India Islands, from which, when colonies they derived large supplies of gold and silver, was forbidden to them in their new capacity of independent states. Their fisheries received a severe check, from their being excluded from several ports in which, when colonies, they had found a ready sale for the fruits of their industry, which they drew from the ocean. These evils were still farther aggravated by the stoppage of the bounty on whale oil, to which, when British subjects they were entitled. To add to their other misfortunes, they could no longer sail with safety in the Mediterranean, a privilege which they had always enjoyed, while they were a part of the British empire. Unable to defend themselves from the Algerine corsairs, they were obliged either to quit that beneficial trade, or ensure it at a ruinous premium.

The United States from the want of power in their common head, were incapacitated from acting in concert, so as to avail themselves of their natural advantages. Congress called once more upon the States to enlarge their powers, and particularly to entrust them with the regulation of commerce for a limited number of years. Some states fully complied with this call, but others fettered their grants with such conditions, as prevented the formation of an uniform system.

From the combined operation of these causes trade languished; credit expired; gold and silver vanished; and in consequence thereof, real property was depreciated to an extent equal to that of the depression of continental money, in the 2d or 3d year of its emission. Instead of imitating the wise policy of Great Britain, in making an artificial medium of circulation, by funding their debts, several of the states to alleviate the differences [340] arising from the want of money, adopted the fallacious expedient of emitting paper, to supply the place of gold and silver. But the remedy increased the disease. If the funding plan had been adopted, the sum due by the United States, was so much within their resources, that by the establishment of efficient funds, for the punctual discharge of the interest, the public debt might have easily been made a public blessing. It would have been a capital for the extension of agriculture, commerce and manufactures, as well as an honest and effectual substitute for real coin. But these advantages, which would have lessened much of the sufferings of the inhabitants, were lost by the imbecillity of the general government, and the want of concert in the state legislatures.

When the people on the return of peace supposed their troubles to be ended, they found them to be only varied. The calamities of war were followed by another class of evils, different in their origin, but not less injurious in their consequences. The inhabitants feeling the pressure of their sufferings, and not knowing precisely from what source they originated, or how to remedy them, became uneasy, and many were ready to adopt any desperate measures that turbulent leaders might recommend. In this irritable state, a great number of the citizens of Massachusetts, sore with their enlarged portion of public calamity, were induced by seditious demagogues, to make an open resistance to the operations of their own free government. Insurrections took place in many parts, and laws were trampled upon by the very men whose deputies had enacted them, and whose deputies might have repealed them. By the moderation of the legislature, and especially by the bravery and good conduct of Generals Lincoln, and Shepherd, and the firmness of the well affected militia, the insurgents were speedily quelled, and good order restored, with the loss of about six of the freemen of the state.

The untoward events which followed the re-establishment of peace, though evils of themselves, were overruled for great national good. From the failure of their expectations of an immediate increase of political happiness, [341] the lovers of liberty and independence began to be less sanguine in their hopes from the American revolution, and to fear that they had built a visionary fabric of government, on the fallacious ideas of public virtue; but that elasticity of the human mind, which is nurtured by free constitutions, kept them from desponding. By an exertion of those inherent principles of self-preservation, which republics possess, a recurrence was had to the good sense of the people, for the rectification of fundamental disorders. While the country, free from foreign force and domestic violence, enjoyed tranquillity, a proposition was made by Virginia to all the other States to meet in convention, for the purpose of digesting a form of government, equal to the exigencies of the union. The first motion for this purpose was made by Mr. Madison, and he had the pleasure of seeing it acceded to by twelve of the States, and finally to issue in the establishment of a New Constitution, which bids fair to repay the citizens of the United States for the toils, dangers and wastes of the revolution. The fundamental distinction between the articles of confederation and the new constitution lies in this; the former acted only on States, the latter on individuals; the former could neither raise men nor money by its own authority, but lay at the discretion of thirteen different legislatures, and without their unanimous concurrence was unable to provide for the public safety, or for the payment of the national debt. The experience of several years had proved the impossibility of a government answering the end of its institution, which was dependent on others for the means necessary for attaining these ends. By the new constitution, one legislative, executive, and judicial power pervades the whole union. This ensures an uniform observance of treaties, and gives a stability to the general government, which never could be attained while the acts and requisitions of Congress were subject to the revision of thirteen legislatures, and while thirteen distinct and unconnected judiciaries, had a constitutional right to decide on the same subject. The people of the United States gave no new powers to their rulers, but made a [342] more judicious arrangement of what they had formerly ceded. They enlarged the powers of the general government, not by taking from the people, but from the State legislatures. They took from the latter a power of levying duties on the importation of merchandise from foreign countries, and transferred it to Congress for the common benefit of the union. They also invested the general government with a power to regulate trade, levy taxes and internal duties on the inhabitants. That these enlarged powers might be used only with caution and deliberation, Congress, which formerly con-sisted of only one body, was made to consist of two; one of which was to be chosen by the people in proportion to their numbers, the other by the State legislatures. The execution of the acts of this compounded legislature was committed to a Supreme Magistrate, with the title of President. The constitution, of which these were the principal features, was submitted to the people for ratification. Animated debates took place on the propriety of establishing or rejecting it. Some States, who from their local situation were benefited by receiving import duties into their treasuries, were averse from the giving of them up to the union. Others, who were consuming but not importing States, had an interested inducement of an opposite kind, to support the proposed new constitution. The prospects of increased employment for shipping, and the enlargement of commerce, weighed with those States which abounded in sailors and ships, and also with seaport towns, to advocate the adoption of the new system; but those States or parts of States, which depended chiefly on agriculture, were afraid that zeal for encouraging an American marine, by narrowing the grounds of competition among foreigners for purchasing and carrying their produce, would lessen their profits. Some of this description therefore conceived that they had a local interest in refusing the new system.

Individuals who had great influence in state legislatures, or who held profitable places under them, were unwilling to adopt a government which, by diminishing the power of the states, would eventually diminish their own [343] importance: others who looked forward to seats in the general government, or for offices under its authority, had the same interested reason for supporting its adoption. Some from jealousy of liberty, were afraid of giving too much power to their rulers; others, from an honest ambition to aggrandize their country, were for paving the way to national greatness by melting down the separate States into a national mass. The former feared the New Constitution; the latter gloried in it. Almost every passion which could agitate the human breast, interested States and individuals for and against the adoption of the proposed plan of government. Some whole classes of people were in its favor. The mass of public creditors expected payment of their debts from the establishment of an efficient government, and were therefore decidedly for its adoption. Such as lived on salaries, and those who, being clear of debt, wished for a fixed medium of circulation and the free course of law, were the friends of a constitution which prohibited the issuing of paper money and all interference between debtor and creditor. In addition to these, the great body of independent men, who saw the necessity of an energetic general government, and who, from the jarring interests of the different States, could not foresee any probability of getting a better one than was proposed, gave their support to what the federal convention had projected, and their influence effected its establishment. After a full consideration, and thorough discussion of its principles, it was ratified by the conventions of eleven of the original thirteen States, and the accession of the other two is soon expected.* The ratification of it was celebrated in most of the capitals of the States with elegant processions, which far exceeded any thing of the kind ever before exhibited in America. Time and experience only can fully discover the effects of this new distribution of the powers of government; but in theory it seems well calculated to unite liberty with safety, and to lay the foundation of national greatness, while it abridges none of the rights of the States, or of the people.

[344] The new constitution having been ratified by eleven of the States, and senators and representatives having been chosen agreeably to the articles thereof, they met at New-York and commenced proceedings under it. The old Congress; and confederation, like the continental money, expired without a sigh or groan. A new Congress, with more ample powers and a new constitution; partly national and partly federal, succeeded in their place to the great joy of all who wished for the happiness of the United States.

Though great diversity of opinions had prevailed about the new constitution, there was but one opinion about the person who should be appointed its supreme executive officer. The people, as well anti-federalists as federalists, (for by these names the parties for and against the new constitution were called) unanimously turned their eyes on the late commander of their armies, as the most proper person to be their first President. Perhaps there was not a well informed individual in the United States, (Mr. Washington himself only excepted) who was not anxious that he should be called to the executive administration of the proposed new plan of government. Unambitious of farther honors he had retired to his farm in Virginia, and hoped to be excused from all farther public service; but his country called him by an unanimous vote to fill the highest station

* North-Carolina since writing the above, has acceded to the union.

in its gift. That honest zeal for the public good, which had uniformly influenced him to devote both his time and talents to the service of his country, got the better of his love of retirement, and induced him once more to engage in the great business of making a nation happy. "The intelligence of his election being communicated to him, while on his farm in Virginia, he set out soon after for New-York." On his way thither, the road was crouded with numbers anxious to see the Man of the people. Escorts of militia, and of gentlemen of the first character and station, attended him from State to State, and he was every where received with the highest honors which a grateful and admiring people could confer. Addresses of congratulation were presented to him by the inhabitants of almost every place of consequence through which he [345] passed, to all of which he returned such modest unassuming answers as were in every respect suitable to his situation. So great were the honors, with which he was loaded, that they could scarcely have failed to produce haughtiness in the mind of any ordinary man; but nothing of the kind was ever discovered in this extraordinary personage. On all occasions he behaved to all men with the affability of one citizen to another. He was truly great in deserving the plaudits of his country, but much greater in not being elated with them.

Of the numerous addresses which were presented on this occasion, one subscribed by Dennis Ramsay the Mayor of Alexandria, in the name of the people of that city, who were the neighbours of Mr. Washington, was particularly and universally admired. It was in the following words:

To GEORGE WASHINGTON, *Esq.*
President of the United States, &c.

Again your country commands your care. Obedient to its wishes, unmindful of your ease, we see you again relinquishing the bliss of retirement; and this too, at a period of life, when nature itself seems to authorize a preference of repose!

Not to extol your glory as a soldier; not to pour forth our gratitude for past services; not to acknowledge the justice of the unexampled honour which has been conferred upon you by the spontaneous and unanimous suffrage of three millions of freemen, in your election to the supreme magistracy; nor to admire the patriotism which directs your conduct, do your neighbours and friends now address you; themes less splendid but more endearing, impress our minds. The first and best of citizens must leave us; our aged must lose their ornament; our youth their model; our agriculture its improver; our commerce its friend; our infant academy its protector; our poor their benefactor; and the interior navigation of the Potowmack (an event replete with the most extensive utility, already, by your unremitted exertions, brought into partial use) its institutor and promoter.

[346] Farewell! Go! and make a grateful people happy; a people, who will be doubly grateful, when they contemplate this recent sacrifice for their interest.

To that Being, who maketh and unmaketh at his will, we commend you; and after the accomplishment of the arduous business to which you are called, may he restore to us again, the best of men, and the most beloved fellow citizen!"

To this Mr. Washington returned the following answer:

GENTLEMEN,

Although I ought not to conceal, yet I cannot describe the painful emotions which I felt in being called upon to determine whether I would accept or refuse the presidency of the United States. The unanimity in the choice, the opinion of my friends, communicated from different parts of Europe, as well as from America, the apparent wish of those who were not entirely satisfied with the constitution in its present form; and an ardent desire on my own part to be instrumental in connecting the good will of my countrymen towards each other; have induced an acceptance. Those who know me best (and you, my fellow citizens, are from your situation, in that number) know better than any others, my love of retirement is so great, that no earthly consideration, short of a conviction of duty, could have prevailed upon me to depart from my resolution "never more to take any share in transactions of a public nature." For, at my age, and in my circumstances, what prospects or advantages could I propose to myself, from embarking again on the tempestuous and uncertain ocean of public life?

I do not feel myself under the necessity of making public declarations, in order to convince you, gentlemen, of my attachment to yourselves, and regard for your interests; the whole tenor of my life has been open to your inspection; and my past actions, rather than my present declarations, must be the pledge of my future conduct.

In the mean time, I thank you most sincerely for the expressions of kindness, contained in your valedictory address. It is true, just after having bade adieu to my domestic connexions, this tender proof of your [347] friendship is but too well calculated, still further to awaken my sensibility, and increase my regret at parting from the enjoyment of private life.

All that now remains for me, is to commit myself and you to the protection of that beneficent Being, who on a former occasion hath happily brought us together, after a long and distressing separation; perhaps the same gracious providence will again indulge me. Unutterable sensations must then be left to more expressive silence; while from an aching heart, I bid you all, my affectionate friends, and kind neighbours, farewell!

Gray's bridge over the Schuylkill which Mr. Washington had to pass, was highly decorated with laurels and evergreens. At each end of it were erected magnificent arches composed of laurels, emblematical of the ancient Roman triumphal arches; and on each side of the bridge, was a laurel shrubbery. As Mr. Washington passed the bridge, a youth ornamented with sprigs of laurel, assisted by machinery let drop above his head, though unperceived by him, a civic crown of laurel. Upwards of 20,000 citizens lined the fences, fields and avenues between the Schuylkill and Philadelphia. Through these he was conducted to the city, by a numerous and respectable body of the citizens, where he partook of an elegant entertainment provided for him. The pleasures of the day were succeeded by a handsome display of fireworks in the evening.

When Mr. Washington crossed the Delaware, and landed on the Jersey shore, he was saluted with three cheers by the inhabitants of the vicinity. When he came to the brow of the hill, on his way to Trenton, a triumphal arch was erected on the bridge, by the direction of the ladies of the place. The crown of the arch was highly ornamented with imperial laurels and flowers, and on it was displayed in large figures, *December* 26th 1776. On the sweep of the arch, beneath was this inscription, *The defender of the Mothers, will also protect their Daughters.* On the north side were ranged a number of young misses dressed in white, with garlands of flowers on their heads, and baskets of flowers on their arms; in the second row stood the young ladies, and behind them the married ladies [348] of the town. The instant he passed the arch, the young misses began to sing the following ode:

Welcome mighty chief once more,
Welcome to this grateful shore:
Now no mercenary foe
Aims again the fatal blow,
Aims at thee the fatal blow.
Virgins fair, and matrons grave,
These thy conquering arm did save,
Build for thee triumphal bowers,
Strew, ye fair, his way with flowers,
Strew your Hero's way with flowers.

As they sung the last lines, they strewed their flowers on the road before their beloved deliverer. His situation on this occasion, contrasted with what he had in Dec. 1776 felt on the same spot, when the affairs of America were at the lowest ebb of depression, filled him with sensations that cannot be described. He was rowed across the bay from Elizabeth-Town to New-York, in an elegant barge by thirteen pilots. All the vessels in the harbour hoisted their flags. Stairs were erected and decorated for his reception. On his landing, universal joy diffused itself through every order of the people, and he was received and congratulated by the Governor of the State, and officers of the corporation. He was conducted from the landing place to the house which had been fitted up for his reception, and was followed by an elegant procession of militia in their uniforms, and by great numbers of citizens. In the evening, the houses of the inhabitants were brilliantly illuminated. A day was fixed, soon after his arrival, for his taking the oath of office, which was in the following words: "I do solemnly swear that I will faithfully execute the office of President of the United States, and will, to the best of my ability, preserve, protect, and defend, the constitution of the United States." On this occasion he was wholly clothed in American manufactures. In the morning of the day appointed for this purpose, the clergy of different denominations assembled their congregations in the respective places of worship, and offered up public prayers for the President and people of the United States. About [349] noon a procession, followed by a multitude of citizens, moved from the President's house to Federal Hall. When they came within a short distance from the Hall, the troops formed a line on both sides of the way, through which Mr. Washington, accompanied by the Vice-President Mr. John Adams, passed into the Senate chamber. Immediately after, accompanied by both houses, he went into the gallery fronting Broad Street, and before them and an immense concourse of citizens, took the oath prescribed by the constitution, which was administered by R. R. Livingston, the Chancellor of the State of New-York. An awful silence prevailed among the spectators during this part of the ceremony. It was a minute of the most sublime political joy. The Chancellor then proclaimed him President of the United States. This was answered by the discharge of 13 guns, and by the effusions of shouts, from near 10,000 grateful and affectionate hearts. The President bowed most respectfully to the people, and the air resounded again with their acclamations. He then retired to the Senate chamber, where he made the following speech to both houses:

Fellow Citizens of the Senate,
and of the House of Representatives.

Among the vicissitudes incident to life, no event could have filled me with greater anxieties, than that of which the notification was transmitted by your order, and received on the 14 day of the present month. On the one hand, I was summoned by my country, whose voice I can never hear but with veneration and love, from a retreat which I had chosen with the fondest predilection, and in my flattering hopes, with an immutable decision, as the asylum of my declining years; a retreat which was rendered every day more necessary as well as more dear to me, by the addition of habit to inclination, and of frequent interruptions in my health, to the gradual waste committed on it by time. On the other hand, the magnitude and difficulty of the trust to which the voice of my country called me, being sufficient to awaken in the wisest and most experienced of her citizens, a distrustful scrutiny into his qualifications, could not but overwhelm with despondence, one, who, inheriting inferior [350] endowments from nature, and unpractised in the duties of civil administration, ought to be peculiarly conscious of his own deficiencies. In this conflict of emotions, all I dare aver, is, that it has been my faithful study to collect my duty from a just appreciation of every circumstance, by which it might be affected. All I dare hope, is, that, if in executing this task, I have been too much swayed by a grateful rememberance of former instances, or by an affectionate sensibility to this transcendant proof of the confidence of my fellow citizens; and have thence too little consulted my incapacity as well as disinclination, for the weighty and untried cares before me; my *error* will be palliated by the motives which misled me, and its consequences be judged by my country, with some share of the partiality in which they originated.

Such being the impressions under which I have in obedience to the public summons, repaired to the present station; it would be peculiarly improper to omit in this first official act my fervent supplications to that Almighty Being who rules over the universe—who presides in the councils of nations—and whose providential aids can supply every human defect—that His benediction may consecrate to the liberties and happiness of the people of the United States, a government instituted by themselves for these essential purposes; and may enable every instrument employed in its administration, to execute with success, the functions allotted to his charge. In tendering this homage to the Great Author of every public and private good, I assure myself that it expresses your sentiments not less than my own; nor those of my fellow citizens at large, less than either. No people can be bound to acknowledge and adore the invisible Hand, which conducts the affairs of men, more than the people of the United States. Every step by which they have advanced to the character of an independent nation, seems to have been distinguished by some token of providential agency. And in the important revolution just accomplished in the system of their united government, the tranquil deliberations, and voluntary consent of so many distinct communities, from which the event has resulted, cannot be [351] compared with the means by which most governments have been established, without some return of pious gratitude, along with an humble anticipation of the future blessings which the past seem to presage. These reflections arising out of the present crisis, have forced themselves too strongly on my mind to be suppressed. You will join with me, I trust, in thinking, that there are none under the influence of which, the proceedings of a new and free government can more auspiciously commence.

By the article establishing the executive department, it is made the duty of the president "to recommend to your consideration, such measures as he shall judge necessary and expedient." The circumstances under which I now meet you will acquit me from entering into that subject, farther than to refer to the great constitutional charter under which you are assembled, and which, in defining your powers, designates the objects to which your attention is to be given. It will be more consistent with those circumstances, and far more congenial with the feelings which actuate me, to substitute, in place of a recommendaton of particular measures, the tribute that is due to the talents, the rectitude, and the patriotism which adorn the characters selected to devise and adopt them. In those honorable qualifications, I behold the surest pledges that as on one side no local prejudices, or attachments— no separate views, nor party animosities, will misdirect the comprehensive and equal eye which ought to watch over this great assemblage of communities and interests; so, on another, that the foundations of our national policy will be laid in the pure and immutable principles of private morality; and the pre-eminence of free government, be exemplified by all the attributes which can win the affections of its citizens, and command the respect of the world. I dwell on this prospect with every satisfaction which an ardent love for my country can inspire. Since there is no truth more thoroughly established, than that there exists in the oeconomy and course of nature, an indissoluble union between virtue and happiness; between duty and advantage, between the genuine maxims of an honest and magnanimous [352] people, and the solid rewards of public prosperity and felicity. Since we ought to be no less persuaded that the propitious smiles of Heaven, can never be expected on a nation that disregards the eternal rules of order and right, which Heaven itself has ordained. And since the preservation of the sacred fire of liberty, and the destiny of the republican model of government, are justly considered as *deeply,* perhaps as *finally* staked, on the experiment entrusted to the hands of the American people.

Besides the ordinary objects submitted to your care, it will remain with your judgment to decide, how far an exercise of the occasional power delegated by the 5th article of the constitution, is rendered expedient at the present juncture by the nature of objections which have been urged against the system, or by the degree of inquietude which has given birth to them.

Instead of undertaking particular recommendations on this subject, in which I could be guided by no lights derived from official opportunities, I shall again give way to my entire confidence in your discernment and pursuit of the public good.

For I assure myself that whilst you carefully avoid every alteration which might endanger the benefits of an united and effective govenment, or which ought to await the future lesson of experience; a reverence for the characteristic rights of freemen, and a regard for the public harmony, will sufficiently influence your deliberations on the question, how far the former can be more impregnably fortified, or the latter be safely and advantageously promoted.

To the preceding observations I have one to add, which will be most properly addressed to the House of Representatives. It concerns myself, and will therefore be as brief as possible.

When I was first honored with a call into the service of my country, then on the eve of an arduous struggle for its liberties, the light in which I contemplated my duty required, that I should renounce every pecuniary compensation. From this resolution I have in no instance departed. And being still under the impressions which produced it, I must decline as inapplicable to myself, [353] any share in the personal emoluments, which may be indispensibly included in a permanent provision for the executive department; and must accordingly pray, that the pecuniary estimates for the station in which I am placed, may, during my continuance in it, be limited to such actual expenditures as the public good may be thought to require.

Having thus imparted to you my sentiments, as they have been awakened by the occasion which brings us together—I shall take my present leave; but not without resorting once more to the benign Parent of the human race, in humble supplication, that since He has been pleased to favor the American people with opportunities for deliberating in perfect tranquillity, and dispositions for deciding with unparalleled unanimity on a form of government, for the security of their union, and the advancement of their happiness; so His Divine blessing may be equally *conspicuous* in the enlarged views, the temperate consultations, and the wise measures, on which the success of this government must depend.

The President, of Congress, then attended on divine service.

In the evening a very ingenious and splendid shew of fire works was exhibited. Betwixt the fort and the bowling green stood conspicuous, a superb and brilliant transparent painting, in the centre of which was the portrait of the President represented under the emblem of fortitude, on his right hand was justice, representing the Senate of the United States, and on his left, Wisdom, representing the house of Representatives.

This memorable day completed the organization of the new

constitution. By this establishment the rising generation will have an opportunity of observing the result of an experiment in politics, which before has never been fairly made. The experience of former ages, has given many melancholy proofs, that popular governments have seldom answered in practice, to the theories and warm wishes of their admirers. The present inhabitants of independent America, now have an opportunity to wipe off this aspersion, to assert the dignity of human nature, and the capacity of mankind for self-government.

[354] Citizens of the United States! you have a well balanced constitution established by general consent, which is an improvement on all republican forms of government heretofore established. It possesses the good qualities of monarchy, but without its vices. The wisdom and stability of an aristocracy, but without the insolence of hereditary masters. The freedom and independence of a popular assembly acquainted with the wants and wishes of the people, but without the capacity of doing those mischiefs which result from uncontrolled power in one assembly. The end and object of it is public good. If you are not happy it will be your own fault. No knave or fool can plead an hereditary right to sport with your property or your liberties. Your laws and your lawgivers must all proceed from yourselves. You have the experience of nearly six thousand years, to point out the rocks on which former republics have been dashed to pieces. Learn wisdom from their misfortunes. Cultivate justice both public and private. No government will or can endure which does not protect the rights of its subjects. Unless such efficient regulations are adopted, as will secure property as well as liberty, one revolution will follow another. Anarchy, monarchy or despotism, will be the consequence. By just laws and the faithful execution of them, public and private credit will be restored, and the restoration of credit will be a mine of wealth to this young country. It will make a fund for agriculture, commerce and manufactures, which will soon enable the United States to claim an exalted rank among the nations of the earth. Such are the resources of your country, and so trifling are your debts, compared with your resources, that proper systems wisely planned and faithfully executed, will soon fill your extensive territory with inhabitants, and give you the command of such ample

capitals, as will enable you to run the career of national greatness, with advantages equal to the oldest kingdoms of Europe. What they have been slowly growing to, in the course of near two thousand years you may hope to equal within one century. If you continue under one government, built on the solid foundations of public justice, and public virtue, there is no point of national greatness to which you may not aspire with a well founded hope of [355] speedily attaining it. Cherish and support a reverence for government, and cultivate union between the East and the South, the Atlantic and the Mississippi. Let the greatest good of the greatest number be the pole star of your public and private deliberations. Shun wars, they beget debt, add to the common vices of mankind, and produce others, which are almost peculiar to themselves. Agriculture, manufactures and commerce, are your proper business. Seek not to enlarge your territory by conquest. It is already sufficiently extensive. You have ample scope for the employment of your most active minds, in promoting your own domestic happiness. Maintain your own rights and let all others remain in quiet possession of theirs. Avoid discord, faction, luxury and the other vices which have been the bane of commonwealths. Cherish and reward the philosophers, the statesmen and the patriots, who devote their talents and time at the expence of their private interests, to the toils of enlightening and directing their fellow citizens, and thereby rescue citizens and rulers of republics, from the common and too often merited charge of ingratitude. Practise industry, frugality, temperance, moderation, and the whole lovely train of republican virtues. Banish from your borders the liquid fire of the West-Indies, which while it entails poverty and disease, prevents industry and foments private quarrels. Venerate the plough, the hoe, and all the implements of agriculture. Honour the men who with their own hands maintain their families, and raise up children who are inured to toil, and capable of defending their country. Reckon the necessity of labour not among the curses, but the blessings of life. Your towns will probably e're long be engulphed in luxury and effeminacy. If your liberties and future prospects depended on them, your career of liberty would probably be short; but a great majority of your country must, and will be yeomanry, who have no other dependence than on Almighty God for his usual blessing on their daily labour. From the great excess of the number of such independent farmers in these States, over [356] and above all other classes of inhabitants, the long continuance of your liberties may be reasonably presumed.

Let the hapless African sleep undisturbed on his native shore, and give over wishing for the extermination of the ancient proprietors of this land. Universal justice is universal interest. The most enlarged happiness of one people, by no means requires the degradation or destruction of another. It would be more glorious to civilise one tribe of savages than to exterminate or expel a score. There is territory enough for them and for you. Instead of invading their rights, promote their happiness, and give them no reason to curse the folly of their fathers, who suffered yours to sit down on a soil which the common Parent of us both had previously assigned to them: but above all, be particularly careful that your own descendents do not degenerate into savages. Diffuse the means of education, and particularly of religious instruction, through your remotest settlements. To this end, support and strengthen the hands of public teachers, and especially of worthy clergymen. Let your voluntary contributions confute the dishonourable position, that religion cannot be supported but by compulsory establishments. Remember that there can be no political happiness without liberty; that there can be no liberty without morality; and that there can be no morality without religion.

It is now your turn to figure on the face of the earth, and in the annals of the world. You possess a country which in less than a century will probably contain fifty millions of inhabitants. You have, with a great expence of blood and treasure, rescued yourselves and your posterity from the domination of Europe. Perfect the good work you have begun, by forming such arrangements and institutions as bid fair for ensuring to the present and future generations the blessings for which you have successfully contended.

May the Almighty Ruler of the Universe, who has raised you to Independence, and given you a place among the nations of the earth, make the American Revolution an Era in the history of the world, remarkable for the progressive increase of human happiness!

NEW-HAMPSHIRE

Atkinson, George
Bartlett, Josiah
Blanchard, Jonathan
Folsom, Nathaniel
Foster, Abiel
Frost, George
Gilman, John Taylor
Gilman, Nicholas
Langdon, John
Livermore, Samuel
Long, Pierse
Peabody, Nathaniel
Sullivan, John
Thornton, Matthew
Wentworth, John, Junr.
Whipple, William
White, Phillips
Wingate, Paine
Woodbury, Mr.

MASSACHUSETTS

Adams, John
Adams, Samuel
Cushing, Thomas
Dana, Francis
Dane, Nathan
Gerry, Elbridge
Gorham, Nathaniel
Hancock, John
Higginson, Stephen
Holten, Samuel
Jackson, Jonathan
King, Rufus
Lovell, James
Lowell, John
Osgood, Samuel
Otis, Samuel Allyn
Paine, Robert Treat
Partridge, George
Sedgwick, Theodore
Ward, Artemas

RHODE-ISLAND

Arnold, Jonathan
Arnold, Peleg
Collins, John
Cornell, Ezekiel
Ellery, William
Gardiner, John
Hazard, Jonathan J.
Hopkins, Stephen
Howell, David
Manning, James
Marchant, Henry
Miller, Nathan
Mowry, Daniel Junr.
Varnum, James M.
Ward, Samuel

CONNECTICUT

Adams, Andrew
Cook, Joseph Platt
Deane, Silas
Dyer, Eliphalet
Ellsworth, Oliver
Edwards, Pierrepont
Huntington, Benjamin
Huntington, Samuel
Johnson, William Samuel
Law, Richard
Mitchell, Stephen Mix
Root, Jesse
Sherman, Roger
Spencer, Joseph
Sturges, Jonathan
Wadsworth, Jeremiah
Williams, William
Wolcott, Oliver

NEW-YORK

Alsop, John
Benson, Egbert
[358] Boerum, Simon
Duane, James
Duer, William
Floyd, William
Gansevoort, Leonard
Ghelston, David
Hamilton, Alexander
Haring, John
Jay, John
Lansing, John Junr.
Laurence, John
Lewis, Frances
L'Hommedieu, Ezra
Livingston, Philip
Livingston, Robert R.
Livingston, Walter
Low, Isaac
Morris, Gouverneur
McDougall, Alexander
Paine, Ephraim
Pell, Philip
Platt, Zephaniah
Schuyler, Philip
Scott, John Morin
Smith, Melancthon
Wisner, Henry
Yates, Abraham
Yates, Peter W.

NEW-JERSEY

Beatty, John
Boudinot, Elias
Burnet, William
Cadwalader, Lambert
Clark, Abraham
Condict, Silas
Cooper, John
Crane, Stephen
Dayton, Jonathan
DeHart, John
Fell, John
Frelinghuysen, Frederick
Hart, John
Hopkinson, Francis
Hornblower, Josiah
Houston, William Churchhill
Kinsey, James
Livingston, William
Schureman, James
Scudder, Nathaniel

Sergeant, Jonathan D.

Smith, Richard

Stevens, John

Symmes, John C.

Witherspoon, John Doctor

Armstrong, John

Armstrong, John Junr.

Atlee, Samuel J.

Bayard, John B.

Biddle, Edward

Bingham, William

Clingan, William

Clymer, George

Coxe, Tench

Dickinson, John

Duffield, Samuel

Fitzsimons, Thomas

Franklin, Benjamin Doctor

Galloway, Joseph

Gardner, Joseph

Hand, Edward

Henry, William

Humphreys, Charles

Ingersoll, Jared

Irvine, William

Jackson, David

Matlack, Timothy

McClene, James

Meredith, Samuel

Mifflin, Thomas

Montgomery, Joseph

Morris, Cadwalader

Morris, Robert

Morton, John

Peters, Richard Junr.

Pettit, Charles

Reed, Joseph

Reid, James R.

Roads, Samuel

Roberdeau, Daniel

Ross, George

Searle, James

Shippen, William

Smith, Jonathan B.

St. Clair, Arthur

Wilson, James

Wynkoop, Henry

[359]

Bedford, Gunning Junr.

Dickinson, John

Dickinson, Philemon

Kearny, Dyre

McComb, Eleazer

McKean, Thomas

Mitchell, Nathaniel

Patten, John

Peery, William

Rodney, Caesar

Rodney, Thomas

Sykes, James

Tilton, James

Van Dyke, Nicholas

Vining, John

Wharton, Samuel

Alexander, Robert

Carrol, Charles of Carrolton

Carrol, Daniel

Chase, Samuel

670

Contee, Benjamin
Forbes, James
Forbes, James
Forrest, Uriah
Goldsborough, Robert
Hanson, John
Harrison, William
Hemsley, William
Henry, John
Hindman, William
Howard, John E.
Jenifer, Daniel of St. Thomas
Johnson, Thomas
Lee, Thomas Sim

Lloyd, Edward
McHenry, James
Paca, William
Plater, George
Potts, Richard
Ramsay, Nathaniel
Ross, David
Rumsey, Benjamin
Seney, Joshua
Smith, William
Stone, Thomas
Tilghman, Matthew
Wright, Turbutt

VIRGINIA

Adams, Thomas
Banister, Mr.
Bland, Richard
Bland, Theodorick
Braxton, Carter
Brown, John
Carrington, Edward
Dawson, John
Fitzhugh, William
Fleming, William
Grayson, William
Griffin, Cyrus
Hardy, Samuel
Harrison, Benjamin
Harvie, John
Henry, James
Henry, Patrick
Jefferson, Thomas

Jones, Joseph
Lee, Arthur
Lee, Francis Lightfoot
Lee, Henry
Lee, Richard Henry
Madison, James Junr.
Mercer, James
Mercer, John Francis
Monroe, James
Nelson, Thomas Junr.
Page, Mann
Pendleton, Edmund
Randolph, Edmund
Randolph, Peyton
Smith, Meriwether
Walker, John
Washington, George

NORTH-CAROLINA

Ashe, John B.
Bloodworth, Timothy
Blount, William
Burke, Thomas
Burton, Robert

Caswell, Richard
Cumming, William
Harnett, Cornelius
Hawkins, Benjamin
Hewes, Joseph

Hill, Whitmil
Hooper, William
Johnston, Samuel
Jones, Allen
Jones, Willie
Nash, Abner
Penn, John

Sharpe, William
Sitgreaves, John
[360] Spaight, Richard D.
Swan, John
White, James
William, John
Williamson, Hugh

SOUTH-CAROLINA

Barnwell, Robert
Bee, Thomas
Beresford, Richard
Bull, John
Butler, Pierce
Drayton, William Henry
Eveleigh, Nicholas
Gadsden, Christopher
Gervais, John Lewis
Heyward, Thomas
Huger, Daniel
Hutson, Richard
Izard, Ralph
Kean, John
Kinloch, Francis

Laurens, Henry
Lynch, Thomas
Mathews, John
Middleton, Arthur
Middleton, Henry
Motte, Isaac
Parker, John
Pinckney, Charles
Ramsay, David
Read, Jacob
Rutledge, Edward
Rutledge, John
Trapier, Paul
Tucker, Thomas Tuder

GEORGIA

Baldwin, Abraham
Few, William
Gibbons, William
Habersham, John
Hall, Lyman
Houstoun, William

Howley, Richard
Jones, Noble Wimberly
Langworthy, Edward
Pierce, William
Telfair, Edward
Walton, George

Presidents of CONGRESS, from 1774, till 1789

Peyton Randolph
Henry Middleton
John Hancock

Henry Laurens
John Jay
Samuel Huntington

Thomas McKean
John Hanson
Elias Boudinot
Thomas Mifflin

Richard Henry Lee
Nathaniel Gorham
Arthur St. Clair
Cyrus Griffin

THE END OF THE SECOND VOLUME

Index

Articles of Confederation (*cont.*)
  expiration of, 656
  inefficacy of, 648–54
Asgill, Charles, 605, 606
Ashe (Ash), John, 442, 604
Atlee, Colonel, 282
Atlee, Sam, 540
Atwater, Dr., 339
Augusta, Georgia
  engagement at, 567–68
  occupied by British, 441
Augusta, 353

Bahama Islands, 624
Baird, James, 426
Balcarres (Balcarras), Earl of, 380
Baltimore, Lord. *See* Calvert, Cecilius
Barbados, 62
Barber, Colonel, 542
Barclay, David, 149
  and conciliatory plan, 157, 160–69
Barlow, Joel, 636
Barré, Isaac, 54
Bartlett, Josiah, 321
Barton, William, 357
Baum, Friedrich, 375, 376
Baxter, John, 563
Baylor, George, 423–24
Bennington, Battle of, 374–77
Berkeley (Berkely), John, 13
Biddle, Nicholas, 428
Bienfaiscent, 527
Bills of credit, 453–62. *See also* Money, paper
Bingham, William, 358
Bird, Lieutenant Colonel, 338, 351
Bland, Richard, 634
Board of War, 600–601
Bollan, William, 140
Bonetta, 588
Bonner, Colonel, 414
Boston
  and board of tax commissioners, 74–75, 87
  British troops in, 75–76, 83–85, 114, 148, 173, 242–43
  British withdrawal from, 246–48
  evacuation of, 277

Boston (*cont.*)
  and fortification of Boston Neck, 118, 120
  and Hutchinson letters, 86
  as mother of rebellion, 95–96
  and nonimportation, 79, 133–34
  siege of, 176–77
  and Tories, 625
Boston Massacre, 84–85
Boston Port Bill, 95–97, 99, 100–101, 104–5, 107, 312
  colonial reaction to, 104–35
Boston Tea Party, 92–97
Botetourt, Norborne Berkeley, Baron de, 78, 82–83
Boudinot, Elias, 600
Bouillé, François-Claude-Amour de, 610
Boyd, Colonel, 442
Braddock, Edward, 37, 202
Brandon, Colonel, 563
Brandywine, Battle of, 343–47
Brant (Brandt), Joseph, 467, 473
Bratton, Colonel William, 563
Braxton, Carter, 322
Brazil, 5
Breed's Hill. *See* Bunker Hill, Battle of
Breyman, Heinrich von, 375, 380
Bricole, 478
Bristol, 271
Brodhead (Broadhead), Daniel, 473
Brown, Colonel, 608–9
Brown, John (Major), 216, 224, (Colonel), 377
Brown, Thomas, 567
Brunswick (Brunswic), Duke of, 268
Bryan, Colonel Morgan, 486, 487
Buford, Abraham, 483
Bunker Hill, Battle of, 187–91, 246, 264, 276, 283
Burgoyne, John
  at Bennington, 374–76
  at Boston, 186
  at Freeman's farm, 377–79
  and Indians, 361, 362, 370
  and invasion of New York, 342, 361–74, 377, 382–83
  and Laurens (Henry), 597
  at Saratoga, 379–81, 383, 384

D'Almodovar, Marquis, 439
Danbury, raided by British, 339
Darby, Admiral, 527
D'Arcon, Chevalier, 612
Dartmouth, Lord, 141, 142, 166, 192, 199
Davidson, William, 557
Davis, Isaac, 175
Dawson, Captain, 419
Dayton, Isaac, 505
Deane, Silas
    and French alliance, 392–94
    and provisions for Continental army, 392
    and Ticonderoga, 210
De Barras, Comte, 579, 582
Debt, national, 649–53
Declaration of Independence, 318–22
    arguments for and against, 317–18
    army's reaction to, 274
    and necessity to organize an army, 286–87
    reaction to, 322–25
Declaratory Act, 69, 72, 80
De Grasse, Admiral, 582, 583, 615
    at Chesapeake, 578, 582, 584
    and Congress, 589
    vs. Graves, 579–80
    vs. Rodney in West Indies, 610–12
    sails for Martinique, 581
    and Washington, 584–85
De Jean, Philip, 470
DeLancey (Delance), Oliver, 340
DeLancey family, 626
Delaware
    and exemption from parliamentary coercion, 158
    settlement of, 13
    and Stamp Act Congress, 64
    Tories in, 343
Delaware, 349
Delaware Indians, 475
Demarara, 610
Demosthenes, 112
Denmark, 532
Dennison, 468
De Peyster, James, 564

D'Estaing, Comte, 476
    at Battle of Rhode Island, 418–20, 422
    at New York, 417–18
    sails for America, 412
    at Savannah, 447–49
    in the West Indies, 447
Destouches (D'Estouches), Chevalier, 547
De Villier, Mr., 35
Dickenson, General, 307
Dickenson, Major, 414
Dickinson (Dickenson), John
    and Congress's petition to the king (1775), 198
    on Declaration of Independence, 317–18
    as distinguished writer, 634
    "Farmer's Letters," 72, 633
    and Townshend Duties, 72
Digby, Robert, 579, 585
Divine right of kings, 26, 27, 312
Donop, Carl Emil Kurt von
    at Red-Bank, 352–53
Dorchester Heights, 245
Drake, Admiral, vs. De Grasse, 581
Drayton, William Henry, 634
    and conciliatory bills, 405
Dulany, Daniel, 634
Dunmore, Lord, 110, 228–36, 271
Duportail (du Portail), General, 582, 589
Dwight, Timothy, 636

East Florida, 440
    British campaign against, 424, 426
    ceded to Great Britain, 39
    Spain presses for, 616
East Haven, raided by British, 432
East India Company, 81, 87, 89–90, 92, 93, 96–97, 171, 264
Easton, Colonel, 216
Eden, William, 403, 409
Education, colonial, 20
Effingham, Lord, 147
Elbert, Samuel, 442–43
Elizabeth I (of England), 5, 6

INDEX

Revolution, advantages of (*cont.*)
  improvements in surgery, 632–33
  improvements in weaponry, 632
  promotion of arts and sciences, 632
  promotion of literature, 635–36
  religious tolerance, 631–32
  spread of knowledge of political
    science, 633
Revolution, disadvantages of, 629
  failure of national justice, 637
  injury to religious institutions, 637–
    38
  loss of reverence for government, 637
  violation of private rights, 637
Revolutionary War
  as civil war, 601–2
  financing of, 184–85
  patriots vs. Tories, 603–4
Rhode Island
  Battle of, 418–22
  British occupation of, 294, 310
  and campaign of (1778), 411
  evacuation of, 450
  French assistance to, 515, 516
  Hessians in, 411
  petitions for Continental army, 277
  and provisions for the army, 542
  seizes military stores, 122
  settlement of, 9, 11–13
  and Stamp Act Congress, 64
  and Stamp Act riots, 62
Richmond, Lord, 137, 142, 147
Ridgefield, 339
Riedesel (Reidesel), Friedrich Adolf von
  and Burgoyne's invasion, 361
  at Saratoga, 380
Roberts, Captain, 446
Roberts, Colonel, 446
Robertson, Archibald, 246
Robertson, James, 521–22
Robinson, John, 8
Rochambeau, Comte de, 520
  and Arnold, 521
  and Congress, 589
  marches to Yorktown, 584
  at Rhode Island, 514, 515
  and Washington, 582
Rochefontaine, Captain, 589

Rockingham, Lord, 137, 147, 619
Rocky Mount, 487
Rodney, Caesar, 322
Rodney, George
  vs. De Grasse in West Indies, 610–12
  and relief of Gibraltar, 527, 528
  at St. Eustatius, 536, 538
Roman Catholicism, 102
  in Canada, 221–22
  and settlement of Maryland, 11–12
Romney, 74
Romulus, 547
Rose, 280
Ross, Brigadier General, 529
Ross, George, 322
Royal George, 366
Royal government, 76–78, 138–39, 228,
    236, 239, 240. *See also* Campbell,
    William (British); Dunmore, Lord;
    Martin, Josiah; Wright, James
Rudgley (Rigely), Colonel, 550
Rudolph, Captain, 567
"Rules for Reducing a Great Empire to a
    Small One" (Franklin), 86–87
Rush, Banjamin, 321, 634
  and cure for lockjaw, 633
  and military hospitals, 427
  on Warren (Joseph), 191
Russia, 531–32
Rutherford, Griffith, 486, 492, 495
Rutland, Lord, 147
Rutledge, Edward, 285, 322
Rutledge, John
  and defense of Charleston, 477
  as governor of South Carolina, 443,
    447
  negotiates for Continental army, 486
  and prisoners of war, 604
  promotes Sumter, 497

Saba, 536
Sag Harbor, 340
St. Christopher. *See* St. Kitts
St. Clair, Arthur
  at Battle of Trenton, 299
  and Burgoyne's invasion, 363–66, 369
  and invasion of Canada, 251, 254–56
  and New Jersey campaign, 293

This book was set in Caslon 224, a typeface
derived from one originally cut by the distinguished
English letter-founder William Caslon (1692–1766) and
known for its legibility, delicacy, and variety of design.
The Declaration of Independence was printed in the
Caslon letter, and until about the time of the American
Revolution, when local foundries began to produce type,
most books, newspapers, and broadsides printed in North
America used the Caslon letter.

Editorial services by Harkavy Publishing Service,
New York, New York
Book design by Madelaine Cooke, Athens, Georgia
Typography by Monotype Composition Co., Inc.,
Baltimore, Maryland
Printed and bound by Worzalla Publishing Company,
Stevens Point, Wisconsin